ON FILM

True seeing is believing
What sight can never prove.
There is a world to see:
Look outward, eyes, and love
Those eyes you cannot be.

W. H. Auden
"Precious Five"

ON FILM

Unpopular Essays on
a Popular Art

Vernon Young

Quadrangle Books

Chicago | 1972

Library of Congress Catalog Card Number:
72-156335

International Standard Book Number:
0-8129-0188-6

A quotation from the poem "Precious Five" by W. H.
Auden is used by permission of Random House, Inc.

For the poet who supplied my pre-text:
he doesn't like movies.

Acknowledgments

I am here faced with a problem similar to the one I encountered when completing my book *Cinema Borealis:* adequately to thank the numerous people who have shown me films I have never written a word about, as well as films I have. To itemize the film distributors and producers, the archivists and film-museum directors and national-institute officers to whose generosity I owe the appalling quantity of movies I have burned daylight to look at is well-nigh impossible, if only because I can't now remember who they were! To those who have remained in the forefront of my memory I have sought to convey my gratitude, in person or by post, with greater effusion than the convention normally tolerates.

Beyond these indispensably pragmatic considerations, there are deeper thanks to bestow. If it were not for the interested and resourceful attention paid me by Frederick G. Morgan, editor in chief of the *Hudson Review,* I would more than likely not have achieved a tenth part of my European expeditions. And if it were not for his stubborn loyalty to (more than that, his solicitation of) my efforts in a peripheral zone of criticism, I don't know how many of these essays would have seen print in the first place. I have also to thank Hilton Kramer, art editor of the *New York Times,* and Nathan Glick, editor of *Dialogue,* for their unshakable defense of my back-bench voice—even while, I feel certain, they were often made nervous by the asperities of my accent.

Most of these pieces originally appeared in the *Hudson Review,* and I am grateful for permission to reprint them. I should like also to acknowledge reprint permissions granted by the following publications: *Accent: A Quarterly of New Literature,* for " 'Hardly a Man Is Now Alive': Monologue on a Nazi Film" and "Fugue of Faces: A Danish Film and Some Photographs"; *Art Film Publications,* for "Program Notes for Two Classics"; *Arts Magazine,* for

"A Festival of Art Films" and "Nostalgia of the Infinite: Notes on Chirico, Antonioni, Resnais"; ARTS Year Book (1961), *Perspectives on the Arts,* for excerpts from "The Sound of Silence"; *Film Quarterly,* for "The Moral Cinema: Notes on Some Recent Italian Films"; *Industria Annual* (1964), for "The Wilderness Art of Arne Sucksdorff"; and *Southwest Review,* for "Footnote to a Cinematic Primer" and "Long Voyage Home with John Ford."

Preface

The essays on film in this book—I think of them as "Unpopular Essays on a Popular Art"—comprise those I am grateful to see reprinted from twenty years of divided but feverish attention to a provocative subject. Excepting the initial essay and the "Parentheses" at the end, the material is arranged chronologically as written; no other organization was feasible. "Our Local Idioms" was written, upon request, as an informal summary of my conclusions about the relation of film art to its cultural sources, hence it is at the same time a statement of my premises. The essays that follow thereafter might be read as so many thematic glosses on that somewhat euphemistic outline. (If these pieces illustrate any unifying principle, however, they do so coincidentally, since—needless to add, perhaps—they were never designed to compose a book.) On that leading subject, film as a cultural phenomenon, I need say no more in this Preface, or I should be writing an introduction to an introduction.

Yet something may pertinently be said of the circumstances under which these several essays were produced. When I look at them from the standpoint of Now, I am all too aware that they suggest an integral, heavy-weight thesis I never attempted; or, to be accurate, I was at one stage prepared to do so, in the form of an international film history, but I was never encouraged by a publisher to make the attempt, except on a speculative basis which neither inspired my confidence nor promised to sustain my existence. For some time I was bitter about this; today I no longer care. Having paid my respects to the "solid historical study" with my book on Bergman and Sweden, I am on the whole happier, looking backward, to have been able to treat film in the unsystematic and insolent manner represented by these articles than to have sacrificed such a method to the slogging accumulation (and equalitarian handling) of hundreds of utterly boring films—the inevitable fruit of any attempt to write a history of the cinema.

To be sure, the choice was not that clearly cut, not wholly a matter of either-or; another circumstance, quite as decisive, intervened. For precisely during the period when I was most indefatigably hunting films I had never seen—or had seen when I was too unripe to regard them with any sense—it fell to my chance to earn my living (I speak in hyperbole) as a critic of art. Upon returning to Europe, therefore, at the end of 1957—with a *Hudson Review* Fellowship by way of the Rockefeller Foundation, with no specific obligation save to follow my bent, and functioning also as contributing editor to an art magazine in New York—I was simultaneously trying to catch every film any unreliable writer had called "memorable" *and* trying to overtake, as far as my budget would permit, every historically important building and picture in Europe. The result of this hectic double quest needs not to be emphasized: my energies were radically dissipated and my output in both areas of concentration was curtailed.

When contributing my earliest articles on film to the few American magazine editors for whom, in the mid-forties and for a decade following, the art of film was a tolerable subject, I was by the same exclusive token under no command to keep abreast of the current commercial distribution or to restrict myself to films made in the U.S.A. It seemed to me then—as it still does—that under such conditions the best I could do was to say what I could about some of the *essential* aspects of film by way of those movies, past or current, in which the essence was, to my mind, clearly embodied; or to cast a colder eye than most on certain received reputations: always, of course, dependent for my evidence on films which were *available,* a contingency few people not professionally immersed can appreciate.

If you are studying paintings or architecture and cannot reach the site of your subject, you can at least, rather easily, get hold of photographs and reproductions of any building or picture in the world. When you need a book not locally available, your helpful librarian (most have been helpful in any place I have lived) will order it for you from a source more extensively equipped; if it is exceedingly esoteric you can advertise for it in the appropriate journals. I presume that in the world of musicology if you want the score of a piano sonata by Clementi or of a choral mass by Bruckner you will encounter no major problem and that the theater researcher, while unable to resurrect a notable performance, can at least find and read the text of a play, since he is normally concerned not with a specific interpretation but with the drama itself as a form of literature.

With films, however, it is quite another matter, quite maddeningly another matter. For if a vintage film you are determined to see *does exist* (this is the first thing you have to find out, never taking a ready no for your answer), you may discover that the only surviving print is in Lausanne or Prague—when you are in New York or London. This situation improves slightly every year, because of the increased policy of exchange among archives. All the same, some archives are more breachable than others; many remain as difficult to transact business with as a bank—a subject I shall not develop here, since it is not conducive to that sunny state of mind in which a preface should be written. In addition there are, it is true, an astonishing number of film schools and film clubs everywhere today, offering film series alleged to epitomize the history of the motion picture. Few of them do so, even approximately; few collections are not characterized by serious gaps; few anthologists or entrepreneurs observe any but an unsurprising chronology derived from the far from unarguable opinions of a film historian who acquired authority because he had the enterprise to unearth or remember a host of films and to write at length, and obtusely, an evaluation of them.

So far I have referred solely to the difficulty of acquiring a frame of reference within the primers of the art. But even when you feel that you have become reasonably acquainted with those "classics" of cinema on which most explorers might agree, there is a far more knotty problem ahead of you when you begin to look for films which no archivist has bothered to purchase because they're not old enough, not "important" enough, not sufficiently admired, and of which there is no print available, for all you know, within two thousand miles. Let me give two examples, among hundreds.

When in London in 1958 I wanted to see a completely forgotten film (more than forgotten, it had aroused no undue attention to begin with!) made in 1949, *Temptation Harbor,* directed by Lance Comfort from a script by Rodney Ackland based on a novel by Georges Simenon, *Newhaven-Dieppe,* featuring—almost exclusively—Robert Newton. I was curious to know if it was as distinguished as it had seemed when first I looked at it nine years before in New Mexico. Because there was no demand for the film, the distributing company, it turned out, had long since placed the only print they had in their vault, about twenty miles outside London; further, they had no screening room of their own. Clearly, if I had insisted on seeing the film, it would have cost me something like forty dollars to recompense the distributors for obtaining and returning the print and for renting a screening room for an hour and a half. Since they would not profit in any way from my curiosity, why should they foot the bill—and how could I? Or, you must see the point, if I had been on this occasion willing and able, just how many films could I pay forty dollars to disinter?

Again, in Germany three years later I was trying to recover in-between German films, i.e., those made under the Third Reich, not *verboten* for public showing, and those made in the immediate postwar period. I presume that the situation today is the same as it was then, a decade ago; even a certified film critic on a German newspaper had to pay a fee if he wished to see a film rarely in circulation. (Closer to forty marks than forty dollars, true. *Quand même!*) During three months in Munich I was able to recover some of the films on my list and I found a few more at the Copenhagen archive. Today it is possible to see most of the Third Reich productions at the East Berlin archive, I believe. What a choice! Rather than go in and out of East Berlin every day for probably three weeks, I would take a beating. In short, if you are researching a film unsponsored by a foundation or a very liberal publisher, you will have an adventure. God knows I don't believe adventure should be shunned. I am only trying to explain its nature.

As a consequence, my pursuit of films, during the late fifties and early sixties especially, assumes in my memory the character of a nightmare odyssey. The recall of any particular film from the middle past is associated with the places in which I saw it. As if caught in a montage, I am again sitting day after day in Rochester, New York—during a wintry March—watching the brute phantoms of UFA and Soviet films loom and grimace soundlessly; when I emerge at day's end, though at four o'clock only, the landscape—like Sweden's, too far north to be lived in happily by man—is leafless, lightless, dirty-snow-banked, as gloomy as the film I have just left, likely, and I rush with relief to my bottle of Black and White. Or I am in London, traveling in the fag-butted underground, alone of course, hoping yet skeptical, headed toward a remote and dismal suburb where, in a schoolhouse, a local film society is showing a French film from 1931; probably not worth seeing, but sundry chumps with reputations as annalists have affirmed its uniqueness and there is no way of settling the case except to see the thing for myself. Or I am struggling up at six-thirty A.M. in Rome (I'm not at my best in the sane light of early morning), hoping to be properly awake by nine when, after breakfast (not too heavy) and a journey which might better have been to Orvieto (it wouldn't have taken much longer) than to Cinecitta, I am to see four films, two on a movieola (which increases one's anxiety since the concentration is thereby more intense), following a lunch which must be solid enough for sustenance but with not so much antipasto and wine as to induce an overpowering desire to sleep around two o'clock! Or I am in Milano, arriving bright-eyed and bushy-tailed, nine-fifteen sharp, as arranged, *at the wrong studio* (the right one being at the exactly opposite end of town), owing to our old friend and crippler, "language misunderstanding."

After listening to other anecdotes similar to those above, someone asked me, "Is it worth it?"

Great heavens, what a preposterous question! Life under any conditions is filled with idiotic excursions, false goals, prodigal waste, disappointed loves, galling personal insufficiencies, half-witted associations. Is it worth living? The object of experience is education; the fruit of education (even in poor movies) is experience. We think it's all worth it when the *immediate* experience is more than commensurate with the effort involved. Upon acquiring a fairly encyclopedic knowledge of films, I was faced with the absurd fact that for any large-scale purpose, such as the writing of a history, it was thoroughly superfluous, because I was no longer interested in such an application of the knowledge. I had instead the satisfaction of being able to dismiss most films from my admiration while recalling, sometimes with decent accuracy, those which were what all film should be, an imaginative entry into another world than our own. A further necessity was acquired, one familiar to the critic of any art: for me, to see any single film is to be aware of all other films that relate to it which I have seen. (At least I delude myself with that presumptuous consolation!)

How does the foregoing narration concern the essays that follow? In this way, simply: the total experience, in which I include my personal experience as a theater director and as a sometime actor in film, together with sessions of watching movie directors at work, impressed on me the dissimilar *social* and *psychological* atmospheres wherein theater and film are created. The experience showed me how radically the motion picture (more than any art because it is in a sense impure, it is contingent, it tells a story in a social context, and social context is behavior) —how radically it can be misinterpreted by the "foreign" observer, who is necessarily seeing the particular film with assumptions alien to those on which it was made. (I'm sure I need not point out that a film can be misunderstood by the citizens of its own country; this merely complicates the question and does not alter my inference.) The experience confirmed my native tendency to resist the popular pressures of an hour or a place, prohibited any exclusive infatuation with the work of an individual director, discouraged partiality—had I ever been tempted—toward a single species of subject matter such as those which fanatical coteries, either of the left or of the *avant garde,* are forever trying to impose on us. Since I have had no obligation toward a daily newspaper or a weekly magazine, I have been free from jumpy editors who have advertisers to mollify, equally free from the tacit intimidations of crowding colleagues. But I have had to face the fact that being a film critic at all entails the vocal presence of those responsible for showing you the films. Early, I learned to be undiplomatic on principle. To be a critic is to be prepared to say no to anyone. When, for the first time, an exhibitor fixes you with gimlet eye as you leave the screening room and asks, with a soft threat in his voice, "Well, what did you think of the movie?"— this is the moment that determines how well you are going to live with yourself henceforth. You must answer him, if this is your opinion, "I think it was trash!"

In another direction I confess that my anomalous position has been subject to a disadvantage. A critic, however footloose, however unimpeded by editorial tyranny, local prejudice, or fashions whipped up at film festivals by influential journalists, *is* a member of a community somewhere, or, fragmented, everywhere. He *is* a man talking to other men; else he is a voice in the wind. Presumably he is talking to those who share something of his education, of his beliefs and, as strongly, his disbeliefs, and to a degree his disposition. I have never, or rarely, known for whom I was writing. It was made pretty clear to me for whom I was not writing—among others, most "film people," who never read opinions expressed outside the film publications or the columns of the wide-circulation press. As I was principally published in the *Hudson Review* or in magazines with a comparable, if not identical, readership, I could infer the status of my reader up to a point. He was very likely affiliated with a college, either as a student or as a teacher; he was closely interested in the arts; he was worldly by inclination; he was not the sort you talk down to, and he would welcome a minority voice (otherwise he would not be reading that magazine). Yet I never knew how much I might assume of what he knew about movies. I was never sure to what extent I should be explicit and footnotey or, on the other hand, how casual I could be with my side references to the field. I have an unholy fear of insulting a reader's intelligence. For a while this worried me until I realized that the anxiety did not improve my communication. Then I began to discover that numerous people read my criticism (not just mine, of course) who never, or seldom, went to a movie! They simply liked to read about movies if they found the critic's point of view interesting and the content vividly re-created. I felt better after that.

But this nervousness accounts for the instances where, in the following essays, I have added a "footnote 1971" if I thought some point needed a more generous explanation or a *mea culpa*. In passing, let me just mention that although I have, here and there, altered a solecism which my increasingly snobbish ear will not accept, or corrected a mis-attribution (naturally!), I have in no case substantially falsified an opinion as originally stated. Where my own view has most shocked me, I have acknowledged it. There are films discussed here which, by my present standard, I feel I have overrated and those which I feel I have undervalued. "Even if it's Sunday may I be wrong."

If there is a single genre of film art I most regret not having chronicled more often, it is that of the short film—the non-theater film, as it has been called—by which I mean films that may run five or forty-five minutes, since alike they are condemned by the utility of things to quick oblivion, to the fugitive approval of a few critics at festivals, or to re-purchase by television interests ten years later when they just go on by, unassimilated by the mass of viewers to whom inevitably television is a time-killing flow of images among which those of documentary, drama, vaudeville, and political encounters are fairly indistinguishable.

I have sometimes a remorseful feeling that in defining the character of film art I should not be writing at all about the feature-length releases which most people see. (If I did not, of course, I would speak to an even more restricted audience.) When I recall the prodigious number of short films I have seen and the scores among them of perfectly enchanting and unkillable records of life in its immense and mysterious variety, it strikes me that their creators are unsung heroes, quite as much as those who in literature confine themselves to lyric poems or short stories. A man makes a film lasting fifteen minutes, sometimes as few as five, about the building of a spider's web; the contest between primitive belief and Christianity, shot entirely with alternating figures of idols and crucifixes; the mountain landscape of Iceland; a tree-felling ritual in Calabria; wild horses on the delta of the Camargue; the education of deaf-mute children; tumbleweeds blown across a drouth-land (nobody in the film but tumbleweeds!); a ferryboat after its last excursion being methodically broken up, taken apart like a living creature, limb by limb. He creates a poem, a whole, a faultless sequence, expressive and authentic, a statement in which there are no large extrinsic supports for his effort—neither the personality of an actor, the familiarity of a popular social pastime, nor the age-old sanction of a story. His film is but half observed, save by other film-makers or by specialists in his subject (if it's of a kind that invites the specialist), and is frequently ignored, plausibly enough, by reviewers in harness who have insufficient space for alluding to his achievement. If they manage to recommend his film with some enthusiasm, what is the practical result? Nobody is going to pay a full admission price in order to see an eight-and-a-half-minute masterpiece about sea horses or a Florentine painting which is being shown with a feature-long film of no merit whatever.

The problem is in truth being settled, even as I postulate it, the way many problems are settled: by eliminating the factors. All over Europe, at any rate, the short film as prologue has vanished, either replaced by advertising snippets or omitted to make time for features which are everywhere getting longer (to say nothing of their getting wider). No doubt the short-film maker will be saved by the television; like so many artists today he will gain a far larger audience and one far less attentive. I can only reiterate my regret that so much exemplary film-making has been blindly scanned and that personally I have not often enough been able to celebrate, as they should be celebrated, these minor masters of a fine ambition: to recreate in a schooled handful of images a small dominion of the arts or sciences, a precise gesture of the human spirit, or one of the countless and haunting marvels which daily pass in territory most of us barely look at and never touch.

We who write about the movies in our several ways, each sneering at the other, are largely concerned—over and above the simple
power of cinema to entertain people for whom we don't write—with
the moral inferences, the public utility, or the esthetic singularity
of a given film we criticize. The emphasis varies from critic to critic;
it will vary within the critical work of a single writer. I think we
tend to take for granted the most obvious yet the most precious contribution of the film-maker. (With such statements, I have in mind
always and only the namable, gifted few among the ten thousand
who are there to make the whole thing pay.) So often an object invoking disdain (I have expressed my share), the film—and the short
film most purely, perhaps—is in nothing more wonderful than this:
it brings us not simply a world we never made but worlds we would
not otherwise glimpse. It compensates us for all those lovely dawns
we slept away, the sycamore trees under which we never awakened,
the rivers we never crossed, the fugitive friendships that never
ripened, the Southwest canyons or Bavarian churches we never
reached.

Contents

ACKNOWLEDGMENTS   vii

PREFACE   ix

Our Local Idioms   3

Footnote to a Cinematic Primer   15

Adventures in Film-Watching   22

"Hardly a Man Is Now Alive": Monologue on a Nazi Film   34

Fugue of Faces: A Danish Film and Some Photographs   44

The Japanese Film: Inquiries and Inferences   51

La Strada: Cinematic Intersections   59

A Festival of Art Films   68

Love, Death, and the "Foreign" Film—1957   77

Long Voyage Home with John Ford   88

International Film Scene: Asia, Italy, and Mexico   95

A Condemned Man Escapes: Five Films on the Subject   104

The Hidden Fortress: Kurosawa's Comic Mode   115

From The Sound of Silence   122

The Moral Cinema: Notes on Some Recent Italian Films   126

European Film Notebook   138

Eisenstein's Third Eye: "The Swede"   147

Of Night, Fire, and Water   157

Kinds of Loving in the International Film   167

Program Notes for Two Classics   177

Nostalgia of the Infinite: Notes on Chirico, Antonioni, Resnais   184

After Bergman . . .   196

Films to Confirm the Poets   205

One Man's Film Festival   217
The Italian Film: Left Hand, Right Hand   228
The Wilderness Art of Arne Sucksdorff   240
Some Obiter Dicta on Recent French Films   253
Films from the Perimeter   263
The Verge and After: Film by 1966   273
Three Film-makers Revisit Themselves   284
International Film: Tensions and Pretensions   293
Poetry, Politics, and Pornography   305
London Film Chronicle: Variation on a Personal Theme   314
I've Been Reading These Film Critics   322
Children and Fools   331
War Games: Work in Progress   340
Film Chronicle: Notes on the Compulsive Revolution   347
Films from Hungary and Brazil   357

Parentheses for Reviews Never Written   365

    Knife in the Water   366

    Harsh Awakenings   369

    My First Love   373

Thoughts After Attending Another Film Society Buñuel Series   377
Some American Films: A Modest Proposal   387
"A Sad Tale's Best for Winter": On Re-seeing *The Third Man*   400
The Brave American   405

    INDEX   415

ON FILM

Our Local Idioms

Once, following a Venice International Film Festival at which I had seen too many films, heard too many voices, and brushed too many elbows, I recovered by sitting ruminatively for hours at a time, gazing at the façade of San Giorgio Maggiore across the water, as its depth of relief changed while the day washed away. I was neither seeking nor avoiding company. To the family proprietors of the restaurant near Santa Maria Della Salute, where I indulged my daylight-burning, I was a very odd specimen, indeed—all alone and apparently content to be so. They took to calling me "Signor Solo."

I concluded that theirs was a generic attitude, consistently expressed in Italian films. The Italian has small appreciation of the solitary ego. His natural observation post is the family bosom, so to speak. His preferred habitat is a gregarious one and society is simply *famiglia*, writ large; anyone outside the family is in effect outside society. In Italy, to be *private* still has much of the old Roman denotation: to be *deprived*. Who, when traveling, has met a lone

Italian—I mean happily alone? When we recall the Italian film, we summon a *populated* world—if not a crowded one, a world in which the group, the village, the local empire, is the assumed human condition: workers in southern rice fields, fishermen on the delta of the Po, the Mafia of Sicily, sheepherders in Sardinia, the unemployed of Turin, Milano, or the Trastevere, a faction of midwives in the backlands of Calabria.

Italy is enormously rich in occupational variety and in tribes of people at discrepant levels of education, skills, economic status, even of language; and the Italian film is drenched with the human, thronged with the fallible, bewildered faces of *homo vulgaris,* observed unsparingly by a compassionate eye crowned with a sardonic eyebrow. No Italian could have conceived *Last Year in Marienbad,* for Italians have a health that forbids the reduction of people to equations. No doubt Italians are less sophisticated than the French: also it is true that they can't be bothered to play such abstract games.

The films which have fed our inference of Italian life are based on a conception of total community; the subject involves an outrage to that community or a defection from it. The object is to restore the broken balance, expel the intruder, mollify the prodigal son, mourn the outcast. Consider *The Bicycle Thief, Bitter Rice, I Vitelloni, La Dolce Vita, Rocco and His Brothers, The Bandits of Orgosolo, Seduced and Abandoned.* For this reason, the Italian's translation of loneliness as a state altogether inconsolable is often more rending than that of any other film-makers.

The isolation of the individual has been a master subject in Western literature for the past century and a half. In Northern countries, to be alone in one way or another is fairly inescapable, and anyone of stout heart will confess that isolation has often a positive value, a compensatory relish, unknown to peoples of the Mediterranean. We invite it as a necessity of the soul. We can cope with it. The Italian cannot cope with it. Fellini's *La Strada* is of course his most ardently poetic statement of the tragedy, symbol and situation inseparable, but the chronology from De Sica's *The Children Are Watching* and *Umberto D* to Olmi's *Time Stood Still* and *Il Posto,* or (the most refined latter-day version) Antonioni's *L'Avventura* is unbroken witness to the catastrophe that ineluctably overcomes the man who is cut off—from his family, from his fellows, from himself.

When the young Marcello of Fellini's *I Vitelloni* finally leaves his home town he does so, not with chin up toward a beckoning future but with regret, as if fearing to sever the umbilical cord. *La Dolce Vita* has been here and there misunderstood by those who fail to see the gravity, for a nourished Italian, of a displaced society-within-a-society, like a floating kidney in the organism. And from the Northern point of view, it is certainly not inevitable for the other Marcello (in *8½*) to resolve his folly by returning to it, ostensibly chastened because he has understood it; he might have as inevitably turned his back on the man he was, on the women he has overvalued, and on the profession in which charlatanry has so great a dominion. Renunciation is not a therapeutic in Italian life: it is a scandal.

We should expect the Italians to be *simpatico* with the comparable misery that screams from such Japanese films as Kurosawa's *Ikiru* or Ozu's *Tokyo Monogatari*—an agonizing desire to communicate and be touched, together with an ambivalent attachment to the family which at one and the same time protects and suffocates. While this is a familiar concern in Japanese films, one would not say that it predominates. Loneliness is but one of several misfortunes imposed on the Japanese by themselves and by the logic of modern history. The filmgoer whose acquaintance with Japanese cinema is limited to samurai films may not realize the scope of the Japanese-film subject matter. He should first be reminded that the greatest flowering of the Japanese film has accompanied the post–World War II period, in which the surviving Japanese has experienced to a degree probably unequaled in any other country the vitiation of every authority and ego fortification maintained for centuries: his social pyramid—family to shogun—his traditional ethos, his ceremonious exchanges, and his domestic integrity.

Since the national mind has been perpetually conditioned to anticipate order, the Japanese talent for creating order in obedience to a new set of codes has been as evident as the deep-going shock to its previous suppositions. What is now the older or vanishing generation of film-makers proceeded to celebrate, not without critical misgiving, the feudal values governing Japan for ages and now being swept away, the nobility and beauty with the inhumanity and the terror. They sustained and perfected the samurai genre and, besides, made a host of films in which the breakdown of traditions, during the Tokugawa period or later, was regarded with a mingled share of regret and relief. A later generation, deracinated and superficially Westernized, appears to be more thoroughly disenchanted of nostalgia for ancient custom, yet skeptical of benefits to be accrued overnight from the chaos wrought by Western technological liberalism.

What is remarkable, however, is the tenacity with which nearly all these directors, of whatever vintage, have retained *style* in a medium that encourages merely technical facility and under conditions which have radically questioned the culture in which that style was nurtured. Arthur Koestler has described Japan as "a country that compels one to think in images and to write with a brush." Japanese films confirm his belief, for even as, psychologically, the Japanese themselves are struggling with heretical influences and with self-division, their age-old cult of precision is intact. In the films of Kon Ichikawa, scrupulous color harmonies and impeccable composition assume greater importance as the content becomes increasingly schizophrenic. Heroism is Kurosawa's subject; things as they miserably are in constricted middle-class circles was Ozu's; blank disbelief is Teshigahara's. But in common their eye for stylistic interpretation is never blurred.

No Japanese director is casual (if he appears to be, he is probably incompetent) ; none is indifferent to effect. The last films of Ozu construct human relationships which are as little dramatic as in any mode of naturalism that has succeeded Chekhov. But the passivity, like the camera's position, is severely calculated; metaphor is so minimized as to be barely discernible. Teshigahara's *The Case* may be thought to exhibit the oblique time-sense of Alain Resnais and a form of moral relativism fetched from Kafka or French existentialism, yet what is more Japanese than a palpable ghost? And the landscape depicted is indelibly of the Japanese persuasion, as clean as a pebble garden or a print by Hiroshige. The same director's *Woman of the Dunes*—incisive, nihilistic, staccato—is visually pure and edited with analytical severity. The result is somewhat antiseptic; it has the attraction of a nude you might appreciate without desiring.

All Japanese films are not lovely; they are all *composed,* Kurosawa's least obviously, since they are more dynamic. The grotesque plays a prominent part in the Japanese movie, but we may imagine that only disorder is considered ugly. The loving scrutiny of the Japanese is impartial: almost equal pictorial value is bestowed on the skirt of a roof, wrinkles around the eye, a dragon on a lacquered box, polychrome parasols lanced by rain, shirts flapping in a slum compound like the banners of defeated samurai. Despair, reconciled by formal beauty—the Japanese answer to life resembles that of the ancient Greeks, or of Nietzsche.

There are certain obvious similarities between the Japanese film and the Swedish. In both, a powerful inhibition is externalized by an overanxious attention to surface clarity. In both, suppressed violence is channeled into vindictive personal relationships, or contained by inordinate tensions that frequently break and recoil as acts of suicide (ergo, the Japanese fondness for Sjöberg's *Miss Julie*). And in both, nature is never for long absent from the screen —but the Japanese variety is alternatively more decorative and more baleful than that of the Swedish. Cultural conditionings intersect at special junctures: when the Japanese, of traditional temper at any rate, loses face, he commits hara-kiri; when, according to Herbert Hendin's psychiatric study of Scandinavians under stress, Swedish "performance anxiety" becomes unbearable, the victim commits suicide, if not ritualistically! Beyond this it is a matter of common observation that the Swede is supersensitive to adverse criticism—like the Japanese, we have been assured both by Donald Richie and Arthur Koestler.

Anxiety—frequently in excess of what appears to be justifiable— and a bred-in-the-bone affection for wilderness: these are the conspicuous features of Swedish life and Swedish film. Nothing more consistently stamps the Swedish movie—either the television documentary, the films made for children, or those made for export— than its touching, beautiful fraternity with unspoiled nature (birch trees, rocky peninsulas, waterfalls), usually photographed with a sensitivity to minor tones which not even the French can surpass. To be sure, there is nothing mysterious about the Swede's devotion: for centuries nature has been the overbearing element of his surroundings. Seven-eighths, or thereabouts, of his country is rural today, and, excepting a small section of the population, all daily experience until forty years ago was a pastoral experience. The Swedish film at its purest is, whatever else, prevailingly a film about Man in the Open Air: all the films of Sucksdorff, 1942–1965 (whether set in Sweden, India, or South America); Bergman's *A Summer with Monika*, 1953; Mattsson's *Salka Valka*, 1954; *The*

Virgin Spring, 1960; and the newest link in the continuity, Jan Troell's first feature-length film, *Here Is Your Life,* 1966, the epic story of a country boy's growing pains during World War I years in northern Sweden that richly sums up the cherished hour of the bucolic tradition.

The latest films of Ingmar Bergman purchase their internality at the cost of excluding scenic values by an act of will, utilizing only so much of the natural world as shall serve the action and cast no affirmative spell. In his *The Hour of the Wolf,* 1968, and *The Shame* landscape is reduced to its most spare denominator—an island. When the Swedish mind (whether we speak of the mind that creates the film or of a character therein conceived) fails to discover adequate insurance against moral confusion and is otherwise unsupported by its living source in nature, it falls back, becomes claustral, suffers hallucinations, approaches madness: *Torment,* 1944; *The Silence,* 1964; *The Hour of the Wolf,* 1968, and Troell's *Ole Dole Doff,* 1968. By a Spaniard the subject of these films might be described as Man Shut in With the Bull.

With Swedish film as a reminder, it is perhaps the more surprising that in the country of Wordsworth, Keats, Emily Bronte, Hardy, Housman, and D. H. Lawrence, the cinema is all but devoid of earth poetry. The British film came of age late and in an hour when English nature as a correlating symbol was a luxury for poets. The traffic of an established metropolitan tradition was closer to the interests of those who pioneered in English movie-making, and today the nation's films are recognizably the children of their postponed and urban origin: the international spy story of Alfred Hitchcock and, a little later, the documentaries of the John Grierson school. From Hitchcock the English film received its essentially empirical approach, quite literally: the camera as protagonist, the incorporation of no more in a scene than the principal observer, at a given moment, is likely to see. (Hitchcock modified his practice when he changed his residence and subsequently saw too much!)

If English film directors have not been limited to a single technical method, they have imposed limits on themselves in another sense, for tacitly they agree with Edmund Burke: "To be attached to the subdivision, to love the little platoon we belong to in society is the first principle (the germ as it were) of public affections." True, "to love the little platoon" has not been the reaction of yesterday's Angry Young Men—it is certainly far from the mood of *Satur-*

day Night and Sunday Morning or *Room at the Top;* but this wave of panic and disgust may have already passed over into the half-burlesque of films such as *Georgy Girl* and *Morgan.* Exposures of the grumbling classes had their last word, perhaps, in the cheerful complaint of Morgan's mother—and *cheerful* is the cue here: "I'm miserable in this world and I don't believe in the next."

All art is a game played with ethnic rules. Those of the British are empirical. Since the English distrust ideas, no harassed schoolmaster in an English film could have become an archetype in an expressionist world, like Professor Unrath in *The Blue Angel;* instead, the British made *The Browning Version* and *Term of Trial.* Empiricism shuns the symbolic, cordially surrenders the universally significant to the familiar, exploits what it knows best. What English writers and directors know best is their scaled society, each class or vocation in possession of its own manners, its own aims, its special avenues of escape, its exclusive absurdities (of idiom, dress, or custom—which gives to English comedy its touch of bright and endearing malice). The full range of British film production can best be appreciated by including the television programs (there are no better anywhere), since the content of films distributed to the international cinemas is on the whole less explorative. In fact, contemporary English commercial films are not nearly so various as those of the immediate postwar years, when Carol Reed made *The Third Man,* Lance Comfort filmed a splendid adaptation of Simenon's *Newhaven-Dieppe* (*Temptation Harbor*), Thorold Dickinson made *The Queen of Spades* (by Pushkin), and David Lean that masterpiece of film Gothic, *Oliver Twist.*

Under any circumstances, no English film is likely to embody a generalization powerful enough to be called great. There is no home equivalent of *Los Olvidados, Rashomon, La Strada.* England's ambassadors are *Tight Little Island, Brief Encounter, Billy Liar, A Taste of Honey, Tom Jones, The Whisperers*—socially aware, even-tempered, genial under pressure. The passions and prognostications of the past are more often consigned to the theater. Russia has contributed the most exuberant *Romeo and Juliet,* as well as the most haunted *Hamlet,* to filmed Shakespeare. (In exchange, Englishmen have staged perhaps the greatest Chekhov ever seen—the Redgrave-Olivier *Uncle Vanya.*) If many British today are repeating to themselves, "Milton! thou shouldst be living at this hour," to date there has been no cinematic rehearsal of the sentiment—

and they left the martyrdom of Sir Thomas More in the capable hands of the American, Fred Zinnemann (American by way of Vienna!), who made *A Man for All Seasons*.

The more complex a country's intellectual heritage, the harder it is to account for the polarities of attitude and disposition we find there. In the case of France, it would be foolish to try, unless we have unlimited time to spend. One can only suggest a key, with no certainty that it will fit all the doors. Most people have a ready-made definition of the Frenchman which seems to satisfy them, derived from the travel folder—"If you love life, you will love France" —and its conventional implications: the Frenchman is superficially gallant, he is *insouciant* toward domestic morality, he is a master of the soufflé, he quotes Montaigne whenever pressed, and he dismisses all political contradictions with "an eloquent shrug" (or by quoting Descartes instead of Montaigne). These attributes could probably be assigned to a number of Parisians, but they will not take one very far when trying to explain Cardinal Mazarin, Henri Poincaré, Marie Curie, the French penal system, Jacques-Yves Cousteau's propensity for staying underwater, or the art criticism of M. André Malraux.

Confronted with the French film as with any other department (the term is nothing if not French), you should not deduce from its abundant inflections that the Gallic consciousness is self-contradictory. Alexandre Astruc's tribute to baroque, by way of Max Ophuls, in that perfect film *Le Rideau Cramoisi;* Jacques Demy's bow to the spirit of neoclassicism in *Lola* and *Umbrellas of Cherbourg;* Robert Bresson's clerical austerity and preoccupation with little circles of cruelty; the late Jacques Becker's extraordinary empathy with the criminal mind; Truffaut's confident, if unflattering, view of women and children; François Reichenbach's perpetual balance, whether making films about provincial schoolboys, the U.S. Marines' training program, the secret life of a West Indian boxer in Paris, or Brigitte Bardot intercontinentally touring—all these are simply aspects of that admirable, and to anyone else incredible, phenomenon: the French mind.

I am led to suppose that intellect and intuition are, in the French, less separable than in other peoples, which suggests that the French film-maker is likely to be a poet apparently using prose for his immediate purpose. The infusion of these delicate properties we call *wit,* the single word that perhaps explains the French film art-ist's genius for endowing any subject with a tone peculiar to it, yet keeping his distance from it, as it were. Just as the sauce tends to make every ingredient of a French meal taste of all the others yet retain its own piquancy, so a French film, while indubitably French, is at the same time a specific film about a prison break or a queer sexual triangle or the retreat from Dien Bien Phu or the life and death of a donkey.

The French film-maker is above all, and as a consequence of this gift, never at a loss for a subject. He hasn't to wait for history, the weather, or a local crime in order to think of "an idea for a movie." Since he is a realist—never doubt it!—for him things always exist; hence there is always a something to make a movie about. The rest is style, which is commonly in his nerve ends. No French film direc-tor was born yesterday, or twenty-five years ago, or sixty-three years ago, however his dossier reads. Every talented Frenchman is a thousand years old, a thousand years of a civilization which has pre-cisely striven to fuse the intellect with the senses. There is nothing supernatural about the Frenchman's ability to discriminate wines —it has been acquired by a practiced palate.

Had I but space enough and time—to say nothing of sufficient authority—I might venture more than a few sweeping assertions on the unifying character of films from India and South America. I do not know if the films of Satyajit Ray represent *the* Indian film, and I have seen few others. I found *The Music Room* and *Charulata* more Indian (more Eastern, let me say) than the *Pather Panchali* trilogy. But at the later films, strangely spangled with an incessant and (to my ears) bizarre musical accompaniment, I felt myself in the presence of an alien rhythm, with a completely un-Western feel-ing of duration, and of an emphasis that never fell where I expected —not an uninviting experience, merely one not instantly compatible with my nervous system or my cultural reflexes. The subject matter was as distilled as that of Henry James. *Charulata* was especially rich in nuances of grief and in dialogue quite extraordinarily allu-sive. A languorous afternoon spent swinging in a shaded patio, with the world that doesn't really matter making a faint sound as of wind-bells far away: this is the impression that remains with me.

I should like to try explaining why Luis Buñuel is unmistakably Spanish and why Leopoldo Torre-Nilsson is patently Argentinian, but this would open up the whole South American subject, on the real nature of which I am ignorant. I suspect there must be perceptible differences among the films of these countries, derived from ethnic origins, from political directions, from basic social attitudes formed historically.

Black God, White Devil, from Brazil, seemed to me a stirring echo of that cruel and fabulous film of 1951, *O Cangeceiro (The Bandit)* with the weird concatenations of a ballad, a ferocity of incident that was breathtaking, and scenery that imposed on the characters something of its own cloud-topping arrogance and savage indifference to the smaller interests of reason. *Vidas Secas* was nearer the human scale but no less dominated by space: the patient, arid journey of a peon, his wife, their two children, and a dog, who trek from one dessication of land and spirit to another, hostages to nature and man alike. The amplified groan of a cart axle with which the film opened and closed was one of the inspired sound metaphors of contemporary film-making.

Similarly, *Voice of Anxiety* (made in Colombia) will be for some time memorable to me for one sublime moment when, in a dying sky-high village, a man who has had half his leg sawed off (without anesthesia) sits singing into a sunset over what looks like a planet-full of mountains, grateful for the gift of life. The spare, bold images in these films, however different their national and regional provenance, are reminiscent of the Swedish, but the lyric note is less often touched—and temperamentally, of course, these films are gods apart. Their peoples ask no mercy from the sky, fate, or their kindred; in the teeth of adversity and death they stand erect with pride.

As for the work of Torre-Nilsson, it is in my opinion too little esteemed in the North; there is no director more overdue for intelligent evaluation in his own terms (which few critics seem to comprehend). His films—the few I have seen—substantially define a society: its thick palisades, its courtly manners, its handsome men and women registering infinite gradations of conduct, its shockingly cruel concealments. My composite image of this world has been formed largely by Torre-Nilsson—monuments and cypresses and tense erotic music in narrow back streets, a frightened girl crouched in the food-lift of a Jane Eyre mansion, men passionately contending across the baroque waste of a vast courthouse, a rakish political henchman shot down before an elegant ironwork gate, staggering to his unscheduled death in ankle-deep water.

Articulate Americans have long since agreed that even their best films do less than justice to the variety of American life and thought; the candidates represent a single party—the pragmatists. We find the most authentic American experience in documentary films or in those with a documentary stance—*The Plow That Broke the Plains* and *The River* (about the Tennessee Valley Authority) ; the greatest of combat documentaries, *The Battle of San Pietro; The Quiet One* (of a Negro boy's rehabilitation) ; and a short film made a few years ago, *Time Out of War,* calm, laconic, plausible.

These were not Hollywood films; in the popular product there have been hints of the real thing—moments or sequences, rarely the whole, rich but disconnected scenes in a few westerns, a high degree of zest and some rhetorical cynicism in the Hecht-MacArthur films made on Long Island in the early forties (*Crime Without Passion, The Scoundrel, Angels over Broadway*) and, a little later, Hollywood's life-is-a-jungle films about battered detectives and twisted lives: *Murder My Sweet, The Blue Dahlia,* and Nicholas Ray's *They Live by Night.* Just yesterday there was *Bonnie and Clyde,* a dehydrated version of the Ray film referred to but, for all that, electric, properly callous, comic in a ghastly way, a film with a *style*—if with no more moral sense than its protagonists. Men doing their jobs with no horizon beyond the job, a soured dry form of social accusation without crusading fervor, sometimes a neo-Elizabethan relish for life lived sub-socially or beyond the fences. All very energetic, uncouth, good for a sardonic laugh. But where in these films is there any conception of man as more than a merely instrumental animal? When does one ever see the majestic ranges of the West as anything but a backdrop to preacher-man tall tales or juvenile-fascist hostilities? Where, in short, is consciousness?

A recent American movie—John Huston's *Reflections in a Golden Eye,* from a novel by Carson McCullers—helps locate what has been missing. If the characters in this film are as warped as any in the surreal world of Poe, O'Neill, Faulkner, Williams, and Albee, they are unarguably cogent; they convey the spook-ridden essence of much American literature, an atmosphere of spiritual infirmity and moral caprice quite as present in the American scene as the robust virtues favored by the extroverts of American expression. The film is about a man who fails to master a white horse. To describe it as the story of a murder at a Southern garrison or as a clinical inquest of a regional ailment is to leave it where Miss McCullers and, later, John Huston found it.

Tangibly—and so beautifully—the film takes place (rather, I should say it seems to; it actually was shot in Italy) on American earth, sauterne sunlight kindling the tamaracks, as if at the dawn of habitation. This is a false dawn. The numb tranquility stretching between the outbreaks of violence reveals in a transparent medium, "like gold to airy thinness beat," the dehumanizing of life where mind has never been domesticated and a species of manic innocence reigns. With the removal of Miss McCullers' narrative prose, for many a barrier rather than an illumination, the real territory of the novel is disclosed as a form of meditative, visual poetry. Happily, the "name actors" have been subdued to the element they work in; we would call that element *life* if it were not lucidly art.

Huston had come close to the life-and-death sounds before. Made nervous by movie critic James Agee too soon calling him great, he tried lifting the veil (with *Moby Dick*) twelve years ago but, all the same, remained outside—holding the veil. Here he is in the domain of Antonioni or of Joseph Losey's *Accident* (and more confidently than Losey), where the air is charged with a radiation of something never revealed until too late to forestall its consequences. To achieve this effect and permit symbols to emerge as though unbidden, a director must sacrifice urgency to eavesdropping. Characters in most American films are so engrossed by the world of fact that they seem not to exist at the psychic level at all. In Huston's film the *only* connections are psychic, for these people speak to each other across sunken continents of meaning. Huston's achievement should be instructive, a clear insinuation that unless you have inherited a number of lifetimes with your mother's milk, it takes your own lifetime to make a work of art. *Reflections in a Golden Eye* was made by a grizzled veteran, "withering into truth."   1968

Footnote to a
Cinematic Primer

The recent circulation of D. W. Griffith's films throughout the *avant garde* movie houses of the nation is a shocking as well as instructive phenomenon. Since the apotheosis of Griffith is one of the most prominent features of the belated minority interest in the art of the motion picture, the revival of such prodigies as *The Birth of a Nation* or *Intolerance* is valuable if it does no more than demonstrate the provenance of a certain kind of cinematic ingenuity in this country rather than in Russia or Germany—and, what is more, in Hollywood itself, the despised suburb of cinematic achievement. But the reminder cuts more than one way, and as we watch the fabulous and seemingly interminable unwinding of *Intolerance*, particularly —made in 1916—we experience, if we are not pedantically restricting ourselves to observation of montage, a peripheral but steadily contracting discomfort.

There is no denying that this film, if taken with historical sympathy, is an inordinate technical accomplishment. Filmed under "paleotechnic" studio conditions on a few miserable acres of now-haunted ground where Los Angeles for no organic reason becomes Hollywood, *Intolerance* was a synthesis in advance of the essential language of the motion picture: rapid cutting, the dissolve, the iris, the dolly shot, the crane shot, the punctuating closeup, and the flashback. Arriving only a decade after Thomas Hardy's epic poem, *The Dynasts,* it gave cinematic sanction to Hardy's esthetic of ubiquity, and it moved not simply terrestrially, as Hardy's work (with celestial detours) did across a continent, but back and forth in time, with an alarmingly accelerated frequency in its final crescendo. A contemporary story of the suffering, downtrodden industrial worker was sliced up and intersected by other dramatizations of "intolerance"—a moderate epitome, indeed—in the Christ story, in the Babylon of the Persian conquest, and in Paris during the Huguenot War period. Each of the historical plots, besides being a moral hitchhiker, was made an excuse for lavish spectacle projected by fantastically bad miming and through a gruesomely shoddy, if ambitious, archaeological paraphernalia, accompanied by cautionary texts, footnotes on French Renaissance history and cuneiform writing, quotations from Walt Whitman, Oscar Wilde, and the Bible.

All this is surprisingly impressive—perhaps more to us than to the 1916 spectator who was very likely as much stupefied as impressed—because of the sheer sweep and unfaltering visualization of the three-hour narrative. (We are told that a half-hour's worth, at least, of the original print has been lost over the years.) Despite the interlarded texts and subtitles (these the lowest incarnation of the written word before radio advertising copy), Griffith made a *motion picture,* which is to say a product wherein the relationship of paced visual images not only tells a story but creates thereby an esthetic intrinsic to its mechanistic means. *Intolerance* moved, with energy, suppleness, and variety astonishing for its time; it moved by way of coordinated, counterpointed, and juxtaposed images to a polymorphous finale in which the several motifs were consummated in weird but conclusive wedlock. It was a spectacular preview of the *kind* of experience the motion picture, alone among the arts, is fitted to give—the experience of mobility, perhaps the cardinal experience of our time.

A multiplex of vulgarity, unreeling at approximately four hundred and eighty separate images to the hour (a phenomenally fast rate of cutting), *Intolerance* was in many respects a disquieting prophecy. While it represented in crude form the amalgamating and boundary-leaping urge of the modern mind, it foretold also the terrorizing factor in high-powered industrial organization; anticipated the assembly-line method in commodity art; preshadowed, in general, those processes and surrenders by which modern art expression has imitated the conditions of technology. For the certain consequence of the motion picture as exemplified here in all its inceptive powers is the subjection of histrionic and intellectual virtues to the ranging omnipotence of the camera (and, in its latter-day development, to the discriminatory requirements of the sound mixer). From this initially dehumanizing operation has developed a new wonder, fraught with sublimities of audio-visual analysis all too rarely executed.

Unfortunately co-evident with its fulfillment of the motion picture dynamic is the film's revelation of the wasteful ancestry of that absurdity and pretension which has been more often than not the focalized content of the American film ever since. The limitation, as well as the genius, was inherently American in an especially energetic, lowbrow fashion (although, to be fair, we recall that Italian producers had already found the epic idiom sympathetic to their own Roman-holiday instincts and, independently of Griffith's influence, made *Quo Vadis,* 1913, and *Cabiria,* a D'Annunzio production, 1914). From the mind of D. W. Griffith, a mind at once enterprising, imaginative, original, but completely shallow, there emerged this extraordinary cinematic corollary of the New American's passion for multiplicity, his rootless hunger for an opulent past, his gauche sense of the present's relation to the past, his sentimental version of political and economic inequality, his wistful craving for de-civilized orgy, and his puritanical denunciation of orgy. It is absolutely fitting that the recurring shot of a mother "endlessly rocking" a cradle (as if the cutter had been afflicted by a traumatic maternal compulsion) should have been suggested by a sentiment from Whitman, for the abolition of formal clarity by a confusion of stridently sentimental detail which is so often the effect of a Whitman poem is precisely the effect given by *Intolerance.* (And the hand that rocks the cradle has been ruling the world of American mass art from then out!)

The strike sequence comprised a masterpiece of dialectical cutting—from the battling workers to the increasingly isolated tycoon at his desk—but it was vitiated by the subsequent infantilism in the "mistaken innocent" turn of plot and the generally unrepentant bathos of the ensuing action. It is not too far from the gist of this film to detect in its gratuitous scope that cult of the anachronistic which, at different levels of behavior, can be found in the literature of Melville, Thoreau, and Pound (*Intolerance* as a cine-Minsky edition of the *Cantos?*), in the contemporary musical comedy, and in Los Angeles County architecture. The continuous procreation of sublime and ridiculous in American art is a perversity as well as a sly technique. To crosscut, as Griffith did, from the Siege of Babylon and/or the Massacre of the Huguenots to a speeding train pursued by motorists trying to secure a last-minute pardon from the governor was neither relative nor ironic—it was just damned silly! And we are then and there reminded that if, as the cinema historians tell us, Griffith provided examples of craftmanship for Pudovkin and Eisenstein, he himself was heir to David Belasco and a blood brother in taste to that other dean of disjunctive theater, Eugene O'Neill.

Master of circuses without bread, Griffith fathered a line of producers who to this day and tomorrow primarily conceive of the motion picture as ubiquitous rather than analytic. Actually, there is no such simple alternative; epic, fantasy, and enclosed psychological drama are on equal grounds for movie interpretation. An embarrassment of scenic riches or bare walls may equally well serve the camera's skill. Scope, restless movement, *and* isolation of detail can all be indispensable elements in the composition, whether they serve a thesis saga like Eisenstein's, a Weimar Republic surrealist exercise, or a Hollywood western. They are constants. Any film is necessarily a compilation of single shots. There is no other method from which to begin. The final question lies in the propriety of their combinations. The difficulty of the *panoramic* movie has always been that in the average studio ringmaster's hands ubiquity has become a license for quantity without discrimination. The Griffith precedent has too often encouraged range for its own sake, either the range characterized by constant change of glamorous scene—a travelogue device to keep the patrons awake—or the operative range of the camera *within* any given setting, hungry to taste every item in view, prone to dwell upon the symbolic prop (a crushed rose, a crying baby, a crucifix, an overturned glass) at the expense of the narrative line.

Almost any Hollywood film made from this formula—and a formula it has become, whereas with Griffith it was simply a glib dramatic sense working upon experimental ingenuity—will show us a hundred details superfluous as exposition and unwarranted as emotional index. Moreover, they are usually implausible in terms of visual logic. They are included not because any character in the scene *saw* them that way but because it was so easy for the camera to include them en route. Which is why the early Hitchcock treatment is such a chastening influence whenever applied—that treatment of approach from the single protagonist involved at the cinematic instant. Carol Reed, who was Hitchcock's immediate pupil, has never forgotten the lesson. Cruising the ruins of Vienna or an outpost in Malaya, his cameraman is never allowed to abandon the selective viewpoint to hunt for gratuitous trophies demanded by the gluttonous mind for the rampaging eye. The best directors work with this kind of integrity; but Hollywood practice in the main, dictated by budget-minded producers, will flatter the general spectator's inability to concentrate on logical succession by underlining the relations between objects or by multiplying the spectacular features of any sequence which can be thought to afford it. Any 20th Century–Fox "special" will give you ample evidence. So long as the motion picture is encouraged as a commodity for perpetuating the mass moviegoer, to whom the cinematic ideal is maximum elaboration of scene with minimum necessity for close attention, just so long will it display its adherence to the mercantile bazaar of Griffith's inspiration. Not only *Intolerance* but also *The Birth of a Nation, Way Down East,* and *America* definitively set the pattern for that Hollywood mélange of colossal banality and expert organization which Henri de Montherlant has called "technical perfection in the service of cretinism."

But Griffith would have been no genius worth footnoting if one were unable to rediscover in his primitives those other advantages of cinematic form remarked above. That, in movie-making, ellipsis may be a more valuable art than inclusion Griffith was not the first to expound, although he was one of the first to organize the discovery as a full-length narrative principle. That a single, telling transitional image is more effective, very often, than a half-dozen shots composing a stagelike scene is a commonplace now, if still insufficiently acted upon. To watch *Potemkin,* made some years after *Intolerance,* is to appreciate how much Griffith had already invented without the dialectical rationalization which guided Eisenstein. As a result of this discovery, Griffith as well as Eisenstein very nearly eliminated all cerebral interest from the motion picture. The eye is bombarded with the most explicit of possible images, espe-

cially since neither simultaneous speech nor sound effects are present to relieve the eye of its sole responsibility. (Ergo the appalling
subtitles!) Even with sound, this is still a permanently challenging
problem: how to keep a movie moving and primarily visual without
robbing it of the intellectual (I do not say didactic) ingredient that
must be present in any complex art form.

In attempting to make the film procedure autonomous, Griffith
encountered an esthetic problem without solving it; but his attempt earned our respect. He did put into cinematic practice
Braque's definition of the art of painting which, with slight modi-
fication, indicates the first task of the film-maker: "not the *reconsti-
tution* of an anecdotal fact, but the *constitution* of a pictorial fact."
If Griffith's pictorial facts were so constituted and synthesized as to
necessitate a depraved psychological shorthand for their intellectual continuity, they can nonetheless be credited with having widely
promoted the film's most important independent mutation. From
this selective point of view, we may then admit that the battle for
a purist film art, achieved in directions as various as those taken by
René Clair, Cavalcanti, Cocteau, or Carol Reed, was won, in part,
on the playing fields of Hollywood. If *David and Bathsheba, Duel
in the Sun,* and *Ivanhoe* are contemptibly legitimate offspring of
Intolerance, then *Carnival in Flanders, Beauty and the Beast,* or
The Third Man may be said to bear that unacknowledged distinction which so often belongs to the bastards of a line.

From *Intolerance,* which is simply the most egregious of his pre-
sentations, we can define D. W. Griffith as a Hollywood Faustus
who, with no philosophy and no ideas, with bad taste and a middle-
class apprehension of history, nonetheless established a magical
point of departure, not only for the puerile Cecil B. DeMilles who
have followed in his piously florid steps, but also for whatever
newly equipped visionaries are now fighting, with batallions of experts in their laboratories and on their sets, to create from the chaos
of cinematic juvenility a mature art in which the paraphrasable content is worthy of the informing style.   1954

Postscript 1971. Having long ago restored the rightful credit due
D. W. Griffith, it is now necessary for critical researchers to catch
up with James G. Card's demonstration, with film and lecture, at
the Museum of Modern Art (November 13, 1955), that the art of
cutting to express simultaneity of action in an artistically sustained
film sequence was independently discovered by the Danish director

August Blom in the film *Atlantis*—four years before *Intolerance,* two years before *The Birth of a Nation.* Mr. Card, curator of motion pictures at George Eastman House, Rochester, New York, subsequently published his findings on this subject, which included comparative stills from the films of Blom and Griffith, illustrating unarguably the superiority of Blom's spatial definitions and lighting effects ("Influences of the Danish Film," *Image,* George Eastman House, March 1956). I think it would be difficult to dispute Mr. Card's contention that *Atlantis* was "a film in every technical respect superior to any other motion picture in the world that has been preserved for study from the year 1913." But nobody has attempted to dispute the contention; nobody is aware that it was ever made. Since Mr. Card's lecture was sponsored by the Danish Embassy in New York City, Manhattan "film people," notoriously indifferent to any sources off their beat, were conspicuous by their absence. And since *Image* is read principally by subscribers who are not film critics or historians—it would appear—Mr. Card's contribution was ignored.

I have never subsequently read an acknowledgment of Mr. Card's convincing exposition and in no film encyclopedia, published in any country, which I have consulted have I read any evidence that anyone else was aware of Blom's pioneer achievement. (The Danes had not been, before James Card called Blom to their attention!) I have tiresomely repeated this information, to no avail. I shall tiresomely repeat it until somebody sees the film for himself and ratifies Mr. Card's assertion in the appropriate annals. The influence of Blom on Griffith is purely speculative, and Griffith's accomplishment is in any case not seriously assailable. From the national standpoint, I couldn't care less who discovered or invented what, in the motion picture. But a decent regard for truth is the first principle of scholarship. The petty chauvinism and the simple negligence of those who claim to be film historians are notorious.

Adventures in
Film-Watching

Let every eye negotiate for itself, and trust no agent.
Claudio in *Much Ado*

CHILDREN OF PARADISE *(Les Enfants du Paradis)* —1945*

Although it introduces no fresh mutation of cinema techniques, Marcel Carné's film is expressively superb, conceived symbolically and acted with histrionic elegance and feeling—a rich parable of the uses of love. The subject is masks, enacted against the background of theater (Paris, c. 1840), where all is simulation and dissimulation. Garance, the lunacentric figure of the story—she is first seen as a sideshow attraction, Naked Truth in a well—emerges from the crowd, from the masses of masked anonymity, the pseudo Pierrots and, at the end, disappears into and beyond it, vainly followed by Baptiste, the real Pierrot. Everyone finds in her what his nature and needs dictate: to Forestier, the criminal, she is someone

---

*The date following each title designates the year of the film's release.

who asks nothing and cannot be mastered; to Lemaître, the actor, she is a night in bed (he would like to feel tragic about her but cannot) ; to Monsieur Coudray, the count, she is a possession—he buys yet never owns her. To Baptiste, the mime, she is the moon, the unattainable, the Idea of Love; her carnality he at first refuses but eventually embraces, thus precipitating her flight.

Natalie loves Baptiste who loves Garance who (Baptiste believes) loves Lemaître (who simply loves himself and the simulacra of himself, the parts he plays). Everyone, for an arrested moment as it were, has what he wants; for everyone the possession is a chimera. Natalie has Baptiste, Baptiste has Garance, Lemaître plays the part of Othello (performing a fatal passion which, in reality, he would be too cheerful to undergo!). Coudray, an Othello without love, tries to satisfy his frigid lust-to-avenge by challenging Lemaître to a duel. But Forestier—for whom truth is finally violence, since everything else is unreal—saves Lemaître by murdering the count, and therewith satisfies his own consummate nihilism; it is the most important gesture he has ever made. (The murder takes place in a bathhouse; we see Coudray at last unclothed—which is to say, unmasked.) . . . The pantomimes of Baptiste are commentaries on his own status and on leading themes in the film. With dumb and tragicomic eloquence, he saves Garance from arrest, holds up a clothes line for Natalie, yearns for the moon, and chases butterflies. Lemaître has greater prestige, a more fashionable fame; *he speaks lines.* Yet Baptiste is the real thing—the silent voice of poetry. Real? Impalpable as a gyration of smoke; an epicene clown who impotently thrashes the count's flowers and to whom life and the dream are one. He is left with the dream.

An informer—perhaps the greatest rogue in this allegory—skulks through the film preaching morality, announcing his own spurious identity at every entrance, sweating with self-pity, serving as cynical chorus to the tragedies of others, finally impeding Baptiste's pursuit of Garance in the milling crowd.

LOUISIANA STORY—1948

Twenty-five years ago Robert Flaherty had the courage and skill to film an enthralling and unprecedented documentary on Eskimo life; since then critical opinion has widely agreed that he can do no wrong. The fact is that he has learned no more since than the best men in films everywhere have learned—about exposition, continuity, cutting rhythms, lighting, or narrative suspense. *Louisiana Story:* Any of the boys in the back room—say Rossen, Curtiz, Walsh, Huston, Milestone—could have done as well with less (i.e., with even less money from Standard Oil). And they might have found in the material a subject, a point of view, a treatment.

Subject: As is, confused and neutral. Flaherty meets boy meets coon meets alligator meets oil derrick—loveless love among the bayous. What *should* be the controlling stress? The conditions of backwater life? The impact of machinery on this life? No significant comment is made on either and the two themes never merge. The people themselves seem scarcely viable for documentary treatment: the Cajun family inarticulate, inexpressive (and so unconvincingly polite with one another!) ; the workers on the oil tender so dry and laconic. No suggestion is made of even a banked-down conflict of interests. *Technique:* No rhythm. No meaningful progression of shots. Yards of waste footage, based on the pedestrian assumption that what goes up must be shown coming down or must be seen going all the way to the top. On the other hand, gratuitous cuts to irrelevant images: a madonna on the wall, boy's wiggling toes, and so forth. For transitions, Flaherty still favors the slow fade (he seems to have forgotten the existence of the dissolve). Not a "faked" shot in the whole film, and that's the trouble, because cinema-wise, to fake, in its best sense, is simply to prepare for a sequence under the best condition of angles and light and then to edit it carefully into the montage scheme. By Flaherty's own admission ("Robert Flaherty Talking," in *The Cinema,* 1950, Penguin Books), he is opposed to "pre-visualized" continuity. The result, in this film, is an effect not of spontaneity but of unintegrated odds and ends. The music is no help either. Virgil Thompson makes no such synchronizing contribution as he did to *The River* (1937) ; the score, allegedly derived from Cajun folk tunes, is thematically uninspired, almost as simpering as a Victor Young concoction.

Poet and *poetry* are terms persistently applied to Flaherty and his films. Would anyone care to define the analogy at this point? Flaherty has fought against great odds, earning heartbreak as well as prestige, and the development of the nonfiction film has prospered through his initiative and sacrifice—but let's keep distinctions clean. A poem is a disciplined rhythm with some kind of lyrical direction. Flaherty has been an educator but never a poet. His films have had poetic touches (intrinsic to the scene, as in *Moana* or *Man of Aran*) , but there was never one with anything like the conceptual beauty of Basil Wright's *Song of Ceylon,* which, as well as being a document, was a dance of life.

S.O.S. SUBMARINE (*Uomini del Fondo*) —1950

Made in cooperation with the Italian navy, this enacted or "pseudo" documentary of a sunken-submarine rescue operation is a model for precision and beauty in film-making of this kind: movement all the way, with every detail adding up to montage speed and design, achieved by rapid and ingenious crosscutting, dramatic use of light and perspective. Bulkhead doors closing one by one from distance to closeup; the accelerated sequence where P.T. boats, hydroplanes, and cruisers race to the rescue area; strange, glassy light through fog and the blank light of late dawn on a flat, waveless sea; the interrupted program on Radio Rome and the subsequent shots of suspended activity among the listeners: a billiard ball's slow roll not followed up; a spoon halted over soup; a waiter with an arrested plate of hors d'oeuvres; dissolve from baby in crib through bubbles from the submarine's escape cylinder; the abruptly fantastic ascent of a diver, attired in science-fiction costume, hoisted against a cyclorama of pale sky. And the glorious finale of lined-up sailors grouped in the rigging of waiting ships—black, white, black, white (consummation of a structural dynamic first attempted, perhaps, in *Potemkin*). No shot is ever lingered over; the waiting girls behind the dock gates and the mother talking by telephone to her boy in the submarine are given no extra stress. The film editor keeps his distance while retaining his necessary balance of the human and the accessory, the event and the emotional overtone.

In some neo-realistic quarters, the formalism of Francesco de Robertis' procedure is considered passé; a new snobbery of film criticism is arising that seems to despise directors who know exactly what they are doing with every foot of their film. If, in any instance, the art of montage were to banish the emotional experience which is, after all, the final test for the spectator, reservations would be justified. But in *S.O.S. Submarine* the narrative is not cold, it is simply well ordered; the brilliance of de Robertis' assembly enhances the eloquent central fact—man doing his dangerous job. I would advance this film as substantial evidence against the incoherent method of a *Paisan,* a *Farrébique,* a *Louisiana Story,* in none of which, to my feeling, is there a comparable effect of human endeavor boldly reconceived and rhythmically understood.

CAUGHT—1949

To date, I have never seen a film better directed. . . . Which is not the same as to say that *Caught* is a great film. . . . That a power-driven, psychopathic millionaire (Robert Ryan) should marry a model he encounters casually (Barbara Bel Geddes) in order to spite his psychiatrist, and that subsequently the model, after vainly trying to perform her part in the useless alliance, should learn love and social usefulness from an overworked doctor to the poor (James Mason), may sound like a more promising outline for soap opera than for a brilliant film. But a brilliant and frequently cogent film, thanks to Arthur Laurents, scenarist, and Max Ophuls, director, the outline has become. Ophuls, with years of European film-making behind him, shaped the uneven material into a sardonic essay on one aspect of American social aspirations. The adventure of Leonora Ames in search of a fortune, if inconclusive, reverberates with acutely interpreted undertones. Always beautifully deployed in terms of approach, camera-wise, every scene establishes, sometimes lightly, sometimes searingly, the atmosphere of need become greed—from the beginning, with the camera moving in over the girl and her young roommate, lying on their stomachs in their low-cost apartment, appraising the ads in a snob-appeal women's magazine, to the millionaire Ohlrig's climactic heart attack (neurotically induced) when, as Leonora advances to the door behind which she hears Ohlrig struggling, the camera moves back smoothly to include in the foreground of our view a sculptured lion, rampant, on the hall table.

Although virtually every sequence has its own perfect timing and wryly observed milieu, it is in the goings-on at Ohlrig's mansion that Ophuls' direction is seen at its most expedient: in the ignominious strategies of Franzi, the millionaire's "secretary" (Kurt Bois), a little dancy man with a Continental veneer covering up his worm's function until the moment he, too, has had more than the remains of a man can take; in a home-movie showing (itself a gem) and its acrid aftermath—Leonora shouting at the tyrannical Ohlrig across the vast space of the manorial game room. Ophuls has an astute way with the moving camera, employing it to involve the spectator in the nervous tension of a scene. On one occasion, Franzi is awaiting Ohlrig's late arrival home, sitting blandly at the piano, playing the same tune over and over, while Leonora lies on the couch, a mile away, complaining of Ohlrig's neglect of her. Franzi responds by monotonously repeating, in a suave Viennese accent, "Tough, darling, tough!" and continuing to pound out the waltz tune. The camera accompanies Leonora's indignant progress across the room, her destination the relentless piano; by the time she has reached Franzi, slapped his face, and slammed the piano lid down on his fingers, we're right with her, lending kinetic support. . . . Of such details is the film made: If, as a story line, it fails to meet the full requirements of its socially sinister possibilities—Leonora's dilemma is far too simply resolved—it succeeds as a qualitatively rich lesson in the art of the film director: the art of making an unexceptional story count for more than, in its preliminary form, it would seem to suggest—or even to deserve?

THE THIRD MAN—1949

To analyze *The Third Man* strictly by the logic of literature (an improbably impudent exercise at one's first bombarded exposure to it) is to sacrifice an intense experience of a far different order. Within the framework of commercial film-making, the film is exceptional for the quality of its rhythmic structure, achieved by Carol Reed's supple interlacing of effects: the profusion of low-level, tilted, and oblique shots; the short duration of separate images in narrative sequences; the almost exclusive use of the cut (there is very little tracking camera and few dissolves) ; the sharply selected "off-mike" sounds; and by the urgency of the zither—not an accompaniment merely but a counter-figure that contributes its own special pattern, as every good film score should. These means to fluidity, surprise, and persuasion, combined with the unreal reality of war-stripped Vienna and the incidental locales—a cemetery, a Ferris wheel, the sewers, the wide boulevards—give the whole film a percussive fluency, like a plausibly scripted nightmare. Seldom has the actor seemed less important (which is not to say that Cotten, Howard, Welles, and the Austrian contingent are not *effective*) ; seldom have the concatenating shocks of sound-and-visual seemed so justifiably vehement. Realism, nominally the category under which one would classify this picture, is not somehow the final impression received. A melodrama of an American pulp-writer trying to solve the death of a black-market friend assumes the character of a Hoffmanesque charade. Actuality here has a pitch reminiscent of certain early Eisenstein episodes or the opening sequences of *Variety,* wherein what is being told finds such aggrandizement by style that its essential shallowness (as idea) goes unacknowledged.

Criticizing seriously *The Third Man's* particularities, one may easily conclude that the intellectual content is glib, and go on from there to beg the question of the kind of psychological melodrama Graham Greene has been writing for years, in which serious problems of man's fate are resolved by violence and luridly devised irony. I'd rather not assist at such a digression in this context; the burning question is whether or not *The Third Man* as a *movie* experience overcomes whatever reservations one may entertain of its synopsizable content. For me it does; it left me, besides an esthetic lift, a moody sense of tragedy muffled—as when someone is murdered next door.

Assuming the continuity of the scenario as given, there are perhaps three really superfluous moments: the teddy-bear closeup in the hospital, the parrot-biting episode when Holly Martins flees the lecture room, and Orson Welles's overplayed finger-grappling through the sewer grille. These will be superseded in my memory by the electrical climaxes—the zither tune rising with ominous jubilation as the light flashes on to illuminate the resurrected Harry Lime; the porter's cautious revelation to Martins from an upper window, while street sounds recapitulate the earlier "accident" that "There vas a *third* man"; the small boy with a face like a smooth, ancient planet, blank with mindlessness, giving the hue and cry with his imbecilic, "Der wars. Ja, papa, der ist der mörder"; and by the last shot, where Anna walks away from Martins and from life—Who'll be chief mourner?—and Martins lights his cigarette as all the leaves in Vienna, it seems, fall from the sad and stately trees.

THE QUEEN OF SPADES—1949

At the second climax, the ghost of the Countess Anna visits the penurious Lieutenant Hermann to give him the dread secret of the cards which she had been too terrified to give him that snowy night he had forced himself into her solitary presence and frightened her to death. The moment depends for its great effectiveness on what has been prepared in the film up to this point. We've become accustomed to seeing the ancient countess, a towering wig on her riveted head, supporting herself by a stick and dragging yards of skirt train behind her, looking for all the world like an overdressed snail—you can almost see the trail of slime—as she takes her painfully slow way down the halls and across the lobbies of her palace, her punctuating stick and sliding skirt making a sound best described as BOMP-pause-SWOOSH. Fittingly, then, her ghost is a *sound* ghost. Hermann's door bursts open before a blast of swirling wind; a presence, a *something* bears down on him; photographed from his witness point, table and chairs rise from the floor and fly out into space. He retreats, almost crawling to the wall; we hear the familiar BOMP-pause-SWOOSH of the stick and skirts—then the spectral voice of the old ruin, gratifying his desperate obsession!

The texture of the film throughout has to be so designed as to make inevitable our intercourse with the macabre and the supernatural; it *is* so designed, sumptuously, with fine resources of dramatic irony, symbolic impositions of image, metaphorical cuts, relational arrangements within the scene or from one scene to another. Lizaveta, the young ward stifling in the service of the withered countess, is shown freeing birds from their cages in the market; at night she tosses in her bed and the voice of Hermann (who is actually wooing her solely to gain access to the palace) murmurs in her dreams, while a spider web is superimposed across the screen. . . . A flashback to the countess' youth, when she had visited the fearful castle of the necromancer, St. Germain, tracks her down corridors to the ultimate, self-opening door, and an impact of the unspeakable is achieved by an abrupt cut to her waiting carriage horses, rearing in panic against the night sky. . . . Similarly, as Hermann gropes for the secret panel in the countess' florid bedroom after she has died of fright (early in the film she crabbily asserted, "I might die of sudden shock"), the startling cuts from Hermann's back to her open but sightless eyes enforce the terror of his position; when he stumbles away from the palace in the snow, the whole world becomes, in an overhead shot with another superimposed image, the dead woman's frozen, staring eyes.

Although it would be invidious to slight the multiple skills that organized the complex wonders of this picture—the skills of the writers (Rodney Ackland and Arthur Boys), of the designer and set decorator (Oliver Messel and William Kellner), of the cinematographer (Otto Heller), and, naturally, of the director (Thorold Dickinson)—it must be allowed that their manifold efforts would have missed fruition without the compelling performances of Anton Walbrook and Edith Evans. Film criticism can usually afford to disregard actors in a film's total effect, unless they are grossly bad or overwhelmingly good. Evans and Walbrook *are* overwhelming (the supporting players are perhaps too sharply British to sustain a complete sense of Russian society at the turn of the last century). Dame Evans' cracked-voice petulance, her goggling eyes and stiff neck, the mute vividness of her fear, temptation, and resistance when Hermann invades her sanctuary; Walbrook's passionately mobile voice, whispering, trumpeting, lingering on vowels with love, with disdainful emphasis, or with contempt; his economy of movement, the relaxed eloquence of his hands and shoulders, his swaggering pride, and his broken despair (all of which casts into outer darkness the frigid Olivier) : this is the very ecstasy of acting—*cinema* acting, precisely adjusted to the nuance of closeup or the bravura of distance.

A baroque film version of an occult fantasy by Pushkin—neither socially relevant, nor *avant garde,* nor Disney. I suspect it will go right on by without anyone's giving it a second look, even assuming they give it a first one.

FORBIDDEN GAMES *(Jeux Interdits)* —1952

> *. . . after the first death there is no other.*

The opening is a concentrated classic of exposition by terror. . . . Fugitives from Paris on a country road, 1940. Hundreds of them, in cars, in carts, on foot. Murmur of mingled sounds. A jam at the bridge crossing a river. Blowing of horns, altercation. Messerschmidts zoom from the sky. The people break, scatter, flatten themselves, flee down embankments into the fields. A rasping clatter from the strafing planes; crescendo and diminution. . . . The planes disappear and a moment's hush takes over before the fugitives surge back to the road. In that hush, the camera frames a dilapidated car with its engine left on, shuddering like an accordion or a failing heart. Again the rhythm of feverish flight. The bridge is cleared, but an ominous drone disturbs the lull. A five-year-old girl runs across the exposed bridge in pursuit of her escaping dog. The parents run to catch the child. Messerschmidts again. Couple, child, and dog drop in an embracing heap. A spray, like purposeful hailstones, whips a path across the bridge and the couple rear up like galvanized frogs, with sudden and swiftly terminated grimaces of pain. The Messerschmidts vanish. . . . The child stares with incomprehension at the inert couple, touches her mother's face with experimental curiosity. She walks away, holding the dead dog by its front legs; its hindquarters dangle, shuddering spasmodically like the abandoned car. The girl wanders along the riverbank, puzzled by the odd behavior of her pet. She stands indecisively at a path from a field. A cow lumbers down it toward the river. . . . She cries. . . .

Thereafter, the film takes up the child's adoption by a clownish farming family, most responsibly by the eleven-year-old son, Michel, with whom she becomes merrily implicated in a game of Burial. This innocently macabre pastime brings to a climax the grotesque feud existing between the family and its neighbors. Over the vehement protests of Michel, the waif is subsequently removed to a city Red Cross distribution center. Here, the world she never made—where love and death are the two most shattering facts for the living to survive—enters her consciousness with a burst of illumination, and on her heartbreaking screams—"Michel! Michel! Michel!" —the picture closes.

Summary is inadequate to convey anything but the general conception, surely the most extraordinary blend of tragedy and ferocious comedy ever achieved in the history of film-making. The child's adventure is but the nucleus of a richly unsparing comment on the pathos of the irrelevant: a children's game of Graveyard and the rivalry of oafs, while the juggernaut of war thunders by. Statement and texture are all of a piece, in the interests of which analysis can credit without hoping to define (of the acting, in every case, it is superfluous to speak, for this is not "acting," and Brigette Fossey seems to be the child of all time for whom the dreadful word *poignant* was devised—her presence is spun gold) ; the lighting of René Clément's compositions is a miracle of craft; the synchronization and editing of the sound are meticulous; the guitar themes arranged and played by Narciso Yepes constitute the most unique scoring since *The Third Man* or *Los Olvidados*.

LIMELIGHT—1952

Inside Chaplin

A creative cinematic imagination gone to seed. *Limelight* cruelly exposes the limitations of Chaplin as producer, for it is everything, most of the time, a movie *shouldn't* be: overwritten, underdirected, slowly paced, monotonously photographed, fumblingly cut—and oh so *dreary,* far beyond any justification from the milieu, a penury of the soul. . . . . The first ten minutes, roughly, are good Chaplin, relatively pure cinema: camera tracking from the street into the rooming house, around the gas-filled bedroom where the dancer lies in a coma of attempted suicide; Calvero's raffish entrance, his blurred alcoholic dignity; pantomime with the doorkey, unsteady progress upstairs, business of smelling gas, inspecting his cigar and the sole of his shoe—all shopworn but disarmingly executed trifles; his resolute rescue of the girl, absurd strategy with the landlady, the lecture to the ailing dancer on the cosmic glories of Consciousness while she retreats into a snore. Up to this point, or shortly thereafter, the situation is managed with a fine balance of tragic and comic, dramatic and ludicrous, theatrical and cinematic. But from here on, Chaplin abandons all effort to keep his invention within these disciplined commutations of method. The whole gorgeous potentiality breaks down, washes away in a welter of tears, archness, smut, coincidental meetings, Pagliacci closeups, and in *talk, talk, talk.* For interminable stretches he either sets his camera while two or three actors play out a scene virtually face front, with no cuts to benefit either their comfort or the scene's modulations, or he simply moves in to a close shot from middle distance. These are almost the limits of his *motion.* When, during a ballet sequence, he suddenly gives us four overhead shots in as many minutes, the change of perspective is so unprepared for as to seem completely out of key.

Chaplin should have long ago—as far back as *Modern Times,* for instance—placed his idiosyncratic genius for pantomime and his occasionally seminal ideas at the disposal of a sympathetic director who might have created a context in which they were neither dissipated nor overdeployed. But this is to imagine a totally different personality for an artist who has increasingly become his own worst enemy from the deluded notion that it is not enough for him to be an ingenious comic—he must also be an entrepreneur with a message about faith, hope, and charity who can yet afford to ignore the finer details of everything but his own performance. (He was once a master of cutting and timing, but that was in another country and the muse is dead.) In this film, where he has so much to say about pride and imagination—"My dear, you are *such* an artist!" Calvero tells the dancer, with luminous sincerity—it is all the more pitiable that during these verbal protests he is betraying the very art which has given him fame by dishonoring its fullest and liveliest possibilities and reducing it to a showcase for his personal uneasiness. (There's an embarrassment of riches here for the analyst of Chaplin's bifocalism. In the person of Calvero, he airily mentions five marriages, flaunts the name of Freud, stands before his own youthful photograph in the same pose, confesses ambivalence toward the public, and has nightmares of an audience walking out on him!)

1954

"Hardly a Man Is Now Alive": Monologue on a Nazi Film

You hear that the Museum of Modern Art is to show a film of the Olympic Games, made at Berlin in 1936: in two parts, for God's sake!—two afternoon sessions of an hour and forty minutes each! You ask yourself, "What's in this for me, besides the occupational compulsion of the critic to see everything? Three hours and twenty minutes of the extrovert ideal? Strictly for mesamorphs!"

Supervising director, Leni Riefenstahl. The name rings a cracked bell: a German actress who became a Hitler favorite. Memory prods: called by some a genius, by others an upstart given credit for the achievements of her production staff. She received especially high praise from Robert Flaherty, did she not, in a footnote to an article on film-making? You're not in agreement with the orthodox, who believe in Flaherty as the Holy Ghost of that Trinity which allegedly comprises D. W. Griffith and Eisenstein as well. Still, you look up the reference (Penguin-Pelican: *The Cinema,* 1950)—"Robert Flaherty Talking":

> Hitler was a very clever fellow. . . . He spared no effort to make films and use them . . . wonderful films made by Leni Riefenstahl, but terrifying like her *Triumph of the Will*. Here was a film made in 1934 in which you saw even then that the Nazis were a psychopathic case with whom to reason was impossible. But that film, which because of its revelation could have had a vital influence on subsequent events, was suppressed. . . .

Instantly you're intrigued, if not intimidated. Whatever you think of Flaherty's place in the hierarchy of film-makers, you believe him to have been a decent, humane personality who would scarcely have extended compliments lightly to a Nazi-ess. You can argue privately and some other day as to whether the cinematic "revelation" of Nazi psychosis would have had any influence on anything whatever. For the present you are going to see an Important Film— unquote. But two days' worth of the Olympic Games! The knees boggle. How documentary can you get?

Sunday afternoon and it's raining on Fifty-third Street. Everywhere else, too. Not without misgivings, you enter the wet crush in the museum's own bargain basement and wait among the aquatints and the lithographs with all those others: the look-at-me contingent from the Village, the earnest (heavily or mildly) boys and girls from Columbia (or N.Y.U., or C.C.N.Y., or the New School), the neutrals who pardonably just want the most from their sixty cents' worth of admission—and perhaps even an aging hero or heroine who competed in the Games of 1936. . . . You take a seat within reasonable distance of the door, just in case. The girl next to you opens a pocket-book edition of *The Life of the Bee*. Maybe she's smart. The house lights go down; small, subtle ones come on in the ceiling. Just enough light for taking notes—*if* it's necessary.

Olympiad, 1936! Part I. Martial music. The introductory credit informs you that this colossal reportage was undertaken by a horde of photographers who employed everything from pocket Leicas to telescopic lenses and took their vantage points in towers, in underground pits, on wheels, in underwater compartments, and in balloons (also, as you will later infer, hanging by their thumbs). Four language versions of the film were made, and two years were occupied in the cutting process. . . . All right, so it's thorough. You can just bet it's going to be thorough!

The opening image is a mass of clouds or murk which the camera slowly penetrates. Boulders. Slabs of stone. A fractured landscape, wuthering. . . . Broken columns. Weed-riven steps. A collapsed cornice.

You get the point. Greece: ruins of the Olympiad site.

Flames. A naked youth apotheosized to carry the torch in relay. Leisurely cutting, as a succession of beach boys trots across the Grecian landscape, down to the verge of the sea, and then, by way of "dissolves," up through the ages. The four elements—air, earth, fire, and water. Inevitable? All the same it's pretty damned impressive. Within five minutes you're more enthralled than patient; within twenty minutes it dawns on you that if this keeps up you're seeing one of the very great cooperatively made fact films on record. . . . And it keeps up.

Much of it is Siegfriedian; all of it is imposing. . . . At the top of a spectacular flight of steps a Nordic male animal lights a caldron which is to burn throughout the Olympiad. They've placed the caldron where the sun will set directly behind it (like Reinhardt, who timed the striking of all the clocks in town for a scene in his open-air production of *The Miracle*) ; and there is one stunning shot of the flames licking and consuming the molten star as it sinks: a terrifying conceit when you recall the date—1936. *Morgen die Welt!*

After the fanfares, the shots of Hitler, the panorama of flags, and the release of about a million doves (what a touch!) , *Olympiad* gets under way. From now on you're in the hands of an excellent (if, at times, unconsciously comic) British announcer, of you don't know how many hundred cameramen as ubiquitous as Mercutio's Queen Mab, and of a film editor (or staff of them) brilliant as they come. The announcer gets his first laugh from the audience (let's agree, there's nothing sharper than a New York audience) ; naming the entrants for the first event, he declares cheerfully, "Another American! They keep popping up!"

Now the strategy, generally speaking, is established. Wide-angle shots of the event, the particular stage, so to speak: the stretch, the pit, the circle; move in, oversee, participate. From the total action to the detail. Whole to part, part to whole. Medium-distance shot, closeup face on, profile, low level, overhead.

Jesse Owens' jaw muscle tightens; a vein throbs in his temple; he swallows.

The man in the white coat (he looks like a village butcher) warns, with an upward inflection, *"Fertig!"* Runners up on their toes and fingertips. Two seconds of dry-mouthed tension. The gun goes off, and the sprinters leave with a velocity suggesting they've been shot from its barrel.

The cameras do their jobs, methodically, and with unflagging variety of witness point, reporting their subject—competition. The track event, the shot put, the discus, the hurdles, high jump, broad jump. You're overhead, underneath, running parallel, out in front, or standing by politely. Cameras pan, swivel, tilt, track, or just wait. You confront the pole-vaulter as he begins his run, or you concentrate on the pole's point, merely, as it goes into the ground. Or you wait and crane your neck as the vaulter comes over on top of you. Or you go up with him on a pole of your own and just grunt. And in one shot you remain focused on the pole pit, and see the action in shadow only.

Slow motion. The weight throwers bounce in an unearthly levitation, spongelike, straining to keep their momentum from carrying them over the chalk line.

The girls take the high jump; legs almost horizontal scissor suggestively before your eyes.

Faces: Nordic, Celtic, Mediterranean, Oceanic, Asiatic. Monkey faces, dog faces, horse faces, pig faces. And bull necks.

Heads: Dolicho-, brachy-, and mesocephalic.

The look of strain.

The set of determination.

The expression of surprise.

The controlled elation.

Chewed lips, knit brows; the shrug and the faint smirk that says, "Take *that!*"

The British announcer again: "It's a serious business, this putting the shot."

Tensions of the Olympics audience, inter-cut. Italians jump into the air, gesticulate, and yell. Germans look stolid or allow themselves a quiet, triumphant tic, one side of the face at a time. Hitler grins (Germany has just won something). The German rooting section intones *"Sieg Heil"*; the Japanese chant *"Nish-i-da, Nish-i-da"*; the French project crisply something resonant you don't quite catch; an American claque gives its rah-rah-rah, though not as intensely organized as on native ground. And somewhere in the middle of it all, a tidy group of English youngsters enunciates: "We want you to win! We want you to win!"

Fertig!

Most of the music (by Herbert Windt) sounds like Richard Strauss (even when it's good) and the rest like the Mars movement of *The Planets Suite* by Holst, most effective where it accompanies the flight of the javelins—a trembling roar and a high-pitched chord as they plunge, quivering, into the ground. The Japanese and the Filipinos look atavistic as they grasp their javelins weapon-wise— suddenly centuries (or at least oceans) removed, spearing a boar in the jungle or a seal from a hide boat.

Sieg Heil! We are the great companions! What do you see, Doktor Freud? *I see men and women everywhere*—mutually exclusive. The primary sexual inhibition of our time here gets conditional sanction. Never has there been so much public intrasexual hugging and kissing as the vicarious embrace the victorious, and not all of it unconscious. A German girl, the favorite in the high jump, leaps to success, the focus of hungry female eyes, caught by the cameras with their usual impartial pertinence (or shall you say impertinent partiality?). She throws herself to the ground and is covered by a blanket; a minute later the camera pivots back as she watches her competitor. In the corner of the frame you glimpse another girl's arm moving to encircle her. . . . Behind you in the theater a woman's startled voice asks, "Who's *that?*" and her male companion answers knowingly, "Her *coach,* I suppose!" . . . You hear a low rumble, apparently from the sound track, which you can't quite identify in the context—premonitory, subterranean. Later you realize it was merely subterranean: the Eighth Avenue subway train on its way to Jamaica, reverberating beneath the museum's auditorium.

Night comes down over the Berlin field. The caldron burns brightly, illuminating the hopes of thousands, heating the sinister ambition of millions. . . . The pole-vaulters carry on. A record must be broken. Up and over! Hands leave the pole only at the last inch of moment, as if the pole were being gently planted, while its planter rises reluctantly to the dark sky. A weary Japanese boy shakes his head in the flickering light, resigning himself visibly to the fates before he starts his brief run; you can feel him calling up all his reserve of adrenalin. Up!—and over. Not quite! He dislodges the bar and the film audience, well in it now, expresses disappointment with a kindred groan. The British announcer says, extenuatingly, "Oh well—he must be tahd!"

Shot of empty stadium, ringed by searchlights, like a mountainous shower curtain. Dissolve to a tolling bell, from the bell to the caldron, from the caldron to the flags of all nations, revolving, ascending, and descending in double exposure. The Olympics flag with its linked circles. The caldron again and smoke rising. Berlin, 1936. Trumpets.

Lights . . .

Indubitably you are still at 11 East Fifty-third Street. You rise, disoriented but surcharged with vicarious energy. The girl in the next seat is finishing another paragraph in *The Life of the Bee*. You wonder if she comes here to read. Why not? Probably it's more comfortable and no more distracting than where she lives. . . . Swaggering from the auditorium, you take the stairs to the street floor, three at a time, potentially invincible. You consider inspecting the authentic Japanese house which has been reassembled in the museum's garden, but the consideration is short-lived; your Sagittarian impulses resent being Librafied. Corrupted by kinesis, you want nothing so much as to broad-jump the pond or to pole-vault over the garden railings into the middle of Fifty-fourth Street. You telephone a friend with whom you're to have dinner. You ask him if he has any liniment.

Second day. No rain, but the streets are damp. The quiescence of the Japanese house seems more appealing—the uncluttered life. . . . The museum theater is not as full, and the Monday audience has a more distinct air of professional curiosity. The *Bee* girl is not in attendance. Perhaps she has resumed her studies in the more cavernous privacy of the Radio City Music Hall.

Olympiad, Part II, is clearly the object of more artifice than Part I. Reportage is giving way further to poetry. . . . The opening is pastoral: a Siegfried idyll or an ode to matutinal joy. Dawn; beetle on a dewy leaf and birds caroling. No Disneyizing. No editorial comment. The camera speaks, unaided. . . . The houses sleep. Only the lawn sprinklers are active. Contracted sun rays splinter, making crosses and stars in the interstices of the trees, and a lone youth lopes through the woods. The community stirs itself—not yet to compete but to limber. Men shadow-box, relax their necks, kick soccer balls, walk with ludicrous short steps, raising their knees high, like herons. Others merely have their calves massaged while they lie smiling at the sun. Even the Germans look happy. The girls enact similar prologues, but since on the whole they are less attractive, clouds and sunbeams are wisely superimposed on the montage.

The stadium fills again; the preliminary exhibition is an unstinting display of *Kultur*. This is gymkhana with a vengeance. Battalions of German man- and womanhood (but you can barely tell women from men without a program) perform a joyless if intrepid ceremony of calisthenics. They leapfrog leather-bound horses and indulge in tendon-pulling feats of skill on horizontal bars, evoking every moment an intent, if unintentional, political myth: tempting the precarious balance, straddling the pit, suspended cruciform in mid air with horizontal arms clutching iron rings. The women distend their thigh muscles, clench their jaws, knot their biceps, split themselves through the pelvis, as if to see how far they can submit their femininity to the test of rupture. . . . Hitler smiles. (He's got doves in his gloves.)

International rivalry is resumed, and the swimming matches are as fleet, as breathtaking, as anxiously observed by the omnipresent and nimble cameras as everything else. . . . With the high-diving event, objectivity falters; the provocation for a sortie of expressionism was too strong. At this point, Fraülein Riefenstahl, or whoever, must have decided, with sweeping disregard for the nominal subject, "To hell with the Olympics! Let's just make a glorious movie!" . . . Shots, low level and diagonal, of a diver impelled from the springboard, hinging in air against a sun-edged cloud. Crosscut to another. Increase of pace by cutting the duration of each shot. The sequence becomes a fantasia of springing divers, outlined against the chiaroscuro sky, "not to eat, not for love," but only diving. You no longer know or care who is diving for what team or with what score. Surely these flexed and soaring figures are meant to poise themselves, step tiptoe, bounce, jackknife, twist in half gainers, spiral, swallow-flight and swan eternally, with trumpets to herald their abrupt ascent and their plummeting fall. The camera as Wagner? Yet more to the point of analogy you are reminded, by way of Malraux, of the clay models of divers Tintoretto used from which to paint his cloud-borne angels.

After hours (or should you say miles of footage) at a nervously dynamic *presto,* modified only by intermitted snatches of slow motion, an *allegro moderato,* nautical, sets in with the yacht races on the Kiel Canal. In order to preserve the necessary ratio of tension, since to the eye a racing sailboat has a totally different rhythm of suspense from a running man, a zooming javelin, or a bounding diver, the camera's witness point and the tempo of the cutting are artfully manipulated. As the boats veer into the wind around the buoys with gunwales almost under, you move in suddenly to get the vertigo sensation of a slumping list to port and glimpse the quick action of hand-over-hand hauling or a scramble for the tiller; and in one magnificent head-on shot, with a convoluting wave in the foreground, the victor's bow rights on a swell to perpendicular and the spinnaker sail bellies out like a triumphal banner, beautiful and strange as a sea-borne flower.

There is no breaking of stride in this cinematic ingenuity. Still Aquarius bound, you are next parallel with and abreast of the shell-racers, whose brief, synchronous, exacting efforts compose one of the most rhythmically exciting effects in the world of organized sport. Here you can only guess, wildly, how some of the shots were obtained, for during one explosive sequence you are in a half-dozen boats within fewer seconds, each time squarely confronted by a face-less coxswain with a megaphone strapped over his mouth like a gas mask, yelling "Stroke!" in six different languages! . . . Surely this is the climax, you hope, since you are by now solicitous of the film editor's ability to keep this material going with sustained interest. You need not be. After this, the cross-country bicycle grind, the appalling steeplechases, and that punishing trial of versatility, the decathlon, captured in a walkaway by a prodigy from California, Glen Morris—now a name in a sports almanac (after an inglorious interlude as one of Hollywood's Tarzans) .

Not the least remarkable job of photography (again challenging your credulity and your inferences) is the exhausting marathon, cross-country, where, in one instance, you conclude that the camera-man is either sitting on the contestant's shoulders, like Sinbad's Old Man of the Sea, or is spying from a low-flying balloon that casts no shadow. (Nothing would surprise you; Abel Gance, a French film director, once tied his camera to the tail of a "runaway" horse!) But in this case the plausible (and more prosaic) explanation is that the runner (the plodder) was followed by a car from which a camera was suspended from a boom over his head. (This is your guess and you're stuck with it.) Anyway it's uncomfortably astonishing to look down and see those feet as close as if they were your own, lifted up and set down in a grueling battle against fatigue and spots before the eyes. You wonder if he felt like a donkey, with the carrot above instead of beyond his reach. Or was he past feeling anything but the unyielding ground and the cruelly receding finish line?

The finale involves more swirling flags, the stadium in a long shot, and again the tolling bell. . . . *Never send to know—*

Well, what *have* you seen? A documentary record of the Olympic Games—it says here. You can do better than that. The organization of a life force made into art by the collaboration of sensitive instruments. . . . But as you leave the auditorium you overhear a skeptic saying, "With all those cameras, you couldn't miss!" The hell you couldn't and the hell they don't! Try to find an equal five minutes in the billion feet you've seen of Fox Movietone, Pathé, and Paramount, the Eyes, Ears, Nose, and Throat of the World. You saw nothing like this. *Olympiad, 1936* is not a newsreel; it is history, estheticized. And what else? For the hindsight implications are rampant while you smoke your cigarette among the lithographs once more. Berlin, 1936—made possible by Berlin, 1934—the Reichstag. The flames rise as they'd risen before and would again: 1939, 1941, 1945. . . .

The participants. What happened to them? Where are they now —the ones who didn't play Tarzan or who didn't survive to cherish the fallen arch, the fatted calf, the varicose vein? *By brooks too broad for leaping?* . . . All that prowess and mindless agility. The gratuitous beauty of keeping fit. Two thousand sets of coordinated muscles dedicated to an exhibitionism where victory (apart from the scoreboard) is so often a collapse, a speechless gasp, or an ugly convulsion, like a parody of sexual ecstasy; where the reward is a wreath of myrtle placed on the brows, in this case by the Reichsführer's Rhinemaidens, in khaki with overseas caps. *Sieg Heil! Allons enfants! Of Thee I Sing!* Images of humanism disporting not only for national aggrandizement but also for the edification of a piece of human filth who will subsequently break their limbs on the beaches of Normandy, bury their torsos under the leaves of the Ardennes, splinter their javelins on the coasts of Italy, shatter their swan dives over the fires of Kiel. *Pro patria mori.*

The massive folly of the physical. Organized athletics, a perennial structure for collectivizing the beautiful, the belligerent, and the hollow; valid symphony of and for Hydra; and pandemic rationale of the third sex for whom, like Whitman, life can be verified only by the smell of sweat from a million armpits.

All the same, you've seen a great movie, and you wonder whatever happened to Leni Riefenstahl. (*The Thane of Fife had a wife.*

Where is she now?) Did Adolf the Hammer ever realize that *Olympiad, 1936* was an act of treason? The redemption of the adrenal cortex by the creative eye? The vindication of mass by perspective?

The aim was to win. The Americans won—that is, the contest. But Germany won, too. You've just seen the winner, a lyric wrested from the enemies of the lyrical.

The bust outlasts the citadel . . . sometimes.

Outside the museum, it's raining again.   1955

Fugue of Faces: A Danish Film and Some Photographs

Those of us for whom the written word is after all the sustaining expression to which we turn for statements of the imaginative and intellectual life must deplore the contemporary abandonment of reading in favor of those shortcuts to culture which are actually endless detours: the picture magazine (see, look, and live!), television, and the movie. For a film critic, this is an especially troublesome acknowledgment, since his function is precisely to discover and relate in motion picture art those concerns which are basic to all the expressive arts. If he is honest, he will admit that instances of a film, in its own esthetic terms, supplying the spectator with an experience equal in serious definition and in style to the arts with which it is contemporary, are distressingly rare. Carl-Theodore Dreyer's *The Passion of Joan of Arc,* a silent movie (this, one hour after you've watched it, seems hard to believe), is one of those instances; it forces our consent to the proposition that *to see* is as fruitful as *to know,* when the object of our seeing has been invested with the form that inspires knowledge. Knowledge of the poetic order, let us say.

Ideally the cinema, like painting in this respect, is not a substitute for verbal revelation. It is an art with its own responsibilities and its own means for extracting, as in the Dreyer film, the sum of tragedy from a unified visual experience. It is in the highest sense an illiterate art. The least impressive films are often those that affect literacy. These may entertain; they may flatter the pretensions of the word-snob; they accomplish nothing—nothing that the theater can't accomplish. They attract the eye without opening it, and if they are "sound" films they assail the ear without attuning it. The pure film constitutes a world of feeling before which, as audience, our senses are sharpened and our minds stimulated as they would be in scrutinizing great plastic art or in apprehending the ideas of a critic or novelist. The relative immediacy of even an exceptional motion picture is deceptive. Easy enough, in many cases, to follow the visual story line, but extraordinarily difficult for most people to recognize the selective and complex means by which a sequence of photographs, moving forward in time as variously as water or as music, has become the instrument of a moral imagination. *The Passion of Joan of Arc,* made by a Dane with French actors in 1928, narrated almost entirely in closeup, vindicates the cinematic ideal.

Not the least remarkable feature of this film is the daring curve that Dreyer took—backward, so to speak—in the direction of the manipulated still, and away from the more eclectic methods of the greatest among his contemporaries, such as Epstein, Murnau, Ruttman, and Eisenstein (though one does wonder whether his sharpest point of departure mightn't have been conceived after studying the mesmeric Odessa Steps sequence in *Potemkin*). Especially during the first long inquisition passage, his method is deliberately *successive,* rather than fluid or percussive. In the process of fashioning a film which to this day has few equals in uniqueness of conception (or in depth of feeling), Dreyer risked sacrificing the quintessence of cinema: interfluent motion. He took the risk and made a masterwork, incomparable and inimitable: a play (in the fugal sense) of photos—a *photoplay* (what a pity the term has been otherwise appropriated!). And the austerity of its means is the controlling factor of its greatness. Cutting from closeup to closeup was already, in 1928, one of the accepted ellipses of dramatic continuity in films, but it had simply never occurred to anyone to try sustaining the device, with but few variations, for the full length of a movie.

Dreyer opened his film *in medias res*. No preliminaries; no exposition of where and when. (We all know about Joan of Domrémy-la-Pucelle!) A hand thumbs a legal volume, closeup, and we are thereupon moved abruptly into the courtroom (into *a* courtroom—medieval, perhaps; the furnishings roughly denote the period, but the clothing of Joan's inquisitors is timelessly ecclesiastic, and the British soldiers wear World War I helmets with chin straps!). A stool is contemptuously set down for the prisoner, who from here on is the almost unrelentingly focalized object of the camera. We are placed *in* Joan's world, which consists of little else but facial reflections of her inner conviction assailed by the faces of her enemy—*men*. Importunate men: leering, skeptical, fanatical, stupid—or pitying, from a complacent distance. Under Dreyer's supervision, Rudolf Maté bears down with the camera as if he were going to devour the actors with it, stressing the mystic's unbridgeable isolation and magnifying, to the point of grossness, the fidgeting mortality of her prosecutors. An inquisitor picks his nose, scratches the bald top of his head, or pulls at a tuft of his sweating tonsure. A monk, fuming and obscene, vituperates the prisoner in a visible shower of spittle. . . . A fly settles on Joan's face. . . . The "trial" becomes a fugue of faces—beleaguered Maid and predisposed tribunal —subject and counter-subject circumscribed within a visual polyphony, unabating and nobly monotonous. Yet there is development, crescendo, statement, and restatement. For rhythmic variety, Dreyer employed both the cut and the laterally moving camera (i.e., panning), and his closeups are fabulously varied—taken full face, profile, slantwise, overhead, from below, and from the back. Sometimes a head occupies the whole frame, sometimes one side or a corner only.

As the film advances to its terrible climax—by way of the torture chamber and preparations in the marketplace for the burning of Joan—the action grows more inclusive, and the cutting rate is faster. The world *is* larger than a courtroom or a dungeon—but not much larger—ringed by walls, guards, moats, stern towers, and the machinery of execution. But there *are* people in it besides inquisitors; ordinary people, curious, frightened, obdurate, wanting (perhaps) to understand, to sympathize, to feel, above all to believe. The sky is like a steel helmet, yet there is room in it for birds to fly, unimpeded, from the prison to the church. The gravedigger shovels up a skull. A flower blooms. In the crowd a baby feeds at the breast, gulping on plenitude, then turns to stare at the doomed woman with neuter eyes that offer no solace from the comfortable world of its innocence. The birds fly over, unrestricted by chains or by self-imposed fictions of the spirit which are nonetheless all Joan knows of truth. The impossible doubt invades her. If *no one* shares her conviction, could she not be mistaken? She has but to declare that there were no visions, no visitations, that there can be nothing beyond the touch, the smell, the look, the accustomed relationship of substances in space. . . . She recants, eager to repossess the natural world. But this alternative is denied her; instead she is condemned to imprisonment and returned to her cell, where her already manwise hair is shaved off to the bone. The people celebrate with a carnival. One man shouts, "Long live Joan!" and he is pitched into the moat. In the dungeon the sight of her shorn locks swept up like wood shavings is the final affront that restores Joan to the sanity of her insanity. Her expression plainly tells that if she has traversed so far the road of the denatured she must go all the way. In revulsion and exaltation she reaffirms her visions, and the faces swing again like pendulums. . . . They rush her to her death.

Once more the daylight and the sky—and a freer ranging camera. Life at the decisive moment is more than a pinpoint of solitude and persecution. It includes protest from anonymous faces in the crowd, combat, defense, and suppression with iron knouts. And a pile of faggots. The birds take their flight. . . . For refusing to say "Yes," one human being—a great fool? a divine? a mortal sick unto hallucination?—is to be roasted alive in a small, cramped space of the monstrous earth by a corps of armored bullies who are breaking like straws the bones of the pitiful few who would deliver her. (Where else have we seen this spearhead of time on a shield of space? Isn't it in Brueghel's "Massacre of the Innocents"—the tight phalanx of power, the frantic cluster of villagers on a frozen earth with no conceivable hope of rescue under a steel-plated sky?) Joan does not cry out, but her head falls forward. Obscured by smoke she is no longer a face, a profile, a closeup, a note sounding. She is a silhouette, a shadow of Man. Now she no longer has even the sensation of being alone.

The remnants of the resisting crowd are pushed back and struck down, as the soldiers retreat over the drawbridge to the tower. The bridge is raised. The people kneel on the far side, lamenting. . . . The fugue is resolved.

The Passion of Joan of Arc is one film among probably less than a dozen of which it can be said that it adds deeply to the sum of one's experience. It exposes the nerve-root of a spiritual dénouement which Bernard Shaw's play, *St. Joan,* for all its complex of ecclesiastical and political forces, never glimpsed. The historical ramifications that contributed to the prestige of Shaw's drama were precisely what Dreyer put aside; in so doing he met his subject literally face to face. Strangely, it has bothered not a few critics (I believe Iris Barry was the first in this line of disparagement) that Dreyer's Joan is not *in* history, that she is a beleaguered face merely, without social attachments or precedent dimension. Such paltry objections to Dreyer's artistic ruthlessness should be dismissed with a high hand. As a matter for the record, it might be pointed out that details of the trial itself were researched from original documents, and it is difficult to imagine how a crisis in the remote past could be recreated more concretely or with a more austere selection of data than this one. But personality is beyond the reach of documents. We don't (or shouldn't) give a hang whether this *is* the Joan of history (whoever that may be). Maria Falconetti impersonated her as one distinctly "possessed." Further than this, we may construe as we please. The absolute social context is irreclaimable. Jeanne d'Arc does not historically exist—any more than Jesus or Cleopatra or Napoleon or, very soon, Gandhi. She belongs to imagination, not history; she is a figment. In Carl Dreyer's movie she is simply a subject born of metaphysical drives and temperamental probabilities. . . . It is always too late to know *the truth;* it is forever possible to experience that truth which it is the overbearing privilege of art to enact for us.

By a coincidence providential for the delight of the comparative eye, Dreyer's curious and superlative film was revived at the Museum of Modern Art simultaneously with the opening of Edward Steichen's photographic exhibit, "The Family of Man" (now on world tour and reproduced in book form). In this compelling association, the reciprocal values of still and cinema photography were given prominence and vitally enhanced, the more so as the two media seemed bent on exchanging identities: the photographs all but conveying motion, the film so concentrated on a single cinematic element as to appear relatively static. On the one hand, an aggregate of separate moments coerced into vivid succession; on the other a succession crystallized into an anguished moment. Insofar as the photographs had for their theme Man in Crisis—

and this was the overall effect they gave, even though predications less critical were on view—their impact was a consequence of drama suspended, of a challenge to one's inferences and one's curiosity. . . . A mud-spattered war infant, scarcely beyond the age of toddle, awaiting, with no visible concern, sequels unpredictable to his insensate misery. (Where? Anywhere!) . . . A small, neat boy going tranquilly down steps to school in a city of rubble. . . . A girl tied to a tree, caught in a twist of fear that she may be the victim in a game that has gone too far. . . . A pair of lovers embracing good-bye on a railway platform, cornered by the inexorable (and Ernst Haas) in a composition any cinematographer would applaud. . . . Youth: on the make, on the prowl, on the beach—on the run . . . Old men on farms with hopeless eyes. Old (before their time) rural women with calculating eyes . . . The traceries of time and of something more than time in the faces of the late Werner Bischof's Indian women ("Do these bones live?") . . . Cartier-Bresson's four sibylline figures invoking Brahma . . . And one of the most powerful emblems of human protest ever captured by a roving camera: Anna Riwkin-Brick's Israelite Cassandra, with accusing arm raised high, fingers spread—an avatar of outrage.

These are achieved photographs. Also, they are fragments for a cinema. Our response to them is unstinting, beyond the pull of identification, because the *motion picture,* more than any single esthetic agency, has trained us to appreciate the still moment that isn't still, the "artistic shot": artistic exactly when it returns life to us stripped of the accidentals that would otherwise vitiate the purity of its emotional appeal, whether the appeal is of hunger, physical grace, despair, or of one of the terrible ultimate things. When photography has reached the limit of its dramatizing resources so that you wait spellbound for something further to ensue within the single print—for the Japanese lad to swallow the snow-flake; for the hands in stop-motion to finish threading the bolt; for the Peruvian Indian boy either to sound a note from his flute or put it aside and elaborate the charm of his smile while he talks to you—when it has reached this brink of sentience, you may well feel that it has already exceeded its own powers and entered, ironically, a limbo of the incongruous. However persuasively it may enlist our humanity, the documentary photograph is bound to desert one's kinetic anticipation; born of art, it yet remains umbilical to life, crying out for its gesture to be developed or terminated, for its form to be depersonalized altogether or extended in space-time. By its assumption of mobility it is condemned to supersession by the motion picture.

Under the immediate spell of *The Passion of Joan of Arc,* one recognized that the force of Steichen's collection was largely the result of derivations. The artful arrangement, topical and biographical, involved the several photos in a *cinematic* chronology; the quotations from world literature edited their universality. In a rush of sweeping ingratitude it was possible to regard the exhibit as synthetic and unnecessarily multiple, since Mlle. Falconetti's superb art (in her first and only screen role) had already identified these fugitive notations of the human drama—these and others, past and to come, sustaining in a unified ordeal by closeup all the times and places where men, women, and children have hoped, feared, defied, and been defeated. The Joan of Falconetti and Dreyer is Ishimoto's girl tied to the tree, beginning to exchange apprehension for terror. She is the psychotic, dejected, and self-embraced under a towering blank wall, locked forever in the extremity of a riven ego. She is Ernst Haas's pair of lovers overtaken by time. She is the anger in the bones of all who, like the gnarled Israelite woman, raise a hand in rebellion.   1955

The Japanese Film:
Inquiries and Inferences

Most of us who write about films may as well relax and confess that
we know nothing at first hand about Japanese movie production;
that all we have as data has come to us from press sheets, from
quick consultation with the nearest Japanese bystander, or from a
handful of factual essays; that whatever else we may know of
Japanese art is the sum (probably meager) of having taken an "intelligent interest" in Japanese prints, of having been exposed academically to the matter of Japanese influence on the architecture
of Frank Lloyd Wright, of having read two Japanese novels and a
few slim volumes of poetry, of exploring, post-*Rashomon,* whatever
we have been able to find useful in the way of analogy, and of seeing
the "unaccredited" performances of Kabuki. Beyond this, except for
the fortunate few who may have been in Europe with sufficient
frequency since 1951 to see others of the dozen or more Japanese
films exhibited there, we have been shown precisely five in the
United States on which to establish generalities. (Of these, two—

The Impostor and *Hiroshima*—scarcely merit extended consideration, and we owe the selection of the big three to the enterprise and
good taste of Mr. Edward Harrison.) This little piggy stayed at
home, and he is by now somewhat wearied by those who primarily
see the Japanese motion picture (let's just say *Rashomon, Ugetsu,*
and *The Gate of Hell*) as a by-product of Japanese decorative and
theater arts. He is equally wearied by the Orientalists (home grown
or otherwise) who are patently well informed on the minutiae of
Japanese culture but who know little or nothing of cinematic art.

There is a prevalent and not altogether accurate analogy in emer-
gent use between the Japanese film and Japanese "painting." Before
this easy observation goes much further, we should plainly ask *what
kind* of painting is implied for reference and which of the three
films usually invoked actually exemplifies, in more than a superficial
way, such a comparison. We have been specifically informed that
Kazuo Miyagawa, the cinematographer of *Rashomon* and *Ugetsu,*
is a student of traditional Japanese art, and we may assume that a
large number of the technicians on these films share his absorption.
By reference to single frames in *Ugetsu,* I would infer that both
India-ink drawings and the wood blocks of Hiroshige might very
likely have been Miyagawa's inspiration. But a specialist would
have to confirm my inference and further specify the models, if any,
for the photographic style of *Rashomon,* which, to my view, nowhere suggests Japanese painting in any media. And in *The Gate
of Hell* quite dissimilar effects are achieved by Kohei Sugiyama,
owing as much to their composition in Eastman color and to their
formal derivation from the constructs of Eisenstein (in the opening
episodes, especially) as to their kinship with kakemonos, wood-
block prints, or folding screens. I am now prepared to add to the
confusion myself by contending that the film which to me egregiously suggests Japanese watercolor-and-ink textures is not a Japanese film at all, but Arne Sucksdorff's occult documentary of Swedish wild life, *The Great Adventure.*

Both the photography and music of the Japanese films have come
in for a certain amount of cavil. Here the purist struts and frets his
hour. I have heard an allegedly responsible teacher of esthetics
claim that the lighting in *Ugetsu* was "too dim." And in the magazine *Film Culture* (March–April 1955), an excessively disgruntled
"Oriental critic" (he was so programmed), Ben Pinga by name,
after donning a hair shirt, took to task the producers of *The Gate of
Hell* for their failure to make the Buddhist message more explicit,

for not being consistent in their musical scoring, and, above all, for having "played up the visual splendor of the subject at the expense of its ideas and meanings." Leaving to someone with more time on his hands that charming cognate "ideas and meanings," I'll content myself with fearing that the accusation of which it is the nub will meet with scant agreement. Without conceding that generally held opinions are more valid than minority ones, I find Mr. Pinga's downright perverse, but I dare say that the degree of beauty one can support in a given context is not measurable. The more recherché quibbles fall strictly within the province of the experts, but I am not intimidated by Mr. Pinga's self-identification with this category, in the face of his innocent belief that the cameraman of *The Gate of Hell* was also the cameraman of *Ugetsu*. Nor am I much more impressed by the scolding, every bit as stern, administered by Gordon Hendricks (same magazine, same issue) to the musical director of *The Gate of Hell*. In considerable detail and with an air of authority as indisputable as his petulance, Mr. Hendricks discoursed on the nature and social usages of the *koto*, the *samisen*, and the *shakubyoshi*, and crushingly deplored the occasional employment of Western strings and of drums "played in a Western scale." I would be willing to knuckle under to Mr. Hendricks' agitated defense of authenticity, and I'd even promise myself to listen more objectively when I see *The Gate of Hell* again, if it were not for the very grave impasse into which the writer led himself by his retrospective criticism of the *Rashomon* sound track.

Proudly involving Archer Winsten of the *New York Post* in his shock reaction, as if this agreement certified his sense of outrage, Mr. Hendricks fulminated against Ravel's *Bolero* used "to back up a 13th-century legend" (a description which, while we're brushing the subject, requires qualification; the literary material on which Kurosawa based his adaptation came from two short stories by Ryunosuke Akutagawa, who committed suicide in 1927). I think we must all have been alarmed by the *resemblance* of the bandit theme to the *Bolero* (that it is literally the *Bolero*, note for note, I doubt), but I hope a majority of the baffled suspended their judgment in favor of the belief that Kurosawa might reasonably be trusted, like any serious artist, to know exactly what he was doing. That Kurosawa did know is ably supported by James F. Davidson in a most edifying article, "Memory of Defeat in Japan: A Reappraisal of *Rashomon*,"*

Antioch Review, XIV, December 1954.

which is indispensable reading for any further speculation on Kurosawa's masterly film. To summarize a single point of Mr. Davidson's exposition: at one level of interpretation, the bandit represents—the West! From this clue, you may deduce the ramifications for yourself, but I urge you to read Mr. Davidson. In any case, you can see at once the sardonic function of the music's alleged impurity.

Stylization is probably the most ambiguous conception currently overexercised. A semantic difficulty, I'm sure. No one bothers to distinguish between the stylized, the conventional, the generic, the abstract, or the stereotypical. Japanese milieu, in art and life, being what it is—rigorously fashioned with a consistency which in our world occurs only under special conditions of place, economy, temperament, and influence—our interpretation of its quality is pardonably confused. *Sometimes* pardonably. Into an aperitif served to the readers of *Fashion and Travel*, "Style: and the Japanese," Truman Capote stirred a doubtful ingredient: "A half-comparison might be made with Restoration comedy: there is at least the same appreciation of the artificial; *and it is true* that in the gangster thriller and cowboy genre Americans have produced *a classically stylized form* of code and behavior." (The italics are mine—believe me!) Mr. Moritoh, meet Little Caesar and Mr. Shane. I'm sure you three gentlemen will have much to discuss. . . . Mr. Capote is in safer hands when he repeats Arthur Waley's observation that a principal characteristic of the Japanese esthetic is dread of the explicit. But I am certain that different levels of esthetic and, conceivably, different occasions, are here involved. *The Gate of Hell* affords many instances of this dread, expressed with lovely indirection, but it also features that extraordinary moment when the samurai spits a mouthful of water into the face of the unconscious Lady Kesa. Sexual insight has not often been rendered so ruthlessly, with no dread whatever of the explicit. And *Rashomon* is as fearlessly expounded, which brings me into argument with another authority.

Since Harold Strauss has the support of past residence in Japan, I have read with some attention and even humility his recent articles on the subject, but when he describes Machiko Kyo's laughter (in her taunting of husband and brigand in *Rashomon*) as stylized, I am prompted to challenge further what seems to me an increasingly general misuse of the term. Quite simply, stylization implies a *reduction* or a *crystallizing* of elements, but I appeal to Elie Faure's elaborate definition (evoked, incidentally, by this very matter of the Japanese principle, in Volume III of his *History of Art*) to assist the relevance of my objection.

An erroneous distinction has often been made between the process of reason which consists in stylizing a form and the process of instinct which tends to idealize it. Idealization does not re-form an object; it reconstructs and completes it so as to deduce the most general, the purest, and the most hopeful meaning that the object has for man. Stylization adapts it to its decorative function by systematizing the characteristics which appear in practically a consistent manner when the form is studied. The artist saw that all forms and gestures and all architectures in repose or in movement retained certain dominant qualities which defined them in our memory and which, when accentuated by schematic processes, could be applied to decoration with the utmost exactitude. . . .

If this distinction is as acceptable to others as it is to me, the application of "stylized" to the scene designated can surely be called into question. To my feeling, that moment of laughter is the almost intolerable climax of a sequence characterized by primordial realism. Miss Kyo's laugh may well ring in one's ears after the last film has faded from the last screen as a consummate outcry of sub-human derision. . . . I would say that this actress' face makeup was conventionalized, if you like, as it was for *Ugetsu* and for *The Gate of Hell,* and that the court sequences of *Rashomon* (where the film audience is the tribunal), in passive face-front contrast to the restless movement of the camera in the woods, were formalized, after the suggestive mode of the Noh drama, as Mr. Strauss pointed out in his *Harper's* article.* The meticulous relationship of figures to the architectural spaces wherein they sit or move, a conspicuous feature of *The Gate of Hell,* but not uniquely Japanese, is simply a theatrical, or plastic, sense of proportion; it would illustrate Faure's sense of the stylized if its gestures and other elements were submitted to an elliptical and unrealistic continuity. (Yesterday's European expressionist theater was, in its own way, as stylized as Noh.) Only in *The Impostor,* among the films shown here, a commodity item of the Shochiku Corporation, owners of the Kabuki-za, is there considerable, if not subtle, treatment of this kind (the mock duels, the fixed character traits, and so forth).

The reception of Japanese film acting has not been unanimously charitable. Embarrassed by the vehemence of the Japanese actor, and even by his repose (notable in Kazuo Hasegawa—Moritoh in *The Gate of Hell*—who generates tremendous force while sitting completely still), many Westerners attempt to account for their dis-

---

*"My Affair with Japanese Movies," July 1955.

comfort at the phenomenon by some such explanation of it as stylized or "artificial" acting. When the performers, seized by paroxysms of violence or anguish, throw themselves on the ground, bellow, grunt, and gnash their teeth, embarrassment may give way to facetiousness. From unexpected areas of the critical world, where you would suppose some effort might be made to rise above a subjective reaction to alien manners, have come unwarranted disclaimers, of *Ugetsu* markedly. John McCarten's flippant review of this film in *The New Yorker* was the least excusable; I make this assertion not from any belief in the balefulness of wit (I usually find Mr. McCarten quite funny) but from an assumption that jeering at an unfamiliar mode is not a vice permissible to a critic. At least not without more authority than I suspect Mr. McCarten can lay claim to. The most unflattering verdict on Japanese histrionics was delivered long since by the French poet, Henri Michaux, in his ferociously brilliant travel memoir, *A Barbarian in Asia,** but it was the fruit not of a single film but of several months of theatergoing in the Orient.

> No actor in the world bawls like the Japanese with so little result. He does not speak his part, he mews it, belches it, and he trumpets, brays, neighs and gesticulates like one possessed, and in spite of it all I do not believe him.
> All this is done on the side, "to decorate." The frightful contortions he makes in the effort to represent his sufferings merely express the hell of a trouble he is taking to express suffering; it is suffering expressed by a man who no longer knows the meaning of it (a lot of esthetes, all of them) in front of an audience of esthetes, equally ignorant of the subject.
> A loud voice that reeks of prejudice a thousand miles away, of life taken up by the wrong end, a background of ancient impostures and obligations, and a series of second-rate notions, but spelled with a capital letter, in the midst of which like the voices of the Categorical Imperative (the great master of Japan) the poor characters move about, victims, subordinate creatures, but giving themselves, as one might expect, great swashbuckling airs, with a peculiarly decorative type of courage, and there is such a lack of variety that one sees why in the *No* plays they wear a mask and why at Osaka the actors are simply wooden marionettes, lifesize.

There is much more of this, very amusing, very perceptive, and very cruel. If I had less respect for Michaux's fabulous gift for

---

*New Directions, N. Y., 1949. Translated by Sylvia Beach. First published in France, 1933.

psychological impressionism I would hesitate to present such a persuasive corroboration of the latent xenophobes among us. As it is, I am willing to accept his prejudice for the sake of his vivid accent, but I reserve the right to claim that I've not been similarly affected by actors in the Japanese film. Furthermore, I am strongly convinced that however "decorative" Kabuki-trained actors may have seemed to Michaux on the stage in the early 1930's, they have been forced by the exigencies of the interior drama which has constituted the screenplays to substantiate their emotions by a more complete involvement. Clearly the principals of the three films under discussion understand the meaning of the suffering *they* are expressing! And this, I think, is not the least wonderful result of the Daei company's so-called compromise with the West. If the psychological realism and the dynamic editing of these films is a consequence of Western influence on Japanese style, we cannot but be gratified by their instinctive conquest of our domain. The motion picture is by its nature and its origin Western. A *pure* Japanese film is a contradiction in terms, for it could only be an even more awkward compromise between film and theater than *The Impostor* has verified. The "stylized" theater of Japan—Kabuki and Noh, if not Bunṛaku—will presumably survive in its own right, but the Japanese film will have to develop away from the broadest theater conventions in order to be film at all, and a transformation of the acting technique is naturally of initial importance.

As a matter of related fact, many people find a full expression of emotion equally intolerable in our own theater and movies. I have seen audiences highly disturbed by a passionately committed Shakespearean actor or one from the Yiddish theater, and I am neither referring to nor defending the elocutionary high style. Blanche Yurka in classical drama, Katina Paxinou's animal outcries of grief in the otherwise farcical film *Mourning Becomes Electra,* Peter Lorre's grinding falsettos, Anton Walbrook's broken-voiced speech before the curtain in *Red Shoes*—the popular aversion to these strenuous displays of feeling is less than a rational distaste for an art démodé; it is fear of vitality. In his projection of strong emotion, the "natural man," with few regional exceptions, uncalculatedly brings into operation a distinct physical style, determined by factors of his physique, his occupation, and his social conditioning. Any crisis-acting not founded on the re-creation of such emotion and such style, skillfully heightened, is inadequate to its source. But a population grown effete finds the shallow-breathing Olivier, for glaring example, a suitable vehicle of tragic feeling. Toshiro Mifune, the bandit of *Rashomon* (a soldier whom Kurosawa "discovered" and then Kabuki-trained), has more kinesis in his feet—literally in his feet—than Olivier has in his entire body.*

I have not elaborated these details for the sole purpose of outflanking the cognoscenti. I think it advisable for the unprepared viewer of Japanese films to beware of the footnoters before he has assimilated his own unguarded experience, and to discriminate for himself between what is deeply universal in these films and what is special to them. Further considerations of décor, lighting, color, histrionic subtleties, and so on will present themselves for analysis when we have seen not only *Musashi* but also *The Tale of Genji, The Life of Oharu, The Seven Samurai,* and *A Woman's Life,* all period pieces. The extent to which we have been charmed by costume films will be tested when we have seen the best of Japan's films on contemporary subjects, which will probably be a long time off. That these will pass the test there seems little question, judging by reports on such films as Kurosawa's *Living* or *Drunken Angel.* We consider Kurosawa a man apart, but many Japanese critics will not have it so and assure us that directors whose work we've seen no samples of are equally significant. We await the evidence. Meanwhile, on the evidence available and beyond the reservations of the experts, we can acknowledge that the heart of the Japanese film is animated from below the luminous surface. No matter what contingencies of the world market Daiei productions have been designed to meet, they have touched—above all, in *Rashomon*—the deepest and most implacable concerns of man, with cinematic values unmatched by any present body of film-makers.   1955

Footnote, 1971. The reader who has only this context to go by may reasonably feel that two successive disparagements of Olivier's acting were gratuitous. He should be reminded that the previous remarks (on Walbrook in *The Queen of Spades*) had been jotted down some years before; moreover, the reputation of Olivier then was so universally, adamantly, and complacently defended that one had to raise one's voice in order to oppose it with any hope of a hearing. Today I endorse the view I held, and perhaps the contemporary filmgoer who has lately seen Olivier's *Hamlet* or *Henry V* is readier to agree with me than almost anyone was in the forties and early fifties. This does *not* constitute my opinion of Sir Laurence's later performances, on stage or screen, when he had developed the flexibility too soon ascribed to him. Unquestionably he is now one of our greatest character actors. He was always extremely facile, but I never believed in him as a "romantic" actor. When he passed the age of romantic appeal, he acquired the quirky but impressive reality he now displays.

La Strada:
Cinematic Intersections

Who hides his fool dies speechless.
Henri Michaux

Fellini is the new princely name in films—Federico Fellini: seven syllables, like Vittorio De Sica, to be pronounced lyrically or fatefully. Associated in the immediate postwar years with the more widely known Roberto Rossellini and Alberto Lattuada, he has lately won recognition as a creatively important writer-director; yet the recognition is secure, and subject to revision even so, among Italian and French critics only. *Lo Sceicco Bianco* (*The White Sheik*), his first independent directorial achievement and the most artful Italian comedy short of *Miracle in Milan* with which I am familiar, was hooted down by political factions at the Venice Film Festival, 1952. It fared little better in New York City this April, where, despite generally cordial notices, it was dismissed with arrant condescension by Mr. Crosley Bother, who keeps moviegoing safe for the film-page readers of the *New York Times*. A widespread assumption among entrepreneurs and exhibitors attributes to Mr. Bother the power of making or breaking a foreign film (exceptions acknowledged) in Manhattan, which determines its subsequent distribution in the country as a whole. Not that he speaks with any authority demonstrable by reference to a film's visual or intellectual content, but that his unmistakable sincerity is so essentially middle class as to be accepted without question by the multitude in search of its own image. *I Vitelloni* (1953) was equally a slow starter in Italy, which obliged Fellini to sell the film outright, whereupon it unforeseeably became a national success, though it did not escape vilification in all quarters. *La Strada*, a Venice prize-winner, 1954, has proved either baffling or irritating to every British reviewer I've come across, while *Il Bidone* (1955), excoriated in Venice, was exalted to the rank of "masterpiece" by certain Parisian critics. For the United States, the latter film, retitled *Con Men*, will be the victim of voice-dubbing, that process clearly derived from the principle "Nothing alien is human to me." . . . All of which suggests that Fellini is a dangerous man, and makes one wonder if he mightn't be a great one.

In *The White Sheik*, Fellini, like the Shakespearean wag, uses his folly as a stalking-horse, under which cover he shoots his wit. A newlywed provincial couple arrives in Rome, he to ingratiate himself and to support his husbandly authority with the official aspects of the imperium, she (secretly) to pursue a glamorous phantom, "the white sheik" of a weekly photograph-serial (*fumetti*). After twenty-four hours of misadventure, during which the stifled wife suffers infatuation with and then abuse from the preposterous "sheik" and his absurdly vulgar consorts, and the husband, distraught by her disappearance, winds up a harrowing night in the company of a prostitute, the pair are reunited in time for the climactic event of their visit, a papal audience. Flustered, each uninquiring of the other but shakenly repentant, they march quick-step toward the Vatican. Tearfully the erring wife clings to the abused husband's arm, worshipfully declaring, *"You—you are my White Sheik!"* . . . Farcical in detail, directed with smartly interfused sounds and images and musical insolence, acted with a range of styles sardonically attuned to the subject (e.g., Brunella Bovo's wife and Alberto Sordi's shiek: but Leopoldo Trieste, husband, is wildly a creature of fun and pathos)—the film is basically terrifying, in more than its social ridicule. Only the Italians, I think, can produce comedy so piercing as to complicate our laughter with anxiety. A brief scene between Giulietta Masina (of whom more, *infra*) and a fire-eater, in a plaza at night, upset this writer beyond his ability to account for the reaction coherently.

"Neo-realism" has been parroted without recess to define the post-World War II Italian novel and film. As a result, although the sociology of Giuseppe Berto, Vasco Pratolini, and Carlo Levi, as well as the psychological masochism of Alberto Moravia, has received adequate consideration, in the U.S. at least, far less attention has been paid to the lyricism of Elio Vittorini. The film *Bitter Rice* was applauded or scorned solely as a melodrama; no one has yet observed the relationship of Umberto D's watch (to say nothing of his dictionary) to the unifying symbols in *The Watch* of Carlo Levi. Ennio Flaiano's superb allegorical novel, *The Short Cut* (despite paperback circulation five years ago), has escaped serious discussion. That Flaiano is also a co-scenarist of *The White Sheik* and *I Vitelloni,* and that De Sica and Zavattini persistently qualify their formal announcement of "social attention" with another plane of relevance, should by this time have aroused more than a suspicion that "neo-realism" will not suffice as a clue to the art of the Italian film at its best.

Fellini's short masterpiece, *The Miracle* (his conception, directed by Rossellini), will survive in the minds of the just as a more profound and powerful achievement than most of the war protest films in the temper of *Open City* (another Fellini collaboration).* Those who recall its theme of ecstasy-in-madness will be better disposed to appreciate *La Strada,* if not *The White Sheik,* and in *I Vitelloni*† they will recognize the inescapable Fellini touch (unless I'm modifying the force of his co-workers, Flaiano and Pennelli) in a brief interlude from the nominal action: a village idiot, left to guard a gilded angel stolen by one of the *vitelloni,* props the statue on a mound and seats himself twenty feet away to stare at it, enraptured and moronic. Its setting an Italian city of moderate size, not identifiable by this writer, *I Vitelloni* inscribes a saltatory curve in the lives of four young men—five are named, one never significantly differentiated—loitering at the reluctant threshold of manhood. The latent personalities which will infallibly overtake them in the daylight of legal maturity are less distinct to their sense than the fantasy image each has conjured for his ego in the mirrored halls of adolescence. Over a year's passing, we watch the separate and in no

---

*Torn soon after birth from its twin film, *The Human Voice,* by Cocteau, then removed again (largely through the influence of the unsleeping inquisitorial Church) from its loose fraternity with films of Renoir and Pagnol under the embracing title *Ways of Love, The Miracle* is at present a smothered and outcast paragon.
†Literally "the sucklings"; in France, titled *Les Inutiles,* but "The Unused" would be a more appropriate reading than "The Useless."

case conclusive reaction of each as he meets himself, or fails to, in a trial by exposure.

Fausto, a would-be Casanova, is forced into marriage with Sandra, Moraldo's sister (introduced at the opening as Miss Siren, *enceinte,* in a beauty contest); his disgruntled evasion of marital responsibility takes the form of pursuing other sirens and evading labor, until his wife's precipitate flight reveals him to himself as an insecure boy. (The pathos of inadequate or perverted ideals is a major concern in Fellini's films.) In a sheepish frenzy of love urged by guilt (and his father's strong right arm) his story "ends," but we know by then that in all probability his future will resemble the status of the average male in his social world—that of a questing rotter who is a lost baby at heart. . . . The plump Alberto, satirical and happy-go-lucky, is nourished in his gaiety by dependence on his mother and sister; when his sister elopes unexpectedly, the shock undermines his bolstered frivolity, leaving him to face the stonewall prospect of going to work and thereby laughing less often. . . . Perhaps the weakest characterization, because it is too farcically projected, is that of Leopoldo, the poet; his place in the design is stronger than the bizarre particularities given him as a person. But fittingly, he offers his major effort (a rhetorical play) to an aging bravura actor, storming the provinces with a variety show. In one of the more characteristic Fellini sequences the aged actor, sparse hair wild and eyes bulging like a distraught prophet's, strides against the wintry blast of a seacoast area at night, mouthing platitudes into the wind. Leopoldo, mistaking this genial charlatan for the demonic muse, flees in terror when the old man beckons him to recite at the sea's edge.

Moraldo is the lonely one, always sympathetically detoured by the problems of the others. Sad because he has no exterior involvements of his own, or for reasons of which he is unaware, he establishes deep rapport with a small, rugged angel of a boy, a rapport maintained with fearful tenderness never quite acknowledged by either. (Ironically, the nine-year-old is the only "gainfully employed" youngster in the film.) Driven by a compulsion he cannot understand but must obey, Moraldo abruptly quits town on a train at dawn. There, at the station, like a bird or squirrel who, when you've given up all attempt at reaching for him, comes to your hand unbidden, the boy appears to bid Moraldo goodbye. "Weren't you happy here?" he asks, in a burst of annihilating candor. And Moraldo can only smile and shrug in wonder. The train leaves (its sound and movement combined with shots of the sleepers whom Moraldo is deserting without farewells), and the last vignette—one of those finales for which Italian and French film-makers seem to have special feeling—frames the boy, already dismissing the other's melancholy as irrelevant to his own fledgling survival, walking away down track, balancing himself on the single rail, greeted by arriving workmen.

Narrated with an almost novelistic abundance of detail, the film is seldom allowed to relinquish its visual melody of the five. Arms linked abreast, the wastrels dance down the street at night, or split up and pair off (Moraldo always odd man) to race each other or to dawdle at shop windows, kick empty cans, or wolf-strategize a startled girl. Contemplative, they watch, from a breakwater, the relentless waves; fretful, they sip at a sidewalk cafe. The oceanic background, prefigured in *The Miracle* and *The White Sheik,* unequivocally employed in *La Strada,* is moderately thematic here. The film opens on a beach casino; Alberto first discovers his sister with her illicit lover at the beach. The absurd poet flees from the risks of art by the sea's verge, and by the sea Fausto meets again the seductive woman, for whom he had once left Sandra in a movie house, who tells him she is his fate. (Literally she isn't; confronted by the climactic opportunity, Fausto turns away, remorsefully seeking the other Miss Siren, now but an abused wife.)

And always the distance, behind the lonely, short-sighted figures of men: the sea, the railroad track, the street—*la strada.* Alberto comes home from a masquerade ball in the grey hours, drunk and maudlin (supported by the loyal Moraldo), to encounter his sister eloping at this incongruous moment (his fat body is attired grotesquely in woman's clothing). Before he can explain or receive explanation, the girl cries a quick, regretful farewell, jumps into the waiting car, and is driven out of sight. Stunned, but barely sober enough to grasp his sudden desolation, he sways in Moraldo's arms and we are given a long view of the otherwise empty road, the vanishing car, and, in the left foreground, the transvestite rear end of the ludicrous Alberto.

From the actuality of the Italian middle-class family's tyrannical cohesion and bankrupt aims, Fellini derived the social substance of his unspectacular milieu. But he is a film poet, which is to say one whose images mean more than meets the eye. To a poet the social situation is never a closed system; the phenomenal opens to vistas, terrible or inceptive. *I Vitelloni,* circumscribed by its modest subject of incomplete illumination, nonetheless flashes with light from sources beyond the circle. Fellini's direction of this film was supple and alert, as if he were restraining impulses more intensely lyrical and searching for conveyances more stark.

La Strada is the consequent testimony: the most uncompromising fable yet evoked from the material of Italian naturalism, a timely reproval of the deaf who have missed the deeper resonance in its voice. Not *cinematically* remarkable, for it is directed and photographed with a conventional technique, the film is metaphysically astounding; longitudes of implication extend as awesomely as the ocean, on the strand of which it begins and ends. As a crystalline conception it belongs with much of the pure literary art of our time —with *Death in Venice,* for instance, or *The Man Who Died,* with a lyric by Jeffers or Yeats. Like any deeply felt and realized symbol, *La Strada* is at once nuclear and radiating; within its deceptively simple span, an eternal pattern and a prophecy are established. Since my superlatives have already been disputed, in much the same spirit as that which denied the complexity of *Rashomon,* a somewhat detailed synopsis of what happens in *La Strada* may be in order; I trust that a measure of editorial underlining will not be out of order.

The opening scene presents a dismayed household by a remote seashore. Zampano, a consummate physical specimen of Hobbes's primal Man—nasty and brutish, if not short—has offered to buy the services of Gelsomina to assist his "act," wherein he struts fearsomely in a circle before bucolic audiences, swallows fire, and bursts a linked chain by expanding his chest within its constriction. As a sister purchased many years before by this same Zampano had never returned—she died somewhere, the *fauve* explains with a grunt—Gelsomina, a clown of a creature, scarcely verbal, dressed in sexless clothing, with feet like those of a duck, is idiotically uncertain whether to laugh or cry when sold by her family into the bondage of this stranger who tours the back country with a motorcycle-driven wagon. But after facing the ocean, to commune in some fashion we are not permitted to see, the girl departs with her master who thereupon ignores her existence, giving her only the recognition of abuse because she fails readily to learn her part in his performance. Gelsomina is required to prepare his act by the loud and rhythmic proclamation, "*Zam*-pa-no is here!" and then to accompany the chain-breaking with a drumbeat crescendo. She learns slowly, and Zampano's brutal impatience ill elicits her concealed talents.

Insensible to the female under the shapeless rags, to the eyes mischievous, eager, luminous, and occult, to the wild invention of the clown girl's fantastically expressive motions, Zampano takes his pleasure from whores and bottles, while Gelsomina waits in a world of her own, imbecile and germinating, alternately downcast and irrepressible. When Zampano snores drunkenly on the ground by the covered wagon outside a village, she dance-struts over the bleak *campagna* and picks flowers, watched by a small, astonished girl. Though she and Zampano are leaving the spot immediately, she plants tomato seeds, and this gesture, more than any, incites the man's jeering contempt. Unable to stand his cruelty and his indifference, Gelsomina runs away, following three single-file trumpet-and-fife players on a country road. Once in the city, she is lost and amazed in a louder music, the pomp and bell ringing of a church processional, and a street carnival where she is entranced by an equilibrist wearing paper wings, who eats spaghetti from a table on a high wire above the crowd. Teased and made drunken by wastrels in a windy trash-blown square at night, she is reclaimed, with violent blows and curses, by the pursuing Zampano.

In dire need of a better income, Zampano begrudgingly attaches his act to a circus, where the equilibrist Matto ("crazyhead") is also a featured performer. This "fool" (Gelsomina's term for him) has known Zampano before and delights in taunting the brute's vanity and his sluggish strength. But Gelsomina he finds comically beguiling and teaches her, as part of a farcical ground-act he is working out, to blow a sentimentally haunting air on a bugle. When his derisive merriment lands him and the outraged Zampano in jail for brawling, he is dismissed by the circus company. Before going his way, he tries to coax Gelsomina, stubbornly waiting for Zampano, into going with him, but she is unable to convince him that she is useful for anything—even for loving. She is sure that Zampano really needs her but that anyone more particular could not. Bidding her look to her own value and blithely discoursing on his own mortality, Matto dances out of the scene. The circus group, after offering to keep Gelsomina but not Zampano, resigns the obdurate girl to the mercy of her choice. Zampano is released from jail; the traveling partnership is resumed. They reencounter Matto by the roadside, trying to mend his broken-down car. Zampano, to avenge past insults and from resentment of the fool's unique influence over Gelsomina, attacks him with a savagery which is fatal to the equilibrist. Panic-stricken and disgusted at the bad luck invoked by his uncontrolled strength, Zampano hides the fool's body and his wrecked car under a bridge. (Matto's only words in this scene, uttered with weary surprise, are "He broke my watch!")

Gelsomina now loses the little articulation she is mistress of; she babbles inarticulate terror, and to remove her from the locale of the crime Zampano has to trounce her as if she were a mule. Paralyzed by fear and confusion, she subsequently refuses to sleep under the tarpaulin with the fleeing Zampano, preferring to make her bed on the ground in sight of the stars. Her presence in the act is futile; she can no longer open her mouth to cry, "*Zam*-pa-no is here!" or bring her quavering hands to beat the drum; instead she makes anguished animal noises and succeeds only in whimpering brokenly, "The fool is hurt! The fool is hurt!" . . . Early one morning, on the summit of a snow-covered pass, as she sleeps by the embers of a fire she has made, Zampano drives away.

Five years go by. Zampano, his hair greying, still treads his circle, threatening dangerous feats to mildly curious villagers. Drumless he struts; transparently his confidence has left him. In his idle hours he drinks himself senseless and is thrown out of taverns. . . . Passing a house one day, where a woman hanging out sheets whistles a tune which he remembers as the one taught by the fool to the clown, he asks the woman where she learned it. She tells him that the girl who sang that tune had once stayed in her house, but she was ailing and had soon died. In a drunken daze, Zampano staggers to the beach. There he collapses, to stare hopelessly at the encroaching waves and to dig in a tormented stupor at the foundationless sand. He lifts his head like a wounded animal to scan the infinitely remote and empty sky. The waves roll in. . . .*

---

*Something, if only by way of parenthesis, should be said at this point to extol the fabulous performance of Fellini's wife, Giulietta Masina, as Gelsomina. The obvious comparisons will have already been made, for this woman is patently linked with the great clowns of repute, and her art must be apprehended, not subsumed, by the relation it bears to the art of Chaplin or Barrault or Marceau. Her miming goes through vicissitudes of movement in this film; the more Gelsomina is needed, the less strictly puppet-like her physical reactions. After the fool has been murdered, she becomes altogether limp, human but no longer taut, drifting toward catalepsy. Yet it is the interior spirit which Signora Fellini expresses with such terrible veracity, sometimes through a stylized mockery of pain or joy that pierces like a knife: the way she walks blindly to the middle of an expanse of wall and stands there as if she were in a corner; her manner of sinking to the ground when crushed, using no more circumference than she needs to squat in; her furtive, metronomic eye movements when experiencing something, grave or gay, which she would like to share with an audience that is never looking at her. Above all, she illustrates accurately this profound interpretation of the clown's facial singularity by André Suarès (from "Yorick: An Essay on the Clown—Fragment"). "One looks at the mouth or the cheek of the clown as one looks at the brow of another man. Frequently, the mouth is the brow of a farce . . . Many children have the same expression: they laugh while crying and cry while laughing. But the will has nothing to do with this. The mind is absent. . . . The grimace's hesitancy between laughter and weeping is the principle of an aesthetic theory" (*Verve*, I, January–March, 1939).

Since action, in the classical canon, confirms the qualitative nature of the plot, my rehearsal of the action in *La Strada* has been offered as a guide to the integrity of its composition.

From the one foot of water into which they have plunged, the performing seals of social outlook (who bark and clap flippers only when promised a literal fish) have retrieved the discovery that *La Strada,* like *Umberto D,* has something to do with "problems of communication." Indeed it has. Very likely it would yield a wealth of analyzable (or unanalyzable) problems for classification by the tools of motivational research. . . . Beyond the reach of McCann-Erickson and David Riesman, *La Strada* is nothing less than a rite of passage, a vision of perennially failing pig-man.

Zampano is *here,* at the center of a debased culture once again: a spiritually abandoned savage who, trudging in a circle, makes a show of breaking voluntarily assumed chains—his destiny to burrow at last in shifting sand with the tide coming in and the sky bereft of illusion, having rejected the Clown and destroyed the Fool in himself.   1956

A Festival of
Art Films

In April—notoriously "the cruelest month"—there took place this
year at the Metropolitan Museum of Art (the institution serving as
host only) an event which should have—could have? might have?
—been a cultural landmark, applauded, widely discussed, and
analyzed, and its next occasion universally anticipated, with pleasure. That event was the Third International Art Film Festival.*
Since, however, this august-sounding title was belittled by an atmosphere of diverted purposes, confused standards, and provincial
preoccupations, the event can scarcely be memorialized as a successful realization of its possibilities. For this reason, although I
should prefer to come directly to the point—the films on art which
were shown—and although I am personally grateful for having seen

---

*The first and second festivals were held at Woodstock, in 1951 and 1952. As I
understand it, the festival was then shelved until its security was assured by a
grant from the Rockefeller Foundation. The sponsoring bodies listed are the
American Federation of Arts and the College Art Association of America.

the few worthwhile exhibits which transpired, I am persuaded that the forensic issue is of first importance. The value of the end products, as so often in these affairs today, suffered drastically from the unmerciful accompaniment of trivia which our puritan context (I'd welcome another interpretation) seems to delight in imposing on us as the price of any possible enjoyment.

I am sure there were many more operational difficulties than those I am aware of connected with the staging of the festival. I am certain, by instinct and past observation, that lieutenants did whatever dirty-detail work had to be done, and that sundry people can explain (indignantly, perhaps) the inside reasons for this festival's poor integration of interests, its small proportion of good films, its tedious conference addresses—delivered during the day, when spring, beyond the doors, was bursting out all over—the incompetent projection of the films. From an offside position, the object of the festival seems clear enough in basic outline: to present films which have as their subject the fine arts to a larger audience than is customarily reached and, incidentally, to bring new films in this category to the notice of commercial distributors and noncommercial exhibitors (i.e., officers of schools, museums, film societies, and whatever). Obviously, the principal purpose of the individual art film is to display, analyze, and/or interpret a work, or works, of art. And since a movie camera is obviously a more complex instrument than a slide projector, *ipso facto* the art of film-making is an instantly provoked consideration, and the film will be judged, by a simultaneous exercise of one's sensibilities, on the basis of how successfully, in cinematic terms, it expresses its specific subject. Variously, the effectiveness of such a film may derive from its analytic function, its director's subtlety of perception, its historical scope, or its researching of a hitherto unobserved factor in the art which is undergoing scrutiny. In short, an art film is an esthetic construction, to be received attentively like any other, preferably with some degree of foreknowledge regarding the subject. And since it *is* an esthetic construction, it can reasonably be required to have a discernible form and meaningful content. But its responsibility is mandatory: to elucidate imaginatively a phase or instance of that protean blessing, the art experience.

Nothing so evident saved time, won friends, or influenced people at the Third International. Despite the ostensible continuity of the festival's dedication, wrangling over what *does* constitute an art film consumed half the time of the two-day conferences in the auditorium. One good soul from a New England museum delivered a report, warm with civic pride, based on the erroneous impression that an art film was an *arty* commercial film; for the repertoire she was extolling as evidence of home-front cultural improvement consisted of films starring Alec Guinness and Laurence Olivier. Serious conference participants were shocked by such irrelevance, but their own engagements of the topic were frequently as far afield. The appropriateness of art films in secondary education, the precarious profits of commercial distribution, the librarian's view of it all, and the inevitable "long-range enterprise" suggestion for subsidizing an army of art film commandos to storm the world's museums: these "problems" were inextricably mingled, with no one the least interested in any problem but his own and the whole superstructure of the occasion ignored. Taking place, as it was, in a museum housing multiple treasures of the human spirit, the festival conference proceeded at the level of a department of education council meeting in Keokuk.

In this environment the sedulously prepared report by Mr. Francis Bolen, the European representative from Brussels, on the short, happy life and vicissitudes of the C.I.D.A.L.C., the I.I.F.A., and F.I.F.A. (these are Unesco-assisted European art film federations) seemed almost oppressively thoroughgoing, and the expository finesse of Amos Vogel (Cinema 16's president), in defining the various cinematic techniques used in the making of an art film, was a disastrous incursion of pertinence. His address fell like a stone into a hundred-foot well. Not the least astounding derogation from the heart of the matter was Meyer Schapiro's perplexing defense of a film on Miró by Thomas Bouchard, shown *hors concours,* so to speak, as an exemplum of noteworthiness! The film is purported to be a gesture of friendship toward the painter by the filmmaker, and I am sure this is an honorable justification for making a film. But it's insufficient justification for exhibiting the film as a seriously finished achievement, either as art interpretation or as movie production, and it's certainly an insufficient reason for Mr. Schapiro to duplicate Mr. Bouchard's *beau geste* by defending his limitations. "Bouchard rarely calls attention to the direction of his thought," declared Mr. Schapiro, euphemistically. In the Miró film there are fine photographic fragments, but the sum is an unrealized miscellany indicating, even more than Bouchard's incapacity for editing a film, his inability to edit his mind. There were many films on display which lacked Bouchard's evident sincerity and qualified for more severe negative criticism; I dwell on the Miró incident chiefly because it seems to me regrettable that Mr. Schapiro (for whose critical eminence I have enormous respect), in denying the value of cinematic method (which he claimed, overmodestly, I'm sure, to know nothing about), thereby assisted the indifference of the general public toward the integrity of a craft—a curious position for the appraiser of one art to take when confronted by another.

Meanwhile the evening audience, undisturbed by these ancillary conflicts of interest, was having its own mixed experience with the contest waged by Helen Franc's program notes against the films they were intended to introduce. Although it's a novel idea to be provided with a program in which the items are criticized during the course of description—and Miss Franc's light handling of a heavy responsibility cannot but evoke our admiration—questions did stick in the throat. With the offended assurance of a knowledgeable scholar, Miss Franc assaulted Enrico Fulchignoni's script on Leonardo, *The Tragic Pursuit of Perfection,* scorning its adoption of the Antonina Vallentin view (not hers alone) of Leonardo as a failure in his own eyes. This view, we are told, is a "misconception" —and Miss Franc's repudiation of it found favor with a number of bystanders at the festival, for I heard it repeated on all sides, complacently. I suspect that the overemphasis on what was thought to be Fulchignoni's overemphasis—i.e., the possibility of a "successful" painter and inventor (he predicated *us,* didn't he?) experiencing disenchantment—arose from the fear, beneath our contemporary optimism, of swallowing so unpalatable a notion. Be that as it may, Miss Franc's concurrent support of Arcady's irresponsible excursion with Brueghel, and of Block and Berg's *Goya,* is even less an arguable verdict. The Goya film is one of the poorest on a great painter —produced outside of Hollywood—with which I am acquainted, thoroughly banal in conception and treatment. Among others of the twenty-one making up the program, its inclusion urged one's suspicion that of the 175 films previewed, many worthier were eliminated under the pressure of "democratic" voting. (I was witness to one inexcusable omission, of which more hereafter.)

The voting procedure seems to have been a free-form one, involving whichever interested parties happened to be around at preview time—among them teachers, education officials, film renters, "critics" (including the present writer, on one such occasion)—and their friends, who may or not have been qualified to cast an independent vote at this ceremony of innocence. Ergo the oddly assorted levels of discourse and genre officially presented; for example, two animated cartoons were sneaked in; highly entertaining—but on what grounds? Among those films, below the top level which were meritorious, I would include the Jan Hulsker *Vincent van Gogh*, which, if it didn't meet the impossible conditions adumbrated by this writer in a previous "discussion" (see *Arts*, November 1956), applied the biographical emphasis with more expertise than any attempt to date. The opening, with an auction of a Van Gogh painting, cut in over his gravestone, and a letter appealing for financial help, was bitterly effective; on the whole this film, property of the Netherlands Information Office, was a tasteful effort. But I think we're ready to agree that the next film on van Gogh could afford to insist on what distinguishes the paintings themselves, rather than the personal conditions under which they were produced.

Personally, I am not enthralled by the art of Willi Baumeister, but Will Grohmann's exposition of the abstract painter's work won my respect as a conscientious half-hour study of its kind. I found *The Tragic Pursuit of Perfection* intensely interesting—which I didn't two years ago, when I thought the *musique concrète* more disturbing than helpful (perhaps the sound system was better at the Metropolitan). What seemed, to my sense, to vindicate the accentuating of comparative details in Leonardo's *oeuvre*—and this is the principal mode of Fulchignoni's treatment—was the degree to which this method got under the skin of Leonardo's prodigious anatomy of the world.

Within my ken, the most undeserving victim of the laissez-faire voting policy was the film *Royaumes de Ce Monde* (*Kingdoms of This World*), written by Yves Bonnefoy and directed by Roger Livet, which is, I think, the single most penetrating film on art I have seen. Its concern is the ironic duality of the ostensible subject and the unconsciously primary one in paintings, from the eleventh to the seventeenth century, on a single theme, that of the Annunciation. The producers have not scorned spoken commentary and subtitles as well as real and unreal landscapes, used in judicious antiphony, to effectuate their artful thesis. The intrusive worldly interests of painters who were supposedly rendering a traditional iconography, and in some cases the essential ambiguity of their portrayal, are searchingly exposed by the acute perception of the poet-scenarist and by the irrefutable lens of the poet-cinematographer. As the film progresses, the commentary, as eloquent as it is subtle, shifts emphasis. From the terrestrial and decorative aspects revealed in the paintings—details of landscape, ornament, garden perspectives, flowers, to say nothing of the occasionally striking carnality in the poses of the Angel and the Virgin—the authors of the film move into considerations of the unmistakable melancholy and passivity which so often pervaded the subject, expressed in one picture as a matter of detail or general atmosphere, in another by the demeanor of the two figures (notably in those of Grünewald, Piero, Titian, Tintoretto, Poussin). Here the critical insight of the film-makers recognizes the growing intensification of that sharp Renaissance anguish before the phenomenon of change and dissolution (the prevailing subject of Ralph Roeder's magnificent study *The Man of the Renaissance*). The Christian symbol of joy gives way to the secular feeling of doubt; the tidings brought to Mary suggest a mortal world of splendor and decay. At the end, the film's formal unity is fulfilled by a return to landscape details, the first image of the film having been announced by the spoken *"Au point du jour . . . ,"* the last introduced by *"A la chute du jour. . . ."* Dawn and twilight. And in Leonardo's Annunciation the Renaissance is vindicated. *"C'est la réalité profonde et immédiate que cet ange évasif semble symboliser. Il se tient au seuil d'un royaume: celui du monde retrouvé."**

This film, within its seventeen-minute span, is a superlative instance, one of the few, of the psychologically creative art film. The little scenario, with its rigor and texture as of a fine poem, is itself a prize; it clarifies and enriches the subject, while the visual means enforce its claims overpoweringly, leaving the spectator with an experience and with a question. How many films of any length or any genre do as much? But unless a commercial distributor is more venturesome than the festival jury, you will see no more of this fugitive masterpiece than I have attempted to install in your mind's eye—and MM. Livet and Bonnefoy will have to console themselves with the uncorroborated taste of those who awarded their film the Grand Prix at the 1955 Festival of Tours.

Noblesse du Bois (*The Majesty of Wood*), which, to date, has received no commercial attention here either, was one of three Belgian films which constituted the festival's best offerings. (The other two were both executed by Paul Haesaerts.) In ten minutes of

---

*"It is reality, immediate and profound, which this elusive angel seems to symbolize. He is poised at the threshold of a kingdom: that of the world—rediscovered."

beautifully synchronized images and music (a Vivaldi concerto and a French choir), Charles Dekeukeleire, with a commentary only slightly less resonant than that of Bonnefoy—its burden is not profound—unreels a succession of sculptures in wood, all from Belgian churches and museums—from the Gothic Christ of Tancremont to an eighteenth-century pulpit representing Adam and Eve, by Verhaegen, at Notre Dame d'Hanswijck. Actuality-shots of living trees, of the kind which yielded their branches, and sometimes their very heartwood, to the varying needs of religious sculptors for eight centuries, are lyrically inter-cut or dissolved, and the director makes loving and skillful sorties among the changing styles, closing with a triumphant moment of cutting as, with the Eve figure, his camera focuses in turn on a single eye, the face, the entire head, then glides like a lover's hand down the grain-swirling baroque curves of the body. Again the trees return—naked branches of maple and elm, material of man's habitation or his imagery: "forest of symbols, forest of man: a reservoir eternally renewed."

One section only of Paul Haesaerts' *The Golden Age of Primitive Flemish Painters* was shown (during the daytime conference program), but I feel justified here in taking an opportunity to recommend the full version (about an hour), which comprises, besides the "Jan van Eyck" viewed on this occasion, studies in color (for the most part fully adequate) of the art of Roger de La Pasture (Van der Weyden), Dirk Bouts, Hugo van der Goes, Bosch, Memling, Metsys, Brueghel, and, in brief, Rubens. The van Eyck is the most satisfying self-contained section (partly, perhaps, because more of his work was immediately available for demonstration). The father of the Flemish continuity, the master of space-in-depth, seems to have fired Haesaerts' imagination to more vivid strategies of presentation. Yet all the others are resourcefully and patiently cine-illustrated. Haesaerts is one of the rare art film producers who consistently respect the totality of a painting, before and after the analytical operation of examining its particulars. His admirable narrative, fastidiously spoken for this film by Pamela Brown, never over-informs his unhurried isolation of visual detail. *The Golden Age* is particularly valuable because it calls attention to works not often encountered in reproduction, and it discriminates the esthetic *raison d'être* of each painter. My only quarrel is with the Brueghel résumé. It seems to me that, since Tolnay's study especially, there is no warrant for maintaining the view of Brueghel as a painter who was "after all" a celebrator, principally, of rustic pleasures and the meliorative view of things. In fact, this characterization can be substantiated only by falsifying, as I fear Haesaerts does by implication, the chronology of Brueghel's pictures. Inexcusable above all is the employment of that masterful stormy seascape, the enigmatic climax of Brueghel's art and one of the great Flemish achievements, as an incidental shot in a sequence depicting the painter's delight in scenic and occupational variety. (The same solecism was committed in another film shown at the festival, from France, *Peter Brueghel the Elder*—but the conception of this film was totally beneath contempt.) However, Haesaerts' lapses of insight are rare; this is otherwise a splendidly produced nine-part film, ennobled throughout, I might add, by glorious salvos of music from the contemporary sources.

Humanism, Victory of the Spirit (thirty minutes, black and white) is another victory for Haesaerts, a film of imposing intellectual vigor, wherein is defined, by a veritable crescendo of paintings, the transition from the conception of medieval man, God-ridden, guilt-ridden, and physically unimpressive (at least in the samples chosen, which treat of the Creation and the Temptation), to the humanist-plastic assertion of Man as measure (and measurer) of all things—and usually handsome, whether represented as poet, scholar, or man with a club. Certainly the initial images of this film were chosen to subscribe to a monstrously simplified deprecation of pre–High Renaissance man; yet the evidence selected *is* startling. With the assumption of the heroic subject, Haesaerts is in his element, performing a brilliant synthesis of humanist aspiration and conquest; correspondingly his purely cinematic flexibility is altogether daring and appropriate. The earlier paintings are modestly introduced at a medium-distance perspective, with a split-screen device for juxtaposing comparative examples. As the dynamic world of volume, tactile foreshortening, closeup, and multi-perspective dominates the walls, the domes, and the canvases of the sixteenth-century masters, Haesaerts' camera involves itself, perforce, with the implicit movement and the penetrable space.

Defending the kinetic principle in architecture, Geoffrey Scott has affirmed in *The Architecture of Humanism* that "we adapt ourselves instinctively to the spaces in which we stand, project ourselves into them, fill them ideally with our movements. . . . We transcribe architecture into terms of ourselves. . . . The tendency to project the image of our functions into concrete forms is the basis, for architecture, of creative design." Is there not an analogy here by which we can declare that to project the image of our *movements* into concrete forms is the basis, *for the motion picture,* of creative design? This, at any rate, is what Haesaerts has done, through the intermediary of cinquecento painting, even more boldly than it has been done before, even in *The Titan.* His most virtuoso feat is a plunge from the summit of that epic *Paradise* of Tintoretto, in the Ducal Palace, where the viewer, close in at first, is drawn swiftly back and down, obliquely from the figure of God and across the incredibly figured expanse, with the whole composition sailing away and opening out in all its breathtaking spacious complexity. And the finale is a further tour de force, in which a massive male figure by Michelangelo appears to contemplate Earth itself, one of those period globes known as armillary spheres, a shape with no substance save its centripetal structures, revolving backward into endless night.

Most ambitious film of the three-day program, *Humanism, Victory of the Spirit,* was almost too colossal a reminder, by the Sunday afternoon, of how far the spirit of the proceedings and the general diffidence had been from anything which conceivably might have been termed an idea about (or a feeling for) art—or, for that matter, from an idea about creative film-making, whereby such an interpretation as Haesaerts' was accomplished and for the encouragement of which, one supposes, the project was originally promoted and financed. 1957

Love, Death, and the "Foreign" Film—1957

> *Man always lives among graves, and we can recognize the future in store for him by the dignity with which he moves among them.*
>
> Franz Marc

In a review of Pierre Braunberger's film, *Bullfight* (*The Nation*, August 4, 1956), Mr. Robert Hatch, with visible effort keeping diffidence from becoming contempt, implicitly decided that whatever merits the movie had he wasn't interested in appraising them, so shocked was he by the subject and by those for whom that subject (death—in Mr. Hatch's flat view of it) exercised any fascination. His disdain was summarized with this, to me astounding, declaration:

> The world is full of incompatibilities—you cannot, for example, feel akin to both *Walden* and the ritualistic slaughter of wild beasts in the hot sun.

In passing, it should be noted how unfairly Mr. Hatch has loaded his brush: "ritualistic slaughter" is calculated to stress the quantitative, negative aspects of the bullfight at the expense of any other meaning to be discovered therein; "wild beasts" cannot accurately be held to define carefully bred and conditioned bulls—and "hot sun" seems to be a puritanical intensive for characterizing the event as disagreeably pagan. Beyond these rhetorical maneuvers, the statement illustrates a prevailing point of view—embracing subjects other than bullfights or films of them—among those who spell their liberalism with a capital L, and points to the probability that the progressive American of our day is as disingenuous a chauvinist as the world has seen for some time. Of course, there is something incidentally comic about an editor on a Manhattan political weekly asserting sympathy with a rural New England anarchist, whose pantheism alone represents the negation of every social value to which *The Nation* is ostensibly dedicated.

I have no long-buried bone to pick with Mr. Hatch. He simply happens to have outlined, with uncommon candor, a generic complacency, and he's brother under the skin, whether he says yea or nay, to the word acrobat of *Time's* film review page who, concealed by editorial anonymity, sneers at foreign decadence from a column adjacent to a display advertisement of *Tums*.* From our exponent's defense of healthy-mindedness it should logically follow that if liberal American values are more life enhancing than those which underlie the bullfight, for instance, American movies might be expected to profit from them artistically—an inference that requires no lengthy refutation. Our films—the exceptions barely justify the courtesy of a concession—are worse than incompetent and lower than juvenile; they are meretricious where they're not massively vulgar; they serve beauty or use as little as any popular art in the history of mankind. Every shallow Hollywood film is shallow precisely because it travesties an existing cultural shallowness: the tacit belief that it's both desirable and possible to legislate passion and death from the scheme of things, and that social security alone can bring the good life into existence. Every good imported film is not merely technically better, it's in another world of art. It *is* art. Especially when it deals potently and in cinematic terms, as it does often, with those irreconcilables which our population at large is too terrified by to confront: the co-extension of life and death, of attraction and revulsion, love shaped from the shock of death, material sacrifice for the peace of personal dignity.

---

*As a complex instance of moral chastisement administered through a *first-the-pleasure, then-the-guilt* pattern, note *Time's* review of *The Wages of Fear*, February 21, 1955, where an attack on Henri-Georges Clouzot was unmitigated by any distinction between the conception, a novelist's (Georges Arnaud), and Clouzot's principal role of director.

Needless to say, the Braunberger film does not engage all these universals, but the evident thoroughness with which it explores its subject has been sufficient to stimulate that compulsive counter-reflex, the crux of Mr. Hatch's protest. If one is a forward-looking American, one *shouldn't* enjoy bullfighting, even though it is sug-gestively comparable (without for the moment estimating its es-thetic value) to every large-scale arena combat known to our de-mocracy—the political campaign, the congressional investigation, the prizefight and the World Series, the radio or TV "quiz"—differ-ing in a single major respect: its calculated object is not simply the humiliation but the death of the baited victim.* Man, universally, lives by the death of others, but it's not democratic to acknowledge the murder which roams in the pandemic heart, or to confess its symbolic sublimation; above all, it is not progressive to relish, or even to appreciate, its ritualistic celebration in another cultural mode.

Bullfight is essentially a sensitive editorial feat, like the other two films produced by Braunberger—*Paris 1900* and *Life Begins To-morrow,* a nonfiction movie assembled entirely from existing ma-terial (which is to say that nothing was specially photographed for this film) —as a graphic means of explaining the principal com-ponents of the art of bullfighting, with historical examples, from the training of the matador to the *corrida* itself. I am amazed—or would be if I hadn't encountered this indifference to craftsmanship among sociologists before—that anyone, any critic, let's say, could fail to be enthralled by the film's sustaining details, which include remarkable shots of a bullfight made in 1895 (!), a sequence photo-graphed in Peru which has that keyed-up vibration of light as in-stantly recognizable in kind as the light of our own high-altitude Southwest, an absolutely fabulous display of style by Conchita Cintron, who fights from horseback in a compact enclosure, and an impressive moment, utterly silent (narration and guitar music other-wise accompany the film), when Manolo Gonzales prays before leaving his dressing room, while his manager, in the background, smokes with controlled nervousness . . . Personally, I find many aspects of the Spanish psyche incomprehensible, and *Bullfight* did not make an *aficionado* of me. But it did project for me, more viv-

---

* Curiously, opponents of the bullfight always pity the bull, not the man. When, in their private arenas, they are themselves gored, do they, one wonders, accept the penalty of their complicity in the fatal action?

idly than any prose description or verbal proselytizing ever has, the significance of the bullfight's profound attraction; it elucidated, beyond question, how acutely the Spanish have understood—since long before Wagner—the phenomenon of the love-death motif.

Bullfight isn't a Spanish film, as I may not have made clear. Braunberger is a Frenchman,* and his film is the best recent importation from France; the most popular have been those "gimmick" entertainments, Jules Dassin's *Rififi* and Clouzot's *Diabolique,* and René Clair's usual champagne-on-shredded-wheat, *The Grand Maneuvers,* so effervescently superficial it is an epitome; while you watch its exquisitely tinted fun, you're beguiled, yet you can't help wondering why Clair has never, in thirty years, really wanted to say anything. Max Ophuls' *The Earrings of Madame De . . .* is the model by reference to which Clair's situation in this film—love taken seriously too late—is sadly vitiated. Proceeding from deeply serious premises, *The Proud and the Beautiful* and André Cayatte's *We Are All Assassins*—flawed, both of them, in the execution—are nonetheless noteworthy. The former, a Sartre invention directed by Yves Allegret, places a French couple in a Vera Cruz pesthole where the husband is instantly killed by yellow fever; the ironic hinge of the ensuing action is the dazed astonishment experienced by the wife (Michele Morgan) in this heat-stinking nightmare, at her own resources for survival, resources which inspirit a broken-down doctor (Gérard Philipe) . Two moments are effectively mordant in the French manner: one where the wife, groping on the cockroachy floor under the bed, cries for the first time during the ordeal; the other, where Philipe dances with grotesque abandon in a cantina, as his payment for a bottle of rum. Truthfully, I was convinced less by the abrupt moral rehabilitation of the ending than by the local-color degradation which preceded it. . . . André Cayatte's film is one you watch with determination to like it, even as it dis-

---

Footnote 1971. Something further should be said. One could almost represent the history of the French cinema, in outline, with films produced by Braunberger, at least since the twenties. His association with film, first as an actor, goes back to 1922. A producer since 1924, he has been responsible in part or wholly for films as various as Cavalcanti's *Rien que les Heures,* Renoir's *La Chienne,* Buñuel's *L'Âge d'Or,* the brilliant and little known (outside France) documentary *Paris 1900,* edited with a touch of genius by the late Nicole Vèdres; and in the New Wave period he was the sponsor of key works by Godard, (alas) Jacques Doniol-Valcroze, and François Reichenbach, among others. *Bullfight* appears to have been largely his personal achievement; yet no one man could have assembled and "montaged" the profusion of material from which this splendid film was edited.

integrates, continuity-wise, as you watch, for it is concerned with our most fundamental social value—justice. Unfortunately, Cayatte has written a peroration, not a scenario. Despite many harrowing episodes—first with the Maquis, then in the cells of Villejuif, the same milieu as that of Bazin's paralyzing novel, *Head Against the Wall*—the film breaks down under a surfeit of exhortations and climaxes. One is finally unpersuaded that we are all assassins; the guilt here seems less that of man than of the appalling French penal system.

Guilt is also the *bête noir* of German film-makers. *The Last Ten Days* and *The Devil's General* deal, as squarely as at present it is possible to hope for, I suppose, with the Hitlerian sector of the German madness. But they chiefly confirm the German mastery of cinema techniques, of lighting especially, which redeemed their early films when nothing else did. *The Last Ten Days* proves what one had long suspected of the highly praised director, G. W. Pabst, that his head continually interferes with his artistic sense. Again and again the film falls short of the concentrated horror it climbs to; but the performance of Oskar Werner makes it entirely worth seeing. We have no single film actor with such warmth and such articulated vehemence. Similarly, Curt Jurgens is the dominating presence of the literate (and a shade too literary) adaptation of Carl Zuckmayer's more or less biographical play. I fear the film will not gratify those who would have preferred the Nazi obscenity to have been indicted by another standard than that of the officer class, but that's the subject as given, ending with a self-liquidation in Siegfriedian style, untrue to the derived facts but dramatically plausible.* Like the Pabst film, this one is enlarged beyond its scenario by its trenchant depiction of a man realizing too late that he has bartered his soul for an unspeakable political shibboleth. If German producers can find subject matter in which the strain of making public speeches is not omnipresent, they may well assume a position as eminent as they are falsely supposed to have occupied in the twenties. However, it will demand a resiliency not native to them to equal the cinematic sophistication of the French, an effort of humanity to rival the Italians at their best, and a supreme control of taste to match the clarity of the Swedish.

---

*In reality, Ernst Udet, the anti-Nazi flyer, model for Zuckmayer's General Harras, was killed by the party before he had the opportunity (or the desire?) to kill himself; they planted a bomb in his plane.

The greatest European film to be shown here in the past year—
always excepting *La Strada*—is *The Naked Night*, directed by the
virtually unknown Ingmar Bergman who, at the age of thirty-five,
has a dozen (I believe) film credits to his name (as scenarist or
director or both) and whose script for Alf Sjöberg's *Hets* (*Torment*), 1944, put the Swedish movie on the international map, insofar as it is there at all. Since for many years the Venice Film Festival committee prohibited Swedish films on the same prudish
grounds for which they are either barred from, or excised for, the
United States, the work of Bergman and Sjöberg, who have no su-
periors in the art of film-making anywhere, has received little attention outside of Scandinavia.* The fate of *The Naked Night* in New
York last year is unhappily characteristic of the treatment accorded
Swedish films. Our press reviewers, unprepared by prestige clues,
were baffled or bored by the production, which ran nine weeks at
its first showing only because the theater owner also happened to
hold distribution rights to the film. Sparse bookings nationally will
be the likely consequence, instead of the wide, and close, attention
the film deserves. Like most of Bergman's scenarios, *The Naked
Night* (title designed to suggest the Swedish proclivity for undress?) turns an unsparing scrutiny on the struggle between the
sexes, its contingent subject the self-punishing efforts of a couple—
the aging owner of a traveling circus and his young mistress (this
is Sweden at the turn of the century) —to liberate themselves from
an intensely possessive relationship: he by way of his deserted ex-
wife, she through an impetuously willful affair with a sadistic actor
of equivocal sexual tastes. They are both rejected and return to
each other before the circus moves on at the end of the film, but not
before the man, Albert, has been exposed to a relentless humiliation
of his sexual pride, and the filmgoer has been submitted to an almost unendurable laceration of his sympathy. Bergman has a perfectly hellish understanding of what goes on, psychically, between
male and female, and since his craftsmanship is equal to his psychology, he is probably responsible for Hilding Bladh's crystal cam-

---

Footnote 1971. This is simply not true. Probably I accepted this opinion from
Swedes before finding out what bad losers they are and to what lengths they will
go to justify their inability to compete. During the war, certain Swedish films
were banned or scolded by the Venice authorities (under Mussolini) for political
reasons. Thereafter, if any Swedish films were found unacceptable for competition, the reason would have been the same that obtained for films from any
country.

era-eye, which catches images of beauty and of crucial desperation as if it were balancing precious water in a goblet.

One of the most creative passages in film since the great Russian experiments of the twenties is a thematic prologue, as it were, wherein the pathetic Frost (a supporting character), dressed as Pierrot, staggers across a rocky beach to rescue his wife from the consequences of her own exhibitionism. The film print is treated in such a way (possibly double duplicated?) as to present an etiolated texture, thoroughly macabre, and although laughter and imprecations are mouthed, no sound is heard save a terrible drum accompaniment. That such cinematic inspiration should have been promoted solely on the pulchritude (indisputable!) of its leading actress, Harriet Andersson—and even so fail to make a stir—indicates the poverty of film criticism and promotion alike.

The only film of recent release that competes with Bergman's for sheer force of impact, with another kind of rhythm, is *O Cangaceiro,* usually referred to as *The Bandit.* Edited by a German and photographed by someone with the un-South American name Chick Fowle, the movie was written, directed, and produced by Lima Barreto, Portuguese Brazilian, and financed by the Bank of São Paulo. For two years the film has been in circulation—limited, I would presume, judging by the few people I have been able to discover who have seen it. Just as the guillotine in *Casque d'Or* was a climactic image for the tone of the whole movie, a garotte would be the appropriate ideogram of *O Cangaceiro,* although death by strangulation is the one kind not represented in the film (it would have been kinder than any that are). An introductory title specifies, "The time is indefinite. When there were still outlaws." After this sardonic subterfuge, Barreto and his cameraman proceed to show Hollywood the meaning written in the scorched dust under their big, nerveless feet since the western was born as a category.

The jaguar, enticed by the simulated whistle of his mate, meets death instead. . . . Or, in synopsis: a band of outlaws under the leadership of Captain Galdino Ferreira (as filthy-stiff-with-pride a little beast as you ever saw on the screen) raids a defenseless village— somewhere on the pampa—and carries off, among less reluctant female captives, a schoolteacher of relatively patrician background whom Galdino spares from indignity, ostensibly in order to collect ransom money. Teodoro, a lieutenant with Christian memories, without waiting for the issue of his suspicions, escapes from camp with the lady and after a cross-country "journey perilous" returns her to the civilization where she belongs. He then stoically awaits punishment from his compadres. He receives it. That's all. . . .

In outline that's all. A hint of the level at which the film is conceived will be suggested by Teodoro's answer to Olivia's question, "Why are you risking your life for me?" His reply: "A man wouldn't have asked." But this gives no hint of the visual excitement of the movie, of the raffish style of the actors (Milton Ribeiro's Galdino is unimaginable!), or of the pulsating Brazilian folk tunes which animate the score. Or of that breath of the inexorable which, in every interlocking episode, conquers slickness with veracity. One such episode will establish my point. Following the raid mentioned above, a volunteer posse from the surrounding area rides into Galdino's territory to avenge the rape of their families. They seal their doom by a quixotic neglect of strategy, riding straight into ambush, where, to a man, they are implacably picked off. During this briefly tragic engagement they never once see the enemy which is annihilating them, for Galdino's men are indistinguishable from the mesquite and pampa grass in which they have taken cover. With a perversion of courtesy that chills the blood, the banditti respect the principle Rank-Has-Its-Privileges, allowing the leader of the foolhardy contingent to remain erect, untouched, till his company has been dispatched. In response to the screaming profanity with which he then invokes his own reward (this seems to be part of the convention) they riddle him with bullets. While firing in pointless return, the defeated man continues to hurl invective, even as he is brought to his knees and finally to the ground. With a gesture of insatiable impotence, barely able to lift his head, he now rams in his last clip of cartridges, and the gun empties itself with a stutter of futility into the chaparral. Before sinking lifeless over the spasmodic weapon, the man ejaculates, "Filth!"—and it's impossible at this juncture to know whether he is addressing Galdino personally, all of the bandits, humankind, or that God who permits a man to die like a cornered, tortured rabbit under a planetary sky, without succor, with but hostile witnesses. . . . The dreadful, piercing nihilism of this film is ennobled by the weirdly dignified staunchness and fatality from which everyone, Galdino included, derives his strength. In a neglected "fiction" too drily entitled *Southwest*, John Houghton Allen expressed admirably a text for this manner of outcome:

> . . . . there is never anything ridiculous about those who die for
> the shadow, or those who take the losing side, or those who
> stand alone, or those in general who live dangerously—because
> even when you are betrayed, it is with a strange pathos.

Aside from the fact that there's something more bitter than pathos
in the residue of this film, I would say that Allen's gnomic sentence
fairly justifies its general temper.

Surprising as it may be to admirers of Akira Kurosawa, who plausibly expect the master of *Rashomon* to produce only masterpieces,
a comparison of his *The Magnificent Seven* (originally *Seven Samurai*) with *O Cangaceiro* is markedly in Barreto's favor. Kurosawa, unlike the Brazilian, fails to disengage the intrinsic meaning
from the core of his melodramatic commitment. His plot substance
is the preparation for, and defense of, a remote mountain village
from marauders, under the hasty tutelage of hired warriors,* and
his introduction promises great moments: a syncopated drum motif,
and thundering horsemen, outriders of doom, against a dingy sky.
They rein unsteadily to a halt, survey the sleepy mountain village
they intend plundering when the crops are gathered, months hence,
and ominously gallop away. After their staccato dialogue and clat-
tering exit, a hush—gently invaded by a rising bird song. But from
there in, Kurosawa seems to have been told, like Lady Macbeth,
that his undaunted mettle should compose nothing but males, for
he was clearly bent on developing the most virtuoso action movie
ever attempted, without benefit of chariots, galleons, buffaloes, pyramids, or whales. Nothing up his sleeve but five barley loaves and
seven small samurai. Filmgoers who are easily overcome by operational genius will assert that Kurosawa performs his miracle. Cinematically, the film is certainly adroit, a succession of pyrotechnics:
variable speed-cutting, close-in work, dynamic panning, overheads
—and underfoot!—wonderful sword-and-spear prowess, horseman-
ship that unseats you from nervousness. More filmic ingenuity is
shown off in a thousand feet of shooting than in the annual cinemascopic output spread end to end. And physiographically the movie

---

*Unemployed samurais, as a result of the deposition or elimination of the noble
families on whom they were customarily dependent, were common in the fac-
tional period represented by this film. Known as *ronin* (i.e., men without masters
—literally *wave-men*) , they were often willing to fight for room and board, so to
speak—i.e., a roof and a rice allowance.

is all there, too; it establishes a scene, a rugged, hill-trapped, rathole kind of settlement, ringed by fitfully lighted forest under permanently sullen skies—houses with dark, primitive interiors that suggest corncribs rather than the dwellings of man. The guerrilla contest which takes up fully the last half of the film (and I saw the uncut version—you're actually lucky) is a vortex of rain, mud, bamboo spears, redundant skirmishes, and banners that flap in the wet wind with a sound of drumheads. All this is cinematic muscle, equaled in tensility by few films ever; *Alexander Nevsky* is the closest contender.

But the film has no heart. It narrates compellingly the rigors of subsistence-level creatures fighting to maintain a bare foothold; human awareness is absent. No sentiment is internalized by a single character long enough to command our anguish as well as our suspense. If it were *real,* it would be affecting; a documentary can afford to forgo internalization to a degree not permissible in a fiction movie. Nothing is at stake here but survival, and if it can be retorted that survival is, after all, everything, it is also true that a narrative work of art must make survival count by incarnating its imaginative values through a consciousness. The heroic clown played by Mifune (the bandit of *Rashomon*) is stoutly a man; he is scarcely a consciousness. His death does not move us; at the last he's what you see: a corpse on a bridge, with bare buttocks. The interjected love interest cannot move us, either. Renunciation will be simple for the young samurai, for we don't believe he has touched anything—except his sword. Only in the closing shots does something like epic stature emerge, as the surviving samurai prepare to move on. Standing before the graves of their buried confederates, as the villagers in the fields below resume their eternally earthbound ritual of planting for a dubious harvest, "They have survived," one samurai observes, "and they have their earth. What do we have?"

Anywhere but in Southern California, it would seem, a movie director can still try, at least, for the great themes and the small winnings. Only where "money is no object" are no risks taken for the sake of a decent perception, for an adventure which may be unpopular but isn't fraudulent, for ninety minutes, more or less, which might add their cinematic sum to the statements about man which evade neither his inordinate folly, his complicated chivalry, nor his dirty, unanswerable pain. If I terminate these remarks by again invoking the esthetic of the bullfight, I ask to be absolved from any taint of obsession, pleading pertinence as my excuse. My epilogue is taken from the "Mexican Journal" of Rico Lebrun, the Italian painter. I find it sharper than vintage Hemingway.

> "Do you work close?" asked Simon [a *torero*] superciliously, staring at me. "Do you work close to the picture?"
>
> "Of course he does," said Paco [a doctor]. "I have seen him do it. Close it is, boy. He ruins many an effect because he is a mule against fear. He can paint out a whole house in a picture and replace it with a firefly."
>
> "No me diga!" said Simon. "Don't tell me! He doesn't know what he's doing. I don't change my mind in the middle of a veronica."
>
> "It's not the same thing, stupid," answered Paco. "Can't you see that it is not? The way they work they never see the animal until it's all over. You could say that they work blindfolded like horses and stay in close. Others, the not-so-good painters, work away from the animal and save their glass posteriors with great precision. They live longer, they paint worse."

1957

Long Voyage Home
with John Ford

John Ford has been prominently installed in the Musée Imaginaire of the American Cinematic Way since 1924, when he produced *The Iron Horse*. Since 1934 an alarming number of critics have apotheosized him as Film Artist. Under the present condition of downward-spiraling national taste, when it is possible and even unremarkable for the motion picture editor of the *New York Times* to betray his own modus vivendi by undertaking a "biography" of MGM, and for the Museum of Modern Art to issue a membership-edition apologia for Samuel Goldwyn's films—wherein not a shadow of adverse criticism, selectively quoted, is suffered to rest on its own accusations—we may very soon expect an official memorial of John Ford's fortieth year as a commercial film-maker. In the course of this memorial the sparse merits of that loaded and pedestrian parable, *The Informer*, already worn threadbare by overattention, will again be rehearsed and the handsome scenic backgrounds of *Stagecoach* or *She Wore a Yellow Ribbon* will be extolled as justification for the puerilities enacted thereagainst.

The Searchers reenacts and summarizes—with finality, one would like to hope—the more shocking of these puerilities. Throughout the movie, set in the immediate post–Civil War Southwest (Monument Valley, for the most part), the rogue male played by John Wayne, whose antecedent excuse is never clarified, snarls or sulks in the face of any advice or opposition; hates Indians and even part-Indians even more vehemently than he hates Yankees; and is nauseated by his Kiowa-abducted niece, to the point of wishing to destroy her, upon realizing that she has slept with a "buck" and possibly enjoyed doing so. Be it noted that in the original frontier case from which the novel (and Ford's scenario, further denatured) was drawn, the thirteen-year-old white girl *refused* to be rescued from her Indian captors. When, fifteen years later, she was forcibly liberated and her adopted tribe wiped out to a man, including her warlord husband, she died soon after of a broken heart. When John Ford is willing to engage so grim an irony, he will partly vindicate the contention of his defenders that, if nothing else, he has sophisticated the western.

Ford's frontier is actually but a *point d'appui* for his flattery of the homespun aggressions of the democratic ethos. And his esthetic, for momentary want of an unkinder word, is appropriate to that content. *My Darling Clementine* (1946), an inconsequent narrative artistically photographed in terms of period and occupational mannerisms, and in places stunningly acted, showed Ford at his visual best and suggested a latent charm he has nowhere else freely expressed. But *The Searchers* is more characteristic, exploiting, as it does, every quasi-Flemish literalism of the Ford milieu: the interminably "panned" symmetry of mesas; the stilted closeups of the patiently waiting girl who, though allegedly withering for want of a male "yes," maintains a henna rinse, smooth hands, and a radiant face unlined by sex hunger; the impeccable dressed-stone house, with gleaming copper pots and freshly waxed restorations of American provincial furniture; and the swept-tidy oases into which canter dustless thoroughbreds with milky-clean fetlocks (promptly picketed in a bunch to make it easy for a troublesome Indian to cut them all loose simultaneously).

Moviegoers who don't really want *movies*—they like action within the frame, but they don't want the frames to progress too elliptically—welcome the Ford film. In line with common Hollywood practice (the more so now that the wide screen encourages the return of the full-tableau shot), Ford has maintained the picture-frame or stage-set composition. Like Thomas Hardy, in one sense, he stands us off while his creatures assemble on a dressed landscape. This is very effective at special moments, as in the preparations for the O. K. Corral gun battle in *My Darling Clementine,* tiresome as a general habit of substituting panorama for logical continuity of perspective. (Obviously he learned no distinctions from Pudovkin or Dovzhenko in this direction.)

Somewhere—I can't cite chapter and verse—Ford has been quoted as believing that it is more "natural" for a man to approach a camera than for a camera to approach a man. (Early-Hitchcock students please note.) The dogma is witless in view of the fact that a motion picture isn't a natural phenomenon, it's an art; the terms of cinematic imagination will confer naturalness within the context. But the pronouncement is revelatory, a clue to Ford's peculiarly decorative realism—seldom convincing, since the art of film realism consists, paradoxically, in avoiding an obviously pictorial attack on the pictorial. Ford, at his most pompous, is reminiscent of Albert Bierstadt, whose grandiose landscapes with fated buffaloes focused in amber (painted around 1860) sold at unbelievable prices. Bierstadt was no calendar artist; he was lurid, in the finer sense. Like Ford's, his *kitsch* was confused with the real thing, and his example dominated the execution of western scenery on canvas for almost a century. Ultimately he took to drowning single figures in a tempest of peaks merging with the heavens. Ford seems never to have been tempted by an equal degree of impressionism, if you can call it that. The elements of reality, as Ford sees them, are never atmospheric, never indistinct. A bold chiaroscuro, shot from dead-center level and prolonged unduly, is his furthest risk.

Similarly his groupings are next of kin to those of George Caleb Bingham, the Missouri painter of the 1850's, who reacted to the Jacksonian social spirit of uniform accent by modeling his flatboatmen, hunters, squatters, and electioneers with equal definition within a scene. Each figure stares from the canvas with an unsubordinated claim to attention. Gradations of low-keyed color punctuated by whiter facial and sartorial areas often lend a muted monumentality to the painter's compositions. Ford's are rather less subtle of impact; they are Bingham at his most stilted. (There are times in *The Long Voyage Home* and *The Grapes of Wrath* when the deck crew of the S. S. *Glencairn* and the grouped Joad family are all too heroically posing for a destiny mural to be unveiled at a courthouse.) Compare almost any relational cluster in a Ford film with, for instance, John Sturges' strikingly casual disposition of his indolent Black Rock conspirators as they gather in loose-limbed vigilance at the railroad track. Ford has never so cunningly achieved the ominous natural moment of decision. The failure is symptomatic of his basically undistinguished contribution to film art.

When pressed, his admirers submit *The Informer, The Long Voyage Home, The Grapes of Wrath,* and sometimes *Stagecoach, The Fugitive,* or *How Green Was My Valley* as their principal support of Ford's attainments. Since critical judgment is nothing if not comparative, and since these films were produced after 1934, when the major experiments in creative movie-making had long been consolidated, evaluation is futile unless it acknowledges that Ford was simply one of many inheritors who synthesized, in the commercial-entertainment area, discoveries made elsewhere. This definition, far from contemptible, leads to sensible questions. Beyond the general decency of their pretensions, what is uniquely interesting in *The Informer* or *The Long Voyage Home?* What depth of psychological perception or cinematographic freshness affirms their value in the memory of those who seem utterly to have forgotten even the lesser masterworks of the decades preceding these films? Surely to ask such questions is almost to cancel them before an answer profitable to Ford's reputation can be framed.

Ford neither introduced nor developed a vitally differentiating style. Those who make him responsible for the acutely lighted and tightly knit compositional surface, his sole warrant for above average skill, are unjust to a host of claimants among whom, in Hollywood, I am content to single out von Sternberg and Boleslawski. The legend of his courage in handling dangerous commitments during the forties is not a beguiling one to those of us with middle-distance memories. Ford has never tackled subject matter that would disturb your maiden aunt. *The Informer* offered him (and his parishioners, as it were) a piously popular theme of betrayal, guilt, and redemption (melodramatically purchased) . The year of its production does not qualify the film's essential vulgarity of treatment. Good taste then deplored, as it must now, the clumsy overacting of Victor McLaglen (evidently made acceptable to the credulous by years of submission to the gaucherie of Emil Jannings) , the crude insistence of Ford's restatement shots (e.g., the recurring wall patches where the reward posters had been pasted) , and the vile finale, recalling Belasco or Griffith, with Mother coincidentally in the church pew to witness McLaglen's dying remorse. If Ford sacrificed private funds (as it has been asserted) to make *The Long Voyage Home,* he had the compensation of a self-indulgent adventure with "artistic lighting," as well as a prolonged rehearsal of Irish accents—O'Neillized in this case—sweet to his ears but not harps to everyone else's. With *The Grapes of Wrath* he was perfectly safe. The novel was a best seller, its cause was righteous, and by the time his glossy film version appeared, the California migratory worker problem was already a subject of state legislation. No one of these films radically challenged an artistic or commercial status quo. In the case of *The Long Voyage Home,* to conceive of filming a sequence of one-act plays was daring only because it was *in*artistic; the result was as unrhythmic as might have been foreseen. It survives as a curiosity of misbegotten earnestness, heavy-handed and sentimental, its atmosphere continually vitiated by "artiness"—which is to say calculation ill concealed.

Following the war years, after he had done his honest job of battle reporting, Ford returned to, and has remained at, the normal altitudes of Hollywood fare, unless one excepts his disastrous cooperation with Dudley Nichols in the emasculation of Graham Greene's *The Power and the Glory (The Fugitive)* , one step beyond (and lower than) the portentous religiosity of *The Informer*—every window sash a potential crucifix. Since then (1947), Ford hasn't stirred a lion or started a hare. Assuming that his autonomy is limited, so is that of every other Hollywood director; in fact it is reasonable to suppose that his seniority and prestige have been less precariously maintained than is customary, front offices being what they are. The record stands: Ford has not made a film in the last decade which competes seriously with Lewis Milestone's *A Walk in the Sun,* Robert Siodmak's *The Killers* or *Criss Cross,* Edward Dmytryk's *Cross Fire,* Nicholas Ray's *They Live by Night,* or John Sturges' *Bad Day at Black Rock.* He has been content to repeat his stock in trade, the action "epic" picture with a thin varnish of Significance and a thick undercoat of sentiment, embellished by those "characterization" tags successfully displayed in *The Iron Horse* and recapitulated, with improved continuity and timing, in *Stagecoach.* For these purposes the cinemascopic western is ideally suited. Ford's intellectual temper, little different from the prevalent one in Hollywood's cultural vision, is lowbrow conservative. He has never voluntarily chosen a milieu in which it was feasible to depict a complex motivation or a subtle aspiration, or where it was pardonable to question a socially unified shibboleth. The church, the family, the troop, and the forecastle are his emblems. Cowpokes, western cavalry, deckhands, and "Okies" may well represent his democratic affinities; also they suit his psychological limitations, his flair for tribal allegiances, and his allergy to the ironic. Ford's informer had no such endearingly mixed traits as had Johnny McQueen in *Odd Man Out;* and if this monochromism can be explained by Liam O'Flaherty's original or Dudley Nichols' screenplay, what explanation justifies Ford (and again Nichols) for scrapping Graham Greene's harrowed whiskey-tippling and woman-fumbling priest in favor of a soulful prig (in *The Fugitive*)? The Ford social morality is abidingly transparent, little modified by front-office directive or scenarist's whim. His films condescend lovingly to anyone outside the clan of the hour—Irishmen, Englishmen, Swedes, heretics, Texans, or Northerners. His chosen heroes are dumb oxen, "good guys," or, at best, thoughtful and unworldly professional men—Doctor Mudd in *The Prisoner of Shark Island,* young Lincoln, the priest in *The Fugitive,* Mister Roberts. Clearly he was most uncomfortable with Martin Arrowsmith, whose dedications were intellectual. He is most at home with characters who can be played by John Wayne, epitomes of the strong outdoor nonverbal extrovert, preferably over forty-five, patronizingly contemptuous of the inexperienced, the sensitive, and the "foreign"—and basically misogynist. (Ford's movies, like Howard Hawks's, are masculine, but Ford is less interested in the *frisson* of the male-female contest which, it may be confessed, contributes to the prevailing verve of Hawks's movies—for instance, *Only Angels Have Wings, To Have and Have Not, Red River.*) There have been few Ford films in which the women weren't either-ors: either madonnas or tramps.

That Ford's films should be popular with those to whom they cater in the central manner of the Hollywood stereotype is not at all surprising. But it is startling that in ostensibly more knowing circles their routine directorial competence and their sophomoric content should be given a second (and a third) look. Clearly, our pretenders of the film societies are as susceptible to the refabrication of mores (especially of the western frontier) as any high school boy or provincial shopgirl. In the last analysis, where the close observer of popular film art should resent being stranded, Ford's world is mindless, inartistic, and calculatedly false to cultural realities. All the brothers are valiant, Mother could sit for Whistler, retribution is swiftly picturesque (supported by full orchestra), the badlands of Monument Valley are ideal for raising fat cattle or for mining copper, Ireland is a poem, and be it ever so humble there's no home on the range less attractive than a National Park Service lodge. . . .

The shameless last stand of the Ford apostle is to defend the master's generic mythomania as myth.   1957

International Film Scene: Asia, Italy, and Mexico

> *It is our differences that unite us, because we approach each other in order to study them, and because in studying them we discover our resemblances.*
>
> Elie Faure

Like the crystal note of a temple bell sounding over the hubbub of a native bazaar, *Pather Panchali (The Little Road)*, a film of contemporary Bengal village life, has emerged from the fantastic mélange of operetta, melodrama, and anachronistic legend which normally characterizes the movie production of India. A young Bengali girl and her small brother—incarnations, both, of sculptures from an eighth-century grotto—seeing their first railway train and listening to the *sostenuto* of telegraph wires threading the spaces above the paddy fields and bamboo groves; white bullocks drifting through plumed grasses; the surface of a lotus pond prismatic with dragonflies or darkened by ferocious diagonals of rain; the outcry of a bereaved mother suddenly cut off and then resumed, as if in mercy, by the plaint of an unearthly flute: these and other images inveigle us into that most difficult of simulations, the pretense of having shared place and time with a handful of people (in this case an indigent Brahmin family) whose rhythm, customs, and social destiny are alien to ours. But this is a lovely illusion which doesn't stand the test of months. We are not subjugated by Satyajit Ray's film, as we were by Mizoguchi's *Ugetsu* or, in a less personal way, by Basil Wright's *Song of Ceylon*. *Pather Panchali* is a sensitive film, beautifully photographed, indigenously composed; yet it is a film of moments never satisfyingly fused. These moments are given temporal continuity by reference to the changes of season, two deaths in the family, and the final departure of the survivors for Benares. What is missing from the film as a whole is an esthetic principle, intuitively developed from the native source. Ray has chosen to ignore the traditional sinuosity and inter-dissolving identities of Indian art which even Renoir captured in *The River* (whenever he was able to cut loose from the static sequences of the priggish novel he was adapting). Perhaps these would not have been to the point of Ray's particular intention, but something of the kind was demanded, and perhaps all I'm really saying is that Ray was animated by love but had no point of view. He has admitted that he wasn't afraid of the picture's rambling because life in a Bengali village rambles. But the director-artist, while he is making a film, is God; he musn't *permit* life to ramble! I suspect that Ray's caution, assuming it doesn't derive from inexperience, may be due to his conscious attempt to stand outside his material, in the manner of Western sociology. He believes himself to be influenced by De Sica. Like De Sica, he does have a special gift for finding poetry in stillness and for coaxing the lyrical from the everyday—"that light of glamor created in the shock of trifles." Unlike De Sica, and more like Flaherty, he is afraid of imposing on his material. Neo-realism, in the hands of De Sica and Fellini, is more than verisimilitude, and Ray is not the first to misunderstand it. However, this *is* a first film and as such has introduced to the West a film creator of more than ordinary promise whom we should watch with some eagerness.

Mexican films have been shown in the United States for years, usually without English subtitles, in Spanish neighborhood theaters, with the result that any familiarity with them has been limited to the work of Luis Buñuel, a Spanish surrealist (now working in Paris, as he did originally). An enterprising producer, Ponces by name, is probing the gringo market with films that speak uncompromisingly for the native Mexican and more especially for the Indian. Not since Sergei Eisenstein's ill-fated incomplete epic has the monumental, bristling landscape of Mexico been photographed with such impact as in the four-part film *Raices* (*The Roots*); never has the quiescent pride of the submerged Indio been so intensely focalized —embarrassingly so in the first two stories, where an unquestionably driving resentment insults one's intelligence by overstatement. But the edge of this same sincerity is sharpened like the blade of a machete in the sardonic fable *One-Eyed,* wherein a boy named Angel, tormented for his affliction by his playmates, is dragged by his mother on a desperate pilgrimage to a religious festival where, she is convinced, his sight will be restored. No touch more clearly differentiates *Raices* from that other morality film of a small boy's faith, *Marcelino, Pan y Vino* (the Hungarian-directed film from Spain—the Spain of Murillo, not Goya!—shown here last year), than the nature of the "miracle" which ensues. . . . *The Filly,* final story of the four, engrosses a subject of equally concentrated power: the struggle, as silent for the most part as it is deadly, between an Indian servant girl of slim, pristine beauty and her would-be seducer, an aging Spanish archaeologist, pathetically obtuse and headstrong as a burro. I have noted few film scenes more relentless in their intimacy than one in which, against a black-clouded latitude of ocean, the man knocks the girl unconscious by the waves' edge: as she lies, limply graceful on the wet sand, he first arranges her long disordered hair into a tidy undulation, then proceeds to kiss the length of her body, beginning at the feet, the camera unmercifully within an inch of his head all the way! An assertive Mayan pyramid, around and upon which the camera also builds vivid tensions, finally comes to symbolize, with no forced effort from the director, the spirit of a rooted people who have endured and may yet triumph.

Probably the Italians don't half appreciate how kind God is; He has given them De Sica *and* Fellini—De Sica, open, measured, at ease, and deceptively informal; Fellini, raffish and oblique, a revolutionary wit whose moral pity sears as it enlightens, while he enlists madness and the saints in his cause. *Oro di Napoli* (*Gold of Naples*) is a composite film from which one of the five stories was removed before it left Italy, presumably because the Italian government wanted rich Americans (for "rich Americans" read "Americans") not to accept with too great alacrity the slogan *Vedi Napoli e mori.* What remains is still a dazzling example of De Sica's versatility and of his mastery of the tragicomic vein. In two of the four instances he took unusual risks by employing situations in which the climax is an interior revelation; if nothing else, the weight of the burden is then placed squarely on the actor. This is true of the story where the gangster who has held a quaking *petit bourgeois* family under his thumb is suddenly made to reckon with their timorous but resolved unanimity to oust him. Since they are actually as harmless as they ever were, physically, their concerted moral reprise must appear sufficient to break his command of himself and over them. That it does so is a tribute to a great cinematic spirit, not the least of whose achievements has been the restoration of acting to a fully complementary role in the motion picture, without at the same time sacrificing cinematics to theater or to tedious transcripts of anecdote not even theater, characteristic of Marcel Pagnol and of too many British directors. De Sica himself is a featured actor in this film, generously sharing his big scene with one of those small phenomenal boys who seem to exist in Italy and France for no other purpose than to be discovered by the like of De Sica.

But the masterpiece of *Oro di Napoli* is, in my opinion, the closing episode—an entity which should be preserved on supernitrate film for containing one of the memorable sequences of movie pantomime—dealing with the surprise offer of marriage by a respectable and wealthy man to a well-bred prostitute, played by Silvana Mangano. Accepting the proposal with mingled happiness, mistrust, and fear, the girl discovers she is being used solely to support the man's sadomasochistic guilt. The long moment when, having left the man's house indignantly, she hesitates, shivering and torn between two worlds (her own and the partly beguiling alternative) on the lamplit solitary street, is another victory of De Sica's confident genius for trusting the inwardly provoked imagination of his actors, with a minimum of shots exterior to their responsibility for projecting the emotion. The eloquence of this moment was certainly not supplied by De Sica alone: there is abundant preceding evidence in this vignette of Mangano's resources, which up to now have been generally supposed to exist entirely below her waist! My own infatuation has always been more presumptive; I'm satisfied that my contentions, in the face of austerely raised eyebrows, have been vindicated. With opportunities available for responding to actresses who express the very core of feeling, it seems to take a mass neurosis for public appreciation to coincide with a deserving object. Silvana Mangano will never be the universal emblem that Garbo was, yet in this film her expressiveness is of that order—the great silent order. Observe her introductory scene at the café table:

with what nerve-end finesse she expostulates or questions with one free hand—and I know of nothing more wonderful in the context of today's film, insofar as our subject is personality, than the exact moment at which the Mangano face begins to break, either with pain or joy. In fact, confronted with Italian films of this kind, one is reminded of how rarely one sees today that most miraculous conformation in nature—the human face.

Federico Fellini's *Il Bidone* (*The Swindler*) has Giulietta Masina to compound the exceptions, but she is regrettably in the subordinated part of a loyal wife to one of the trinity whose petty but hellbent larceny comprises the subject matter of this strange, tough-textured film. Space does not permit me to suggest the extensions in *Il Bidone* of the Fellini-Pinelli-Flaiano metaphysic. Suffice it for summary that although on a single viewing I would not rate the film equal to *La Strada* in human and evocative appeal, it does show Fellini at his cinematic best, its moral urgency is (dangerously) more explicit than heretofore, its résumé of the struggle for status within criminal elites is a withering social accusation—ultimately allegorical, of course—its substantive details of contemporary Italian society are fresh and syncopated, and it is quietly dominated from beginning to ambiguous end by a marvelous dry-mouthed, utterly sad performance from Broderick Crawford, playing a lonely swindler with such majestic fatigue as to suggest an experience-laden derelict painted by Rembrandt.

During one pellucid interval of Keigo Kimura's *Senhime* (*Princess Sen*) —an interval that follows a fading tableau of red and gold where assassination has been diverted by welcomed seduction (a reverse climax to that of *Gate of Hell*) —in this refulgent hush of daylight, the Princess (Machiko Kyo), flanked by a tulip tree and attendants dressed in fuchsia, inquires artlessly, "Was the world ever so beautiful?" And only a spectator of swinish constraint will fail to murmur, *"Never!"* It is barely open to doubt that no decorative world within the confines of a single motion picture was ever so beautiful, and I declare this mindful of Murnau's *Faust*, Cocteau's *Beauty and the Beast,* and those other nominations from the Japanese, *Gate of Hell* and *Yang Kwei-Fei.* The latter no more than prepared us for the infinities of delicate color orchestration which compose the eventful progression of this feudal, fantastic (if historically grounded) chronicle. Pragmatists, struggling mothwise to evade the splendor of Japanese samurai films, have been heard to broach the supposedly confounding question: "Can you identify yourself?" A swallowed answer turneth away wrath. . . . Identify with whom—with what? With Machiko Kyo's princess, a frozen figurine of green and lavender in the moonlight aftermath of a killing or poised, ivory-still, in the tremulant immobility of mourning, like a Kwan-Yin freshly molded? Identify with a frustrated abductor deserted by his followers, frantically alone, impaling himself on a spear within a cool frame of trees and oyster-white wall?—Or with chromatic shifts from jubilant red-and-white dancers to the menace of gunmetal blue-and-grey guards at an ominous blossom party which ends in slaughter?

If the demand for identification has areas of pertinence (and means more than a failure of imagination on the part of the demander), this film is not of them, any more than a performance of Kabuki or even a Western ballet. We surely know that identification (i.e., participation) can take place at a deeper level of empathy than that of topical recognition. The order of experience represented by Japanese period films is widely misunderstood in a way that ballet isn't, because the cry persists for film art to be exclusively a narrative, newsy art, within reach, and never an art of form. Our public will consume domestic travesties of history where no effort is required of its imagination, since no distance has been established, and it may patronize two or three Japanese films out of curiosity. By and large, however, judging from the poor reception given *Senhime* in Europe, the honeymoon with Japan seems to be approaching the end. Commercial distributors, of necessity open-eyed to what goes on in the movie houses of the capitals, view with caution the launching of another rearrangement of elements which have made up *Ugetsu* or *Gate of Hell.**

Admittedly there's a thin line, where treatment is everything, between the archetype of romance or myth—*Arabian Nights, Tristram and Yseult, Romeo and Juliet, Don Giovanni*—and one of its myriad standardized echoes—the paintings of Salvator Rosa, *The Three Musketeers, Madame Butterfly,* a western, *The Thief of Baghdad.* "Popular art is simply the fixation and perpetuation of moods and means originally expressive, which have lost their former peculiar significance and turned into stereotyped and merely symbolic expressions" (Carlo Levi, *Of Fear and Freedom*). At the Museum of

---

*The prospect may be temporarily improved by the bestowal of the Venice Film Festival Grand Prize on Kurosawa's *The Throne of Blood*—i.e., *Macbeth* in a Japanese medieval setting, September 1957.

Modern Art during Japanese Film Week early in 1957, it was evident to anyone who had retained contrary illusions that the sweep and violence, as well as the almost lapidary surface, of the finer Japanese product are mocked by its lower forms and that a third-rate film from Japan, whatever travelogue assets it may incidentally boast, is a third-rate film, that's all. *Nozo No Yureisen,* to name one among the offerings of the Dismal Week, belongs to a cycle of stories exploiting the master swordsman, Saotome, also known as the Bored Hatamoto; and there we are again, in what we know as the Fairbanks world. Yet the basic historic material supplying the intrigue of *Senhime* and the ethos of *Samurai* (formerly *Musashi*) is the same in kind. The Western sophisticate alerts his conscience against frivolity when he suspects its presence in imported films; while discussing as tolerable the *kitsch* of a *Henry VIII* or a *High Noon,* he has been quick to disclaim *Samurai* as little better than a western, principally in the faulty belief that the swordplay therein is inconceivable!* An ironic circumstance, for this film is part of a trilogy, which nobody bothered to discover when complaining of its inconclusiveness—its subject, the spiritual disciplining of a warrior.

Devotees who have willingly paid a half-dozen admissions now expect the Japanese, without peril and tomorrow, to upset the equilibrium between their thinking and their milieu, which has prescribed the style and matter of their art for centuries. Their twentieth-century theater is negligible, by report, and their current-problem films are far from even Elia Kazan. To the Japanese, this is a genuine crisis, and more than their world film market is at stake. In two issues of *The Reporter* last year, Mark Schorer discussed the conflict in the Japanese psyche as he found it mirrored in some recent novels and in a group of nihilistic contemporary-subject films which will no doubt never reach here. What Schorer found missing in both the fiction and the films was "a central psychic control of a kind to which western fiction, even cheap popular fiction and even our fiction of despair, has habituated us." I agree with Mr. Schorer that in the Japanese literature I've read—by no means abundant—and in the contemporary-problem films I've seen (a slightly larger number), there is scarcely any assumption of the mind's ability to shape action which might change one's personal

---

*The comedy gathers. Actually Kurosawa has stated that with *his* samurai film (*The Magnificent Seven*) he *did* propose to outdo the westerns! But that's not all he proposed, whatever he achieved or failed to achieve. *Cf.* "Love, Death, and the 'Foreign' Film," pp. 77–86.

destiny, or for that matter the immediate prospect; throughout there is a fatalistic self-surrender to a closed cycle of the character.* But this is not surprising. The samurai films, at the level of *Senhime* or *Chushingura* (a superb film I'd love to expatiate on but there's small chance of your exhibitors procuring a four-and-a-half-hour film), have pictorialized the basic pattern: the warrior state, with its sacrifices and Spartan scapegoats, its tribal revenges and set precedents, its ritualistic interdictions and self-mutilation, and, in the Japanese case conspicuously, the primarily sexual alternation of self-denial and orgiastic release. As social anthropology, quite as much as exquisite cinema, Japanese period films are instructive. To the question, "Why should we be interested in the past?" Erwin Panofsky has replied, "Because we are interested in reality." The reality status of feudalism is visible in most of the modern-situated films—containment and cold violence, stiff pride and concern with retribution or renunciation—without the ritualism or the cinematic iridescence to glorify it. (*Cf.* the meretricious *Golden Demon, Undercurrent, Wheat Whistle,* and the Isihara films described by Schorer.) Where the pattern is least discernible, little remains but bare melodrama, family sentiment, and a puerile aping of tame Western formulas (*cf. Okasan, 24 Eyes, Bliss on Earth, Street of Shame*). Toyoda's *Wheat Whistle,* a comparatively attractive film, concentrates, with none of the psychological shadings of, for example, *Devil in the Flesh* or *Torment,* on a painful adolescent triangle. The hero, young son of a Buddhist abbot, cannot bring himself to express love; his ordeal of suppression is an unsatisfactory film experience chiefly because you're never quite sure to what extent the writer understands the sources of the boy's predicament. All but one of the modern films I've seen, in the popular category or not, convey a diffidence next door to frigidity (when characters aren't screaming their heads off) if any intimate exchange—not amorous, necessarily—is called for (especially noticeable in *Tower of Lilies,* the last-days-on-Okinawa film). Poor naturalistic acting is partly responsible; to be contemporary is evidently to be American, with an alien personality.† No, the Japanese actor *has* to be disguised: he *needs* the mask or the samurai sword, and the costume that stylizes

---

*Brilliantly exposed by Akutagawa, the young suicide who also wrote *Rashomon,* in one version of *Gate of Hell*—not the version filmed for the international market! *Cf.* Donald Keene's *Modern Japanese Literature,* Grove Press, New York, 1956.

†*Footnote 1971.* This statement was certainly premature. I wrote this essay long before the arrival in the West of films by Ozu, notably.

him. And the actors symbolize the Japanese at large—invaded by two worlds, the one chimerical yet in their blood; the other a rational wish, inaccessible to the temperament.

Harp of Burma, an etude mistakenly constructed as a didactic symphony, is the single Japanese movie I've seen that expressed a possible mode for their reserving poetic perception within crucially modern content. The harpist of a Japanese Army unit (a bugler in our terms?) is left behind, all but buried alive under a British barrage, during the retreat from Burma. Digging himself out, he commences a staggering trek to catch up with his men, witnessing for the first time, on his death-strewn journey, the full and widespread enormity of Japan's defeat. The shock is decisive: he determines not to rejoin his company but to stay in Burma and bury the Japanese dead. Forty-five minutes of it has the substance of a lyric; thereafter it explains and reiterates itself away. . . . Yet not altogether. A compound image at the film's climax, matching anything of its kind since Dovzhenko's hour, registers indelibly the crossroads of Japanese anguish. The harpist is wearily trudging the wide mud bank of a sluggish river when, high on the beach and slightly ahead of him, he sees a huge, rotting pile of Japanese bodies, a heap of skulls and fragmented carcasses. Covering his face with his hands he runs, sobbing, past the hideous sight, the camera swinging riverward behind him. And into the expanding view, rhythmic, unhurried, and invincibly alive, untouched by the wake of carnage, come gliding boatfuls of Burmese natives—and some strolling, but erect, along the river's margin under the vast sky.   1958

A Condemned Man Escapes: Five Films on the Subject

*We have, because human, an inalienable prerogative of responsibility which we cannot devolve, no, not as once was thought,
even upon the stars. We can share it only with each other.*
Sir Charles Sherrington, *Man on His Nature*

We must love one another or die.

W. H. Auden

In March 1943, twelve British-trained saboteurs reached the Arctic coast of Norway, having sailed from Shetland in a fishing boat, with orders to destroy the German base at Bardufoss. Their mission was a total failure. Eleven were captured and then, or subsequently, killed. The lone survivor, Norwegian Jan Baalsrud, escaped across the mountains of Sweden, a distance of eighty miles which took two months of inconceivable hardship to negotiate and entailed the courageous devotion of many nameless people. Baalsrud began his fantastic journey with half a toe shot off and wearing only one boot. He swam two ice-laden channels, wandered snowblind for three days, started an avalanche which dropped him three hundred feet and left him senseless. Rescued, he languished in a hut, alone, for two weeks with his feet becoming gangrenous, then was hauled to the top of the Revdal plateau strapped to a sledge (where hanging from a cliff right side up was worse than upside down because the blood would break through his damaged toe). Next he was incarcerated under a protective ledge beneath a snow field for twenty-seven days, during five of which he was buried completely. After another move he rested in the "open air" for three more weeks; there, with a bottle of whiskey for anesthetic, he systematically cut off nine of his toes with a clasp-knife. He reached the Swedish border with a band of somewhat reluctant reindeer-herding Lapps, and the last spurt was accomplished because the reindeer stampeded, sweeping his sledge to safety over thin ice which the Lapps had feared to attempt. Eleven years later, an English novelist, David Howarth, accompanied Baalsrud over the original route at the same time of year to reconstruct the incredible stages of his itinerary, and published the resulting narrative as *We Die Alone*. Nord Sjo Film of Oslo has made a film of this miraculous essay in endurance, called *Nine Lives:* it is Norway's first notable motion picture.

Since the physical crises of life breed more anonymous heroes than are usually accredited, Baalsrud's experience, terrifying beyond imagination, is probably not unique in the annals. But the film, distinguished by visual fluency and by rare good judgment in the editing of effects, gives to this man's intrepid achievement an honestly monumental quality unmatched by any similar film epic since Britain's *Scott of the Antarctic* (1949). The Norwegian adventure has perhaps the added force of featuring one man at bay rather than a dozen; further, while the Scott expedition fought only nature and its own mistiming, Baalsrud was in constant danger of discovery by German patrols, with the haunting consequence of wholesale reprisal for all the men and women who were aiding his flight. There is no dearth of movies which deal with extroverted struggles for survival. *Nine Lives* is no deeper involved with subtleties of consciousness than any of them. Yet it is singularly impressive, partly by reason of the fluency I have noted, partly because the setting is, of course, awe-inspiring, and above all, I daresay, because the principal actor, Jack Fjelstad, besides being a creature of physical grace, suggests always a greater range of feeling and of temperamental subtlety than can at any moment be explicitly accounted for. These are attributes of talent no hero in the flesh could be expected to display; they enhance our ready sympathy with the heroic image.

Of Arne Skouen's scenario and direction, a single aspect may be questioned: his unshaded emphasis on the superhuman confidence of both the protagonist and the men who helped him. There is no hint that anyone concerned with this arduous operation ever de-

spaired, an amelioration humanly as well as dramatically implausible. In actuality, the Revdal rescuers abandoned Baalsrud at one
point, with the helpless conviction that since he would shortly die
there was nothing more they could humanly do. Baalsrud himself
would have committed suicide but was then too weak to pull the
trigger of his gun. To skimp the darkest moments of failing will, in
a story which is otherwise sufficient testimony of valor, is somehow
to falsify the humanity of those engaged. Elsewhere, however,
Skouen ably synchronizes his skills with his subject matter: his
montage of the ascent to the plateau and his management of the
delirium sequence have the rhythm of a master, and his minor re-
editing of Howarth's established chronology assists the supple continuity which the art of film narrative requires. Most effective is his
quick termination of the film (omitting the Swedish episode of
Baalsrud's journey) shortly after the reindeer stampede, a glorious
crescendo which at that climactic moment captures visually something of the large musical timelessness of saga. Possibly our clearest
satisfaction with the film derives from our relieved consent to the
wonder that sometimes a single man, in the face of pain and isolation, self-mutilation, and mathematically overpowering terrors of
body and mind, can, if befriended at the right hour, actually win—
and that flights of reindeer will bear him to his rest.

Robert Bresson's film *Un Condamné à Mort s'Est Echappé* (released in the U.S. as *A Man Escaped*) is also a reconstruction from
the World War II resistance. Skouen's setting was an eighty-mile
area of snow-tyrannized wilderness; the limbo of Bresson's French
prisoner of war is less majestic, if less actively painful: a German
cell in which he can walk three paces. Each of the very few films
Bresson has made focuses a prison situation of a kind (his own explanation is that he likes to find "a uniform" for each film) : *Les
Anges du Péché* took place in a convent; the characters of *Les
Dames du Bois de Boulogne* were costumed in a stylized fashion
which hermetically sealed them off from contemporary reference;
in *Journal of a Country Priest,* from the Bernanos novel, the prison
is that of conscience. Bresson, austerely neo-Catholic, composes a
film of essential material only, making no concessions to "entertainment values." When he has edited his essential material, the film is
complete. According to René Briot's recent study of Bresson, he
prefers not to use professional actors; their talent "prevents" them
from giving what Bresson demands—a "moral resemblance" (a

counter-paradox to Henry James's in "The Real Thing") . The hero of *A Man Escaped* is played—perhaps one should say lived—by a civilian, François Leterrier, and not since *The Passion of Joan of Arc* (1928) has a camera been so unremittingly trained on a single face, the face of Leterrier, curiously ill-bred and spiritual at the same time: his face and his hands, whose fingers, in frequent close-up, intimate apprehension, indecision, or stoic resolve as vitally as the prisoner's strange eyes.

Long, deft, and spatulate, these fingers, obedient to the man's frantically stubborn ingenuity (we never learn what previous occupation trained his resourcefulness) , secure his "impossible" escape from a concrete and steel confinement, picking at the wall, handling an improvised file, unraveling a shirt and recomposing it as a rope, and sundry other minute operations as unbelievable as Baalsrud's physical conquest of starvation, exhaustion, and gangrene. When, in answer to his muffled plea for a companion to try escape with him, one man shrugs off doom with the observation that God will decide their fate and Leterrier insists, "But God needs help," one cannot avoid the reflection that all the moral courage notwithstanding, ten nimble fingers were the agencies of his freedom. Leterrier's final test, however, is one of faith in his own perception of human personality, for he has to decide whether the young shaggy stranger unexpectedly introduced into his cell is really a fellow prisoner or a German spy. To include the boy in his painstakingly prepared break for liberty—this is his willing instinct—is to risk betrayal of all his patient effort. He takes the risk, and the film ends abruptly when the pair are safely over the wall . . . the essential material has been utilized.

The East German movie, *Betragen bis zum Jungsten Tag,* deftly translated in Great Britain as *Duped till Doomsday,* is a devilish advocate of the point that for most of us fear (in the vicarious world of theater, at any rate) is a readier emotion than mercy. The closed situation set up in the scenario, and confirmed by Kurt Jung-Alsen's cold direction of the film, maneuvers us into identifying ourselves as intensely with Lance Corporal Lick as with the Norwegian fugitive or the French prisoner. Yet Lick is the murderer of two innocent people. To what extent the screen adaptation reflects the novel (Franz Fuhmann's *Kamaraden*) I have no idea. As it is, the spare disposition of forces within a predicament highly contrived scarcely leaves one an alternative sympathy. Three infantrymen, crack shots of a German regiment momentarily stalled before the Russian front, are excused from the day's duty to saunter in the neighboring fields. Two of them aim and fire at a blue heron which they see descend into a thicket. There follows a distinctly human cry of pain. They have shot and killed the daughter of their commandant, Angelika.

The two who fired, Corporals Lick and Wagner, realize at once they can expect no clemency if their accidental crime is not concealed. Private Paulun, who didn't fire, protests he is not involved and believes the death should be reported; the ensuing battle of nerves is the mainspring of the film—Lick, by sheer force of will, supporting the failing strength of Wagner and suppressing the piteous conscience of Paulun. I presume the characters of the three men were purposely schematized to illustrate the analogous state of Germany under the Nazi dispensation. Paulun is sensitive but weak, and his desire to confess is motivated obviously as much by fright as by idealism. Wagner is not only frightened; he is not very bright as well. Which leaves Lick master of the field, animated by one consuming instinct—self-preservation. In other respects he is not portrayed as inhuman: he is tough but personable. We are forced to commend his enterprise and the authority he assumes, even as we speculate on the uses to which these assets might have been put in conditions with a civilized inducement. Hourly expecting the discovery of Angelika Van der Saale's corpse, he divulges the whole affair to his uncle, a *Wehrmacht* general who arrives to inspect the post just as the hue and cry is raised. This cynical exponent of German infallibility diverts the investigation by a rousing speech to the company, blaming the Russians for the girl's brutal murder and calling for spirited retaliation. When three captured Russian women are shot as hostages, Paulun, his devastated control giving way completely, rushes to Captain Van der Saale's quarters to reveal the truth. But Lick overtakes him, and the private's hysterical confession is countered with an outburst of inspired presumption from the iron-willed corporal. Paulun, he charges, is mentally unbalanced by the recent events and is not responsible for his wild declarations. The distressed father and captain wavers between disbeliefs; Lick pushes his advantage. Hasn't the truth of the matter been satisfactorily revealed by a high-ranking general of the Reich? Will the captain dispute authority in favor of a sick private's hallucinations? At this hour, when national unity is more than ever imperative, is he willing to accuse loyal Germans of murdering his daughter? . . . Fear, bewildered pain, and a *Führer* echo from the mouth of a determined infantryman shatter the poor captain's equilibrium. Crying out impotently and covering his face with his hands, he begs Lick to remove the demented Paulun. Lick resolves to take no more chances. With the hesitating Wagner brought to heel, the dazed private is bundled into a motorcycle sidecar and taken to the edge of the forest. Again overcoming the vacillation of Corporal Wagner, Lick summarily shoots Paulun. The two corporals drive away— liberated.

My synopsis should make it evident that from the naturalistic standpoint the motivational structure is flimsy. The dénouement is inevitable only on multiple conditions: that Wagner and Paulun are weaker than Lick; that the general happens to be Lick's uncle, happens to be visiting at the strategic moment, and is of a type willing to subvert the death of an officer's daughter for the sake of exonerating a relative and for the vainglory of fomenting a wanton massacre; that the captain surrenders authority, reason, and paternal indignation when intimidated by a bulldog subordinate. Yet from another angle of vision the contrivances are artful. Specious in realistic terms, they insidiously support the architecture of betrayal which is the ultimate subject. In a system (political, military, social) dedicated to nothing beyond the maintenance of its structure, any personal issue has fatally constricted limits. Why was Angelika (surely the name is meaningful?) in the fields at the particular moment? Ostensibly she was returning, via the railroad, to town. Actually she was on her way to an assignation with an officer. (In a war economy love is a clandestine luxury.) The three soldiers, given a day's liberty, can find no more satisfying expression of it than to do what they've been trained to do expertly—to shoot. How could they resist so emblematically pristine a target as a blue heron? As for their ethical implication, Lick spells out for each of them the gravity of the consequences if they confess, and not impertinently asks why one accidental killing is important weighed in the universal scale of killings which they are pledged to increase. But Paulun—is he culpable? . . . He was there, wasn't he? He, too, was a prize marksman; he didn't happen to pull the trigger this time. And why wasn't his timorous virtue as persuasive as Lick's bully-boy incentive? On the periphery of the incident, the general and the captain react according to their conditioning, within the terms established by the moment of military tension and by the shibboleths of nationalism under which they have consented to function, now reiterated for them by the efficient end product, Corporal Lick.

In presentation, this deadly shrewd fable is provided with no embellishments to ease our reception. Even the impassive Bresson relieved the severity of his concentrate with the music of Mozart. Jung-Alsen offers no comparable relief: he uses no music—except an occasional marching song—none at all to underline (or mitigate) the astringency of his story line, a more unusual sacrifice than you may suppose. (Try to remember when you last watched a sound film with no musical score whatever.) Nor does he permit his photographer any but clearly defined, unadorned compositions—no chiaroscuro, no untoward sight-lines, no atmospheric lighting. The result, if totally effective once you recognize what he's up to, is not easy to take. The closeup quality of the film is powerful but one does wonder if the statement had to be *quite* this bereft of inflection. Stanley Kubrick's *Paths of Glory* (while it doesn't sustain its lethal integrity to the end) deals with as grim a subject but is richly endowed with tonalities of lighting and cyclical camera movement. Naturally, in *Duped till Doomsday,* the art of persuasion becomes largely the actors' responsibility; they live up to it commendably, with the required fever-pitch tension. Thanks to their performances, the unyielding treatment does compel. (It may be noted that Jung-Alsen has been associated with the late Bertolt Brecht's Berliner Ensemble.) We are so strung up—or nailed down—by our recognition of a juggernaut system to which there is no appeal that it is with almost as much relief as pity we experience at last the offhand decisive execution of an "innocent."

Even more desolate in its conclusions, with no palliation to be complacently recovered from any "larger meaning," a Polish masterpiece, *The True End of the Great War,* directed by Jerzy Kawalerowicz, owes its existence, like Jung-Alsen's film, to the ironies—for it, too, is sanctioned by the U.S.S.R. Kawalerowicz is one of a nucleus of Polish film-makers which, mainly within the last four years, has produced a half-dozen films equal to any which have emerged from Europe since the rise of Italian neo-realism over a decade ago. *The True End* is the most deeply disturbing of those I have seen (and each of them disturbs, by either its crucial violence or its wounding sadness). Were it not for Kawalerowicz' dazzling virtuosity, I would be moved to acknowledge the film as virtually insupportable, since it conveys an ordeal so painful as to refute that vestige of belief which the most professedly disenchanted among us nourish in their hearts—the belief that there is a finally discernible compensation for the infliction of extreme suffering.

Kawalerowicz opens his film with the vehement, uncontrolled rattling of a bedroom door. A woman sits up in bed, patiently admonishes the unseen disturber as if "it" were a refractory child or a monster, to go to sleep, and remains sitting up in absently sad vigil as the camera glides to a dressing-table photograph of an unusually handsome, smiling man; a waltz accompanies the ensuing dissolve in which we assume the witness point of the woman, Rose, dancing with the man of the photograph—Julius, her husband. This waltzing sequence, with the camera (and us) inseparable from the happily dancing man, is prolonged intentionally, so that we make the connection between the debonair Julius and the creature imprisoned behind the door; further, so that eventually we receive the full, nauseating impact of the particular prison-camp experience which has reduced him to near imbecility and which, only through brief flashbacks in a crescendo of horror, we glimpse during the film's progress. That he was a *dancing* man is the excruciatingly cruel feature of his numbed sequel. (He can only mouth words to so repulsive an effect that his distraught wife has told him not even to try.) After a hopeless term in which Rose, divided between loyalty and physical revulsion and by the fact that she is in love with another man (her employer), refuses the effort it would cost her to tolerate Julius and perhaps to restore his faculties, the husband has no decent hope remaining—like a maimed insect who has been permitted for no reason to crawl three painful feet in a tantalizing struggle for locomotion.

A perfectly appalling parenthesis of doom—and interpreted with such sensitivity to all the factors that we are never justifiably permitted the easy way out, of condemning the wife or lover. No contrived advantage is taken in the other direction, either, to evoke romantic sympathy. Rose herself is moderately attractive, alternately selfish and patient, often petulant. Her lover is a man much older than herself, with a tentative personality. Their mutually inhibited disgust with the husband-victim and with the whole hopeless, unbidden situation (which from time to time feebly erupts in exchanges of spite) is neither exploited nor condemned by any directorial bias: these are human beings of no distinguished capacity "caught in the fact"; if their predicament is considerably less agonizing than that of the poor wretch who must watch their discomfort and realize in stifled isolation the inconsequence of his own mutilated survival, we are nonetheless allowed a reasonable measure of sympathy for them as well. Julius takes the only possible way out, which frees nobody but himself, at least not so far as the film divulges. In a kind of trenchant side glance at Carol Reed's ending to *The Third Man,* Kawalerowicz implies an aftermath unresolved. The lover, waiting as is his custom in restless, if resigned, devotion, is ignored with evident finality by Rose and her housekeeper as they leave the scene of the funeral.

As I have indicated, Kawalerowicz has not only a gift for compassion ordered by insight but also a stupendous film technique. The milieu is right, the tonalities are right (I have an impression, probably erroneous, that all the exterior Warsaw scenes take place in the rain) —and the moments when Julius' consciousness spins blurred visions from a fit into gradually decelerating images of the prison camp are shockingly brilliant. This director involves the beleaguered onlooker with resourceful cinema, in the absence of which one would be tempted, long before the end, to escape from the unappeasing spectacle of a cultivated but broken human tortured by a futile extension of his lease on life.

Dr. Walter, head physician of the Trablos hospital, seems equally a blameless sacrifice if you regard one level only of André Cayatte's allegory, *An Eye for an Eye.* In one of those Near East outposts which appear to consist solely of a tacky European café society and a substratum of native squalor, Walter (Curt Jurgens), relaxing at home after a long unstinted day, declines to give personal attention to an ailing woman whose husband, a Syrian named Bortak, phones him for help. He recommends them instead to the hospital, only twenty minutes away by car, where his competent assistant, Matik, is on night duty. The assistant operates, on the basis of a faulty diagnosis, and the woman dies. Walter's subsequent examination reassures him, and the remorseful Matik, that her case was hopeless anyway; her death is regrettable but neither of them is to be blamed. The husband, however, whom Walter has yet to encounter, after a preliminary sequence of mystification on Bortak's part, is of a different mind. To this injured, obdurate man, Walter's guilt is irrevocable: he shirked his professional obligation and the patient died. In a succession which needn't be summarized here but is altogether plausible as it unfolds, Bortak (Folco Lulli) devises a scheme of Orientally elaborate cunning whereby he first puts

Walter under obligation, lures him to a primitive village, and strands him there helpless, then offers to lead him to an ostensible return route across the desert which, day by day, seems to be taking them farther away than ever from the promised last junction of their journey—Damascus.

Penelope Huston, writing in England's *Sight and Sound* magazine, has summarized this movie as "a brutal and unlikely story of revenge [which] has force without substance and falls under the weight of its own pretensions." I believe I'm not generalizing unfairly if I remark that the judgment is of greater significance for understanding the premises of British film criticism than it is for appreciating the film in question. To the empirical mind, there is always something not quite nice in the view that man may be impelled by forces less visible than social agencies. Cayatte's film, far from being unlikely—brutal it may well be to those who wince easily at fateful conclusions—has in it a profoundly dismaying logic when the metaphysic of its melodrama is perceived. (The very choice of Damascus is a fairly explicit clue for the Miss Hustons.) Its real subject Cayatte has previously adumbrated, and the title of his last film was the text, *We Are All Assassins.* At the rational altitude of human response, Walter's dereliction, suavely depicted as unavoidable, is patently justified by the detailed circumstances to which the audience bears agreeable witness. Nonetheless, asks Cayatte (or Vahe Katcha, author of the idea which Cayatte co-adapted), when a man evades an appeal to his moral instinct, no matter how temporizing a case he can make out for himself, is he not likely to initiate a chain of reprisal out of all proportion—as we conventionally see it—to the innocence of his evasion? Cosmic response to human frailty is seldom relevant. The civilized doctor does in truth refuse humanity, and an oaf, Bortak, is the instrument invoked to avenge—terribly—this refusal. Indeed the film's "substance" is more ample than its "force," paced as it is with disarming absence of tension (no premonition-style music, no symbolic colors) until well past the mid point, when you begin to suspect that the nice doctor's detour may never end and that Bortak is fatally more than an aggrieved and knuckleheaded Arab wearing a cheap store suit, a loud tie, and sunglasses: he is the shabby angel of an unseen and dispassionate power of requital (himself executioner and victim, as it transpires) .

Bortak displays the first clear evidence of any calculation on his part when the disciplined but now buckling doctor, tortured by thirst and exhaustion, begs to be left alone to die. The Arab's savage rejoinder is, *"That's* what I've been waiting to hear you say, Doctor Walter!"* Apparently satisfied, he finally promises to take Walter into Damascus without further deviation; the city is only a short distance behind a range of hills where they camp on their last night. But Walter has by now no faith in such announcements, no conviction that his tormentor is appeased. While Bortak dozes, he scrapes the man's arm open with a razor. As Bortak struggles to his feet, clutching at his bleeding arm in amazement, Walter tells him in effect: "Now, *if* we're as near Damascus as you claim, you'll survive the journey and I'll take care of that arm for you when we arrive. If we're not . . ." Bortak, nursing his arm but still oddly impassive, thereupon deals his last card. He points ruefully in the *opposite* direction, assuring the doctor Damascus lies *that* way. They resume their weary trek. Bortak gets rapidly weaker from loss of blood, falls behind, and collapses. "Just go straight on, Doctor," he calls out to his doggedly trudging victim; laughing faintly he repeats, "Just go straight on." Dr. Walter plods straight on. The camera lifts slowly to a panoramic overhead shot (the only occasion which may be said to warrant the use of VistaVision for this film) . Beyond the doctor's mercifully hidden view, the Syrian badlands extend—mile upon mile of dead, sun-baked terraces and twisting, empty riverbeds: not a creature visible in the limitless expanse of plain and rock and chasm, no village, no habitation of any kind whatever, no Damascus —no reindeer. 1959

The Hidden Fortress:
Kurosawa's Comic Mode

On a vast, arid plateau with a horizon of forest clump and mountain peak, two all-but-naked clowns of God take their stumbling progress: vagrant peasants, two remnants among a million scattered in the wake of feudal warfare. Exhausted and embittered by their failure to find either glory or bread, unnerved by their own puny hearts and enfeebled wills, they abuse fortune and, with what monkey-spiteful courage they have left, each other—while the slow-tracking camera at their backs makes eavesdroppers of us all. Their impotent scrapping is interrupted by a Something that freezes them with fear; they break off to stare in *our* direction. Abruptly, a hunted figure lurches into the wide-frame view from the right, twisting his painted and sweating face backward at his pursuers. Another instant, as his legs give way while he fumbles with his sole weapon, a bow, they overtake him—a band of mounted warriors which sweeps over and past the victim, spearing him en route. The miserable pair now clutch each other in belated need while the horsemen race by, yielding to their own impetus before wheeling to canter back again. Scarcely halting to take in the presence of the terrified couple or the doubled-up samurai, they disdainfully ride away, lances at rest and pennons fluttering. The dust settles over the plain, emptied once more of visible life save those two shuddering monkey-men and the fallen samurai—fallen but not at rest: crumpled up, rather like a roasted beetle, one defensive bow-arm still half extended, trembling faintly in the last spasm before rigor mortis. . . . At this precise moment, a huge cloud shadow moves over the landscape, like a delayed and barely sensed ripple over one's scalp.

Such is the opening scene of Akira Kurosawa's latest samurai film, in Tohoscope, *Kakushi Toride no San Akunin,* premiered in San Francisco as *The Hidden Fortress* (called *The Wild Flight* in Sweden, where I saw it). With no time to wonder where we are, in which century—or on which planet!—we are sucked into the event like gulls into a cyclone. And the whole film has this air of wild, cogent invention, of visual shock, and of abrupt outrage. Grandiose, raw, implausible (yet conventional in a sense), *The Hidden Fortress* restates and enlarges, in more than "aspect ratio" terms, virtually every feature of the so-called entertainment film, as we know it, from the Fairbanks genre to *Treasure of the Sierra Madre,* while incorporating stylistic vestiges of the older Soviet masters and a host of samurai films. On the wide screen, Kurosawa reaffirms his already manifest command of the witness point and of its collaborative art, editing, as he cuts brilliantly from latitudinal compositions to those aligned diagonally, uses depth of field and, as it were, distended surface, and concentrates one's obedient eye no less on two or three figures within engulfing space than on a compactly seething mass in the torch-lighted gloom of an earthworks prison. (The latter shots, by the way, are not reminiscent of any other film sequence I can recall, but they do suggest the monstrous episodes depicting the Chinese coolies packed into the hold of the *Nan-Shan* in Conrad's *Typhoon.*) No doubt the following scene, when these captives erupt from their hole in the ground like angry bees, then swarm down a flight of steps to freedom, was inspired by Eisenstein's Odessa climax—but with no such dialectical purpose and in reverse order: Kurosawa's mass moves *downward;* the shogunate guards, facing them from below, and nowise as disciplined as the czar's whitecoats, after emptying one lethal volley into the descending mob, break and run as before a lava flow. (After a dissolve, there's a single impressive shot of the steps, cleared of all but a dozen rag-naked sprawled bodies, glistening like outcroppings of the masonry.)

Kurosawa's modes of action are seemingly inexhaustible, his bravura editing tireless. As a time transition, to indicate rapidly that the two scaramouches have been followed all day by Rokurota, who guards the royal gold they've stumbled onto, he projects two successive frames of their heads against a *daylight* sky, then cuts directly into a night background. Better than anyone now working in film, perhaps, he knows when to hold his camera position and exploit wide screen, not simply as a theater tableau but as a magnitude wherein movement is never absent and space is viable. He frames compelling laterals of horsemen with pennants crossing a distant bridge, from both ends and with variant pace; catches a line of premonitory banners coming up over the brow of a plateau like hawks to the kill; takes traveling shots of a panting race through underbrush or of a horseback pursuit at blurring speed. He involves those sons of Thersites, the two peasants, in marvelous excursions of fatigue, cupidity, false courage, fright, sly desperation, and giggling lust, each a gem of grotesquerie and broken rhythm, enforced by Masuro Sato, whose accompanying score is a fantasia of staccato whistles, hardware squeals and groans, skipping flute melodies. Throughout the action, mainly unified by the trek of four characters bearing gold concealed in bundles of firewood, Kurosawa's sense of the exact faltering gasp and shift of weight, the sidesteps of momentum and recovery, is infallible. Which makes more astonishing the information that he once envied Toyoda for that director's *physiological* emphasis. All the evidence we have defines Kurosawa as perhaps the most physical director in the history of the movies!

This alone may be thought of as a drawback if we're expecting another multi-level masterpiece of the *Rashomon* order. In *Seven Samurai* (*The Magnificent Seven*), which I don't see as the outstanding achievement critical opinion would make it, the exclusively kinetic emphasis vitiated, or just replaced, an implied interior drama (relating to the hero) never conveyed. However, I'm prepared to acknowledge that I've overstated the force of such an implication—in this case. But not in *Ikiru*, where Kurosawa's rage for excess was a seriously distracting indulgence. The moral crisis of a dying man who in his last pitiful months achieves the selfless life (even as he recognizes how little of the self he has ever asserted) should have emerged as uncluttered as the chiming of a clock tower (if not without overtones) or as De Sica's *Umberto D*. But Kurosawa couldn't resist the impulse, especially in the Tokyo-at-night scenes (which *are* apocalyptic) and in the Shavian epilogue, to prove again his talent for anticlimax. In retrospect I will see only that little man, dead in the swing in the empty playground; all else remaining to my mind's eye will be a profusion of effects—as if the little man had been abandoned not only by the impinging and heedless world but also by Kurosawa; as if, in fact, like a cat with a broken mouse, Kurosawa had quickly dropped him upon being diverted by other stimulants to his feral eye, an analogy to which I shall return.

The Hidden Fortress, a less ambitious venture, to be sure, is more consistently adhered to. Like *Seven Samurai* or, from what report insists, the feudal-Japan *Macbeth* (*Throne of Blood*) of Kurosawa, this film is relentlessly exterior: a tall tale—*jidai-geki*, if I know how to read my Anderson and Richie—wherein our two vagrant fools, Matashichi and Tahei, are prodded into being the mule-back saviors of a princess in flight by her loyal ex-general, Rokurota. This superman, emblematically dignified and infinitely resourceful, engineers the strategy which saves all four, despite the truant efforts of the pair to cheat him and escape. At the adventure's end he rewards them with a single plate of gold, which, depending on whether their innate avarice or their rudimentary wisdom gets the upper hand, will allow them to live munificently ever after. As a morality of the proto-human utilized by a disciplined élite, the story is no doubt open to complaint from those who consider themselves too sophisticated for delight in such fables. I wonder if dissenters on these grounds are willing to ask themselves honestly if the latest capers of Elia Kazan, John Ford, or Stanley Kramer are any more worldly or if, to take hats-in-the-air examples, *A Place in the Sun* or *Look Back in Anger* say anything more pregnant about man's management of his destiny? It is fashionable and probably right—for us in our time and place—to assume that a work of art which gets beneath the skin and bone of its subject is superior to one which doesn't. Yet we may be withholding deserved praise by laboring the distinction too strictly and in unhistorical terms. *The Hidden Fortress* is definitive of its kind and not to be identified with the latest western or Ben-Hur-ern: it honors the flow of events and quietly predicates an ethic.

I saw the film in a three-week period during which I also saw three European movies unsurpassed by any shown this season: Bernhard Wicki's *The Bridge,* Truffaut's *The 400 Blows,* and Bergman's crowning masterpiece, *Jungfrukallan (The Virgin Spring).* These, the last named two especially, come from depths of compassion, from articulated sensibility and power which place them, as psychological substance, beyond relevant comparison with any external adventure film, no matter how vividly related. Even with this acknowledgment, I find they did not, by contrast, *reduce* the Kurosawa film, as they would have any meretricious item of a similar category. And I believe that film criticism almost everywhere has failed a discrimination when relegating the better samurai film. Conceivably the just distinction here is not between art and entertainment, a falsely puritan terminology anyway, but between tragic and comic modes, in that broad reading urged by Susanne Langer's summary (see *Feeling and Form,* Chapters 18 and 19). Tragedy is equated with guilt and expiation, comedy with vanity and exposure. "Tragedy is the image of fate, as comedy is of fortune . . . comedy is essentially contingent, episodic, and ethnic; it expresses the continuous balance of sheer vitality that belongs to society and is exemplified briefly in each individual." For my present inference, *ethnic* is a key word here. There are assumptions in the Kurosawa approach we do well to note, since they underlie the singular depiction of personality which, as much as any visual pyrotechnics, gives *The Hidden Fortress* its character. The "continuous balance of sheer vitality" is here "exemplified briefly" within an elemental social scheme, innocent of our concept, humanism.

Donald Richie has alleged that when Kurosawa was filming *Rashomon* he sent his actors to circuses and jungle films to observe the behavior of wild animals. It seems probable that the practice has become chronic: certainly in *The Hidden Fortress* Toshiro Mifune (Rokurota) is as much a soft-padding genial tiger as in *Rashomon* he was a lion, *rampant guardant;* Misa Uehara's Princess is patently, even stereotypically, of the domestic cat family, alternately arch-backed and kittenish—and it's evident I've been unable to describe the peasant couple without recourse to the lower primates! After watching *them* for half an hour you'd not be too surprised by a following-shot fifty feet above the ground, implacably recording their hand-over-hand passage through the treetops! And yet they're monkeys by default: they lack the creatures' coordination, while displaying the bad temper, the amoral cunning, the susceptibility to the lure of the moment. (A parenthesis should be expended on the performers, Minoru Chiaki and Kamatari Fujiwara: their self-effacing talent for being wretched, ludicrous, or loathsome is exercised beyond all conventional boundaries of naturalism.) These analogies are of the essence. Watch Toshiro Mifune, then listen to Henri Bergson:

> Even reflexion itself, the secret of man's strength, might look like weakness, for it is the source of indecision, whereas the reaction of an animal, when it is truly instinctive, is instantaneous and unfailing. Even the fact that it lacks the power of speech has served the animal by surrounding it with a halo of mystery. Its silence, moreover, can pass for contempt, as though it had something better to do than to converse with us.

And in *The Hidden Fortress* both Rokurota and the Princess *simulate* speechlessness when it serves their purpose!

I'm but halfway to my point. Kurosawa's instructions to his actors most intrigue me by what they reveal of his faculty of observation. Does not Kurosawa view his actors as if he himself were a wild animal—a wild animal who happened to have a flair for cinematography? No fanciful supposition, merely: an animal, more so than Bergson's enlightened man, observes in other animals only their governing qualities. To him, man is simply another species of animal, with habits he is unable to "analyze." Had he a degree of esthetic consciousness, might he not see men as Kurosawa sees them, from the outside and principally—i.e., as *animals in motion?* To this end, I believe, Kurosawa, no matter what he claims about wanting to be honored for making films of contemporary Japan, is inevitably attracted by the feudal setting, wherein social man was more broadly, essentially, ethnically differentiated. And it is just this regressive, if you like, purity of vision which sustains the dramatic tensions of his comedy. When the imperious Princess cries, or the stoical Rokurota smiles, or the bondsmen cooperate reasonably, an inhibition of impulses has been temporarily released, and the surprise engendered is a basic element—dramatic relief. (Our own puritan heroes and heroines—in westerns, noticeably—who sulk for seven reels before the fadeout embrace, represent a like instinct for dramatic procrastination. Unfortunately, since they're without style in the interim, they are more often boring than tantalizing—their vacuity is not redeemed esthetically by compensating mannerisms.)

A cliché is reborn as a perennial mode when vitality confounds a formula. The impassive samurai or loyal retainer, unmoved by the sex appeal of the bare-legged (here) Princess he is defending, is a staple of the Japanese period film. As such, Kurosawa makes no attempt to disguise it. He intensifies it. At one juncture, all hope for the fugitive seems lost, in which eventuality death before dishonor, for the Princess above all, is an imperative. Before preparing a final desperate strategy, Rokurota offers her the weapon with which she may have to destroy herself—in a resolute straight-arm gesture. As he does so, their eyes meet and his expression, in a single closeup, is as nakedly complete as any half-dozen reaction shots could ever be: a wordless suffusion of his face with the emotions he has until then suppressed, in which the whole meaning and mettle of the man is made explicit. The human soul has entered the landscape where before there was a type, less human than zoological, a personable creature equipped with pre-potent powers of endurance and specialized prowess who has otherwise belied the warmth his rarely flashing smile suggested. (No such moment of truth relieved the gymkhana of *Seven Samurai*.) The story recovers, so to speak, from this subjective intrusion and terminates in its no doubt generic fashion. But by such touches—in this instance a momentarily piercing recognition of the nobility which crouches in the cage of the heart—Kurosawa restores to man the quality that individualizes him, and reaffirms the actual as a vital ingredient of the unbelievable.

1961

from The Sound of Silence

Now that engineers have learned how to record, eliminate, and re-dub sound with the meticulosity of a goldsmith weighing his dram, more directors have been encouraged to value stillness subtly accented. Silence *is* golden in a sense seldom realized by the silent-film-maker, who rightly feared the paralysis of all motion, and therefore conviction, if he attempted a sequence of any length when nothing was taking place save reflection. Since silence was the normal medium in which he operated, there was no easy way of distinguishing between the condition itself and the condition as a dramatic factor except by multiplying his images to convey the notion of silence! Meanwhile the orchestra in the pit played on, with equal futility trying to symbolize cessation with duration! A

---

*The two sections of this piece—each self-contained, I think—are all I wanted to reprint from a longer, multi-subject article, "The Sound of Silence: Notes on Images of the Real in the Motion Picture" (ARTS Year Book, *Perspectives on the Arts,* 1961) .

movie must *move*—i.e., it must be expressive—and in the absence of physical action suspended motion will serve, so long as there is either sound or an eloquent substitute: an apprehensive face, a gesture, a tension, a hypnotic light, a pregnant shadow.

Paradoxically, silence as a contrasting value had to wait for the coming of the sound track. Directors who care have been thereby compelled to a decent respect for deserts of silence in which any slight stir or audible sound, of nature or of man, has the value of an oasis. So occupied have critics been with seeing Ingmar Bergman as "clever" that they have failed to credit him with an unusually austere handling of sound and movement in crucial scenes. The monumentally tense moment preceding the act of vengeance in *The Virgin Spring* is a potent experience created by infallible camera position and patient listening. Herr Tore enters the *stuga* where the rapists are sleeping, walks with heavy slowness to their bedside, removes the saddlebag, crosses to the table, examines the contents of the bag carefully, moves again to seat himself, and jabs his butcher knife into the table top. I've asked half a dozen people who saw the film if they could recall approximately how many changes of camera position there were during this action—I received guesses of from three to seven. In fact there were *none!* The camera waited for von Sydow while he moved from "upstage" to the foreground, and slowly panned with him from bed to table. That's all. The rest is loaded silence: the snores, the soft hiss of embers in the fireplace, the creaking floor, the knife thudding into the table, the dawn cries outside, the cockcrow, and the smoke ascending through the roof hole, which recall the daybreak opening of the film when Ingeri had summoned the powers of Odin.

There are painfully delicate moments of near-silent communication between the illicit lovers of Chekhov's *Lady with a Dog*, curiously enough a Soviet Russian production (curiously because little in the Soviet film heretofore implied overwhelming sympathy with personal tragedy of an unpolitical nature). The couple's temporary isolation from the binding social world is indelibly registered in a scene where they just sit, untouching, with period conventionality, on a cliff-top seat overlooking the sea at Yalta. While brooding on their impossible devotion, they study the towering cloud banks, concentrate on a nearby tree, listen to the distance, speak but a few helpless words. To watch a similar scene from a silent film is more often than not uncomfortable, precisely because every aspect of the lifelike may be there, *except the sound of silence.* A whole dimension of sense is wanting, for in real life there is never a moment without sound: "absolute silence reigned" is a literary figment. There is always present some infra- or sub-sonic sensation which denotes life *breathing,* and the difference between a man sitting perfectly still in a silent movie and his sound-film counterpart doing so is like the difference between a telephone receiver when the line is dead and when it's merely not occupied by a voice at the other end of the line. . . .

Within the social genre of film whose subject is the vintage one of private morality in conflict with property values, I've never seen a movie closer to the Jamesian realm than *A Matter of Dignity,* made by Michael Cacoyannis in Athens (1959). Certainly there has been no film, not even Fellini's *I Vitelloni,* in which a class environment (here the insulated upper bourgeoisie of contemporary Greece) is more critically examined to a hairline degree, and no film I can recall has with such moral particularity recorded, as on a seismograph, the vibrations of a proud and vitally delicate consciousness as this film does through the portrayal by Ellie Lambetti of young Chloe Pellas, prepared, against the promptings of her deepest self, to marry a rich, unattractive suitor to save her family from bankruptcy. Like the best French and Italian film directors, Cacoyannis cuts open the heart of a world, or reveals its absence, with a few consummate gestures of its style: the manner in which its members play cards or dance, their attitude toward the waiter and the orchestra leader—the rituals of their prestige and of their defense. Throughout this film, "Close the door" is almost a leitmotif. The others mustn't hear. Father mustn't hear. The servants mustn't hear. Every near-crisis is preceded or interrupted by a concealment, actual or symbolic, as when the mother, caught unexpectedly *en négligée* by the picture dealer, covers her barely exposed throat with her hand. And Cacoyannis, too, is a listener to silence: he notes how the dawn breeze over a terrace after an all-night party makes tired banners of the tablecloths and animates the gestures that restrain blown hair or a billowing dress; he hears the sun coming up and the voices of morning that stir offshore; he exposes the daylight reality of commerce and battleships in the harbor. One scene among many of a like mood, between Chloe and her future husband, played in a kind of piazza made by the ashlar flooring of a ruin, is all silent movement and discreet hesitations, with an under-hush of cicadas, a duration in which the "nothing" that happens is of the essence. Cacoyannis has survived the disciplines and arrived at the secret doctrine of the film artist: watch the outside, listen to the inside—and *camera placement, camera placement, camera placement!* When necessary he can discard the objective role and join the fray, as he does at the climactic pitch when Chloe and her mother struggle with the indignant, ill-used family servant. The three women, swaying, pushing, clawing, and crying out, become a carrousel of pathetic combat, and the camera tries to wedge itself in, so to speak, now here, now there, as if it were a fourth person eager to take sides or, alternatively, to unscramble this triple-blurred fury of female protest. Suddenly the wheel stops spinning, the maid collapses, and the other two fall in a heap on top of her. The panting and the cries cease, the camera vantage point cuts to that of a fly on the ceiling, and the silly Viennese waltz from the radio (turned up to cover the sounds of malice domestic) comes to a halt as Chloe, the first to move, discovers that the servant is dead.

Inasmuch as it is Chloe's sensibility, her problem, and her tragic insight which determine the film's point of view, action, and consequence, Miss Lambetti is the decisive measure. If a director needs more than the elemental emotions from an actress (but those too), he must have an instrument that can play itself as well as being played upon. If he needs, as Cacoyannis needed, the conditioned faces of hauteur, forced gaiety, ennui, it's-been-a-lovely-evening-but-this-wasn't-it, and, together with these masks, the candid faces of mischief, regret, yearning, distaste, dread, and anguish, all on a single head!—he needs Ellie Lambetti. No actress since Falconetti (in Dreyer's *Joan* film) has had such a gamut demanded of her—or rather, no actress of Lambetti's probable age has exhaustively satisfied the demand. Her ability to perform for others while being true for us who are watching her *and* the others is nothing short of incredible. We always know why she is doing what she's doing—and for whom. Her "poise and profundity" (to steal a neoclassical formula) are attributes of a very few actresses one sees in a lifetime. . . .   1961

The Moral Cinema: Notes on Some Recent Italian Films*

> *This is the tragedy of tragedies in all time but particularly in our epoch: the killing off of the naive innocent life in all of us, by which alone we can continue to live, and the ugly triumph of the sophisticated greedy.*
>
> D. H. Lawrence's introduction to
> his translation of Giovanni Verga's
> *Cavalleria Rusticana*

The real subject of Italian film realism (the prefix *neo* simply implying a naturalistic mode) is the death of the heart which follows the frustration of vitality. In Italy many of the old barbarisms are only now breaking up, and with them too much of the old instinctual certitude. Western social progress, which has everywhere produced unsatisfying emancipations and a complete urbanizing of the soul, is a relatively recent factor in Italy which has not been immunized against emotional reciprocity by three hundred years of rationalism —not civilized either. Finding themselves committed to the visible benefits and the concealed contradictions of the modern world, the Italians, remarkably naive where they're not exceptionally cunning, have experienced shocks of revulsion and alarm at every social level. By way of the motion picture, the shocks have been expressed

---

*Since Michelangelo Antonioni is obviously in line for the exhaustive kiss-of-death treatment given to Bergman, I'm omitting him from this survey in favor of directors who are more likely to be neglected outside Italy.

in that rising scream of torment which has its climax in *La Dolce Vita;* elsewhere they have emerged as a snarl of fury, in *Riso Amaro* or *I Delfini,* or as a questioning moan, in *Umberto D* and the *ferroviere* films of Pietro Germi. While our commentators have hopped from one leg to the other every year, chirping over the death of *neorealismo* whenever a film has failed to duplicate the supposition they entertained of the term fifteen years ago, the real Italian filmmakers (which exclude the sex-and-circuses inheritors of Nero) have been creatively occupied with a moral definition of man among his fellows.

Eminent among these film-makers has been, and endures, Vittorio De Sica. Like the late Giovanni Verga (and like Pirandello, for that matter, in his Sicilian sketches) he has chosen the settings of the poor where the irreducible motifs of bewildered social man are dramatically evident. D. H. Lawrence summarized Verga's return to Sicily and his adoption of it as the landscape of his subject in terms which are notably applicable to De Sica, allowing for the fact that De Sica is a Neapolitan whose film-setting is usually the streets of Rome. As Lawrence noted in the introduction quoted above, "Verga turned to the peasants to find, *in individuals,* the vivid spontaneity of sensitive passionate life, non-moral and non-didactic. He found it always *defeated.* He found the vulgar and the greedy always destroying the sensitive and the passionate. The vulgar and the greedy are themselves usually peasants: Verga was far too sane to put an aureole round the whole class. . . ."

So is De Sica. And in *La Ciociaria (Two Women)*, another De Sica–Zavattini collaboration, modified from a story by Alberto Moravia, he is less than ever concerned directly with the fate of a single class; more than ever, and with more driving force than ever before, concerned with the fate of people. As before, however, his generalization is absorbed in the particular, through that reconciliation of intense compassion with scrupulous objectivity which is his personal genius—and the particular, in the person of Cisera, the widow from Ciociaria, cries aloud that in "one world" there is no place to hide. Impudent and voluble, Cisera leaves endangered wartime Rome with her thirteen-year-old daughter, Ilena, for the safety of the hill country where she was born. On the way, death from a strafing plane brushes them and strikes down a lone cyclist instead. Peaceful reunion with the Ciociaria villagers is disturbed by Fascist patrols, unpropitious attempts at conversion by an idealistic student of communism with whom the girl falls in love and whom the

mother seduces, and by an air raid. Retreating Germans comman-
deer the student to guide them out of the region (later shooting
him) and Cisera and Ilena start back to the "safety" of Rome, no
longer threatened with bombings now that the tide of war has
turned. Taking refuge for the night in an abandoned husk of a
church, mother and daughter are discovered and raped by "allies,"
a silently grinning troop of Moroccans.

It may become an easy exercise for copywriters to describe the
woman from Ciociaria as representing "the spirit of the Italian
people," in which case it will have to be recalled that if she seems
all but invincible she's far from invulnerable. The question remains
with one as to how much, deep inside of her, has been permanently
broken. Her talent for life has been powerless against violation and
death and she has been confronted with a malice in the universe she
can't comprehend and never before recognized. She might well be
expected to go as mad as the GI's in the jeep, to whom she had vehemently appealed, said she was, if she were not body-committed
to the rehabilitation of her daughter. It's inseparable from the De
Sica view that misery must love company, in order to purge and
renew itself. Faced with a condition wherein the church stands
stripped, our brothers in arms are rapists, the communist at home
is wide of the human mark, and dead cyclists rot in the postcard
landscape, the surviving individual can only turn to something he
can cherish—and may God help those who have nobody to help.
The American who may believe this is a World War II film of
Europe, yesterday, and not a microcosm, will no doubt find my
metaphor exaggerated. There remains the film itself, which is concrete enough in all conscience.

A De Sica film makes demands on one's talent for simplicity, since
it deceptively appears to have no style; for style is the integration
of an artist's temperament in the form of his art, and the De Sica
film is one in which as far as possible the eye behind the camera betrays no consciousness of itself. Which is why De Sica baffles the
esthetic analyst: he directs one's own eye not toward art but toward
life, thereby making pronouncements on the art nearly superfluous.
We know it *isn't* life we're watching, but the cinematic subtleties it's
our function and pleasure to elucidate have been predigested in the
conception of the film, leaving the critic little to say of specifically
cinematic import until De Sica commits an error of judgment. This
is an extremely rare occurrence and the fact that he makes some in
La Ciociaria is no relief to me; all but the terminating one are too

trivial to be recorded, but that one is puzzling enough to be questioned aloud. As in most of De Sica's films, life comes to rest at a fateful moment which is not so much the end of the movie as the point at which De Sica discreetly takes his leave—on tiptoe, as it were—of the characters whom he has been accompanying, making no untoward cinematic flourish that will disturb their moment of truth. This time the effect is shattered, owing to the prolonged finality of the back-tracking shot that frames Cisera with her daughter in her arms, announcing all too heavily, "closing tableau" —a disappointingly sententious touch which might have been less damaging if the preceding content had not been so excruciatingly untheatrical.

De Sica's "lifelike" purism commits him to an exacting degree of consistency. And commits him to what would be in anyone else an anxious degree of dependence on his actors. Perhaps the secret of his success in this direction is precisely that he never expresses anxiety, only confidence. Hence Sophia Loren's Cisera; as if De Sica had said—"You think she's just one of your big-doll stereotypes, amenable only to flesh-peddlers, all bread, love, and a thousand kisses; a *ragazza* playing at *Venus naturalis?* I'll show you where her heart lies—exactly where, but not why, you've been looking all along!" So Loren, like Silvana Mangano and Gina Lollobrigida before her, leaves the International Doll House where the Monroes and Ekbergs still sit in the windows, sucking their thumbs, and reverts to human stuff. She is nothing less than the kinetic center of *La Ciociaria;* she walks in beauty which has no glamor about it, unless untidy ripeness is glamor, and the assumption of insolence as if it were dignity, and the gift of seeming more womanly as she becomes more desperate and more stentorian. She doesn't give a performance; she gives an existence.

The actor, either "found material" or the professional article, is normally the king post of Italian film construction because what happens to people and why is the besetting concern of Italian filmmakers. I'd be more impressed with Luchino Visconti's *Rocco e i Suoi Fratelli* (*Rocco and His Brothers*) if his *why* were clearer to me, but it's only fair to observe that my reservations may have arisen from seeing what I'm convinced is a drastically cut print. (*Caveat emptor!* One copy in circulation is headless and speaks French.) Judging by clues in the version I saw, Visconti's intention is to show the disaster that overtakes the Calabrian family as a consequence of its having left home for the dubious rewards of Milan. In a purely mechanical sense, he does this, but the internal character of the events depicted fails to substantiate his social determinism. The displaced family's poverty is a fact; thereafter the special reaction to this fact of one son, the boxer Simone, is the horrible mainspring of the ensuing chain of ills. And I can't help believing that Simone's bestial retaliations as he rages downward from stealing to rape to murder, no more conscious of his connections with other objects in the world than an angered rutting animal, might as readily have been provoked back in Calabria by the first deeply sensed insult to his blind self-esteem. Naturally, the ramifications would have been different in some directions, but I don't find this as important as the root emphasis: if, when opened up, Simone is rotten inside, life will discover that anywhere. I'm no fit mediator of the question whether Visconti's alleged "intellectual" communism may construe the pathological Simone as a victim of society; on that point I remain unpersuaded. However, I don't want to belabor a point which may not, on Visconti's part, be intended dogmatically. But I'm still baffled by the crucial touch at the end of the film—Rocco's reaction to his brother Simone's murder of his girl (his, Rocco's; she had once been Simone's, and tried going back to him, virtually to save Rocco's life, but she couldn't follow through, and in final effect she offers herself as a sacrifice). Young Rocco goes into a hackles-raising operatic lamentation—not at all, mark you, out of pity for the dead girl but over the plight of Simone, who by killing Nadia has finished himself and torn a gaping hole in the fabric of the family. This fanatical concern for the impaired family group, the closing of ranks against the outsider when the prodigal returns, even as a killer, is a characteristic of closed patriarchal communities in which the family *is* society, society *is* the family. Now, I'd be curious to know if, speaking for myself, Visconti would expect me to take this all on trust—as I did, finding it psychologically fascinating but in my soul nauseated by what reaches me as a perversion of humanity, the more so as Rocco's elegiac intensity smells to high heaven of homosexual masochism. As acted and directed it's a terrifying scene—don't mistake me! But the situation as a whole leaves me somewhat confused, perhaps for the wrong reasons.

I'm no more content with the style of the picture: Visconti's frontal approach and his dominantly center-focus composition are correlative with his dogged social-epic attitude. Gianfranco Poggi, whose article in this magazine last year (*Film Quarterly,* Spring 1960) is the most perceptively sustained estimate of Visconti I've read, made the defining statement of his directorial method. "His camerawork is generally sober, his cutting measured and harmonious. The tensions of his films are usually 'inside the shot.' " This could almost describe De Sica's technique, for that matter, but the result in Visconti, most of the time, is to leave one outside, looking *at* the film pictorially, an effect magnified in this film by the musical score he evidently found tolerable; with no inventiveness whatever, it infallibly yearns or becomes ominous in slavishly direct obedience to the "melodic line" of the story. Before De Sica and Fellini had transformed early *neorealismo* into something respectively more evocative and more plastic, *Rocco* would have seemed more venturesome. Today it's dry, hard, and solemn, except in the few fast-moving sequences; in retrospect it's the characters (i.e., the actors) who compelled me: Katina Paxinou's Rosaria, Renato Salvatori as the barely Cro-Magnon Simone, Alain Delon as Rocco (though I find it difficult to accept this long-fingered faun as a career boxer) — and, not least, Annie Girardot (also French) incandescent with temperament as the ill-fated tramp Nadia.

The solidarity of the tribe is likewise the nuclear source of domestic explosion in Mauro Bolognini's rancorously beautiful study of Sicilian mores, *Il Bell' Antonio*—a sardonic gloss on the pagan text that "the lust of the goat is the bounty of God." Don Alfio Magnano, an old satyr of undiminished sexual appetite and diminishing funds, has arranged a marriage between his son Antonio, just returned home (to Palermo, I think it is) and Barbara Puglisi, daughter of a wealthy advocate. Mutual benefits are expected to accrue; the Magnanos need money, the Puglisis need an heir, and Antonio's fame as a stud on the loose in Rome has crossed the Straits to swell the concupiscent pride of his Dionysiac father. Antonio gratifies everyone, in fact, by obediently proceeding with the courtship and clearly falling in love with Signorina Barbara. Don Alfio himself trembles with vicarious anticipation, padding up and down and lashing his tail like a tiger in the zoo before mealtime. Although Antonio is in appearance a young man of gentle, civilized sensibility, the senior Puglisi is reassured by the principle that still waters run deep, and at the urgency of Don Alfio's recital of Antonio's exploits he sees in his mind's eye countless swooning women in Antonio's wake—flushed with love, delirious with gratitude, and egregiously pregnant. Seven months after the wedding, an outraged Puglisi visits Don Alfio to complain of the bargain. His daughter is untouched! She remains a virgin after seven months. Don Alfio storms in purple disbelief until the terrible news is confirmed. Dionysus has abandoned the Magnanos, and to prevent his world from crumbling, Don Alfio makes the supreme gesture of virility, crowing his intentions to the rooftops. He goes to a brothel in order publicly to affirm the unabated blood of the Magnanos, and there perishes in his pride—the gesture kills him. Antonio's marriage is annulled, he returns to a saddened home. Not long after this, the family maid, Santuzza, is patently with child, and Antonio's sharp-eyed mother quickly deduces the welcome truth—her pride and joy Antonio is the father. Don Alfio's spirit is appeased; there is rejoicing in the family and dancing in the streets.

I understand that in the novel from which the film was adapted Antonio is simply impotent. Without having read the novel, I find the film elaboration much more subtle and certainly more cruel in its irony. For Antonio's tragic secret in the film is that he is impotent *only* when he really loves. The circumstance of his being celebrated for what, under other social conditions, would get him ostracized, is thereby doubly scathing; having paid the family debt to "society," he is bound to a girl he doesn't love and condemned to unbearable loneliness, since he is still deeply in love with Barbara Puglisi. In summary, the film may sound wildly comic, and I saw it with an audience which seemed to think it was. (I suspect that much of the laughter was nervous.) For me it was just about as funny as something by Dean Swift. And I hope that critics don't waste their time discussing the indelicacy of the subject to the exclusion of the film's dazzling richness of texture and milieu. Bolognini's immediately preceding films have leaned, perhaps on order, rather heavily on certain exploitative resemblances to *nouvelle vague* mannerism and to slices of *La Dolce Vita* subject matter. (That great film could supply Italy's film-makers with ideas for the next decade!) Now Bolognini has come home—and he's potent. *Il Bell' Antonio* is lyrical, savage, and astute. A middle-class Sicilian world of stale paternalistic conventions, loaded with stifled vitality, is built up from incidental characterizations, balcony exchanges of gossip, a "stag" business meeting. Throughout Antonio's courtship, Barbara is staid, frozen-faced, formally polite. Once the couple leaves the altar, her face breaks from ear to ear, like a cat swallowing a still-struggling bullfinch.

Bolognini's shot selection is sensitive to mood (Armando Nanuzzi is cinematographer); noteworthy are the occasions on which he isolates Antonio (Marcello Mastroianni) in a car at night confiding his secret to his brother, or at the telephone studying his own unhappiness in a mirror. He gets fine moments from all his actors. Thimble-size Rina Morelli as the mother is a concentrate of fibered shrewdness; her stance when she is divining the lover of the literally prostrated Santuzza is an example of perfect empathy between actress and director—and inimitably Italian. If I deplore the increasing use of French actors, which seems to be a necessary commercial strategy, and disapprove of dubbing, I'll nonetheless concede that Pierre Brasseur's Don Alfio, played with ferocious Capricornism, is probably unsurpassable. Bolognini's first film was released in 1955. With *Il Bell' Antonio* he has broken through; he'll be among the lordly ones of the Italian cinema.

So will Mario Monicelli in his own way. He too is a master of Italian regional idiosyncrasies, revealed with a light touch. For the initiate there must be a wealth of extra humor in the dialects used in *La Grande Guerra,* notably in the scenes that involve Giovanni from Rome with the camp follower known as "La Furiera" (Silvana Mangano). Besides the dialects, however, there's nothing esoteric in this lively film, one among many recent Italian movies that has critically faced a less than creditable moment in Italy's past. The drift of *La Grande Guerra* is fabulous with surprise for it unites documentary vividness with knavish humor, taking a pair of unheroic clowns (Vittorio Gassman and Alberto Sordi) through the bitter fiasco of Italy's defeat in the north (this is World War I), and makes the transition from farce to tragedy with skill unprecedented, save perhaps by René Clément's *Forbidden Games* or Lattuada's *The Overcoat.* Someone—I've forgotten who—said that life could be considered a comedy only if it were never to end. Giovanni and Oreste, the two goldbrickers who charm and dodge their way through a valley of death, are suddenly caught in a movie-comical situation from which the only way out is in life's terms, not cinema's: disclose important military information or be shot by an Austrian firing squad. Giovanni, who had once tried to bribe his way out of this irrelevant war (comically then; Oreste was his untrustworthy go-between), rises to the terminal occasion with a stubborn smirk of defiance, more derisive than purely heroic. He'll be his own fool but not the enemy's, and he goes to his death as to another KP duty. Given an unequivocal choice, Oreste would obviously make no heroic stand, but the fact is he doesn't have any information to impart, which the Austrians naturally disbelieve. Pathos ends the film: with shaking knees before the Austrian rifles he cries out to his already unheeding comrade-in-fun, "Giovanni! I am afraid!"

Directors of comedy are usually the last to be taken seriously. Monicelli's tempered wit makes him a formidable contender for a prominent directorial place in the sun, since *La Grande Guerra* is a funny film haunted by a sickening sense of waste; it's also an adroit piece of movie-making. Giuseppe Rotunno (who shot *Rocco*) and Roberto Gerardi have supplied a fast-moving background of convincing period carnage, and the editing is flawless. Monicelli's handling of Gassman and Sordi has already been the occasion for laurels, in *I Soliti Ignoti*. That he has a way with Silvana Mangano, too, is further proof of his capabilities. Encouragingly (to me, an infatuate from way back), Mangano's exceptional performance in *Oro di Napoli* was no passing sorcery of De Sica; her Furiera, from another social and emotional level—all fireworks, elbows, flaring nostrils, and down-to-earthiness—is no less authentic, and a pendant to Loren's role in *La Ciociaria*, without the grief.

Valerio Zurlini is having as hard a time as Bolognini had shedding his chrysalis. *Estate Violenta,* case in point, was seven-eighths derivative from *A Matter of Dignity* and the films of Jacques Doniol-Valcroze (even to having Jean-Louis Trintignant in the lead). *La Ragazza con la Valigia* at least gets him out into the open where something of his own style and intelligence is apparent. He hasn't altogether escaped French cooperation here in the form of Jacques Perrin, his angelic juvenile lead, and in a script (with four Italian collaborators) that suggests Clouzot's *La Vérité*, minus the tragic outcome. Tenderness is almost the prevailing ingredient of this film (an irreverent translation of the title, by the way, would be "The Bag with the Bag"), the chronicle of two youngsters from polar-opposite worlds whose very encounter is as absurd and as touching as it is brief. Aida, a local nightclub thrush, is picked up and dropped by a young blood from Parma, then befriended by his sixteen-year-old brother, Lorenzo. After a bewildering interlude, like the meeting of two birds of unrelated species in the heart of a New Guinea forest, the girl is claimed by the pressures of her background; the indignant mother of the upper-class scion has slapped his face and terminated his allowance. The last shot watches the departing girl at the railway station, looking less with gratitude than with puzzlement at the money which Lorenzo has given her (he stole it from his allowance). I think I'm not far out if I read her thoughts in this wise: "But that isn't what I *really* wanted! And what exactly was I looking for?" This is as good a place as any for reserving sixty seconds of credit to Claudia Cardinale (Aida). She's in everything these days, as omnipresent as Jean-Paul Belmondo. She was wife to one of Rocco's brothers, she was Barbara in *Il Bell' Antonio,* she's the victimized landlady's daughter in *I Delfini,* she's Assuntina in Germi's *Un Maledetto Imbroglio,* she will be the tantalizing rural ingenue in Bolognini's next film, *La Viaccia,* opposite . . . Jean-Paul Belmondo! The girl is phenomenal. Since she always looks the same, you expect no more from her than you'd get from a mono-faced American or Swedish starlet, but she never *is* the same; she's always different *inside*. I suspect she motivates herself primarily from a feeling for the social stratum she is representing.

And that's a primary asset in Zurlini's *ragazza* film, which is all nuance arising from wonder—the boy intrigued by this creature of curious plumage who exudes, for him, glamor of a kind he's not old enough to analyze or to engage. From her side, Lorenzo, or rather his environment, is just as alien. Thus they circle each other with no genuine clues to communication, since neither knows who he is himself: the boy, because he's socially insulated and very young, the girl because she's just as insulated and not much more resourceful, and whatever personality she wears is a rudimentary job of social dubbing. Zurlini's direction is at its best when, by keeping his camera high in the intimate scenes, he catches the little mobilities of social mannerism and reveals the personal hesitant explorations of the pair. The more's the pity that someone didn't have faith enough in the script and in the actors to subdue Mario Nascimbene's over-insistent "musical comment" (in itself an entertaining harpsichord recital).

The class attitudes in *I Delfini* (*The Dolphins*) yield considerably less charm. Written in acid by the director, Francesco Maselli (his first feature-length film), with the help of three others, among them Moravia, the scenario inscribes a dreary season of discontent and viciousness in the lives of a thoroughly unpleasant group of mostly rich youngsters in a small Adriatic coast city. Some levels of Italian society change very little, it seems, for these are the same young blackguards whom D. H. Lawrence described in *Twilight in*

Italy, gathering at a local cafe in the afternoon and bitching each other up with an assurance born of irresponsible power. As an unsparing closeup of an Italian social groove with which we're not overly familiar to date, the film makes its point (unhappily with diluted filmic means, a wretchedly superfluous narration from one of the group) : the social adhesion that guarantees the values of privilege also undermines the will to reform the corruption of those values. Nobody successfully escapes from the stultifying round; indeed only the principal hostess of the vicious circle makes a strenuous effort, and she receives the circle's parting contempt for the manner in which she does it. A depressing film, but certainly not a nerveless one. It finally excited me to mayhem. Not for many years at the movies have I so wanted to get into the screen and beat a character to death as I did the young Count Alberto. (Why do people persist in believing a critic looks at a movie as if it were the inside of a clock?) I presume this was a tribute to the *acting* of Tomas Milian; he was equally believable as the compassionate brother to the "bell' Antonio."

The crisis of a man unfitted to commit murder but who does (for a price) is not an unfamiliar situation in our crime films. *Il Sicario (The Hired Killer)* makes it seem unfamiliar by treating moral catastrophe with respect and pity. The awfulness of the aftermath is compounded by there being *two* vulnerable killers: Riccardo, the respectable man who hires, and the needy man, Torelli, the hired one. Our assumption is that Riccardo, the thinking man, is sufficiently complicated to rationalize his deed in a way not permitted to the simple Torelli (a moral and class distinction of a kind once pointed out by Pietro Germi as a clue to the tragic fate of his railroad man in *L'Uomo di Paglia*). What actually transpires when the "justifiable" murder has been committed and Torelli, already half destroyed by belated remorse, comes to collect his money, is that Riccardo, desperately concentrating his willpower to hold Torelli together, is himself in a state of near collapse. The outcome is predictable but the film ends before that point with an inspired image of guilt, too good to be summarily disclosed for the reader who has yet to see the film. Much of the film's credibility and power comes from the separate domestic relationships of the two men; Riccardo and Torelli don't exist in a shadow land unimpeded by social obligations. Both of them are married and love their wives, and these connections are amply suggested, not just sketched in. The disaster leaves you wondering about its later effect on the two women. This is Damiano Damiani's second film; since I didn't see the first, *Il Rossetto* (*The Lipstick*), I don't know how much credit belongs to Zavattini, co-scenarist. If I'm tempted to infer a lot of it does, it's because Zavattini has written the scripts of at least fifteen of the outstanding Italian films since 1935, including all the masterpieces of De Sica.

As much as any film I've noted here, *Il Sicario* illustrates the essentially moral sensibility of the Italian film-maker—by contrast with, for instance, that of the British, which is merely social; of the French, which, exceptions allowed for, is intellectual; or of the Swedish (when you can find any that isn't converted to stainless steel), which is lyric. The men who write and direct the serious Italian movies are of a culture in which death is important and murder is a serious business. A full-time ghoul such as Alfred Hitchcock would find no place in Italian film production. Where man is still connective tissue in society, anything destructive that overtakes him, from within or without, is a radically important subject. And that subject forms the basis for those consistent values which we admire in the Italian film.* 1961

---

*Footnote 1971. Ten years later I am moved to comment that most of my misgivings about the Italian film, and few of my hopes, were fulfilled. Some of these misgivings were foreshadowed in "Italian Film: Left Hand, Right Hand" (see pages 228–239).

European Film Notebook

Europe is, perhaps, the least worn-out of the continents because it is the most lived in. A place that is lived in lives.

D. H. Lawrence

England isn't Europe, though she has creatively fed and been fed by it in the past. Today she looks toward America, if with condescension, or toward Russia, in some hours shrewdly, in others blindly. In the film she looks at herself, with an alarming increase of disgust. . . . Johnny Byrne, member for Labour, is required to make a journey to Canossa—in this case the Midland constituency to which he owes his political office. Forced to make an ingratiating speech before an assembly as rancidly ignorant as it is uncouth, Byrne quits the meeting abruptly, at the peak of his humiliation and relief, in order to vomit. In the film *No Love for Johnny* the occurrence is implausibly timed; the whole movie, incompetently directed and confusedly scripted, is a not exceptional hazard of *tendenz*-film production and would bear little discussion if it were not for that climactic event—a sad, harsh equivalent of many others, not always so contemptuously pointed, in what can only be termed the Hate England trend of British cinema. Since circa 1958 there has been a stir in English film-making. General agreement seems to believe the stir is a good thing; it has made gains in critical realism. Petulant or, alternatively, spiteful realism, I'd call it. It opens nothing out, though it opens much up, to dubious advantage. The English-at-home may find themselves titillated by prolonged closeups of tongued kisses and by the liberty of the actor to call someone a bloody bastard. Such gains in artistic freedom are radically unimportant; if a relaxation of mores brings no enlargement of spirit, the only advantage has been expletive. The generic Englishman indicated by his recent film is in a more embarrassed plight than W. H. Auden's Herod: he has performed all the liberal exorcisms and they've brought him no comfort. Having seen through the royal game, the landed gentry, colonialism, and the absurder fictions of the school tie, and having duly registered these in a well-tempered sequence of comedy, he has allowed himself to be led by the nose into the more equalitarian purlieus of socialism. He has apotheosized the Common Man and is just getting the full taste of how utterly common he is, and no less corrupt than the Uncommon one; he can't stomach him. There's little he can stomach when he obediently cultivates the sociological awareness demanded of him, and no matter in how well-bred a voice he expresses his doubts in the weeklies, the film image he projects is both scabrous and desperate. Conditioned by the empirical fathers of his film, John Grierson and Alfred Hitchcock, he is unprepared to make or to receive movies from any but topical sources. Thus walled, he gasps for air, but the windows open to no view. If at large he accepted the "nature" of those wide-screen postcards in *Sons and Lovers* as wholeheartedly as a nucleus of his critics, he is city-pent with a vengeance.

Look them over. The Peter Sellers comedies: mirthless. *Look Back in Anger:* someone's looking over the wrong shoulder. Is the real object of the hero's wrath un-analyzed or merely concealed? *The League of Gentlemen:* a loaded romp, heavy with anti-female malice, and why the homosexual gambit? Fun? *Tunes of Glory:* sheer agony, beautifully acted; an over-literary, of course, exposure of two men used up by life, mistakenly attempting to destroy each other in their disappointment. But the scenarist hung on at the last to the tartan of heroic idealism. *Hell Is a City* and *The Concrete Jungle:* the very titles are Hollywood, but the first benefits from improved styling contributed by the French—and Val Guest directs, bravely, enough plot and buzzing milieu for five pictures; the second is a dismaying departure on the English scene: it takes the criminal for granted. *The Angry Silence:* annihilates all parties with no corresponding hysteria or collapse of film treatment. Probably the best film made about labor-management relations: a distinction, of sorts. And unconsoling. The ordinary decent man has an eye gouged out by Teddy boys, and his shiftless friend's belated admonition to the audience to think about what they've all done to the man who won't say yes is a lost cause. . . .

If the exasperation in the English film is inevitable, given the social terms, it is nonetheless debilitating. All the same, it's painful to watch a country's heart breaking. One wants somehow to reassure the English that since art never solves anything, they have other resources for the movie than the masochistic observation of Saturday nights and Sunday mornings. "For Monday comes when none may kiss," and they've been saturated for centuries with the poetry of earth and with verse, and polemics, that will exalt our language for as long as it's heard. One wants to remind them that rationalism hasn't yet confounded their hearing and sight, nor canceled their instinct for daily kindness. . . . Had they the motive and the cue for self-destruction that Sweden has, for instance, they'd drown the stage with tears, make mad . . . Amaze, indeed. . . .

Sweden, having no self-knowledge, hence has no shame—no tears. But it does (or should) appal the relatively free, and it makes mad the innocent as well as the guilty—if, within so homogeneous a setting, one can be certain of the distinction. The most colossal social hoax of our time is the advertised and widely accepted claim that Sweden has "solved" its human problem—in any direction whatsoever. Social democracy, in Sweden, is the "objective correlative" of its endemic fear of real contact. If a structured system within society will guarantee the charities, the compensations, and the pensions, this will effectually relieve the individual from having to care at all about his neighbor. *Safety* is the sole national value: under that watchword, responsiveness is curtailed, nuance vanishes, enthusiasm dwindles, charity never begins at home. Was there ever a people so *begrudging*—of passion or of pathos? The very day of Hammarskjöld's burial, a letter published in a Stockholm paper warned Swedes against excessive sorrow with the reminder that he had not, after all, been politically infallible. . . .

The English ghost story is said to be a compensation for the national lack of a metaphysic, or the expression of a subconscious need for the macabre in the over-civilized. But say this: ghosts were once *people,* and England is haunted by presences. Who ever heard of a Swedish ghost story? . . . Anxiety is of course driven inward: there it lodges, untranslatable and unredeemed. As ever, on this subject, D. H. Lawrence has uttered the last prophetic word. "It is one of the terrible qualities of the reason that it has no life of its own. . . . Make any people mainly rational in their life, and their inner activity will be the activity of destruction."

Swedish film is no escape hatch. Two recent "crime" movies show how deep lies the inhibition. There must be better stories of murder available than *Lovely Is the Summer Night,* a film in which you couldn't care less who done it because you're never interested in the people to whom it was done. A provincial town, a girl who disappears, a man hanged in a tree: an investigation by detectives as drab as the milieu they're investigating (a Father Brown, an Inspector Maigret, even a Philip Marlowe is inconceivable under Swedish conditions of personality), an incest theme—how the Swedish are obsessed with sex without ever transfiguring it by a vibration or a cadence in their public speech! Directorially, it's impeccable. Given the material, nobody could have done better with the camera angles, the terminal fadeouts, the narrative logic than Arne Mattsson did. But all for what? Not even for Hecuba. Likewise, the film, *Stöten* (but *The Big Job* would be a relevant English title), made by Hasse Ekman, who has been directing films for twenty years without producing more than a single movie which would entitle him to international consideration (that one, *The Girl with the Hyacinths*). In this one he has the benefit of stunning photographic chiaroscuro by Martin Bodin and he keeps the chase going with a skill he has never before displayed. Again, it's the scenario at fault —or, rather, it's the featureless characters, since such a story can only be as enthralling as the people who give it momentum. Two escapees from a Stockholm prison rob the racetrack office at Taby and flounder their stupid way to Malmö, thence to Copenhagen. (Could it be more than a geographical gimmick that dictated their capture by *Danish* authorities? God forbid the suggestion that Swedish policemen are ever unkind to murderers and thieves!) While awaiting capture, one of the witless pair mumbles a confession, recalled from a French movie, about being lonely. The girl, as photogenic as she is socially implausible, has allegedly got into bad company (a shady haunt of criminals and prostitutes in Stockholm) because she had come to the big city from a repressive country-town environment and couldn't get a job! This is supposed to be

1960, not 1916. One look at this *flickan* and you know very well that within a year of arriving in Stockholm she'd become the *second* highest paid fashion model for Swedish women's journals to gloat over. . . . These films are symptomatically at the center of the Swedish crisis: all technics, no content. A scenery without a drama, a landscape undefiled because in any root sense it remains uninhabited. Acres of granite, pine, birch, and meadow challenge architects to a new style for a new horizon. They plant tower-blocks—pylon apartment houses with balconies that resemble lookouts on a whaler. From the middle distance these buildings look as if they'd been left by someone with his arms full who's coming back to pick them up.

Without Bergman, there would be no Swedish film to speak of. And I think Bergman has now passed the cape where his art can enlarge our perceptions. With his latest film, *Såsom I en Spegel* (literally *As If in a Mirror,* but of course it's the biblical reference, *Through a Glass Darkly*), he is about his father's business. The fourteenth-century *Virgin Spring* cupped the whole world—lights and shadows, snow and sunshine, joy and the terrible, food and poetry, the stench of men and the wrath of God. Twentieth-century Sweden is unavailing as a source of rich, visible life. Four people on a dark Baltic island, and the Swedish situation flickers out once more in approaching madness, incest, and an offshore gleam of faith—"God is love." A somber, depressing film, as monochordic as the Bach cello which, at brief intervals (probably three minutes' worth in the whole film) vibrates as a deep but laconic undertow: an intensely private, unadorned film—all the more Swedish, just so. All Swedish expression finally retreats, with less inner justification than Bergman's, into the barest possible essentials of situation and design. Not the apples of Cézanne, but three sour grapes.

Robinson Jeffers once wrote, "It is good to look westward as to look upward." In Sweden it's good to look southward, and across the straits. Little of the German vitality, curiosity, and dynamo-driving enterprise, which you feel at every hand, has entered the post-World War II German film, however; for too many probable reasons to explore here. It's too simple to conclude that because their best films in this period *have* been war films—*08/15, Kermesse, Am Gälgen Hangt der Liebe, Die Brücke*—their abiding impulse is belligerent. In fact these films convey humane values more successfully than any other films they make. There's of course always the possibility that in any country movie-making may not happen to be the medium through which the nation best interprets itself. Without reviving here the single most popular explanation of Germany's post–World War I films, I'll risk my conviction that the German early twenties produced many great film-makers who never made a great film. But did Germany ever? Not any you'd celebrate without reservation of one kind or another. The unifying energy which gave rise to the Third Reich seems also to have been the energy which invoked their best films, between 1929 and 1939. None more impressive, that is to say, have since been made there than Fritz Lang's *M*, Walter Ruttman's *Berlin* and *Melodie der Welt,* the Nürnberg and Olympics films of Leni Riefenstahl, the diabolic *Die Alte und die Neue König* of Hans Steinhoff.

For me the most memorable piece of film made in Germany since World War II is a ten-minute episode in Helmut Kautner's *In Jenen Tagen (In Those Days)*, a multi-story film from 1946. The most pressing sentiment then for Germans, out of which to make movies, was not how wrong they'd been but in what ways they had suffered and survived. *Night Journey in Russia, 1943* concerns the resolution of a *Wehrmacht* officer, new to the Russian front, to be driven by a corporal to his battery, perhaps 200 miles distant. They must start *now,* i.e., before night comes down; at which the corporal, an older man and a veteran in the territory, demurs. The distance is great, it will be completely dark, they must drive through partisan-spotted areas, the landscape is disquieting. The officer is not intimidated; he's unafraid, he has a destination, they must utilize time and the cover of night: it's an order. Unwillingly the corporal complies; they drive, and that's your eight or ten minutes of film—it could have been five or twenty-five minutes, for all I was aware. Two men in a car at night, and Kautner never, I think, leaves their faces, from one angle or another, except perhaps to reverse-shoot the nothingness in their headlights' glare. He's inside, or looking through the windshield outside, at a side door, or between them. There's no world but that of the two vigilant men, the sound of the car engine, the flowing darkness, the increasing smell of fear, the huddle toward *Kameradschaft.* They exchange civilities, smile; the officer hitches himself closer to the corporal; faces light up above glowing cigarettes in the purring blackness. Then the sudden ambush: the driver is shot through the head, the car veers, swerves wildly, crab-skids off the road onto a low embankment. Somehow the officer manages to clear the foot pedals, maneuvers the car back into the road and onward, with the dead man slumped against him, on past the firing and the moment of doom. He holds the other man closer to him as he drives on and the episode fades.

New Wave is not a half-bad term. If I remember my primary lessons in oceanography a single wave, retaining the mother-elements of which it is composed, travels headlong until its inertia is checked; whether it subsides or breaks, its elements are re-merged in the matrix. There will come a day when a French film from the turn of the sixties will simply be an experience with a title: few will know that it was once called New Wave, and it will have to be judged on what merit it then intrinsically displays. I'll have to trust growing decencies of perception to outweigh the nimble affectations of the hour. I believe that *Les Quatre Cents Coups* and *Le Trou* will be seen to have more importance than *Hiroshima, Mon Amour* and *Breathless,* which are just now the latest thing and the last word. When I say more important I mean they'll stay alive longer because they've been lived in as well as thought out. In America, where readable-at-all film comment is largely in the hands of collegians, the syncopated, the spastic, and the discrepant are understandably the qualifiers that recommend themselves. Young people are subjective but also frigid; it takes an oblique sensation to arouse their respect. In most of the rhapsodic critiques I've read of *Hiroshima* (not all of them American) the question of whether or not it engages a deep response hasn't arisen; the film has been praised solely on its declared novelty value. The crux of the novelty seems to be the disjunctive cutting, where, for instance, an ostensible reference to someone in the present is then precipitously visualized by cutting to an image from the past—or where a line of dialogue is given irony through a succeeding image which refers to an unrelated subject. This is not, to begin with, a discovery of Alain Resnais, nor is its employment in a full-length film unprecedented. I don't personally care if a method is yesterday's or the day after tomorrow's if it brings me a kindled sense of life. I was not engrossed by Resnais. His subject was love and death and his treatment seemed to me analogous with Edith Sitwell's in poetry. Marvelous diction; her vocables are as calculated to arouse nuances of emotion as variably ground lenses—and I don't believe in her. . . . I believe in Kenneth Clark (on *The Nude*) : "The exploitation by the intellect of a theme usually governed by the emotions must always be disturbing to a normal sensibility."

There will always be those who believe that *Zéro de Conduite* and *Blood of a Poet* are not just historically remarkable but are absolutely greater than, say, *Crainquebille* and *Amore*. There will always be a film-maker for whom the naturalism of the moment lacks the formalism which for him confers art, and another for whom the current naturalism is insufficiently natural. The contest has been waged, exemplified, and argued over before. Today Resnais is at one pole and I'd say, without having seen *Shadows,* that Cassavetes is closer to the other than any French director. The distinctions are not often purely formal; a social attitude is implied. The most sophisticated review I've read of *Breathless* tells me in effect that a beatnik subject is best rigged in a beatnik style. Which is really unarguable; it has no premise for me to engage. . . . The odd thing is that in the American magazines "New Wave" has been applied to at least three styles divergent from each other, and the work of a director I'd personally characterize before all others as wearing the new impudence hasn't to date (Fall 1961) been seen in the U. S. That's Jacques Doniol-Valcroze, with his tongue-in-cheek experiment, frivolous use of romantic idiom, underlying classicism. Is he important? I don't know. Is a crab cocktail important? Is a martini important?

When a man can make a film that breathes reverence for life in a setting constituted for nothing but imminent death, a setting where there's not a single external property or secondary quality we normally associate with life—not a book or a flower, no crack of sunlight or trickle of rain, no food to relish, barely elbow room, no sounds remotely connoting nature or potentially friendly man— when he can make a film without these elements and yet bewitch us with his power to reveal what poetry there is in *tools,* what divinity there may be in the selflessness of outlaws: when he can do this he's an artist and he may die, if he must, with that distinction. The late Jacques Becker opened the fifties with *Casque d'Or,* a ferociously uncanny rehearsal of the Paris Apache underworld around 1900. A suffocating film: its barely contained passion exerted an unbearable pressure on the spectator. During the decade, Becker never produced a film to put beside it and for a while we thought we'd lost him to Arsène Lupin. Before we did lose him, to God, he left us his last film testament, *Le Trou* (*The Hole*), a tribute to the so-called worst among us, as inclement as *Casque d'Or,* as frighteningly intimate with the felon mind, and with neither period costumes nor Serge Reggiani nor Simone Signoret to soften the blows. Prison-break films from elsewhere are made either as exposés or for the sake of the excitement alone (it's a built-in consequence). Becker's film—it recapitulates a Paris actuality of 1947— is, as befits the French art, an exposé of men approaching a zero hour. Acted in the main by "amateurs" (they have nothing to declare but Becker's genius), keyed down to a documentary absence of refined lighting and a measured concentration on implements of escape, *The Hole* in truth opens the very ground under one's safe feet. It has a cloacal smell, it spares us nothing of what we fear all along, it forces us to live with five men so that we tell ourselves we "know" them, and it brings to the screen one of the most arresting inanimate agents of suspense ever contrived: a periscopic toothbrush handle which toys with the inexorable until its very image is evoked.

The European Common Market . . . Becker's condemned, digging their way out under the very eyes of Judas . . . Germany driving into the endless Russian night with its dead corporals in its arms.

1961

Eisenstein's Third Eye: "The Swede"

A certain "Swede," known to students of film usually by his last name alone, like Garbo, is quite as mysterious in his own way as that actress: Tisse, the cinematographer—Tisse, today lying gravely ill in a Moscow hospital, victim of a recent heart attack and stroke, and about whom so little is known for certain that we are justified in doubting the authoritative legend that he *was* Swedish. Tisse is the man who photographed a half dozen of the most revolutionary and influential movies in history, all of them directed by the late Sergei Eisenstein. For veteran filmgoers who are in the know about such matters, to name Eisenstein is automatically to add Tisse, as it is to add Bitzer to the name D. W. Griffith; Jaentzon (either of two brothers) to Sjöström and Stiller, or Zavattini (scenarist) to De Sica.

Yet despite widely circulated references to Tisse as "the Swede" and despite Sweden's normally exhaustive biographical records of its more eminent offspring, there is to date no Swedish book, or even a reliable article, concerning this accomplished expatriate. In Swedish-authored film literature, the only data of any extent on the subject of Tisse are in Bengt Idestam-Almquist's *Eisenstein,* considerably less than may be found in Marie Seton's biography of the Russian director (1951) or in Jay Leyda's history of the Russian film, *Kino* (1960). Repeated inquiries have elicited from official and unofficial Soviet Russian sources the following data: that Tisse was honored for artistic achievements in 1935 by the Russian Federated Republics, that he has been a member of the Communist party since 1940, and that three times—in 1946, 1949, and 1950—he received Stalin prizes. Beyond that, nothing: nothing but the oldest export known to Muscovy—silence.

Edward Kazimirovich Tisse, to give him his full name, is rumored to have been born in Stockholm in 1897. We say "rumored" because despite the assertion by Jay Leyda in *Kino,* a grueling search of all the birth registers for Greater Stockholm in the late 1890's has failed to disclose the name of Tisse among those making their debut. Nor is the place of birth confirmed by either of two directories compiled outside the Soviet Union: the *Biographical Directory of the USSR* (Munich, 1958) and another German-published directory, *Sowetköpfen.* Both of these, however, agree on the year of birth. Idestam-Almquist gives Tisse a Swedish sea captain father; Leyda, a Russian mother. Mosfilm, where he often worked, suggested that his parents came originally from Latvia. Nobody seems passionately eager to claim the man! Leyda's ambiguous remark that Tisse "was educated, first, among the Swedish film-makers," may have been simply a figurative reference to nature films which Tisse is known to have made for a Russian studio on an assigned excursion to "Scandinavia" (most likely to Finland, of course). This must certainly have been after 1913, for in that year he had barely been hatched, according to Almquist, having just graduated from the czarist Merchant-Naval Training School for Navigation. From here on, chronologies are in agreement.

After studying painting and photography, Tisse chose his fate without hesitation; before 1917 he was an accomplished and intrepid newsreel photographer covering a number of European war fronts. The Revolution of 1917 was a tide going his way; it lifted him into history. He joined the Soviet Central Cinema Committee in 1918 and filmed the first May Day celebration in Red Square. During the years when Soviet Russian film-making was as fantastic, as heroic, and as blindly ruthless as the regime itself, Tisse, with his precision instruments, was an active midwife in the birth of a film era. He co-photographed the first Soviet film of 600 meters, *Signal* (1918), and was cinematographer of two films released in 1921. Before his working association with Eisenstein, which began in 1924, he made two other films, one of them an anti–Orthodox Church item about the manufacture of holy relics.

Eisenstein, whom he met in 1923, when the future master was producing a newsreel parody in the theater, evoked from Tisse the talent and the initiative which had so far found no commensurate expression. Together they made *Strike,* the first assured masterpiece in the distinctly Soviet film idiom. Neither the conception nor the elements of this film could be described as unprecedented in Soviet Russian expression: both its theory and treatment had already been pioneered. But this film fused all the latent and fragmentary forces of the revolutionary drive and idiom in "an image of collective action" never before achieved. If *Strike* had been distributed in the West before *Potemkin,* as logically it should have been, much of the admiration (excessive, in our opinion) given the later film would have been justifiably shared with *Strike,* which, while it boasts no episode as fully hyperbolic as that of the Odessa Steps in *Potemkin,* is a more evenly constructed film. And there are few single scenes, even among the many of its kind in Soviet cinema, with greater eloquence than the near-finale of *Strike,* in which mounted Cossacks, having driven the defeated remnant of workers into their ghetto, ride away across tenement-connecting bridges, from which dangle the limp bodies of the trampled and executed. The concluding shots, in which a military attack on the revolutionaries is interspliced with images of cattle being butchered, is perhaps better known, since it became a standard metaphor in the Soviet film. Unfortunately for our present reception of these accusing figures of movie speech, the regime that sponsored them was no less disposed than the czarist to butchering *by the million* those who opposed its decrees. To be sure, we are all wise *ex post facto,* but there is no honesty in those critics who, changing their politics in the thirties, then disparaged the very films they had personally authenticated a decade earlier. If, not of the left, we now make the supreme effort required to see *Strike* and its successors purely as examples of an evolutionary passage in the art of film-making, we absolve ourselves from the troublesome exercise of political judgment. The irony of the situation can nonetheless be ignored only by a closed mind. The most "intellectual" of the Soviet directors composed a film for the appreciation of which not an ounce of intellect was demanded. *Strike* was the germinal propaganda film. It appealed, as all Soviet films of this order were to appeal, to the simplest of emotions—retrospective resentment. It was the masterpiece that prepared the way for all the other masterpieces wherein genius was fanatically, monotonously, and with exceptional clarity concentrated—not without poetry of a kind—on repeating over and over the same message: "Workers of the world, unite!" *Potemkin* and *October* have generally been preferred on ideological grounds. They celebrated victory; *Strike* memorialized defeat. At the same time, all these films came to expose the contradiction in Lenin's slogan, "Film as a political weapon," since they advocated passionately an action which henceforth the regime would find it necessary to discourage—revolt!

The importance of Tisse's contribution to these films can never perhaps be precisely estimated; the warmth of his political commitment can only be inferred. Artists of the camera seldom have much to say for themselves; Tisse is as nearly anonymous as any cinematographer who ever functioned, an obedient phantom, a smiling (perhaps) lieutenant. Marie Seton callled him "Eisenstein's third eye." If we can imagine a man having a third eye, we might suppose it would not be executive; while inorganic, it might somehow function as a mediator for the other two. Eisenstein clearly valued Tisse, not only as a devoted friend but also as a shrewd adviser, especially during the preliminary stages of a production. The pages of Leyda and Seton are profuse with suggestions offered and carried out by Tisse's pragmatic abilities, notably the execution of the great Odessa Steps sequence of *Potemkin* (1925), where the whole effect of an impersonal, resolute massacre, hideously prolonged by single images established and repeated, owed much to his efficient preparations. *October* (sometimes called *Ten Days That Shook the World*), 1928, was the most symphonically elaborated of the Eisenstein films, densely concentrated and syncopated from beginning to end with indelible, if simplistic, metaphors, shock-cutting devices and ultradynamic compositions. Both Vladimir Nilsen (who assisted Tisse and whose origins and later whereabouts are equally obscure) and Thorold Dickinson have written detailed praise of

Tisse's masterful distortions of angle and bold deployment of light. "Tisse strung up his lights all over the square for the attack on the Winter Palace, and he did so in a manner that would make a military tactician shudder. Thus works the artist who has graduated from the school of actuality" (Dickinson, quoted by Leyda). Whether or not Tisse had any opinions about anything or anybody we never learn.

Between 1929 and 1932, Tisse and assistant director Grigori Alexandrov accompanied Eisenstein on a tour of Europe, ending, after a futile stopover in Hollywood, in Mexico. What Tisse did en route has been amply documented. While in Zurich he directed two educational films, one on the legalization of abortion, the other on the subject of venereal disease. (The former was shown in Stockholm, where the exhibitors substituted "still"-sized cards displaying press notices for the more "indelicate" photographs—a display of tact utterly foreign to the present dispensation in Swedish film advertising.) But of Tisse's personal conclusions on any country in Europe, on the United States, or on Mexico, we are not in possession of a word. It is a matter for passing regret that although we have Eisenstein's views on a multitude of subjects and although Marie Seton wrote a lively, well-footnoted résumé of Eisenstein's grim misadventure with Upton Sinclair—the misunderstandings, the malice, Sinclair's testy withdrawal of support, and the subsequent release of footage (for *Thunder over Mexico*) uncompleted and unedited by Eisenstein, himself—she never quotes a single opinion, on this or on any other subject, from the lips of Edward Tisse. Perhaps he expressed none: the more reason for believing that he must have been more than half Swedish!

In Eisenstein's Mexico interlude and in his subsequent career upon returning to Russia, we may discern the outline of a modern tragedy, not unique but of its kind a distinct paradigm. All evidence indicates that Eisenstein committed moral suicide by convincing himself that his allegiances belonged where they did not, ideally speaking, because during a period of crucial frustration he was at a loss where else to place them. His reflections in the library at Oxford (reported by Marie Seton) reveal the aspirations and the misgivings which he thereafter succeeded in burying. Hence, after all, he returned to Russia, having been "rejected," as his defenders would have it, by the West. This was but simple justice. He had rejected the West from the outset (and it takes no advanced Freudian to identify this rejection with that of his German Jewish father, who had escaped again to Germany when the White armies were defeated). Eisenstein has been admired for the intellectual consistency with which he founded a cinematic method, analyzed and defined its principles, and further embodied these principles in fewer than a half dozen films which, together with those of Pudovkin and Dovzhenko (to name the most illustrious of his contemporaries) made an original and lasting impact on film-making the world around. This there is no disputing. Equally indisputable is the fact that in the realm of theory and judgment he was perniciously addicted to the obtuse and tyrannical vocabulary of the Soviet primer, forever branding other directors and their achievements with the epithets, "bourgeois," "decadent," "urban," " imperialistic"—all the tiresome slag of the *Pravda* (or *CIK*) -trained mind. That he chose to return to a Russia which he must have known was dominated by the Cheka and the Purge argues excessive homesickness, extraordinary self-confidence, or stupefying naiveté, or perhaps, by then, a detestation of the West out of all proportion to any misgivings he may have entertained about Russia. Eisenstein was simply one in a long succession of artists or intellectuals, beginning with Jacques Louis David, who have sold themselves to Populism— and thereby to dictatorship.

As we know, the Revolution devours its children. Eisenstein went home just in time for the griddle; his long absence was reproved and any modifications of his thinking were corrected and reconditioned; he was brainwashed; he repented his errors. We doubt that Tisse had to undergo any special treatment, besides standing in the corner. The man who seems never to have expressed a recordable opinion would be in no need of brainwashing. The first serious consequence of Eisenstein's defection from the Way was the sabotage of a film he was making from a Turgenev story, *Bezhin Meadow* (1935–36). Jay Leyda believed that if completed it would have been a new departure for Eisenstein's film rhetoric and with its visual impressionism a vivid tribute to Tisse's sensitive use of variable lenses to subtilize contrasts of emotion. Hereby depends a curious parenthesis. When filming *The General Line* (1926–29), Eisenstein's earliest calamity, Tisse had confessed in an essay his fondness for the photogenic values of landscape (the nearest we get to an avowed temperamental preference) ; strangely, he added that these values were unacknowledged in the films of the West. The observation should indicate that he could have had no familiarity whatever, at that time, with what had been transpiring in Sweden, where nearly all the important films made before 1924 were distinguished by their outdoor settings! (We have no *certain* evidence that any Swedish film was seen by an influential Russian director during the twenties.)

Bezhin Meadow fell victim to an anti-formalism campaign, and Tisse was included with Eisenstein in the Central Executive Committee's warning snubs of 1935. Three years later, however, the party as well as Stalin, personally—so runs the tale—intervened to restore Eisenstein to—should we say grace? He was "permitted" to film *Alexander Nevsky,* which celebrated the defeat of the Teutonic knights by a medieval Russian hero. Too easily deprecated as a propaganda costume epic, the film is nonetheless, for two-thirds of its running time, a *tour de force* of cruel, bone-cold pictorial grandeur and a stunning example of audio-visual collaboration (between Prokofiev and Eisenstein-Tisse). True, it provides no more essential food for thought than a western or a samurai vengeance epic. We recall that in 1938, or whenever we saw it, we tried pointing out to our leftist friends that the subject was quite simply, "My dictator can lick your dictator." We were disdained for our bourgeois chauvinism, or some such term of ready abuse. In 1939, the Soviet-German nonaggression pact was signed.

Technically and artistically, the film was a fabulous contrivance in which Tisse's enterprise played a prominent part. The great battle on the ice was filmed on the outskirts of Moscow during a July heat wave. (A photograph of Eisenstein and Tisse shows them sun-helmeted, as if they were on the Nile.) Tisse devised special filters to alter the brilliance of the sky to a grimmer shade of slate-grey; his snow was *ersatz:* a compound of asphalt, glass, and chalk; to correct the rhythm of the fighting so that it chimed with the gait and grind of the music and gave an impression (at least when depicting the Teutonic knights) of armored robots, he slowed down the hand-turned camera he employed.

Tisse's final contribution to Eisenstein's increasingly formalized world (the rules had been changed) was the siege of Kazan in the first part of *Ivan the Terrible,* premiered in December 1944. In themselves these compositions are some of the most impressive to be seen in a motion picture. It is a pardonable exaggeration to suggest that purely as designs they vie with the battle canvases of Tintoretto. Tisse must all the same have been frustrated, for in a film that runs over three hours, in its completed form, there are only two relatively brief outdoor sequences. With the *Ivan* epic, a transparent justification of the paranoid Stalin (Ivan, as depicted, is never terrible; he is a tortured saint!), the mockery world of Soviet pretensions was finally and committedly symbolized. The artist who began his film career with such items as *Strike* and *Potemkin*, which opposed the forces of man in the crowd to the bristling phalanxes of the White Guard, had now created a spectacular and altogether regressive memorial, loaded with Byzantine mannerisms—slow-moving, portentous, decorative, as unending and as empty of humanity as the winter plains of Muscovy, dedicated to one of the most formidable of the inspired madmen who through the centuries have ruled Holy Russia.

That Eisenstein's rational Sancho Panza had a hand in this grandiose fulfillment remains a paradox for those given to whimsical speculation. And part of the speculation is attached to a persistently controversial image in that film. Few chroniclers have failed to point out that the breathtaking shot of the procession winding across a snow field to implore Ivan to return to his people (with Ivan posed in elongated profile in the foreground) bears an indelible resemblance to the form of the funeral procession across the ice in Mauritz Stiller's *Sir Arne's Treasure,* 1919. The question arises: when, if at all, did Eisenstein or Tisse see Stiller's film? Assuming they had not seen it in Russia, they could have seen it during their years outside the country, yet Marie Seton supplies no clue to what films they might have viewed. The possibilities have now been further complicated by the discovery of a Swedish literary critic, Staffan Björck, who has published a brief article on the work of Selma Lagerlöf, in the course of which he has called attention to an illustration for the Lagerlöf novel, on which the Stiller film was based, by the Finnish painter, Albert Edelfeldt. This illustration, which accompanied the article, juxtaposed with the film-still, depicts a black-robed mass of figures bearing a coffin, as they do in Stiller's shot, a serpentine group accentuating the snowy wasteland. That this is the original of Stiller's composition, "shot" from the same perspective, there is no doubt.

It has now been suggested that Tisse's memory of the illustration from a Swedish childhood assisted his advice to Eisenstein for the shaping of that sinuous column of suppliants! We feel that this is drawing an immensely long bow, the more so since we have already felt obliged to tackle the clear resemblance of the Ivan figure in this shot, not only to the shadow profile of Wotan in Fritz Lang's *Siegfried*, 1923, but also and more so to Conrad Veidt playing Ivan in Paul Leni's masterpiece of murk, *The Wax-Figure Cabinet*, 1924. The latter insinuations being unacceptable to those who would rather die than acknowledge a German influence on Eisenstein (even though Eisenstein's admiration for early Lang has been documented), we have obliged the thin-skinned by conceding that a *Russian* film (White, alas!) from 1917, *Father Sergius*, closed on just such a framed imperious profile!

We who write about films tend to become overinvolved in these resemblances and imputations. We have introduced the concatenation here principally to illustrate how easy it is to translate coincidence into conscious derivation and, incidentally, to prove that whenever we try to deduce something either *about* Tisse or *from* Tisse, we arrive at a blank wall or another problem.

Eisenstein died a natural death, so far as we know, in 1948. Since only orthodox artists under Stalin managed to do so, we are safe in concluding that he had permanently made his peace with the regime—like Pudovkin and Dovzhenko and Tisse. "The Swede," we are told, wept unashamedly at his master's funeral. Perhaps this was the ultimate function of a third eye: to weep for Eisenstein. Somebody had to weep for him.

The genie of the variable lenses survived the war; we have no detailed information as to what he was officially doing, but it must have been something constructive to have earned him the Stalin Prize in 1946. Afterward there were no new titans to sustain his craft at a standard comparable to those enforced by Eisenstein. The last two films he photographed of which we have record are *Meeting on the Elbe*, 1949, and *Glinka*, 1952, both directed by his old *tovarich*, Grigori Alexandrov, the assistant director of virtually all the Eisenstein-Tisse collaborations.

Whether Tisse was Swedish at the roots, yet uncovered, or simply by the osmosis of heritage, his name is integral with the Russian cinema. If indeed Swedish, he represents the country's unconscious gesture of reciprocity for having built a considerable share of its own film tradition on the talents of a Russian: the Garbo discoverer, Mauritz Stiller.*

1961

Footnote 1971. This article was first published, in an abridged form, in the *Industria International* annual of 1961 (Stockholm) under the title *The Revolutionary Eye of Edward Tisse.* Since much of the factual information was used as under-picture text, I have largely rewritten the article in order to incorporate that material. . . . While preparing the article, we still had hopes of getting in touch with Tisse upon his recovery. Following a request made to the U.S.S.R. embassy—a request treated, of course, with excessive suspicion—we had a correspondent from a Stockholm newspaper standing by in Moscow to ask Tisse a few direct nonpolitical questions: foremost among them, "Where were you born?" But he was then too far gone; the correspondent was not permitted to see him. There is no reason to doubt this information. Tisse died at about the time this article finally went to press. His death was reported, without a dateline, on the *Dagens Nyheter* theater page (November 21, 1961), with no further curiosity expressed on the subject of his nationality: "The Russian film pioneer, Edward Tisse, frequently the cameraman of the famous director, Eisenstein, has died at the age of 64. . . ."

Of Night, Fire, and Water

La Notte. The title is figurative, and Antonioni's only abdication of subtlety in this almost perfect film derives from his fear that the metaphor isn't self-evident. (Twice he shows us a book entitled *The Sleepwalkers.*) Half of the film takes place under hot, un-mysterious sunlight—in an international-modern wilderness born yesterday—which accounts for much of the concealed terror one "hears," as if everything were moving through brightness toward catastrophe. Yet there's no catastrophe more crucial than what you see and hear as the sum of the details: the contemporary devaluation of life itself. For me, the most sinister aspect of Southern California was always the mocking consolation of its blanched surface; what one sensed there as a sleeping fury under or beyond the stuccoed villas, the regimental palms, and the malted milk dispensaries was really *nothingness,* no vibration whatever from a living past or a vital present. On the American scene the best literary demonstration I can recall of a spirit of place so negative it seems a threat is in *The*

Great Gatsby, where Fitzgerald captured with lasting accuracy the savagely hot and seedy weekends of billboarded Long Island in the twenties. (Nabokov does quite well with the same sort of thing in *Lolita.*) And this is the principal note in the Milano of Antonioni's film: a humid, muffling *nothingness* punctuated by terrible sounds toward which we're normally heedless but here suggest a Last Judgment we've already had—metallic taunts from the engineering world, a shortwave signal, a distant siren, a jet plane, a make-believe hydrogen bomb set off in a vacant lot.

Giovanni and Lidia drive up to the hospital (uninflected architecture, willfully devoid of "reminiscent detail"). Antonioni cuts from their dying friend, Tommaso, to the bucket of a motorized shovel which collapses, out of control, in the path of the arriving car. Tommaso's impending death further opens the breach that's patently corroding the ten-years-married couple. As they leave the hospital, after giving futile comfort, a nymphomaniac patient, wild with hunger, detains Giovanni. The scene is a glimpse of hell strong enough almost to destroy you before the film is under way, and it features another of those telling cuts: from the black-gowned girl starkly placed against a sheer white wall to the waiting Lidia, crying over Tommaso, also centered in a harsh-light frame of the hospital's facade.

Heat, choking traffic, a man dying sooner than he thinks, love as a disease or a dying fall in a too familiar melody. In a sequence no less fabulous, if shorter, than the aimless island search of *L'Avventura* (the measured *andante,* now a signature of the Antonioni art), Lidia, estranged and restless, walks the city alone—to reassure herself that she's enticing; she conjures only a wolf whistle and the juvenile barbarism of back-street life. At a cabaret, she and Giovanni try again. She tries too hard. She bores him, knows that she bores him, can't restrain herself from boring him, while Giovanni stares at without seeing the eurhythmic orgy of the two black dancers, performed automatically and to scant applause. "Life would be simpler if one didn't think," he tells Lidia, a delusive cliché apparently inspired, but certainly not supported, by the dancers, whose simplicity is that of performing animals. I was reminded of the hired, tired couple in the ocean liner's salon of Bunin's *Gentleman from San Francisco,* reenacting, ad infinitum, their two-step charade of sensual love as the ship bears its secret corpse into the storm and the oncoming night. . . . And so to the party, at the industrialist's country villa, an opulent, well-lighted place, with city-

scapes of another vintage illustrating the wallpaper and a checkerboard floor (enduring motif in painting since the fifteenth century)
clean enough to eat and to play games on. The guests are not the
depraved, or lost, international set of *La Dolce Vita;* they're a parvenu crowd (with no suspicion that they're lost), rich enough to
look smart, sufficiently cultivated to shake the hand of a conversation without wringing it, easy to spend an evening with if you expect nothing. Expecting nothing is their particular hell, but only
Valentina, the host's daughter, coached and modeled for better
things, is articulate on this subject.

The oppression of the day is translated into a torrential rain, a
cue for the guests to jump, fully clothed, into the swimming pool—
a fashionable aphrodisiac. Only for Lidia is it a trial by water. Since
Tommaso, who loved her unrequited, has died at the hospital and
Giovanni seems dangerously engrossed by Valentina, Lidia thinks
to find vindictive release in a quick affair with a previous suitor;
they drive to his place through a blackening downpour, photographed as if traveling through a tunnel of oblivion. Emerging at
the other end, she's purged: as completely as she had been earlier
after walking the Milano streets, subconsciously invoking outrage.
She's too old for vengeance in the hay, or too virtuous because too
wise. Long after midnight, she has already turned into a pumpkin.
Meanwhile Giovanni and Valentina have mutually exposed and
killed *their* tender illusions: the timing is wrong; they're too clear-
sighted to believe; Giovanni has published too many sincere words
in fiction to sound convincing as a suitor. So the three come to an
"understanding" and no one of them is happy with it. Valentina puts
out the standing lamp with her foot (one of those marvelous, absently decisive gestures of Monica Vitti, who has an ingratiating
loose-limbed gift for using her hands and legs as if she isn't sure
they belong to her) : she may well become a Claudia (*L'Avventura*), reconciled with ruins.

Giovanni and Lidia drift away with the night, over a lawn where
the Negro dance band still fumbles with desultory syncopation, to
the golf preserves beyond. (In a remarkable number of European
films, negroid music pipes society to its doom.) The party's over:
what follows is a coda or, if you judge the film from a strictly formal
standpoint, an anticlimax—yet indispensable. Lidia, as of old, im-
portunes Giovanni (he doesn't love her, she's a burden to him, he
should have accepted the industrialist's offer in order to be "free"),
trying for the thousandth perilous time, while wanting him, to prove

how little *he* wants her. Seated on the grass, she reads him an old love letter which, for too long to be plausible, he doesn't recognize as his own to her. When he does, overcome with remorse or re-aroused by his own prose, he embraces his wife fiercely, desperately, trying to assuage her doubt, trying to persuade himself. As they agonizingly cling to one another, she repudiating his love but wanting to believe, the camera's departing movement reveals that they're struggling in a sand trap, and our terminal view is of the pastorale beyond, hillocks in the middle distance, another bunker—another hazard to play through.

Whatever else the art of the film has achieved it has rarely before now found as pure an equivalent of the *Zeitgeist,* in *cinematic* language, as poets, painters, and novelists have, for a half century, in theirs. The scenic art of Antonioni, in its late perfection, was concealed for years in a few lines of T. S. Eliot: "Where shall the word be found, where will the word/Resound? Not here, there is not enough silence/Not on the sea or on the islands, not/On the mainland, in the desert or the rainland. . . ." And in *La Notte* the heartless pavements and buildings, spiritual equivalents of the volcanic shores and islands of *L'Avventura,* are made to express what Worringer has called "that uncanny pathos which attaches to the animation of the inorganic," first discovered visually in our time by another Italian, Giorgio de Chirico. It seems a pity that Italian cities (even Milano), not, after all, deficient in architectural heritage, should be enlisted as microcosms of our debilitated era. But Italian directors have a finer conscience than others. The vitality of this conscience and of their art for reenacting it almost contradicts the social conclusions implied in the films themselves. To be sure, Antonioni principally concerns himself with the dispirited classes. Which suggests to this writer a challenging comparison: Bergman's characters in *Through a Glass Darkly* exist in a world without pigment not because they've been artistically created to exemplify exhausted communication, but because they're provincial. They have nothing to communicate, and have been approved on these grounds by the Swedish audience. "They're so typically Swedish" is the common refrain here,* and no critic has been struck by any serious distinction between Bergman's lifeless treatment and the compassionate culture of Antonioni. (*L'Avventura* and *Through a Glass Darkly* opened the same week: both, be it noted, deal with

---

*I am writing this review from Stockholm.

very few people in a remote setting.) Antonioni's sleepwalkers are dying in a pocket of a sanguine culture and he *cares* about them! So do we, therefore—materially assisted by the lovely Monica Vitti and the beautiful (not attractive) Jeanne Moreau—astute, morose, exuding style from head to foot—who is always giving one of the "best performances of the year."*

By reference to the motion picture alone, you might conclude that only the Italians are deeply ashamed of our civilization. . . . There's at least one Spaniard who has moved, in our time, from nauseated anger to a burning disdain. The measurable distance between the surrealist films made by Luis Buñuel thirty years ago in Paris (with the still unspecified assistance of Señor Dali) and the art of *Viridiana* (1961) spans a distinction between chaos asserted, not indeed for its own sake, but in an infuriated attempt to vilify chaos itself, and chaos represented in terms of a vandalized historical value to which Buñuel, during the interim, had paid little overt respect. Despite the fond reiterations of a Buñuel cult (to the members of which, we may be sure, the subject himself would give short shrift) that every Buñuel film has been either a masterpiece or a manifesto, in some way, of the master's touch, the truth of the matter has qualifiable proportions. Buñuel has been an uneven film director making uncertain progress toward an unknown objective which nonetheless demanded from him terrible risks of life, limb, and taste in order to confront the objective and express it in his own irreducible idiom once (or if lucky, twice) for all. The aim had a beast in view, and barriers of self-indulgence and easy exploitation on the way. One can't deny a consistent sadomasochistic vein in Buñuel's films, frequently gratuitous—a recourse, within commercial assignments, to the props of cruelty without adequate reason for displaying them. But at his creative best, which I prefer to marvel at, Buñuel's sadism is not, *au fond,* of that salacious order to which Clouzot is prone. Clouzot is an entertainer, one step above Hitchcock. Buñuel is a poet, one step above Georges Franju, and the mention of Franju helps me to understand Buñuel in a special direction.

It's my intuitive belief that Buñuel is one of those vulnerable souls to whom the indignity of the universal scene is so overwhelming that his only protection against madness or paralysis is to construct images of the indignity. This is, by definition, a sadistic strategy, for

*Footnote 1971. Gallantry, in film criticism, is a virtue to be exercised in moderation.

it chooses to retain the hated object in effigy rather than to eliminate it; also by definition it's one form of art. The condition is a
perilous one, since it tends to produce monsters as unmanageable
as those that inspired it and may well lead the unwary artist into the
domain of the ridiculous. Buñuel has made some ridiculous films.
But he made *Los Olvidados* (1950), which should have been called
Il Grito, and he has made *Viridiana*, which will be called many
things. Franju said of Clouzot that he had the wrong approach, he
tried to *punch* people's heads off: "one should *twist* them off!"
Franju enjoys posing as an *enfant terrible;* you have only to see the
two fantasy-horror films he has lately made (beside *La Tête Contre
Mur*) and you realize that to a degree like Buñuel (his own favorite
director) he is a haunted soul who has sometimes donned the apron
of a butcher. Resemblance, for the present, stops there. Buñuel is
also a visionary.

And *Viridiana*, without Franju's Grand Guignol tactics, has already twisted off many heads. Buñuel made the film in Spain—that's
miracle number one, from whichever viewpoint you regard it. (Political liberals who lay claim to Buñuel never acknowledge that his
incisive regional documentary, *Land Without Bread*, was banned
in Spain by the Republic; furthermore, that government worked
hard to prevent the film's distribution elsewhere. It was released in
France, 1932.) Shrewd pessimist, he managed to make two versions
of *Viridiana;* while one was confiscated, as he must have foreseen,
the other was in France and, before you could say *misericordia*, had
shared the Grand Prize at Cannes, been repudiated thereafter by
the French authorities, to propitiate Franco, no doubt, condemned
by the Vatican's official journal, restrained and frowned upon at
Bonn (as of April 1962 I don't know what its subsequent fate may
be in West Germany), and greeted with raised oars in the liberal
press of Belgium, Switzerland, and Sweden—an acclaim quite as odd
as its condemnation. From what I read or deciphered in the Brussels and Zurich papers I infer a general agreement with Stockholm's
Jorn Donner, who saw only that the film was anti-clerical and believes, evidently, that Jorge is a kind of New Deal hero. If that's the
fools' paradise filmgoers want to live in, I'd rather not disturb their
complacency. But I can't honor Buñuel by misconstruing his film as
an ode to the brave new world when it's so succinctly, among other
poetic things, an inversion of Lincoln Steffens' oracular epigram: "I
have seen the Future, and it stinks."

Before offering some "program notes" on the film's principal action, I want to insist on miracle number two: *Viridiana* is a mordantly beautiful movie, however you add up its argument. No estimate of Buñuel as a film-maker will ever be more than provisional
which doesn't try to account for his inconsistent levels of execution;
he seems to be extraordinarily dependent on his cinematographer
and cutter, and perhaps at the mercy of his own disposition. *Nazarin,* made barely two years before *Viridiana,* was unbelievably
ponderous; it might have been directed by King Vidor in 1925. *Viridiana* is a work of complete assurance. Despite the ferocity of its
indictments and the unbearably vivid portraits it includes, the film
has a remarkably dispassionate style and is incredibly sustained at
an *allegro moderato* pace. Jose F. Aguayo (on the camera) should
be conceded a large share of the credit. Impressively he repeats a
smooth arc-panning movement, closed by an abrupt pulling back or
a lunge forward. In commonplace terms it's just a syncopated right-
angled motion, but in context it has often the effect of a tango:
slide, step-step-step-step, hesitate, dip, repeat with variations. (I'm
not predicating an intention, only a felt analogy.)

The film has three distinct parts or movements in its development:

I. Majestic introductory passages of Handel's "Alleluia" chorus.
Viridiana (viridian, i.e., green—springlike, virginal) reluctantly in-
terrupts novitiate to visit aging uncle, Don Jaime. The grandee lives
alone, saving housekeeper and gardeners, on a neglected country
estate. Sequence introduced by housekeeper's little girl skipping
rope with unconsciously spectacular dexterity. Don Jaime summons
the past with ecclesiastical music, fondles the trousseau of the wife
he never possessed (she died on the wedding night), tries to persuade Viridiana to forgo her vows and replace the wife she resembles. The novice, beautiful and untouched, graciously refuses all
carnalities, is afraid to milk the cow, sleeps on nails, treasures a
crown of thorns, walks in her sleep and throws into the fire the knit-
ting she has begun, brings ashes to her bed. To indulge her uncle
before leaving, she dresses in the wife's bridal clothes, and Don
Jaime, after drugging her with the help of the housekeeper, tries to
make love to her (accompaniment—Mozart's *Requiem*) and re-
arouse his sleeping passion, witnessed by the ubiquitous child of the
housekeeper. He is incapable of completing the indelicacy but tells
Viridiana she has given herself to him and must therefore renounce

the convent and stay with him. Her outraged reaction is so excessive as to break down his lie, and she leaves without forgiving him. Faced with insupportable isolation, Don Jaime performs a final calculated mischief: he divides the estate between Viridiana and his unacknowledged son, Jorge, before hanging himself—with the skipping rope.

II. Viridiana sets up a hostelry for the "poor," to the wry amusement of Jorge, a personable if slack-mannered young man who claims he would have been an architect if he had been given the chance. He has a mistress he's ready to discard for Viridiana, whom he tolerates, or for the inherited housekeeper, of whom at first he's scarcely aware. Viridiana's miscreants are given prayer and self-expression: led by an evil blindman, they conspicuously feature a cripple who purports to be a religious painter and a scabby hanger-on accused by the others of being a leper (he is offended and insists that he's syphilitic). Jorge sets his own contingent to the useful work of patching up.

The climax is engineered by the absence from the villa of Jorge and Viridiana, with their housekeeper. The "guests" take over, drag out the ancestral linens and glass, stage a swilling, guzzling, food-throwing banquet, while the Handel oratorio from the phonograph washes over them in an unfelt wave. The "leper" does a fandango, wearing the corset and bridal veil of the dead woman; the assembled company poses for its picture, miming the Last Supper (the Leonardo composition), presided over by the blindman and "snapped" by a gypsy from between her legs as she throws high her skirts. Crescendo of abandon: flamencan dance as natively skilled as the girl's rope jumping, incongruity of Handel ignored. A couple fornicates behind the couch, and the blindman, frustrated in his attempt to chastise them, smashes everything within reach of his stick. All but the artist and the "leper" stagger out: this pair investigates the bedroom after the artist has picked up the skip-rope with which to support his pants. Jorge and Viridiana arrive as the belching blindman gropes his exit with the bridal veils clinging to his legs. Housekeeper returns to town for help. Jorge is knocked out and tied up by the "leper" and the artist; the latter overpowers Viridiana in order to rape her. Last image in this passage: her hand convulsively grasping the wooden handle of the skip-rope, which distinctly resembles the cow's teat of the earlier episode. . . . Jorge comes to, promises to enrich the "leper" if he'll kill the artist. With a satisfied grin, the *lazzarone* beats his compadre to death with a small fireplace shovel and, as he retrieves his payment from the cupboard (probably the housekeeping allowance for the month), the Guardia Civil arrives.

III. Epilogue—evening after the morning after? Order has been restored. Jorge is having the estate cleaned up and wired. Viridiana's impedimenta are bonfired, but before cutting to the finale there's a shot of the crown of thorns being salvaged and burning brightly. Viridiana now waits on the pleasure of Jorge: she knocks at the parlor door before entering and her eyes are softly shining with desire. The housekeeper is ensconced as Jorge's mistress, and the three sit at the same table to play cards through the winter nights which are approaching. There's music, too. Handel has been replaced by rock-'n'-roll. The lyric message tantalizes the orchard (as camera swiftly backtracks into the night)—worded, as nearly as I can recall:

> Be she fat or be she thin
> I don' care what shape she's in—
> Shake, shake, oh, shake yo' cares away! (*Repeat refrain.*)

Questioned by a *Paris-Match* representative, Buñuel affected surprise at the international furore over his film. *Viridiana* was only a treatment of certain poetic ideas, he explained, and why, he asked, should its locale be taken for Spain rather than Mexico, for instance? These are suave equivocations by a veteran of censure and censorship. Of no avail to protest against the undying papal tradition which accuses those who depict blasphemy as being themselves blasphemers! And whatever particularities of recent Spanish history the film no doubt reveals (I suspect there are many to be gleaned by the *aficionado*), they are but decoys or a lower court inquisition. The happy heathen who have rejoiced in their discovery that if the Church and the nobility fail to humanize each other their fate is suicide and rape have only gone halfway with the film. (Buñuel provides no easy encouragement to their animosities: Don Jaime and Viridiana are by no means unsympathetically portrayed.) What happens in *Viridiana* is what has been happening to Europe in our time. The remains of our magnificent, sinful culture are being kicked to death by the inheritors—and the provenance of Jorge, the New Executive, should be obvious: he smokes cigars, will sleep with or bribe anybody, is an enterprising mortician and partial to Africa-modern music.

Nonetheless, *Viridiana is* a poem—for what the term is approximately worth—and while I'm obviously prepared to insist on its historical pertinence. I'd be more gratified if I thought I had urged the reader to look and receive before sweating to "understand." Buñuel's images are their own reward. . . . Buñuel, the man, demands no other—even less. Two years ago a *Sight and Sound* critic asked him if he was anxious for the fate of his *L'Âge d'Or* (the single remaining print is perishing). Interviewers spur Buñuel into provocative answers: he expressed the fervent wish that the film in question would vanish altogether, adding that for himself he wanted a like fate—he hopes to be cremated so that he'll leave on this earth not a trace. . . . Say this for the Spaniard. He knows how to live on a plateau beyond self-justification or disgust. *Viridiana* will be Buñuel's clearest trace—for a wink of time, at any rate.

Antonioni and Buñuel can't, as stylists or as individuals, be profitably compared. Compassion, the master-feeling of Antonioni where his characters are the object of our experience, is irrelevant to the purpose of sardonic allegory. Perhaps the two directors have an affinity, however, in their Latin-European conviction that the fall of valor is not a solecism to be lightly shrugged off. . . . As artists, each has offered hostages to victory. Compassion and ruthlessness are dedicated attitudes for which satisfying artistic solutions are almost equally difficult. A lethal weapon is no easier to shape than a memorial urn: Buñuel's took years for its tempering. . . . The forging of a Toledo blade was a ceremony fraught with anxiety and imminent mishap at every stage, requiring, besides the correct wedding of sand and water, the propitious season, hour, and prayer. Paul Horgan has described the creative conditions in an impressive passage of a rich book (*Great River,* 1954).

> The blades were born only in the darkest nights, the better to let the true or false temper of the steel show when red-hot; and of the darkest nights, only those when the south wind blew, so that in passing the blade from fire to water it might not cool too rapidly as a north wind would cool it.

1962

Kinds of Loving
in the International Film

Exordium. When Alberto Moravia was asked, not long ago, if he believed that inter-sexual hostility, a prevailing subject of his own novels, was a consequence of the capitalist condition, he answered: "I think it's a consequence of the *biological* condition!"

Throughout *A Kind of Loving,* one watches with delicate convulsions of horror the short potential love life of a young draftsman in a British Midlands factory town of singular hideousness: his courtship of an office girl with just enough veneer to seem glamorous until the shallow contents of her mind and the thrifty boundaries of her taste are revealed; his doubt that she is indeed worth the trouble of acquiring and his quitting of the field; his subsequent blotting of the doubt because she's sexually enticing—and how much local choice has he?—the predictable consequence and his outraged but dutiful marriage; the couple's mutual servitude, to each other's spite and to the girl's ghastly mother's house and lower middle (class) pretensions; his galled exit from the home that isn't his, and his irresolute kick of autonomy before accepting the life sentence that will erase the enfeebled touch of decency which differentiates him from his mongrel fellows and extinguish the virility which has swiftly served its shabby ends. At fadeout he and his unwanted wife meet on a hilltop in full, stupefying view of the brick-filled crater which does duty as a city of man, where they make a preposterous agreement to "try again."

"When two are stript, long ere the course begin/We wish that one should lose, the other win." After twenty minutes of playing time, I might not have declared, "Loved him, hated her!" but I rather knew which side I was on and what I wanted him to lose. Everything within his ken. Tempted by a friend who confessed to me that his only positive reaction during Bergman's *Through a Glass Darkly* was to yell at the characters through his cupped hands, "Hey! *Get off that island!*" I was moved by an equally remote form of altruism to command Mr. Alan Bates (actor's name), in a loud, clear voice, to take to the hills—since, when all reward is wanting, reconciliation is the abode of fools.

What the scope of director John Schlesinger's intention may have been, I don't know—it appears to have been modest—but he has obdurately restated a century-old pyrrhic victory of competent naturalism. The film cannot conceivably be edifying to such as those who are its dismal protagonists. For anyone else, except anthropologists, who may well be counted on to show the liveliest disinterest, it is not an experience for prolonged moral or esthetic contemplation. Schlesinger's handling of the milieu is what might be called sensitively neutral (like the way of a surgeon with a pancreas), dispassionate, and unobtrusive: never an excited movement, never a falsification to make a prospect pleasing, never a word or a house front that isn't garishly authentic—never more style than the absence of it in the subject dictates. The deadly, patient accuracy with which he has exhumed every shopworn brutality of instinct and reproduced the excruciating syllables of a populace, totally without subject matter in its life, must itself be regarded as a kind of loving.

If I say that Europeans are frequently more coherent when translating the raw material of the American scene into movie substance, I don't expect the remark to be taken as a finality. But no domestic social realism film I've yet seen, expressionist or naturalistic, has caught even a reverberation of the polyglot wonder discovered by

François Reichenbach in his "documentary," *L'Amérique Insolite*. And *Something Wild*, directed by Jack Garfein (a Czechoslovak), is a case in point closer to my present subject.

The setting is one of those jungle boroughs northeast of Manhattan, if mercifully failing memory serves. Summertime in the Great Ooze: the appalling heat, the jagged tempo, the wide-open door, the wide-opened mouths—plugged ears and barricaded minds. A schoolgirl, nineteen, who has been raped and told no one, hugging her fear and revulsion like an animal in a cave. She is rescued from suicide by a big, silent auto mechanic, himself mutely alive between the oblivion of his work and the oblivion of dead-drunkenness. His protection of the girl becomes an imprisonment of her, while he gropes with what little eloquence he has to be saved by her in his turn. Thus they confront each other across an abyss, like two wilderness animals, making feral sounds. When, after a sketchily indicated passage of time, she relents and agrees to marry him, only then does she permit Mother, from whose indifference she has fled, to reenter the picture—a picture altered for life, which Mother can't bring herself to recognize or accept. Self-injured by the girl's disappearance and baffling alliance with a stranger, yet as fundamentally incurious as ever, the fatuous woman can only exclaim, "My baby!—my child!"

And this is the last good touch: the girl, strong in her newfound will, *is* nonetheless child, and before this belated comfort she melts. The man stands dumbly by, one hand holding that of his wife, who is enclosed within the maternal embrace—shut out but docile before the incomprehensible world of woman. One is at liberty to envisage a future not unlike that of the couple in *A Kind of Loving*, wherein Mother will always be on hand to break the maleness of the muddled man, when a scapegoat is called for, by reminding him that he's not good enough for her "baby girl." Yet somehow (and the genuine, unmannered performances of Ralph Meeker and Carroll Baker have much to do with one's indecision) there are grounds for confidence in the decent survival of this odd union of derelicts. Without a verb between them, they do have unquelled instinct, whereas the brass-knocker fragment of culture inherited by the English couple is worse than none, giving them just enough articulation for vulgarity and a bleak eternity of loveless compromise.

Garfein's first film is not unfaulted: he establishes no cinematic rhythm, his incidental characters are as approximate as Hollywood's, and the anonymous montage which provides the living background swill breaks down into static fragments during the last half of the story. However, if his technique isn't safe from reproach, his integrity of meaning is. His lost man and girl are not trying to destroy each other on instructions from a sadistic script-writer (as in so many Hollywood-cum-Tennessee Williams adaptations); they are trying to discover each other—with pathetically limited means. He keeps his eye on this irreducible germ of relationship, with no time out for anti-intellectualism (*cf. Shadows*), exploitation of sub-social hysteria (*cf. The Savage Eye*)—or for an inventive contribution to the art of implied sexual intercourse. (I'd like to think that in this contest Jules Dassin's *Phaedra* has broken the last camel's back in captivity.) Garfein's contribution to an abused genre is a welcome exception to the compulsive effort which seems to be the secretly punitive principle of British and American film realists alike: to reverse Ben Jonson's admonition—"Beware thou, then, render men's figures truly and teach them no less to hate their deformities than to love their forms." Love of deformity, offered as a charitable interest in the depressed classes, may be a more compelling motive than film critics in the democracies have been able to perceive.

Back in 1958, Marcel Carné contrived an adroit facsimile of a high-speed American juvenile delinquent film, *Les Tricheurs*. After exploiting every negotiable sensation of the fast set, from jive to abortion and death in a Jaguar, he added a ten-minute elegy to show that he was morally wounded by the spectacle. An idiotic film, so successful it impressed French financiers and is thus an important factor in the economic liberation of a production phase called the New Wave. Also it initiated an international epidemic of boring-youth films, in which every character has been a local duplicate of the boys and girls in the Carné escapade. We have seen films from England, Sweden, Czechoslovakia, and Poland strenuously attempting the French atmosphere as they conceive it to be, with no social actuality of their own which resembles it, and only imposed mannerisms to compensate for the lack of style.

Perhaps the most cryptic effort has been Andrzej Wajda's *The Innocent Sorcerers*. The ingredients are familiar: jaded young man (or is it a pose?) meets promiscuous girl (or is she?). Both recognize they may be at the threshold of real love, but neither will initiate the gesture or the phrases that will assure commitment. Afraid of a transitory affair at the serious moment, they affront each other instead, play games (strip poker in the Polish movie), and pretend cosmic indifference. Carné's film ended with violence and feeble casuistry; Wajda's, embarrassingly arch, on an inconclusive note. The pair have "respected" each other but still won't give; they separate again, perhaps temporarily, with a drawn question mark between them. To give this eternal recurrence any credence in its immediate variation demands a consistent treatment. In a sense, *Something Wild* is one, grim way of doing it, and the comic way has been exemplified with high charm by Doniol-Valcroze, who played it as a blend of the fantastic and the sardonic. Poland hasn't the nucleus of urbanity for doing a styled job of this fable; the only hope was to keep it within plausible social bounds and be sure that the two were indubitably male and female. But for some flamboyant reason the hero of the occasion is rather obviously a faggot, with a dyed-blond monk's-cut like Olivier's in *Hamlet;* he reeks with coy mannerisms and is at the same time a phenomenally capable extrovert who works hard at a medical lab half the day, spends much of the other half giving boxing lessons, takes a turn with friends in a jazz orchestra evenings, and spends the night watch in a variety of beds.

Fluently directed and edited, but nonetheless a casualty, this film perversely illustrates the crucial problem for the Polish film-maker, having exhausted his Underground theme and forbidden by unworded fiat to make any more films as unequivocally beyond the reach of welfare-state conciliation as *True End of the Great War, Last Day of Summer, Eighth Day of the Week* (only a pirated German print of the last named reached foreign circulation, I think). These three dealt with deeper fatalities of men and women at the severance point. In the first, a woman helplessly watches her husband, reduced to near-imbecility by a war-camp experience, beg to be humanized by the love she has given someone else. While she hesitates, he hangs himself. In the second, two defeated individuals separately arrive at a deserted beach, where each has come to lick his respective life-wounds. They struggle, but fail, to resolve their undisclosed tragedies in each other's arms; the woman retreats again, the man stops trying, and both are swallowed by the ocean as three jet planes, only other sign of life besides sand-beetles, reappear for the last time, trailing their slipstreams, like comets of doom, across the blank heavens. In the third of these films, a young man and girl needing, and pledged to, each other, literally don't have a place where they can make love or even satisfactorily embrace—not a room of their own or of anyone else's (and the crisis can't be seriously appreciated by citizens of a Mediterranean country or of California!). The girl finally meets an older man who *has* extra living space and sufficient charm to make the sharing of it a species of sexual blackmail. She abandons the younger man.

The Pole is a romantic, given to vehement melancholy. He's a European; his history is loaded with betrayal. He's not yet prepared to make carefree socially constructive films without a self-conscious effort, or to envisage a couple free of estrangement. *The Innocent Sorcerers* is an uncomfortable travesty of a nationally rooted skepticism.

Divorce—Italian Style comprises two dangerous jokes: the absurdity of Sicilian mores as viewed by an outsider (a mainland Italian is no less an outsider for being the most qualified observer) and the disposal, by violence, of a tedious wife. Since, in actuality, Sicily is as impossible to laugh off as murder (or a tedious wife), Pietro Germi's success on both counts is a dazzling *tour de force*. Germi has arrived at art by parodying his own derivative career. His first film, of early postwar vintage, was *I Nommi del Legge*, a sort of Sicilian "western," and his next-to-latest was *Un Maledetto Imbroglio*, a sort of Roman Chicagoan. In the years between, while concurrently acting, under his own direction very often, he tried domestic realism with a touch of De Sica. All the while he must have been assimilating technical resources from every available direction in order to enrich the mode he next hoped to personalize. Farce may be the mode for Germi, the instrument best suited to his talent—not an inferior instrument, for how many notable farces have there been? *Divorce—Italian Style* is a film quickly bypassed on the one-way thoroughfare of intellectual opinion, yet it's a remarkably sophisticated product, not only where it meets the eye but also within the labyrinth of its blatant subject. Trick cutting, insolent music, and contrapuntal monologue have been coordinated with a degree of artifice that makes them appear novel, and sundry merciless vignettes provoke you to identify the directorial signatures which are therein being forged (Clouzot, Franju, and Mauro Bolognini are among the recognizable principals)—this is not a patchwork of other men's inspiration, it's an exploitation of their foibles.

Coincidentally suggestive for me, in line with Germi's malice-domestic pleasantry, was a Polish film I saw, shortly previous to my attendance at *Divorce—Italian Style*. Among other travelers on a night train was an escaping murderer, established as a monster (by the audience on the train, at any rate) precisely because the victim was his wife, and despite our knowing nothing at all about the wife and little more about the fugitive himself. With no pain of transition we tacitly applauded Baron Cefalu in the Italian comedy for the ingenuity he was exerting with exactly the same objective. Comedic license as against that of melodrama is not a demonstrable answer to the question—why do we hope Cefalu will succeed? (And I think the Freudian deduction of our personal fantasies is needlessly indirect.) I don't believe we could care less whether or not he weds his pretty cousin—only a simpleton would share his neglect of the probability that she'd be as boring, given the fourteen years he has spent with the signora. (Germi enforces the probability with his parting shot.) At the point of our intersection with the household, we surely find the wife more personable by far—thanks to Daniele Roca: importunacy with a bland Mona Lisa smile, and moustache. No, it's my feeling that we're purer esthetes than moralists believe; we respond to the *art* of the matter, the esthetically patterned expectation. Impelled to identify ourselves with Baron Cefalu's momentum, we feel a kinetic need to fulfill it, just as we would *not* want to have it fulfilled had we been initially placed within the ambience of the signora's sympathy.

While savoring the beauty of hard sunlight on decaying baroque, a parenthetical reminder came my way from *Il Bell' Antonio*. Bolognini's cool handling of Claudia Cardinale had given us a margin for doubting the felicity of which Antonio thought himself deprived. Two realities depicted—the romantic wooer, the bartering bride—without destroying the fragile balance of Antonio's conviction of personal tragedy: subtle feat. I couldn't help suspecting that *Divorce—Italian Style* might be construed as a wry speculation, farcically treated, on what would have transpired if Antonio had regained his potency and kept his Cardinale. The insinuation is made doubly plausible by the choice of Marcello Mastroianni as Cefalu and by the inversion of a Sicilian imperative featured in the earlier film: the Cefalus have been married for years, have no children; yet they're not pariahs, from the community viewpoint! With no reference to the matter in the film, we must assume that Germi has artfully kept one of his loudest jokes implicit.

The human face and the humanized setting—comic or in disrepair—are the persistent irreducibles of Italian film. When Germi's resources of montage and décor have been itemized, the abundant

spirit of *Divorce—Italian Style* hasn't been located without a
special declaration for the actors who exalt the absurdities
Mastroianni's personification of the baron is a masterly vindication
of his release from playing himself so often, mood-indigo, intel
lectual: the pomaded ruffian instead, his coiffure the crown of a
wax dummy containment of personality; the rigidly respectable
stance which to alien eyes is ground itself of outlandish eccentric
ity; the puppy awkwardness when he swings into action, unseen by
public eye; the vendetta twitch of the cheek muscle. And besides
Mastroianni and Daniele Roca there's Leopoldo Trieste, a fastidious
clown, giving his graceful best since his role in Fellini's *The White
Sheik:* the painter-suitor of Cefalu's wife—the gist of the man hi
shy but unruffled conviction of his irresistible personal splendor—a
figure distilled from ages of photo albums and provincial theater
companies.

Three performers also have pride of place in François Truffaut's
Jules et Jim, but they are too interdependent with the film to be
thought of as exalting it: Jeanne Moreau, Henri Serre, Oskar
Werner. Of the three, seen as characters, I'd like a whole film made
about Jules, as Oskar Werner creates him in context: reticent
warm, smiling at ill usage. To summarize is to flounder, and to settle
for less. To say that *Jules et Jim* is the story of a love maintained be
tween three people over twenty years, maintained in the face of
Catherine's marriage to Jules and when, even so, she has Jim as a
lover and Jim keeps Jules as a friend—to say this is a necessary
minimum for conveying the idea at all. Having said it, one hesitate
before the mystifying inferences which a reader, not having seen
the film, would be likely to gather. For *Jules et Jim* is neither
romance nor morality nor pure farce nor psychological epitome, yet
it touches and sometimes invades each of these territories. "Like
life," one is too easily tempted to conclude; the very conclusion can
only be drawn by adopting what seems to be the most embracing
inference of the film, viewed as a story. "Life" has no such tone—
life has no tone at all until endowed with someone's imposed vision
of it. "Be careful how you interpret life," Erich Heller has advised—
"it is that way." Relative to the observer, we have learned: relative
to the observer's constitution, his experience, his cultural presup
positions. *Jules et Jim* is an essay in moral relativism only if you are
content with restricting the film to its *events,* to the separable sub
ject: which is to miss most of the art and therefore be unable to

account for the events; they are given their character from the tone permeating them.

Truffaut, taken too literally at his interviewed word, has impressed critics and young film-makers with his ready invention. Since he admits being ever willing to invite and incorporate inspirations of the moment when shooting, his films are chiefly regarded as an art of extemporization; this is to honor them more in the breach than in the observance. There's no such thing as an extemporized *art:* there is an unplanned opportunity, instantaneously sorted and judged for its aptness by a controlling sensibility—call it intellectual selection, intuitively governed. Truffaut probably can't himself explain, because he takes as given, the secret of his charm, defined by other film-makers who have need of it (in England, the U.S., Poland, it may be) as "spontaneity." What they overlook—I resume my reference to *Jules et Jim*—is Truffaut's premeditated devotion to subject! In 1953 Truffaut read the novel (the first by a seventy-four-year-old man, Henri-Pierre Roché), promised himself that if he made a film he'd make one of this book, made three other films before fulfilling the promise, wherewith he sought to re-evoke the tone of *The 400 Blows:* tragic-comic (i.e., *"triste dans sa ligne, mais drôle dans ses details"*), in the service of a more panoramic subject.

To compose an epic by lyric means was virtually the demand he made on himself and on the rhetoric of film art; to tell an unlikely story of two men and a woman who must appeal to us, singly and by situation, to move the three through time and place so that the one dimension is felt (protracted yet evanescent), the other experienced by sight and hearing, without unduly subordinating the three and without wholly extricating them from the multiple phenomena which illuminate their value and reduce their importance. With Jean Gruault as associated adapter, he made a whimsical masterpiece, seen at middle distance, an exercise in nostalgia assured by "fixing" the action in only-yesterday, 1907–1927. This is a curiously volatile creation: the essence evaporates a few hours after you receive it, yet mind-hovers thereafter like those passages of life which drop away, entire, and when recalled make you wonder if they indeed took place and, if so, why, then, you *cared* so much—or so little—and isn't it all a heart-catching fraud, anyway? I'm not convinced that Truffaut's literary-historical obligation required as many figures of movie speech as he utilized: the meteoric cutting speed at the opening, simulation of silent-film tableaux and grainy print, the shutdown to a still, inserted documentary, overlaps, film-within-a-film—certainly I could have done without the narrative voice—but I'll concede his intrepidity.

And his insouciance—at a special point of stress. I'm puzzled by Truffaut's hope that he has filmed "a hymn to love, perhaps even a hymn to life." The jubilant description all but disarmed me; it puts at discount my perhaps oversensitive disturbance, set up by watching the rapid transit of two high-minded men through a twilight world, in thrall to a woman who appears to constitute the exclusive focus of their lives, a woman who, in any translation one reaches for, is a Medusa wearing the mask of virtue. Catherine is histrionically amusing, flexible, and devoted, so long as both men agree to worship her not wisely but too well and without question, agree not to see through her—not to see *into* her: when one or the other abdicates, for an hour or a day, she strikes to wound—ultimately to kill. In point of fact she destroys them both, and if the Mack Sennett manner in which she literally destroys the more independent one is stylistically part and parcel of Truffaut's evocation by comedy, it's nonetheless, to my taste, a bizarre "Amen" for a hymn to love and life.*

Envoi. A cartoonist, Gahlin—sole Swedish humorist I've ever been moved to quote—has supplied me with the thought that best concentrates my reaction to this aspect of Truffaut's triangle: "Why should I try to understand women? Women understand them—and they don't like them."   1962

---

*Footnote 1971. I have since learned that in the novel the two men were homosexually devoted. Certainly this makes their sustained relationship, unaffected by the disputable Catherine, more convincing; in the film the absence of such a linkage contributes to a somewhat fantastic ethos. Yet I can't help preferring Truffaut's version: if less plausible, it is to my taste more delightful.

Program Notes
for Two Classics

THE BLUE ANGEL (1930) (*Der blaue Engel*)

In a provincial German city (pre–World War I), Professor Rath has been dragooning grubby little boys through the elements of speech for thirty years. As the film opens, he wakes up to a morning which begins like all the dreary others, except for a single premonitory note: the failure of his pet canary to answer his habitual greeting. Fumbling into wakefulness the "Herr Professor" shakes off the effect of this unexpected intrusion of fatality into his insulated routine. He dresses himself and walks to school, undergoing his customary transitions from a frowsy infant to a punctual pedagogue to a bureaucratic tyrant, as step by step he regains his daytime ego. By the time he has entered the classroom and stilled the juvenile hubbub with a trumpeting nose-blow he is Authority, incarnate.

The name Rath suggests the German word for a magistrate and also that of a household article, so that the boys' nicknaming of their professor as *Un*rath implies the opposite status (i.e., under the bureaucratic dispensation of Central Europe before the wars, *no status at all*) —an article no longer needed, something one throws out, either from the house or from the community. . . . Aroused to moral indignation by his pupils' salacious interest in the entertainer Lola, the professor pays a visit to this sub-social Thais and thereby instigates the common fate of the suppressed man, whether Christian anchorite or latter-day puritan. He is destroyed by the image he loathes but longs to embrace. When, as a consequence of his infatuation, the wretched man is banished from the only world he knows, he is helpless; throwing himself on the mercy of Lola and her raffish company of traveling actors, he is speedily reduced to a halfway level between man and beast, for he is rather less gifted than a performing animal. Lola represents something much shoddier than the "pure instinct" with which criticism has often endowed her. She is of a species which shares at least one characteristic of the black widow spider and the scorpion. . . . In a travesty of bourgeoisie ceremony, not the least cynical of her actions, she marries the fatuous sinner. At their wedding dinner the professor's imitation of a crowing cock recapitulates the dead songbird of the opening scene and, as it turns out, terrifyingly anticipates the last cockadoodle, with breaking eggs baptizing his insanity before he attempts to murder the slut whom he has pathetically mistaken as his wingless angel.

This film can scarcely be appetizing to anyone whom eighteenth-century diction would term "a man of healthy parts." But it's an unsavory *magnum opus,* little dimmed by time, and has, above all, the interest of being linked thematically with a host of films produced in Germany between World War I and the Third Reich. Among others, *The Last Laugh* (*Der letzte Mann,* 1924, Murnau), *Variety* (*Variété,* 1925, E. A. Dupont), and *The Blue Angel* form a definitive trilogy of their own, all of them featuring the man who collapses or goes berserk when deprived of status and/or frustrated by sexual betrayal. (Emil Jannings played in all three and was starred in more than one stock version of the same genre during his Hollywood period.) It may not be necessary in these notes to belabor social analogies already elaborated in Siegfried Kracauer's book, *From Caligari to Hitler;* those who haven't read it should do so, with reservations demanded by certain ironies and contradictions of history that qualify many of the simplifications therein. Notable is the circumstance that Josef von Sternberg (b. Josef or

Johan Stern, Vienna, 1894), who returned to the "free climate" of America after directing this film, produced increasingly empty and meretricious pictures thereafter (*Morocco*, 1930; *Dishonored*, 1931; *Blonde Venus* and *Shanghai Express*, 1932; *The Scarlet Empress*, 1934).

Cinematically, *The Blue Angel* restored to the sound film in Germany, after a first flood of Vienna musicals and kindred *kitsch*, the concentrated dramatic values of expressionism and social realism which had been the principal German contribution since World War I. Von Sternberg himself had in America pioneered the "artistic highlighting" of the sordid milieu on which his fame was based. *The Blue Angel* is perhaps remarkable for the selective claustrophobia of its settings; the key moments are visually forced into the screen's dimension, protesting, with the characters, that of course no other social world exists save that of a gaslit stage, a littered dressing room, a cabaret corner, a schoolroom not large enough to breathe in until emptied of other life. Made in 1929, *The Blue Angel* was one of the first sound films of importance to be made anywhere (*cf.* Hitchcock's *Blackmail*—shot as a silent—England, 1929, and René Clair's *Sous les Toits de Paris*, France 1930), surpassed only, in point of inventiveness, by Ruttman's *Melody of the World*, made in the same year.

Emil Jannings (born in New York City, 1886) entered films in 1915 after a stint at Max Reinhardt's Deutsches Theater, Berlin. In 1930 he was just acquiring the great ability with which he had been prematurely credited. Photogenic facially, he had always acted from the outside, and he had a lumbering gait which most directors covered up by giving him characterizations appropriate to the deficiency. Not before the mid-thirties did he succeed in the impersonation of a human being free of facial tics, masochism, or dementia —in such Third Reich films as *Der Alte und der Junge König* and *Traumulus*. His death in 1950 spared "authorities" embarrassment, since he was otherwise eligible for the same fate as that of his contemporaries, Werner Krauss (who was barred from films) and Heinrich George (who died in a Russian prison for certified Nazis).

Marlene Dietrich (b. Marie Magdalene von Losch, 1902, Berlin) had been in films since 1922, before von Sternberg and *The Blue Angel* gave her the international reputation she has to this day maintained as a special variant of the genus *ewige weibliche*. With but a brackish dramatic talent and no versatility whatever, she has been placed by the public in a voyeurs' niche beyond the reach of any qualifications offered by the critical intelligence. Her career has flourished solely from her insinuative capacity for making smut divine.

1962

LES QUATRE CENTS COUPS (*The 400 Blows*) —1959

The 400 Blows is the latest in a succession of masterworks from France on the subject of the child or adolescent which had its first artistic exemplars thirty years ago in Duvivier's *Poil de Carotte,* Benôit-Lévy's *La Maternelle,* and Vigo's surreal *Zéro de Conduite.* The subject of Duvivier's film, as by artistic consistency it should have been of Benôit-Lévy's, was innocence destroyed. The subject of Truffaut's film is closer to that of Clément's *Forbidden Games* or Delannoy's *Le Garçon Sauvage* (both c. 1952) and can best be summarized as innocence threatened.

In his first feature-length production (he had previously made *Les Mistons—The Mischief Makers—*on a tributary theme), Truffaut follows with dispassionate but receptive attention the almost imperceptible drift of an alienated boy from petty rebellions into delinquency. When first confronted with Antoine, we see an ingratiating but insolent youngster bent on defying the world of his vicinity: a trial to his forbearing teacher, a trouble seeker on the street, an evasive nuisance at home. If we're not initially prepared by advance synopsis or by fortuitous personal identification, we are not altogether beguiled by this handsome little monster, since we haven't the qualifying evidence with which to exonerate him. By allowing the situation to reveal itself, as it were, with no special pleading in his edited material, Truffaut exhibits the motivating sources of Antoine's behavior.

This film is not a study in persecution. Antoine's teacher is not tyrannical, he's harassed; Antoine's parents are not brutes, they're thoughtless and not very bright—like most people; society, insofar as it is represented by the law and inasmuch as it is French society, is confined by traditional practice and a degree of cynicism to judicial powers alone. The boy's frustrated vitality is the prime mover that translates indifference into forces of retribution. Antoine's *petit bourgeois* parents, in peevish combat with each other, have insufficient curiosity for understanding or even perceiving the inhibition from which the unloved boy suffers. Antoine's stepfather tries to reciprocate the youngster's need to admire and to be admired, but he is drastically unequal to the demands made on his limited affection and his lack of insight. For Mother, who has more than a hint of the tramp in her makeup, both Antoine and his father are hindrances to the freedom of her affair with another man. The scene where Father, Mother, and Antoine go out to the theater, and afterward, with self-conscious bonhomie, reenact snatches from the movie they've seen, is one of the most incredible passages of domestic naturalism ever recaptured, belonging with a few rare moments of similar veracity in the films of De Sica and Fellini. Even among French films, notable for their flashes of verisimilitude lifted into poetry, this is a distinguished interlude.

The truce is short-lived: mother and son, morally blackmailing each other, remain mutually distrustful. Irreconcilable tensions at home, complications at school, the boy's betrayal of his mother, the wish to escape, the need for means to do so, a suggestion from his best friend and henchman, and Antoine takes the next step: emboldened by his successful rehearsal of larceny in a small way he steals a typewriter from the office of his chum's father. He is thereby doomed to the definition his child mind was romantically seeking for itself: outlaw. Taken to a detention home by way of the police station and a "trial by reason"—the psychiatrist's examination, where he scarcely helps his case by the trenchancy of his answers—he joins the legion of the "maladjusted." Antoine has *put himself* behind bars (with the help of his vengeful mother and his weak father, to be sure), just as he had put himself into the revolving drum and then flouted its magnetic safety by refusing to stick to its side like everyone else. The audience of his schoolfellows and of the anonymous crowd were substitutes for the audience his parents had declined to be. But since his purest instinct is for freedom, not for histrionics, he cannot accept corrective imprisonment and again compensate by playing the clown. He has no recourse but to break out from "society," now become simply a bird-brained tribunal meting out rations and punishment to those of its mystified fledglings, uninstructed how to walk, who have dared to attempt flying.

And Antoine's only audience when he escapes from the detention home is, so to speak, the movie audience. The superb final sequence that takes him to the perimeter of the human world and the opening prospect of the eternally neutral ocean is the verifying instance of Truffaut's sustained harmony of technique and content in this film:

the logic of feeling and the logic of continuity are united in the most inventively beautiful question mark ever filmed (as the end of *Los Olvidados* is the most terrifying one)—the poised foot sampling "the destructive element," the uncreate face (moving into arrested closeup) on which life will either render an increasingly furtive expression or transfigure that fragile and still uncorrupted smile.

To label *The 400 Blows* New Wave—inevitable at the time and under the circumstances of its release—is to ignore the absence of mannerisms otherwise held to be inseparable from that elastic category. Truffaut, a discontented documentary-maker for the government and a malcontent film critic, is nonetheless *d'accord* with the heritage of subtle formalism in French film-making. Behind the opening credits of this film, the camera tracks into the city labyrinth above street level to the constricted, skyless arena in which the action will mainly take place. The climax of this constriction is reached with Antoine behind bars, peering wistfully at the hostile yet brightly lit world in which he expected to retaliate with impunity. After the restraint of the long semi-closeup Examination, the narrative moves forward and outward in gathering momentum for the last loping run and opening view. *The 400 Blows,* abundant with random life, has the consistency of directed art.

1962

Postscript, 1971

When Mr. Jerry Weiss requested these program notes he imposed only the condition that they tell the story of the film in some detail. Beyond that, I was free to add whatever I felt necessary for an understanding of the film's background, and I was encouraged to express my own opinion. Oh, Brother!

An amusing contretemps occurred, I am told, in connection with my notes for *The Blue Angel* at a performance of the film in Los Angeles. By a dazzling oversight, Herr von Sternberg had been invited to make some prefatory remarks and had been provided in advance with my printed résumé. (This is something like handing a diner the bill before he has eaten!) I might add that in my original version I had written that Josef von Sternberg was born Joe Sternberg! I read this attribution in an international encyclopedia of film, published in Copenhagen. While I was indeed extremely skeptical, I didn't conceive it impossible; in any case, I'll confess that it gave me sardonic pleasure to write "Joe," with the assurance behind me that I could produce an "alleged authority." From all accounts, von Sternberg was explosively scornful of this devaluation. (I still don't understand how it turns out as printed: Josef or Johan. Perhaps his parents couldn't agree and finally arranged to call him Josef on weekdays and Johan on Sunday.)

But this was only the beginning. Naturally, the poor man could scarcely appreciate having to face an audience supplied with program notes that named his Hollywood films empty and meretricious. For some reason further, he snorted at my calling Lola a slut and he was understandably far from delighted at my deprecation of Miss Dietrich's acting powers. But since von Sternberg himself had written one of the most scathing, and certainly one of the funniest, evaluations of The Actor (in *Film Culture,* V, 1955), he was no doubt prepared to accept my contribution as poetic justice. . . . Even so, it seems to me that my last line in that description of the actress was a subtle compliment. *Divine* is a very lofty word!

Nostalgia of the Infinite:
Notes on Chirico,
Antonioni, Resnais

"A landscape enclosed in the arch of a portico or in the square or rectangle of a window acquires a greater metaphysical value, because it is solidified and isolated from the surrounding space. Architecture completes nature. It marks an advance of human intellect in the field of metaphysical discoveries."* Thus the painter Giorgio de Chirico. He fathered a *scuola metafisica* on the verge of World War I. As a local development it was short-lived; as a term connoting many species of the *surreal,* it remains illuminating. In those days, when "the integrity of the object" and "the tyranny of appearances" were being newly assailed from all sides, Chirico was accepted as one among the major prophets of the pictorial dissolution then in swift progress. No doubt he fostered the acceptance by declaring, in 1913, his desire to abolish all "recognizable material" and

---

*My principal source for quotations from the writings of Giorgio de Chirico is Marcel Jean's *Histoire de la Peinture Surréaliste* (Editions du Seuil, 1959, Paris).

by signing, in 1920, the dada manifesto. In fact he was never so radical as to dispense with appearances, or even to jest with them. Today it can be better appreciated that Chirico's position was essentially that of a romantic who had annexed the classical properties of Renaissance painting and of the visible architectural survivals (the arches, the tiled pavements, the campaniles) in order to reconstitute them, together with the new profiles of the twentieth century, as settings of anxiety and hallucination.

Perhaps Chirico talked a better painting than he ever achieved. Perhaps it's easier at present to take his art for granted or to underrate it in the shadow of his imitators. Within the idiom of which he was the parent, though never a chartered member—surrealism as the illogical placement of logical objects, or even vice versa—his art cannot be acquitted of facile theatricalism and of a portentousness too often imposed by his wonderful titles. All the same, he created in his best pictures an impressively haunted world (emphasized by caustic draftsmanship and a narrow compass of eerie color) inhabited by lonely creatures—sometimes only shadows of man, or jointed simulacra, like manikins—spellbound among fantasy-classical arcades, threatened by an overwhelming silence made visually evident. Not infrequently he introduced a locomotive into his setting of arches and historical monuments: it was always ominous. His compositions, while geometrically ordered, were artfully falsified by accelerated perspective; his witness point was more often than not oblique—*cinematic,* we might call it now—from an overhead or low-angle plane. Expressionist sight-lines had not yet been utilized by cinema; in painting they had been pioneered by Degas under the twin influences of Japanese prints and still photography. As correlatives of distinctly psychological tensions they were successively exploited by van Gogh, Munch, and Chirico.

Unlike the futurists, Chirico was not susceptible to the lyric dynamism they celebrated as the principle of the new age, "a life of steel, fever, pride and headlong speed." Anachronism, not assimilation, was his prevailing note. He was haunted by the past, disturbed by the present, terrified of the future. For all his lurid, dislocative method, his paintings have a curiously classical repose. (Biography is an unusually relevant factor in the sources of Chirico's art: his father was a railroad engineer, he was brought up in Greece where he painted the ruins of classical antiquity, and, subsequently, the most important inspiration for his artistic maturity was the landscape painting of the German Romantic, Caspar David Friedrich.)

When the main course of painting turned resolutely nonobjective and nonconceptual, Chirico bequeathed his "restorations" and his *Angst* to other painters who have been backwatered in the terminology as "literary." For many years a variety of surrealists and fantasists restated and rearranged his deserts punctuated by masonry, his classical torsos, his black-and-white-tiled *piazzi,* his wooden marionettes, his anachronistic weddings of remote past with empty present and dire future. Yves Tanguy, Dali, Paul Delvaux, and Leonor Fini are alike related to him. The "landscape enclosed in an arch," which Chirico inherited from the Annunciations of the *quattrocento,* was enlisted by the fabulous Belgian, René Magritte, for shock value rather than for metaphysical irony. Inevitably, one now realizes, Chirico turned to the theater where, in the twenties, he created designs for Les Ballets Suédois and for Diaghilev's company in Paris. And not surprisingly his later re-attention to easel painting has been an attempt to find again the lost "figure" of man through the older tradition of "representational" art.*

"Architecture completes nature." Chirico was here reinstating Aristotle; our architects-at-large have not. Look around you. Little contemporary architecture can be said to *complete* nature. On the contrary, it either contests or usurps nature, as well as all the architecture preceding it. To the abstract expressionist painter, completion of nature is also a dead letter: for him the improvised, the amorphous, and the primordial are the generally preferred effects. Theater, insofar as it is a *scenic* art, has long since reduced setting to an exiguous token (Beckett's plays, for instance, are as fruitful heard on the radio). Only the motion picture, among the visual arts, remains dedicated to the habitual phenomena of man and his stubbornly contingent milieu. Conveying "reality" by a more or less representational method, film art in its rare epitomes —the only ones with which criticism needs seriously to be concerned—thereby defends the method from otherwise justifiable contempt. For the very process to which this art owes its existence, that of decomposing and re-analyzing the literal, is the source of a new synthesis, fused by imagination: a synthesis rescued from elementary definitions of the representational. From time to time, during film's brief history, an urge has been expressed by film-makers and

---

*A fascinating speculation on the origins of the Chirico manikin by Dr. Felix Sluys was published in *Connaissance des Arts* (February 1962, Paris) : "Bracelli, le Dessinateur le Plus Excentrique avant Dali."

by critics to increase the effectiveness of the art through extreme departures from chronological sequence and from visually logical associations. Effectiveness, in their reading, seems often to be derived from a false analogy with arts which have not the same principles of composition and have not, therefore, the same potentialities as those of film art. The motion picture, audio-visual, is nonetheless closer to the novelist's art than to any other, in its power to reveal man to himself. At present, the films of Michelangelo Antonioni and of Alain Resnais are notably suggestive examples of the means by which that objective may be assisted or baffled. And they have mutual bearing on the idiom offered by Giorgio de Chirico, in word and picture, as an evaluation of modern man's abstraction of himself.

For most spectators at Alain Resnais's film, *L'Année Dernière à Marienbad*, the chief source of novelty appears to be the incarnation of what Chirico, in his prose expressions, preferred to leave unidentified—or at least incorporeal. "I remember one vivid winter's day at Versailles. Silence and calm reigned supreme. Everything gazed at me with mysterious, questioning eyes. And then I realized that every corner of the palace, every column, every window possessed a spirit, an impenetrable soul." Taking the common run of films as measure, we can grant the novelty of *Marienbad*. But mystery? Nothing so quickly converts mystery into anomaly as the personification of an abstractly intended *presence*. Chirico committed the error himself in many of his persistent attempts to paint correspondences of his unease. In the *Marienbad* film it is not the unseen which is strange—but the *seen*. Even so, once you have reconciled yourself to this company of apparent phantoms, what's mysterious thereafter are their separately nominal identities and the pertinence of the setting (which you are permitted rather fully to explore) to the subject of the film (which you may never succeed in adequately overtaking!). Favorable opinion has pronounced the film subtle, or "suggestive." Might there not be a prevailing confusion of *suggestive* with *mystifying*? There is no absence of clues in either Alain Robbe-Grillet's scenario or in Resnais' film for an interpretation of the "events" therein; one could well complain that there are too many for suggestiveness to be anything but hopelessly diffuse: they cancel serious curiosity. A surrealistic painter is tolerable, even enthralling, so long as he doesn't unduly compound enigmas on a single canvas. A film director is suggestive until he fails to restrain his apparatus of suggestions. Paul Delvaux vulgarized the arcades, checkerboard pavings, and human shadows of Chirico by multiplying them—to say nothing of his erotic amplifications—at which point they achieved the status of absurdity. *Marienbad* is nowhere vulgar, perhaps, but it is certainly, for long stretches, meretricious, so patently has it been designed to express the inscrutable.

Two international wars during fifty years of steel, fever, and headlong speed (the pride was our most easily expendable item of the futurist manifesto) have by no means diminished the worst forebodings of Chirico; nor have the times justified an image of man much more adequate than the stricken manikins he painted. Yeats's amorphous beast still slouches untiringly toward Bethlehem to be born, his swan still drifts upon a darkening flood. But if dread has not been transformed, art conventions have. The principal mode in painting is not involved with illustrative transcriptions of nightmare, since there is a margin of the sensible beyond which prophetic facsimiles of doom become inartistic and therewith unpersuasive. Today most of us, I think, find the dour continents of Tàpies more eloquent (as art) than the aerial Armageddons of Matta. Among the fantasy painters of Chirico's lineage, a landscape from Yves Tanguy's last productions (e.g., *Metamorphosis of the Arcs*), empty of all but mounds of perforated stones, is infinitely more frightening than the contrivances of Dali—the scaffoldings and armatures, the burning giraffe, the screaming, crutch-supported anatomies. Magritte is far more metaphysical when he paints a massive, denuded rock naturalistically than when he traps clouds in a room or superimposes a Botticelli nymph on the back of a man with a bowler hat. Metaphysically speaking, nothingness is more terrible than dislocation; artistically speaking, Braque's relatively classical standard is difficult to refute: "In art, progress does not consist in extension but in the knowledge of limits."

What distinguishes Antonioni among his contemporaries in cinema is the degree to which, by a flawless and quite personal feeling for the *interval* (not only the meticulous duration and pacing of shots in a sequence, but also the spatial tensions within the shot), he infuses his films with steadily mounting suspense. *Suspension* would be as apt a word: the moments hang, the passages of an hour are gravid with expectation; waves of emotion crest but never break; each image threatens to disclose a monstrous withheld truth or to discharge an act of violence forever hinted but always sup-

pressed—heat lightning without thunder. And although the movement of life in his films seems to share at times that random and un-
willed progress by which our own daily lives proceed, it has a
rhythmic beat calculated with extraordinary finesse. Miraculously,
his films have invaded the domain of painting with no loss of cinematic character: each composition seems to have been established
with plastic deliberation, yet no single composition or fugal group
inhibits the narrative stream.

The cinema of Antonioni is *essential* cinema; it is not an invention
but, rather, a purification of possibilities partially realized by other
film directors. Without resorting to scenic fabrications or distortions, with no editorial chiaroscuro as in the old German expressionist films, and without Resnais' triple device of incessant music,
spoken narrative, and discrepant time-shift, Antonioni *penetrates*
the naturalistic surface and sustains a driving undertone of dread.
In *L'Avventura*, at one moment remarkably, the "mysterious questioning eyes" predicated by Chirico recall the spirit, if not the precise
scenery, of his painting. Sandro and Claudia, during their search for
the missing Anna, drive away from an abandoned new town. As
they do so, the camera remains at middle distance from the uninhabited area (which is dominated by a shut-tight contemporary
church), inching forward almost imperceptibly. After the couple
have left, the lone camera continues to creep stealthily forward—as
if a presence were covertly watching (or listening to) the departure. From here on in the film we sense that the terms of the pursuit
have shifted. Sandro and Claudia are no longer looking for something. A something is looking for them. . . . In the *Marienbad* film
one may be finally embarrassed by the equivocal company of the
visible, whereas in *L'Avventura* one is mortally disturbed by the felt
presence of the invisible. "The whole nostalgia of the infinite is
revealed to us behind the geometrical precision of the square. We
experience the most unforgettable moments when certain aspects
of the world, whose existence we completely ignore, suddenly confront us with the revelation of mysteries lying all the time within
our reach. . . ." (Giorgio de Chirico).

Two years ago a French musicologist, André Hodeir, intimidated
readers of film literature into accepting the arcane nature of Alain
Resnais' contribution to film art. In an article first published in
Cahiers du Cinéma, subsequently translated for reprint in *Evergreen Review*, he declared that the historical importance of *Hiro-*

shima, Mon Amour was due to its having announced "the analogy of cinematic construction and musical composition," a statement which should have shocked half a hundred practicing film directors who had been declaring just that for at least thirty-five years! Further, M. Hodeir maintained that "the conception of cutting Resnais employs introduces a notion of specifically musical discontinuity and thereby creates a complex relationship of time organization." One may ask, in passing, why this discontinuity should be thought of as specifically *musical* rather than—for example—*prosodic* or, for that matter, *cinematic*. However, one is more astonished that Hodeir had forgotten, or never knew, that the discontinuity he claims as a Resnais invention is, in one form, as old as Soviet film theory and practice and, in the more sophisticated fashion to which he seemingly refers, was the animating formal principle of Alf Sjö-berg's film, *Miss Julie* (1950). To displace chronology or unity of immediate reference by cutting from an image in sequence to one unexpected by the reason and by the conditioned eye has a long history in the mutations of film narrative style. Sjöberg first sustained the usage with supreme artistic resource throughout a full-length film *in a cyclical manner*. If the disjunctures of Resnais are more abrupt, so to speak, if his elisions demand a greater adjustment from the viewer, this is a matter of degree and of suitability to the style conceived for the whole film. Hodeir could have written an identical justification, with the same terminology, for the films of Dovzhenko, made in the twenties. Obviously he has his own ax of musical *avant garde* fashion to grind and has chosen an unfortunate correlate from the film world to authorize the grinding.

Renais' method then, as such, is by no means original. The two feature films by which he is presently known introduce no treatment not introduced by the first French *avant garde* of the twenties which culminated in the films of Jean Cocteau and has been recapitulated ad infinitum by various U.S. "experimentalists" ever since. They are radically less inventive than many films made by Jean Epstein and by Jean Vigo in the early thirties—to say nothing of the Dali-Buñuel productions of the same period, which dispensed with even the shadow of a story line. If the commercial-theater public has never been exposed to these films, so much the better for Resnais' prestige as a revolutionary movie-maker. We need not try to dispute Resnais' virtuosity; it is conspicuous and entertaining, and his record as a talented documentary film-maker is irreproachable. With respect to his story films, on the other hand, we are beset by doubt when he is defended for a distinction far from self-evident. It's notable that Hodeir nowhere in his article identified passion or depth of perception as attributes of *Hiroshima,* despite the claims which should be made for their presence by the gravity of the subject. Suppose one were to remove the introductory images from this film, those actuality shots which depict the enormity from which the film story takes its point of departure. How closely would Resnais then appear to have embraced the subject, the actuality, on his own terms? Would the closeups of skin texture, the obliquely related dialogue, the pictorial ellipsis, the percussive reaction shots—would these ingenuities convey an authentic human tragedy, specified *within* the situation? Because if they wouldn't, as I suspect, then Hodeir is simply discoursing parallel with his contingent subject, seeking to impose on film the exigencies of another medium. The basic criterion for a film story is not esoteric: any arresting manner of telling it is welcome, so long as the end is served by the means. The end in view for a film that rests squarely on a crisis of the human condition cannot be dodged. And no matter how intriguing Resnais' visual syncopations may have been in *Hiroshima,* he is open to the accusation of having dodged an engagement too crucial for the means he chose.

The difference, in any single instance of visual art, between our negative reception of an image as being merely derived and our pleasurable acceptance of it as an inspired influence hinges on the degree to which it has been assimilated by the artist—probably on the degree to which it has been *unconsciously* assimilated. After noting the reminiscences, from other films and from paintings, aroused by *L'Année Dernière à Marienbad,* I discover that little is left save a generalized glory of baroque interior, which reaches me as intrinsic to Resnais' style. Epstein by way of Cocteau (*Fall of the House of Usher* and *Beauty and the Beast*), if not Cocteau alone, is responsible for the peignoir of Delphine Seyrig wafted by a breeze which has no accountable source. Overhead shots of the boudoir which impose a sense of transient structure, built from stage flats, are straight from Cocteau's *Les Enfants Terribles.* The frozen guests, as tailored and separate as the clipped bushes lining the *Marienbad* vistas, each casting a shadow more solid than himself, is Chirico. Delphine Seyrig, one hand clutching the opposite shoulder, is a direct reminder of Oskar Schlemmer's lathe-turned figures (together with chessboard floor) in the *Römisches* of 1925. And it's surprising that Swedish critics, reverently applauding the counter-forms of living (or is she?) woman with baroque statuary, failed to recall that Sjöberg made exactly the same point in *Miss Julie*—also in a Versailles-type setting, incidentally, that of Drottningholm Palace and grounds. Antonioni also stimulates one's eye for correspondence (oddly enough, he too uses the tiled floor as a token of the Game—in *La Notte*), but his usage of motifs that suggest Chirico or Paul Klee or Henry Moore or those of his immediate predecessors in Italian film are well seasoned and transcend "effectiveness." Whether or not they're derived is unimportant; his films don't stand or fall by exterior patrimonies. He doesn't dodge his subject with décor; décor, *mise en scène* (the island, the city, the villa, the hotel room, the stock exchange), *is* his subject.

Jacques Brunius has written a less specious exposition* of *Marienbad* than Hodeir managed for *Hiroshima*—carefully avoiding any questionable issues, or dismissing them as petty objections, which might reduce the apostolic weight of his counsel. He supplies plausible explanations of the film's paraphrasable content which I've added to three idly ruminated theories of my own. But as much as I'd like to be as impressed by the film as M. Brunius' sensitive apologia for it alone deserves, I can't but conclude that his cogent demonstration leaves the *raison d'être* as he found it; the film is an anagram, very cleverly worked out and left open to the talents of the viewer—where Resnais found it! For confusion reigns here unless it's understood that Brunius is really defending the other Alain (Robbe-Grillet), the "novelist," not Resnais the film-maker. And the best that might be said for Robbe-Grillet's share, for those who are impressed by reputable fellow travelers (and I'm here giving Brunius a line he didn't take), is that the disposition of it is related to certain tendencies in the French theater of the absurd (e.g., Ionesco or Schehade), where the characters are magnetic fields and little more, yielding a variety of interpretations chiefly because they are vitiated personalities or nameless ones without volition—and are so intended. That Robbe-Grillet has seized no more than a chic sector of this theater as a profitable mannerism which he can repeat as often as a gullible audience will accept it—like Buffet and his bottles—is a probability I find confirmed by a review of his novel *Jealousy* (*Encounter*, February 1961), by Burns Singer, who summarizes thus: "One is left in the end with a number of clinical

---

* "Every Year in Marienbad, or the Discipline of Uncertainty" (*Sight and Sound*, Summer 1962, London).

photographs about the geography of a house, the disposition of banana groves, the position of a woman brushing her hair, and so on, but the central situation has escaped between them. We have no clue as to the identity or character of any of the three protagonists. The drama, resultantly, is an affair of puppets, none of whom are known by the reader or indeed give any evidence of knowing one another. Nor is this accidental, for M. Robbe-Grillet believes we should not be interested in such matters. For him, in his pursuit of the thingness of things, the peopleness of people is merely a distraction."*

"The peopleness of people" is a dubious conviction in Antonioni's films (let it be now understood that my reference is always to his late trilogy) ; he deplores the regression, it's the basis of his poignant vision. And since architecture is the most directly referable form of man's social expression, architectonic forms—of nature as well—are omnipresent in his scheme of dehumanization. He has not surrendered to the translation: his ghosts or somnambulists are not incarcerated behind some disputed barricade—Ultima Thule or Marienbad. They inhabit Milan and Rome; their tragedy is that they retain the substantial attractiveness of living creatures, like those mummies in the drawings of Henry Moore which have yet a hint of classically formed fecundity. Their milieu reaffirms that of Chirico, but they themselves are not yet pillars of salt—or of stapled wood.

Anna, the girl who disappears in *L'Avventura*, makes her first entrance from an archway (a pelvic form) , briefly to converse with her father, irritably preoccupied with the encroachment of mass housing. Later, during that halfhearted search for her on the island, whenever she seems near, a certain peak among the volcanic islands distantly visible is framed in the shot. At the film's close, when Claudia makes her decisive gesture of compassion to the calamitously empty man (an entrepreneur of mass housing) , she is given a closeup within the background structure of an arch, Sandro is shown juxtaposed with an erect tower, and in the final shot of the film, wherein the blank wall of the architectural past extends across

---

*I offer the above as welcome collaboration against M. Brunius' oracular confidence: "I am now quite prepared to claim that *Marienbad* is the greatest film ever made, and to pity those who cannot see this." M. Brunius' trumpet voluntary must be taken as an unaffected gesture of enthusiasm, else we should be tempted to construe it as condescension. I personally don't need his pity, the less so as I have never been convinced that the greatness of any work of art is proportional to its assumed intellectual complexity.

one half of the scope, we see through the open half a breast-shaped peak like the earlier one, completing the triumvirate and resolving the leading motifs. A Freudian reading is by no means the only one, and for those who find it reductive, at best, it is well to reflect that the association of buildings, objects in nature, and anatomical features is centuries older than psycho-pictorialism. But it may be worth interpolating that Chirico himself acknowledged the Freudian plausibility of his employment of the structures named above, and André Breton astutely observed that his tower-dominated pictures were named for *nostalgia,* the arcade subjects for *anxiety.*

In *La Notte,* architecture as history has vanished. There remain only the soulless façades of commercial Milan, the sterile interiors of a hospital, the custom-built modernity of a palatial suburban villa; wallpaper views and a golf course as nature. The post-Mondrian nullity of the hospital façade, a waffle in stone, introduces the already faltering action, slithering downward and back again as the camera slowly mounts and descends, implacably bringing with it the high-frequency sound comparable in pitch to the inhuman tonality of the building; as if in obedience to this sonic reminder, Tommaso awakens to stare gropingly at his death. Antonioni uses no musical score in either film, only controlled amplification of sounds that make their own premonitory music: a motorboat engine, jet planes, humming of wires, growl of seawater in grottoes.

The disfranchising of human privilege is all but complete in *L'Eclisse,* while countermanded cinematically by a rigorously formal gallery of compositions which brings Antonioni's masterly comment close to a cerebral impasse. More extensively, and at closer range, than in *La Notte,* the world depicted is one of space dividers, at once transparent and formidable: draped windows, all-glass doors, ironwork grilles, chambered locks, paintings from an innocent age in entangling alliance with the furniture of chic, isolated rectangles of light in cubiform apartment houses. The two leading abstractions of the film—money and love—are represented by the quotation board (proto-Mondrian) at the stock exchange and by the disoriented tower-block communities "outside the walls"—'way outside—of Rome, where Vittoria listlessly initiates one termination and irresponsibly begins a new coupling in the spirit of termination. All outdoor near-distance shots include the unfailing reduction of man's home to a congress of fabrications: stadium, airport, church, and storage tank at first glance indistinguishable. . . . Resnais' baroque vaults, alignments of corridors and neoclassic avenues may have been selected to comment on the divergence between rational, if prodigious, architecture and the ambiguous drama of identities. They are quite overwhelming, the more so as they are fortified by resonant music and by interminable recitation which gratuitously describes what we are seeing. They secure the attention; they do not thereafter possess it, for they carry no such burden of cultural tragedy as the architectural multiplex of Antonioni.

Antonioni arrives, by finite preparations, at "the nostalgia of the infinite." He is not *avant garde,* if to be so is primarily to be a circuit breaker of time and place; he has been exploring displacements more crucial than those of film-narrative chronology. So doing, he has created a new unity, filmwise, of the lyrical, the social, and the prophetic. His setting, indicated as Milan, Rome, a coastal island, a Sicilian cathedral town, is always on the slopes of a dormant volcano.   1962

After Bergman . . .

The film season in Sweden was initiated last autumn by a conference, on television, of producers and directors whose professed program for the future was the creation of a Swedish film industry not dependent for its prestige on the films of Ingmar Bergman—"a non-Bergman film industry," they called it laughingly. The laughter was a trifle hollow; little previous acquaintance with the situation here was necessary to detect the malice which is never far below the marbled surface of Swedish jocularity. Thereafter, the nominations for this reform have appeared at the rate of one or two a month. So far, Bergman's eminence is safe.

The opening spectacle of the year, if we make less trouble for ourselves by excluding Arne Mattsson's *Wax Doll* to begin with (adding "preposterous" to a foreign censor's verdict, "morbid and unhealthy") —the opening spectacle was a film *intentionally* made for juveniles: *The Wonderful Adventures of Nils*. There seemed in ad-

196 |

vance to be no reason why this should not have been an enchanting film, in the vein of Swedish pastoral, the make-believe given wings with all the technical resources which evoked the supernatural in *The Phantom Carriage* (either the 1920 or the 1958 version): an aerial tour of the Swedish landscape, using the subterfuge of a small boy's flight on a wild goose. With a few arch concessions to tourism, Albert Lamorisse had made in *Voyage au Ballon* a poetic travelogue with moments of great beauty and many of rare wit, from a comparable sortie. In fact it was Lamorisse's example rather than Selma Lagerlöf's tale which convinced Kenne Fant, the producer-director, that a Swedish variant might be a good bet. It was—commercially.

What went wrong in every other respect is easier to note than wholly to explain. Everything went wrong. It should be possible when reporting a film promoted with such pith and enterprise to say *something* favorable. But even with M. Lamorisse helping to supervise, the wonderful adventure never got off the ground, so to speak; there is no wonder in it, no adventure, and technically it's a fiasco. To enumerate solecisms—the crude fabrication of the goose, the painful voice impersonations, the bad dubbing, the uninventiveness of camera perspectives, the dreadful color, the clumsy editing and matching up, the bewildering changes of season within a sequence—this becomes really a superfluous exercise. All lift, levity, and wildness, all feeling of metamorphosis—indispensable to a fairy tale—was wanting. The boy, Nils, remained impenitently a product of the Swedish suburb, 1962, clearly unmoved by any phenomenon more remarkable than a moving staircase. The Stockholm reviewers did their shocked best (I can't believe they were genuinely credulous) to meet the demands of an advertising campaign so vociferous and expensive as to constitute intimidation in the American manner. Then the press of cities where mollification buttered no parsnips was heard from and duly quoted (Uppsala, the university town, for instance). Two days after the film critic of *Dagens Nyheter* (Stockholm's leading newspaper) had walked her tightrope of discretion, the publisher of the paper himself proscribed her caution with a boreal but delicately phrased blast of his own. Financially, the film's returns have not been diminished by the minority recoil. The local first run endured from mid-September to the new year; the film had been pre-sold, sight unseen, in Germany —perhaps elsewhere. Perhaps a universal illusion still prevails that the kiddies don't know the difference between one grade of fantasy and another. I could be wrong on this subject; I think they're not yet so debased in hearing and sight. I'd like to say the film is no worse than Disney—but the lie sticks in my throat.

Alskarinnan (The Mistress) is a bid for the international-sophisticated market. Vilgot Sjöman has long wanted to make a French film in Sweden. Now he has made it (well, you know, like "Harris-type tweed"), with liberal assistance from the styles of Bergman and Antonioni. We are not supposed to suggest that Bergman did any more than advise, but this strategy conceals the author about as successfully as a pair of smoked glasses: it doesn't even fool a neutral Swede. About four years ago Sjöman wrote a script, *Play on the Rainbow*, about a youngish couple having a trial run of free love; the girl decides she wants to play for keeps and the young man makes up his mind too late. To the vindictive applause of collegiate females in the audience, she walks out on him (rather, she flies out —she has an exchange scholarship with which she escapes to America). The script, Sjöman's first, had little provision in it for cinematic treatment, an omission not repaired by the director. It owed whatever conviction it projected to the performance of Mai Zetterling and, to a lesser extent perhaps, to that of Alf Kjellin. Intelligent in its analysis, the film lacked all sense of life going on anywhere in places where people meet, talk, eat, work, or study.

Alskarinnan, written and directed by Sjöman, corrects the cinematic deficiency of the earlier film by throwing out virtually all the discursive content and giving a cinematographic summary of a dilemma not appreciably different, except that in this one the difficulty of Bibi Andersson's choice has been complicated by there being two suitors. One of them is married and unlikely to alter the status; the other is a drab youngster (Per Myberg) not forceful enough to be a very interesting problem, though we fail to understand why she regards him as any more inept than the older man, played by Max von Sydow as if he were a pastor in one of those lugubrious communities memorialized by Ibsen. In fact we never learn *who* he is precisely, and while it may not always be imperative to know the occupation of a character it might, in this case, help us to understand the secret of his charm, since this clearly can't be sexual. (At one point he dashes in for an assignation with Bibi, explaining breathlessly, "I've only got twenty minutes!" There wasn't a laugh in the house.) If there were enough content in this film to engage, we might say that the premise is outrageous: that it's important which of the two males this lightheaded and self-important teaser chooses. But the whole affair is so empty and the girl is so sketchily revealed that further speculation is stillborn. What remains are many handsomely mounted and syncopated shots, reminiscent of Bergman's middle period and of late Antonioni—a clean, well-lighted face swimming in rectangles as absolute as those of Mondrian, a train's express progress reflected, for no cogent reason, by its speeding chiaroscuro on a railroad-crossing barrier, Bibi contemplating a tank of tropical fish, presumably analogical.

The social levels of *Chans* (which means *Chance*) —Gunnar Hellström, director—are at least substantiated. Mainly they are circumscribed by the world of the *raggare* (i.e., the female Teddy boy?), that urban freak born of our time in every city of the West, its traits and costume no different in Sweden: the compulsive outsider, the I-hate-my-sex clothing (dirty hair, blue jeans, and a bust-molding T shirt for the distaff side), the pitifully histrionic toughness, the infantile illusion of being both photogenic and a deadly threat, the motorcycle as sublimation of crime and/or sex. The girl in *Chance* comes out of a detention home at the opening of the film and inscribes a circular route back to it—with some relief, one infers. We are given a flashback of how she was first seduced by a big, leering uncle, then we're off on a journey to Skane, in the south of Sweden, but I was never sure this wasn't part of the flashback and neither was anyone else I consulted whose language barrier is lower than mine. Eventually she gets to Stockholm, where she is slapped around by her gang associates, meets a young man of artistic bent and good breeding but gives neither him nor herself a chance to understand why she's doomed to stay in her rut; she gets dangerously involved with an élite circle of narcotic peddlers and is returned to the detention home for not reporting to the parole board.

The makers of this film, which is not, thank heaven, offered as Social Democratic party propaganda (unless they're getting too subtle for me, and if they're getting that subtle they'll earn no votes regionally), nonetheless seemed to fear that it wasn't going to be sensational without a fancy treatment. For the first fifteen minutes there's scarcely a shot which isn't tilted, raked, overheaded, or at doormat level, and the music imposes itself as immodestly. As of 1928 in Germany, it would have qualified as a work of art, with no continuity further. As Hellström gets into the thick of the narrative, however, he relaxes a little, never enough to let us relax, too, but sufficiently to allow reality to pound at us in very skillful closeups and brilliant inter-sequence cuts. The fact is that after a while actuality gets the better of the lighting experts and the scrupulous editor: they are unequal to the task of eliminating a great deal of sordid conviction that breaks through from the content.

There's an especially good close-up scene of the girl during sexual intercourse, an act to which she submits with a mixture of curiosity and of well-here-it-is-again-I-might-have-known. Unlike the famous *divertimento* in *Extase,* there's no removal of focus to photograph poetic correlatives: the camera doesn't leave the girl's face—for what this is worth as a milestone of realism. There's another moment when a "cokie" gives himself an injection, equally immediate, and just as disturbing to watch. What all this adds to, more than sadomasochism and the resolve to be frank at all costs, I don't know. I can't say it lacks drive and tenacity, but I'm not sure how much of it would seem probable to anyone outside Sweden. Personally, I don't doubt that the shabby-criminal fringe exists with much the same style as is shown in this film; yet as I watched it, conceding the plausibility of occasional scenes, I didn't really believe in it. I find all attempts at sub-social realism in the Swedish film fairly incredible—I think because film directors, who, being Swedish, must *urge* passions into being, take it all more seriously than the social principals would. If you are privy to this recognition, you are left with a disparity between the moral indifference of Swedish life and the moral insistence of those who try to give it an edge of damnation it doesn't ever express. Thus Hellström's film, which does grope for social verisimilitude at the only rung where emotion gets a foothold at all, remains on the whole as cold in its dynamics as in its sympathies. We're never given any reason to suppose that the girl could be rehabilitated save by a psychiatrist, which makes the conflict-elements of the story rather futile and one-sided.

Even so, Hellström gets under the skin of his subject, while photographing the skin to perfection. What's very surprising in a Swedish movie is the way the scenes between the girl and the young man of good family ring true. And the film offers a hostage for the future of the industry in the person of Lillevi Bergman, the most unaffected performer since Harriet Andersson came out of Söder. She's the real sullen, quiescently vital thing and she never *acts* during a foot of the way. What can be done with her before she acquires the range and style necessary for playing a human being is everyone's question, including her own. Wisely she's now taking drama training, which argues, besides shrewdness, a confession of limitations quite unusual in the young. If she assimilates training without being overpowered by it, she'll be a boon to Swedish films, badly in need of a youngster to replace their only present ingenue, Christina Schollin.

A short film *reklam* (i.e., advertisement) has been going the rounds of Swedish movie houses, whereof the "gimmick" is a mock-serious study of someone going quietly mad from typewriter noises, or something equally baleful supposed by the scenarist to afflict the nerves of the Swedish office worker. The climax of this little fable, always photographed with enhanced values and haunted features intensely within the close-up plane, is an echo-chamber voice recommending "Dis-pril!" (a local form of aspirin). *Siska,* another of those Independent Woman problem films from the Bergman stable, is a kind of full-length *reklam* of Dispril. Within a very short time you know that nobody in the film is suffering from anything more serious than a headache.

Script by Sjöman and Ulla Isaaksson; story, the same old—girl breaching her thirties who wants to belong to herself but suffers pangs sharp enough to make her try too hard to belong to someone else, too, and naturally picks men who are easy to reject when they get difficult. The ten-year-old daughter of a psychologist without a license for practicing depth psychiatry would find no surprises in the development and inconclusive conclusion of this film. *Siska* (a girl's name) is just as impeccably directed as *Alskarinnan*—by Alf Kjellin—and it submits Harriet Andersson to a trial by close-up re-actions which she undergoes with extraordinary resources for differentiation. To no avail. Siska's anti-male ambivalence is as over-charged as a Victorian defense of the attributes of feminism, which soon leaves us indifferent to the degree of self-understanding she acquires. The young man who is hopefully training her to bit and bridle already has woman problems (ex-wife and mother) to live down or see through. Regrettably for our undivided attention, he is played by Lars Ekborg—the face least likely to succeed with registrations of *Angst* or even with a moderate degree of tortured speculation. As usual, what we hopefully think of as *milieu* is resumed in a few gratuitous exchanges calculated to represent the world at large, one of them during a Stockholm subway rush hour, which no director of whatever ingenuity could succeed in making appear more than mildly distracting. Another, significantly, is enacted at a suburban cemetery.

Pan, or *Short Is the Summer,* as they call it here, is a co-production which goes to show that desperation is not the exclusive property of Swedish movie-makers. The director of this film is Danish, Bjarne Henning-Jensen; he filmed it on location in Norway with a half-Swedish, half-Norwegian cast, and he did nothing to alleviate the extreme improbabilities which characterize the plot of the novel by Knut Hamsun on which the film is based. If my recollection is sound, the novel had a somewhat mystical quality, achieved partly by virtue of Hamsun's not specifying his characters too naturalistically, partly by allowing narrative and nature description to carry more weight than dialogue. The setting is remote, the consequences of human encounter are violent. Lieutenant Glahn arrives at a rather primitive settlement on the Norwegian coast, craving restoration of his spirit in this wilderness. Before the summer is over—that Scandinavian summer which, according to all their novelists, playwrights, and film-makers, brings love and death as surely as it brings back wild geese—he has destroyed one woman, hardened the already adamant heart of another, and been responsible for the death of his own hunting dog, an English setter, the only rational, and the most beautiful, creature in the film story.

Hamsun's tone of remoteness helps, in the book, to reduce the paraphrasable absurdity of the plot. We accept it as we accept the world of Ibsen: intensity of frustrated human relationship becomes psychopathic for want of social liberation. The first thing Henning-Jensen did was to eliminate from the situation all contingencies which would preserve credence. He moved the period of the story from c. 1880 to our own time, thereby exposing the events to a merciless logic which is nonetheless ignored by all the characters involved. They behave as if it were impossible for them to leave their island and as if sexual choice were so limited and hedged by opportunity and convention that only violence could modify it. Nobody ever says the one sensible thing which would prevent a crescendo of misunderstanding from mounting to fatality. Since fatality is indispensable to the story as Hamsun wrote it, the impasse is ineluctable and, in its details, nonsensical. Even granted the willed perversity of contemporary Norwegians and Swedes far from the madding crowd, it's rather unlikely that a half dozen or so people, city bred for the most part, would be quite as untouched, for better or worse, by rational principles of conduct. The basic premise, however, on which the film's credibility is founded, is our consent that Jarl Kulle, as "Pan"-Glahn, is sufficiently Dionysian to be irresistible to every female within range of his invisible cloven hoofs. But it isn't personal prejudice toward Kulle which convinces me that

Glahn must be a pretty feebleminded kind of wilderness man when he can empty a gun into the air in the vicinity of a porous mountain-side and provoke an avalanche which, incidentally, buries one of the infatuated women in his life. If this dim-witted climax came from the Hamsun original—I don't now remember—no director-scenarist is under obligation to retain it.

Otherwise the coastal scenery, in color, is there to be appreciated, and so is Liv Ullman, a young Norwegian actress with a refresh-ingly naive personality who plays the rural wife summarily dis-patched by Glahn's misfire. (I don't think a Freudian reading helps the coincidence very much.) Personally, I loved that kinetic dog and I sympathized with Bibi Andersson's efforts to make sense out of a senseless and utterly selfish young woman, though I do think that Miss Andersson is far from life-prepared to portray the succes-sion of complex pigheads she is being forced into playing.

A film reporter here has recently drawn fire on himself for asserting that Swedish films could not only be made more inexpensively but also that they would be better if they weren't so well-made, so photographically flawless. The opposition knows enough to write him down on that score, but it hasn't the faintest notion of *why* Swedish films are, by and large, bad—assuming that they recognize them to be as bad as outsiders claim. If they did know, the self-knowledge might have long since improved the product. When composition and lighting are the only felicities in a film, there are few critics anywhere who will not hold that formal perfection is the *cause* of the film's insufficiency. Nobody of influence in Sweden is go-ing to arrive at the simple equation that their films have no life be-cause Swedish society has no life. Almost any Swedish director can make a film more expertly than Tony Richardson, but *A Taste of Honey* is a film about love. Swedes know nothing about love; they have made notable films about the death of love.

But there are particular as well as general pressures responsible for the crisis today. Ingmar Bergman, until lately the greatest asset of Sweden's film industry, is covertly recognized as its present great-est deterrent. His own films have been conceived and executed with unmistakable integrity (Mrs. Gilliatt has an unkind belief that when, in her opinion, he errs, he does so from perversity or because he's "intellectual"), but this integrity is a threat if by imperceptible stages it grades into fanaticism. There's a pronounced feeling among Swedish film-makers—never declared publicly, of course—

204 | *Vernon Young on Film*

that Bergman's tacit control of Svensk-Film's policy is in this way limiting. It's commonly believed that a director or scenarist at Svensk-Film who isn't going the Bergman way—and this definitely applies to Hellström—will go nowhere. The situation has its sardonic aspects. Jorn Donner, a political writer who has been trying his hand at film criticism, made a short film himself, not long ago, at the Svensk-Film studio. By protocol it had to be approved by Bergman. When looking at the film with Donner, so runs the tale, he suggested that a certain sequence in it be removed, it was too face-front static, like television (or sequences in Bergman's *Smiles of a Summer Night?*). Donner refused to comply and took himself to the newly reorganized Europa company. It sounds heroic, but one wonders what Donner would have done if Europa had not been there to welcome him.

What bearing *The Communicants,* Bergman's new film, may have on all this, we can't predict. If it's another masterpiece the circumstance will not alleviate the resentful depression which characterizes industry gossip. How many directors might be expected materially to alter the prospect in Sweden if scenarios were available and operation untrammeled is hard to say. Hans Abramson, Ake Falck, and Hans Lagerkvist have done good things on television; there's Gunnar Hellström, and there's Hasse Ekman, who lacks ideas but who has become an adroit technician. And there is Arne Mattsson, who is impressive when given material for which he has a passion (usually low-life and rural) ; in any other direction he gets lost. But it's altogether clear that fewer films of any note can be made in Sweden while the social life from which they must be inspired is so empty of value, so inhibited from any gratuitous expression of concern or of pleasure, and while no film artist as dedicated as Bergman is being developed who can *will* subject matter into film form. 1963

Films to Confirm the Poets

Drama is neither ritual nor show business, though it may occur in the framework of either one; it is poetry, which is neither a kind of circus nor a kind of church.

Susanne K. Langer: *Feeling and Form*

Elektra, a film of Michael Cacoyannis, opens with a ricochet of images unsurpassed, in the heroic mode of exposition, since the decade of the Soviet masters. Not a syllable of speech, only brazen sound, a sort of chthonic *musique concrète*—the gods grinding their teeth. Clytemnestra greets the returned Agamemnon outside the hilltop palace of Mycenae, graciously conducts him indoors to his bath, and promptly lassos him with a net, the easier for her lover to kill him with a trident. The poetic version closest in spirit, if not in imagery, is that of Robinson Jeffers in *Tower Beyond Tragedy,* where Clytemnestra's recital might have done duty as a preliminary shooting-script (allowing for Cacoyannis' having followed the oldest tradition in having Aegisthus do the actual killing—which we don't literally *see*) :

> He came triumphing.
> Magnificent, abominable, all in bronze.
> I brought him to the bath; my hands undid the armor;

My hands poured out the water;
Dead faces like flies buzzed all about us;
He stripped himself before me, loathsome, unclean, with
    laughter. . . .
I threw a cloak over him for a net and struck, struck, struck,
Blindly, in the steam of the bath; he bellowed, netted,
And bubbled in the water;
All the stone vault a-sweat with steam bellowed,
And I undid the net and the beast was dead, and the broad
    vessel
Stank with his blood.

Cacoyannis is less explicit, but he doubly intensifies the passage in his own way, crosscutting with short, nervously variable shots between the death struggle in the bath and the scene outside: the guards, the waiting attendants, the stripling Elektra fearfully hugging her small brother, while in her clairvoyant eyes horror contends with foreknowledge. In perhaps fewer than fifty images the prologue is achieved. An anonymous cry is swallowed by the hills and the low-ceiling heavens; Elektra still fiercely hugs the innocent Orestes and a circling hawk reigns over the isolate scene. Then the single word of the title appears on the screen—and the film "begins."

The subsequent killings (of Aegisthus and Clytemnestra) are even more oblique, in keeping with classical traditions: of Aegisthus' bad end we see only the induction, Orestes' provocation; but the sequel tells all we need to know and makes its own nocturnal pageant: flaming torches in the hills, and Elektra gloating over the body of Aegisthus. Clytemnestra is slaughtered in a hut, with interjected closeups of the shrouded sibyls who function as chorus writhing like outraged Furies: after the unseen deed we watch her supplicating hand relax into lifelessness as she crumples at Elektra's feet. Above everything to Cacoyannis' credit is the equilibrium he maintains—preserving as much of a ritualistic framework as is proper to the classical matrix while availing himself of the kind of poetry film alone can give: the irreplaceable feel of the *natural setting* (after all, if the *Oresteia* "took place" anywhere, this was its very landscape, strewn with white boulders and wind-troubled olive trees!) and the sense of *duration,* fatally and abruptly compressed or numbingly prolonged. With the assurance only a modern Greek, perhaps, can afford, Cacoyannis proceeded as if he'd scarcely heard of sanctions imposed by conventions of the amphitheater or by the clinical glossary of Sigmund Freud. Combining the narrative order of Aeschylus with that of Euripides, he made a film that never for a moment grovels in the dust of statues, never forsakes the dignity of indirection, never fails to convey the drama as at once memorial and actuality. He even brings off the choric feature with no damage to credulity; women of the fields and in the village street stand and cry out from within their individual griefs, or group themselves esthetically, obedient to the crucial subjects of gossip or local misfortune—as in reality they do today in southern countries—and in no film save one from Bengal have I seen people move so unaffectedly from speech to sung lamentation. The virtual development of *melos* is exemplified in this film: intonation becoming incantation, drums furnishing the accent, bagpipes (I think) extending the human pitch into eerier realms.

The principal actors carry out Cacoyannis' intentions with natural candor and a consistency of personal bearing, each of them *inside* the variant of his prototype, convinced, you feel, that he's responsible for his own fate, equally convinced that his responsibility is determined, as it is for the others. There's a moment of divination when Orestes (Yannis Fertes), after the murder of Clytemnestra, realizes how far Elektra herself has yielded to gratuitous vengeance, how irrevocably far he has followed her. It's only a flicker in the eye but it reveals the crisis of his soul. And as many times as I've heretofore tolerated the conventional stalling of the recognition scene, I was for once intimately and deeply stirred—and relieved, as if I had doubted its resolution. Quite the predominant figure is the Elektra of Irene Papas: she is *the* Elektra you'd be bound to expect, handsome and not ingratiating, a wife for no man; inexorably, to all appearance, the Lesbian, consumed from within by a banked-down fire which betrays itself, between outbursts, through the burning eyes and the abundant sultry mouth. Irene Papas doesn't rest on her native equipment: she feeds it with passionate and somber nuance.

The close of the film is as deserving of respect, for in the absence from it of a posed finality with trumpets and camera flourish telling you a great classic has just passed by, the director's unrelinquished act is illustrated: his adherence to the plausible spirit and the dour character of his design. It's all over but the haunting; vengeance has been won and the remorse follows. Elektra, charred but indestructible, is left to face the sudden hostile winds of community, and Orestes is a broken boy who can only turn and walk away over low, rocky hills into a blackened sky, not yet inhabited by Furies but

with room for them. Faithful Pylades trails behind; then, in a long
shot, Orestes stops and signals him to go back, back to the village
to look after Elektra. He walks away again, as the wind rises, and
that's how the film ends: just a few lonely creatures scattered un-
classically, with a crime between them which had once seemed
terribly necessary—and the landscape couldn't care less.

> . . . . *all the arts lose virtue*
> *Against the essential reality*
> *Of creatures going about their business among the*
>   *equally*
> *Earnest elements of nature . . .*
> Robinson Jeffers: "Boats in a Fog"

By reason of another species of beauty, that of paradox, we may
accept the figure of speech. For only from "the arts" themselves
could a poet have acquired the recognition that "essential reality"
is esthetic. If the real, on its own unedited terms, were simply waiting for a cinematographer to capture it and thereby render superfluous the virtue of art, the history of the newsreel alone would be
a prodigious anthology of great moments. "Creatures going about
their business"—automotive freighters on U.S. 66, boats in a fog,
pigeons on the grass?—are the nearest-at-hand phenomena for the
camera, and the most difficult for a film-maker to transmute so that
by contrast all *inventions* (which I presume to be Jeffers' distinction) "lose virtue." There are fewer masterpieces on film of the *real
thing* than of the imagined.

Kaneto Shindo's *The Naked Island* is a good example of the simple expedients to which a director will resort to improve his reality
and, so doing, fatally miss and not achieve art in its stead. Shindo
tried to commemorate the day-by-day existence of a peasant couple,
man and wife, stubbornly gleaning their livelihood from what Kip-
ling would have called an Altogether Uninhabited Island. To grow
crops in the barren soil they must fetch their water, a few buckets-
ful at a time, from another island; hence the principal rhythms of
their activity are, for the woman, those of rowing the boat and plod-
ding, always uphill from the water level, with two buckets strung
from a pole across her shoulders; for the man, sowing and watering
the rows of seed. Man and wife converse hardly at all, which puts
the burden of expression on the suspense of their slow, silent perpetual motion and on the plastic commerce of the tides, the light
and shadow, wind and rain, animal and bird life (almost none).
Drama is in the undertow: the heavy, monodic rhythm of this ele-

mental round, the gait and faces of man and woman, the measured footing, the concentration on not spilling the precious water. It's an imbecile life, this, so obdurately to inhabit the lowest level of effort, within eyeshot of a coastal society with manifold strata of conveniences. Yet it has the dignity of choice and will leave its own imprint. So long as Shindo keeps us inside the occupational cadence, its poetic autonomy is unquestionable. He didn't believe in its self-sufficiency, however, for he added a musical motif, and no harm would be done if this were barely orchestral, if it mingled with other motifs, came and went like a neap tide or a commuting gull. But he uses the *same* motif, over and over, unvarying, like an emperor's nightingale. Also, impressed by the muteness of his couple, he calls attention to his encouragement of it by permitting, on one occasion, a group conversation to get under way, then throttling down on it. Immediately we're made aware of *acoustics* and of the mixer behind the throne. Again, our fascination with this stoical pair, against all inward questioning of their wisdom, depends absolutely on there being no other world visibly available, as in Luis Buñuel's film of *los hurdos, Land Without Bread*. When the boy in Shindo's film catches a fish which the family takes to the Big City to sell and therewith celebrate—they "dine out," walk the streets, stare at television in a shop window—the force of their voluntary exile is vitiated; we are in the world of the travelogue, "Japan— Land of Contrasts"!

Using comparable, if richer, basic material, Vittorio De Seta hasn't missed—in three short films and a feature I've seen. This newcomer is stupefyingly the master of his source—the *real,* which he unhesitatingly enhances by all means at his disposal: flexible camera equipment, the color laboratory, dubbed music. And it works out as a form of grandeur, a life-curve effortless yet electrifying. Implicitly he depends on the survival of work and festivity in anciently founded villages where the traditional unity of work, song, and celebration—religious or no—is still intact. There is no schizoid gulf between the living ritual De Seta records or reenacts —in Sicily or Sardinia—and the incredible distinctness with which he dramatizes it. If your Madison Avenue friend, unprepared by French recommendations, emerges from the playhouse where he has seen *Bandits of Orgosolo* screaming, "But the *hero* is a flock of sheep!", pay no heed except to reprove him for calling an aggregate of sheep a flock, and see the film yourself. I saw it with a band of allegedly jaded bohemians who so far forgot themselves after this fantastic cycle of victimization and revenge (directed *and* photographed by the single man, De Seta) that they rose to a man (hyperbole) and vehemently clapped their tiny hands. De Seta miraculously urged a Sardinian shepherd and his small boy* to "act out" a crucial pattern of catastrophe and reprise which overtook their normally tranquil occupation and, as if it were as easy as lying, he rekindled a theme deeply reminiscent of the Old Testament—and incidentally mindful of *The Bicycle Thief*. All but occult in his photographing of nature—sheep flowing in forest moonlight like salmon under the surface of a stream; fanged rocks and scant bush-cover exposed to the merciless probe of the wheeling sun—De Seta's only peer is Arne Sucksdorff; if he strikes one as even greater than Sucksdorff it's only because, everything else being equal, man is for most of us a more prejudicial subject than the little foxes, a colony of terns, and the booming silence of waterfalls. Bergman screened the film privately for a nucleus of his personnel, and report goes that the company just sat staring in wild surmise—silent upon a pique in Solna—with enough power of speech finally to ask each other, "And just what are *we* doing?" Frankly, I think they're too close to Bergman to appreciate precisely *what* he is doing at present, but *vis-à-vis* the Swedish film at large, they might well ask! *Bandits of Orgosolo* is one of three superlative films released in 1962 (the others are *Elektra* and François Reichenbach's *Un Coeur Gros Comme Ça*), and Vittorio De Seta is the fourth film director of genius to appear in postwar Italy.

The third, Michelangelo Antonioni, has faltered at the summit—we hope not irrecoverably. If I have agreement that *The Eclipse* is the most disappointing film of the last year to come from an eminent director, perhaps the reader will acknowledge that if this film had not followed *L'Avventura* and *La Notte,* it would have been impressive. We know too well now what, with his special treatment, Antonioni is doing and how he is doing it. His point of departure—according to a *Film Culture* interviewer, the Lucretian theme, "The only thing certain is the existence of a secret violence that makes everything uncertain"—has been put through its last mutation; in *The Eclipse* Antonioni deprived us of that value of contrast which

---

*Footnote 1971. This taught me never to depend on secondary sources! I accepted this information from an American film magazine without question. Later, I was able to talk to Vittorio De Seta in Rome. Not in fact related, the shepherd and the boy *hated* each other. De Seta just managed to keep them sufficiently cooperative so that he could shoot the scenes they shared!

in the preceding films exalted the haunted surround—the infernal beauty of the Liparian islands, the dreamlike space and sound punctuations of Milan registered as freshly as a composition of Bartok or of Chirico and Mondrian, when the world was younger. His foremost artistic error in *The Eclipse* was the casting of Monica Vitti again; although she wasn't playing the same girl (this one is utterly empty and frivolously negative as she begins another "end of the affair"), she *appeared to be* the same girl: same beauty, same "naturalness." The stock market as symbol was overweighted and, for me, superannuated, because I couldn't help recalling Pudovkin's more terse, sardonic use of the institution in *The End of St. Petersburg* (1928) and its further comic rehearsal in a short film of Hans Richter (1929). Antonioni has perfected a treatment of space and silence; his control of it made it seem the only way of making a film (for want of knowing how to do likewise, Shindo lost a dimension in *The Island*). But *The Eclipse* is less convincingly an encore of the "metaphysical shudder," and without that one is left with the cold comfort of intellectually calculated footage—precise as a Bach exercise—and incidentally a point of view, toward socially futile creatures going about no business at all, uncomfortably evangelistic.

> *Europe belongs to Dante and the witches' sabbath, not to Newton.*
>
> W. B. Yeats

Among currently showing films there's nonetheless no reduction of emotional bounty so drastic as Robert Bresson's *The Trial of Joan of Arc,* a disconcerting failure of imagination that calls into question the principles if not the personality of the director. Robert Bresson is a self-conscious Catholic with an exceptionally austere conception of film-making. While I admire, without exclusively preferring, the art of *multum in parvo*, I have not always been convinced that Bresson's close-reefed sailing is inevitable to the channels he has picked. I suspect the rig may as likely be an exhibition of self-chastisement, like Samuel Beckett forcing himself to write in French to purge his language of ambiguous overtones. Since Beckett is an artist, this doesn't work any better for him than Stendhal's rationale; he once claimed the Napoleonic Code as his prose model. Cinematically, Bresson has achieved something like Stendhal's ambition and proves what a lousy idea it was to begin with. In his desire, perhaps, to avoid both *ritual* and *show business,* Bresson arrives at a reporter's desk in the police court. Or rather, his film suggests a performance at a charity bazaar given by a women's organization in Orléans (if such there be) for sending a deserving girl to a private school. The deserving girl—Florence Carrez—reads the lines of the historical Jeanne d'Arc, disinterred from the Rouen archives. M. Bresson, being a professional film-maker, was engaged to photograph the girl and not much more (we never see a whole building, even), mostly face-front, slabbed against a wall. For variation he cuts to an inquisitor and includes an "art" shot of an eye looking at Joan in her cell and whispered speculations, in English, about her sex life. At the stake, this Joan is no glorious martyr to her simple faith; she's a French-fried amateur with rather less expression than the woman at the box office who sold me my ticket. This is not an ordinary failure of movie-making, it's the consequence of driving a principle (neoclassic?) to a standstill. And for Bresson to have supposed he was contributing anything sufficiently vivid to the legend (we can scarcely rest with it as "history" by now) to modify Carl-Theodore Dreyer's film version of 1928 is conceit gone wild. To believe, in any case, that a deep-going traditional subject, protean in its possibilities, can be renewed with no emotional commitment, no décor, no taste of the hour or even of the century is simply intellectual perversion as willful in its fashion as the narcissism of Roger Vadim and the frantic hay of Jean-Luc Godard.

> *Who would have thought the old man had*
> *so much blood in him?*
> Macbeth

The socialist countries are finding out that the safe life (only a blueprint in their scheme, at best) is rarely a diverting subject for narrative art, that one more anti-Nazi film may tempt audiences to ask delicate counter-questions, and that the old-fashioned capitalist thrill from crimes of passion can't yet be liquidated for the New Poetics. Andrzej Wajda, a Polish favorite of liberals—having tried the sex-tease, Paris model, in *The Innocent Sorcerers* and attempted again the persecuted-Jew gambit in *Samson*—has made a movie for Avala Films in Yugoslavia from Nikolai Leskov's long short-story of 1865, *Lady Macbeth of Mtensk* (or *Minsk*), which once supplied the libretto for a Shostakovitch opera. The film is socially unconstructive, politically indifferent, and it caters to the animal in us. It's wonderful. In a provincial Russian village which looks like a medieval cattle compound (a church with minaret is sole spooky relief in the dust-blown monotony of the place), a concupiscent woman waiting for her absent husband, a village V.I.P., takes as her lover an itinerant and irrepressibly insolent farmhand, Serjosha I'll call him, no better than he should be—except as a lover. When her father-in-law finds them out, she poisons the old bastard (in the film, with surprising celerity, by putting candle meltings in his soup) and with the help of Serjosha she butchers her husband within an hour of his return. They bury him in the pigpen and briefly enjoy the fruits of their liberty and their fortune. Here there's a magnificent shot of them riding full tilt through the summer fields, recalling all the Tolstoy you ever read. Nemesis appears in the person of a spinster-faced sister of the dead husband (played by an intelligent actress—they're all Yugoslavs—with hands as musical as a Shankhar dancer's), towing her abominable boy who wants to be cut in on the inheritance. Obviously, this little monster must be dispatched, and I'll confess that when the new master of Minsk tries drowning him headfirst in a well, I was uneasily visited by images from the cartoons of Charles Addams. I might have been able to dismiss the rest of the film, wherein "Lady Macbeth" gnaws on her hand to extirpate the blood spots and the impudent Serjosha gets the quakes at the wrong moment, but I was spellbound by Mile Lazarevic as the miscreant lover, by the regal fleshiness of Ljuba Tadic (she would have been an even more potent Clytemnestra than Aleka Catseli), by the authentically grey-waste scenography, and by the unfaltering seriousness of Wajda's direction. It's melodrama, of course; no structure of belief in necessity gives it the transcendence of an *Elektra*—but it's superb film-making, visually indelible.

At home—i.e., in Poland—Jerzy Kawalerowicz has also repaired to the far distant and the long ago in search of the filmable, and produced *Matka Joanna* ("Mother Joan of the Angels") to redeem his feeble entr'acte, *Night Train*. The situation is euphemistically transcribed from the notorious outbreak of fantasy at the convent of Loudun, an episode that inspired Aldous Huxley's *The Devils of Loudun* and was in part the subject of a Danish film of 1922, *Häxan*. Kawalerowicz is the most sensitively dedicated of the Polish filmmakers. During a symposium on "The Human Cinema" (translated for *Polish Perspectives*, August–September, 1962), a shatteringly intelligent discussion of aims when compared with this sort of thing in the Advanced Countries, he answered the question, "What is the principal characteristic of our films?" with the statement, "A certain respect for man. Not love, but respect." An honorable admission, and *Matka Joanna,* no less than his *True End of the Great War* (1957), confirms the helpless compassion and the analytic temper revealed by it. I had gathered from a review by Boleslav Michalek that this film was too polished (no pun intended) for the full release of its emotional content. This was not my experience: pictorially it was not more formal than the asperity of the setting (an early Gothic cloister in an open-view wilderness) would logically dictate. To be sure, Kawalerowicz spends little time on the social periphery—he doesn't "fill in"—working instead close up to Matka Joanna and her "possession" by the Devil. This exclusiveness tends to concentrate the film with almost theater intensity on the prioress herself, her alternating seizures and recantations, and on the dialectic of a priest's struggle with her crisis and his own resulting anxiety. Joanna is played, devastatingly, by Kawalerowicz' wife, Lucyna Winnicka—such acting with the *eyes* I've not seen excelled—but the more important figure is the father, irresistibly tempted to assume whatever aberration of body and soul has subverted the woman. He takes his casuistry to a rabbi (Mieczyslaw Voit plays both men), who snorts in effect, "You think *you* have had experience of the Devil? Let *me* tell you something on that subject, my friend!" From here to the horrifying dénouement, the film drives home what I take to be its unutterable thesis, for the veracity of which the Poles are well qualified to vouch: evil cannot be abolished; it can only be transferred.

> *Now his wars with God begin,*
> *At stroke of midnight God shall win.*
> W. B. Yeats

*The Communicants** might easily warrant the accusation that at last Ingmar Bergman has confused drama (on film) *about* the Church with drama *as* church. The accusation won't come from me. I think *The Communicants* is no end depressing, and I can understand that few friends of mine are willing to take the subject as seriously as Bergman: the secondary subject, that is, for the film is plainly about people suffering—to a degree anyone else is at liberty to consider morbid or in the service of something he may feel is in excess of the amount of anxiety engendered. That's as may be. One

*Released in the U. S. with the title *Winter Light.*

man's Mede is another man's Persian, as S. J. Perelman has reminded us. I'm not easily harrowed by Bergman these days, but I'm
ready to call *The Communicants* a masterpiece. Bergman is the only
practicing director who can make an eloquent film from a rag, a
bone, and a hank of hair. Bresson can't. Antonioni can't now. Bergman can. Everyone (well, most of the "critics," let's say) thought he
had done so with *Through a Glass Darkly*. I stand on my previously
forwarded objections: that in the earlier film Bergman failed to distinguish between the necessarily arid and the factitiously tedious,
that he went too far outside civilized sensibility; and that he evaded
his own truths with a highly specious parable. *The Communicants*
is the film people thought he then made; there's faultless and almost
intolerable harmony here between the major theme—God is silent
—and the environment. Within a span or hollow of time little more
protracted than the running time of the film, the pastor of an area
(you can't call it a community) in north central Sweden presides
over Communion for a congregation of nine, is asked to comfort a
man on the brink of suicide with faith he doesn't himself experience,
confesses to the woman who loves him that he loves neither her nor
anything save his dead wife, listens wearily to plaintively mumbled
burdens or to inarticulate fervor with a face of crumbling stone, and
three slate-grey graceless hours later begins another service of High
Mass with only one auditor—the woman he has tried to cast into
outer darkness. "Holy, Holy, Holy," he announces. "God is
almighty."

Like Conrad's captain in *The Secret Sharer,* Bergman has tested
his craft with the ultimate strategy, sailing perilously near to a
headland, with only a bobbing hat to assure him of the human trace
he has all but repudiated and submerged, full fathom five. The intimate agonies of three or four people fill an hour and a half with a
nagging simulation of eternity. Nothing in this exiguous world is
more present than the close-up, tormented face; the few alternative
images remain on the eyeballs and in the tympani like the hallucinations of a man in solitary confinement: a Lubeck altarscape or a
baroque pulpit glimpsed in an otherwise unadorned church; the
feverish clamor of a dammed-up river under a pewter sky when the
dead man is carted away; a key to the toilet door in the schoolhouse, absurdly notable, labeled *pojkar* (Boys).

Bergman could lay claim to genius for no other achievement than
wringing from Ingrid Thulin such deeply dredged pain and exaltation. For no one else has she given such a performance; for no other

director could she so strip herself of all aids to glamor and drain her poor native capability to find at the bottom these dregs of an uncompromisingly authentic expression. Unprecedented in the history of film, if elephant-memory serves, is the juncture at which she talks in mercilessly held closeup for what seemed to my unclocked sense well over four minutes. In English-language distribution, with subtitles imposed, this may well resemble an animated passport photo; in its pristine form it's excruciating. But by now it's surely not contestable that Bergman knows unerringly how far he can ask any actor to go, how much more he can dig from their already excavated talent. Everyone in this film is better than he has been under anybody's direction: Gunnar Bjornstrand as the doubting Thomas (when life does terrible things to you, said Dostoievsky, you do terrible things to others) ; Alan Edwall, the crippled sacristan whose secular apprehension of time convinces him that he suffers more than Christ did on the cross; Frederik Blom as the hired organist who performs a modest miracle of his own by converting the five barley loaves of his tippling into a perennial repast of facetiousness; Max von Sydow as Jonas (Jonah?) , the terrified fisherman drowned by his own irredeemable solemnity while begging to be told he can walk on the waves. . . . I think I've earned the right to add in conclusion that the film is not without relevance to Bergman's personal case: a pipeline to God, maybe, who doubts his own character as chosen medium, despises those who light his candles and want to believe in his infallibility, and may be left at the last murmuring the ancient texts with a single abused believer for all audience.   1963

One Man's Film Festival

The 24th at Venice, 1963

Preface. These notes on the 24th International Film Festival at Venice last August–September are offered with the awareness that my view of the occasion was indubitably colored by the physical circumstances under which I attended, and on the supposition that *Hudson Review* readers would in any case be more receptive to an attempt, however personal, at conveying the ambience of such an occasion than by an effort to rehearse dispassionately the content of thirty or more films, most of which they'll never see—and should not if I know what's good for them.

Subject-object. Clarifying data are called for if I expect the reader to appreciate the consternation with which, from time to time, the ensuing *obiter dicta* may be animated. At the Palazzo Cinema, within two weeks, thirty new films were on view; twenty of these were submitted or invited *in concorso*, i.e., to compete. Concurrently there was a showing of retrospective films (of Max Linder, of Buster Keaton, and of various Soviet Russians, 1924–1939). Other recent films were offered to the insatiable, ex officio, at a local Lido cinema; these were usually award-takers from less celebrated festivals—Locarno, Karlovy Vary, etc. Altogether, if you had been intent on not missing an item of this abundance, you would have been required to see sixty films in fourteen days! Fortunately for my concentration, to say nothing of my mental health, I had in the recent past (just love that term) seen over half of the retrospectives, and I passed up many of the remainder in favor of grabbing a sandwich. Nonetheless I discover, after incredulous recount, that I saw thirty-five (35) films in the fortnight. Of those in competition I missed only one, *Tom Jones* (regrettably).

Predication. A film festival is no place for a film critic. I write that more in sorrow than in anger. And with no ingratitude toward the organizers of the Venice affair nor toward the incredibly accommodating Press Office staff. This is not a glad-hand parenthesis. I'm convinced that here, as elsewhere, the social and commercial aspects have obscured the loftier intention. For the committee that designs the festival events, the purpose is to exhibit work in progress, an aim intelligently substantiated in the catalogue (edited by Luigi Chiarini, if I'm not mistaken, and a more valuable contribution to film bibliography than many with greater pretensions). For film-makers who have been invited to participate, the festival is a contest and/or a trial of nerves. For the dealers who spend much of their sour time elsewhere saying that Art doesn't pay off, it's frequently Big Business. For the journalist who is accustomed to reporting quantity from the top of his head to meet deadlines, it's News. But anyone who arrives at a festival with some such tag in his mind as "The best that's been thought and said in the world" or "Let's see how these films stand up to the Tintorettos" will shortly discover what he should have already known—that if in any company a critic is a fifth wheel, at a film festival he resembles one of those importunate skeletons in the old Dance-of-Death engravings, reminding commoners and queens alike of their mortality. Even this figure over-rates his importance in the scene. The point is that a film festival is no place for disinterested scrutiny and judgment, or at least it's not an occasion when discussion can be shared on such a basis. There's no *time* for reflection, the atmosphere forbids it, one's acquaintances are embarrassed by it. Everybody is on the make—for a story, for self-aggrandizement, for a contact or a contract. For most "film people," whether or not their job is to write about film, movie-making seems to be a competitive sport. For them, the value of the individual film is not the quality of the experience it yields but its rating in a kind of Grand National—an arbitrarily decided finish line, and hurdles to clear—wherein the current favorite is the director who has most adroitly surpassed his contemporaries at being contemporary—or is ahead by a neck.

The setting. I'll confess that I compounded the attendant pressures at the 24th by committing two strategic errors: living in Venice instead of on the Lido and making a glutton of myself with the program set before me. (One of these is a deadly sin.) To commute daily in those murderously overladen bump-and-grind *vaporettos* during vindictively humid weather, to resist day and night, night and day, *noise noise noise,* to attempt as many press conferences as would give one a fair idea of what transpires thereat, to make appointments with sundry people who don't show up, for conversation which is usually fruitless if they do—all this is the quintessence of instability (it if can be said that instability has a definable essence), no ground on which to base an objective report, whatever that may be! . . . In the wake of the matter, with the amphibious city still rocking beneath my feet, I must nonetheless acknowledge a kind of esthetic consistency to seeing motion pictures—by their nature infirm, dissolving, transitory—in this terraqueous *ambiente.* For Venice is as insubstantial as it is imposing, a beguiling labyrinth everywhere resistant to continuously lucid apprehension. And just as one struggles there to keep in the mind's eye a clear, single unit of scenography to prevent one's sense of the place from leaking away in a montage of interfluent arcades, *loggiati,* humped bridges, constricting alleys, sunset-tinted finials, bobbing gondolas, and incessant upheavals of the insolent, trash-laden sea, even so at the film festival one makes hourly repair of self-control and vigilance in order to salvage from the inexhaustible flow of images, sounds, and meretricious substitutes for vision whatever moments will uphold one's conviction that a film is potentially a work of art and that a work of art is a structure of the human imagination. "Man is a reed," I would tell myself doggedly every day at five as I reached for the double Scotch without which I could have no longer sustained either observation or courtesy—"the frailest thing in nature, it says here, but he's a *thinking* reed. . . . Hold on to that."

Salient impressions.

1. This was a very Italian event—not so idiotic a tautology as it may appear! Italian films on the contemporary program outnumbered those from any other country, and in two of them the setting

was Venice itself, an overlapping circumstance that tended to enforce, naturally enough, the moral solidarity of the largely Italian audience. There were three Italians on the seven-man jury, which meant that if these three were in agreement they had only to convince one of the remaining dissenters. I'm not privy to what went on behind those doors; I only know that almost before the first screening of *Le Mani sulla Citta* (*Hands on the City*) was over, the conclusion was foregone. (The festival had three days yet to run, but only one film remained to be judged *in concorso*, Martin Ritt's *Hud*.) Frankly, I'm inclined to believe that Rosi's film would have taken the Silver Lion without the Italian influence, offered as the single explanatory factor by many who didn't approve the decision. In the absence, otherwise, of a single film so distinguished as to overwhelm all lesser argument, the choice was predictable. For there's no gainsaying the fact that critical consensus, internationally, is unable to resist the intimidating appeal of film as a political weapon. On the Italian side, there were special incentives: the popularity of the communist director, Francesco Rosi; the closeness of his subject (collusion between politicians and business interests in the ruthless promotion of mass-housing schemes) to national feelings of indignation; above all, the Italians' love of public debate, *fortissimo*. I find most remarkable the inference of a fluctuating principle of selection, year by year, since social utility could scarcely have been the criterion by which, e.g., *Marienbad* was honored two festivals ago. Evidently each jury is on its own. This may not be an unwise policy; specified principles have a way of hardening into standardized assumptions. Anyway there are so many counter- and auxiliary awards given, at Venice or elsewhere, that sooner or later justice is done.* (Not to all. *Do not presume. One of the thieves was hanged. . . .*) Rosi's film was a shrewd and probably accurate analysis of political alignments in a hypothetical crisis. As an exercise in forensics, it left little to be desired. Whether or not it was creative film-making was a distinction nobody cared for less than Rosi himself; he made that clear at his conference.

---

*Some instances: *A Sunday in September* (Sweden, Jorn Donner) and Chris Marker's *Le Joli Mai* shared First Film awards; *Il Terrorista*, a first work of Gianfranco de Bosio, received the City of Venice Prize; an association of critics, based in Vienna, voted Alain Resnais' *Muriel* the best festival film; and shortly after the close of the festival, Ricardo Fellini (brother to Federico) , whose *Stories on Sunday* was suddenly disclosed as having delighted Japanese observers, was invited to make a film in Japan.

2. Our age is desperately in love with its own collective image. This familiar and inescapable conclusion was again forced upon the awareness of a critical viewer by a nucleus of films in the festival repertory—they comprised the most popular—exploiting the rage for topical identification. *Cinéma vérité* is the chic term for a new disintegration of style which has taken place everywhere in misguided, if well-intentioned, emulation of certain young French masters of the New Wave. The incorporation of urban actuality, caught on the run, as it were, within a fictional context (*Jules et Jim* or *Cleo*), or the frank use of the real as if it were fiction (*Un Coeur Gros Comme Ça*) apparently looks easy to a host of enfranchised film-makers who haven't the verve or the nuance of Truffaut and Agnes Varda, or the visionary perception of François Reichenbach. In this pursuit of a new personalizing of the documentary method, there is wide recourse to the zoom lens, the concealed camera or microphone, the informal tracking shot, and many other devices. The end result is neither personal nor progressive; it returns the art of the film to a muddled compromise with the newsreel and the TV interview, and we are asked to accept, as revolutionary, films that tell us nothing more about the fragmented life which daily surrounds us than the latest copy of *Paris-Match* or *Life*. Among films at the 24th which more or less fitted this category were *In Capo il Mondo,* an expressionist autobiography shot in Venice by a newcomer, Tinto Brass; *Le Joli Mai* of Chris Marker—a roving nonstory film of a season in the French capital; *La Belle Vie,* first feature of Robert Enrico (you've probably seen the long-short he made of an Ambrose Bierce tale), allegedly the story of an Algerian war veteran's discontent but mainly an actuality editorial of international violence; *Dragées au Poivre*—it means something like *confections,* I gather, and was a parody by Jacques Baratier of practically everybody else's film-making (i.e., of everybody fashionable). Shirley Clarke's *The Cool World* is related to *cinéma vérité*, although the descriptive use of tracking background shots, not directly involved in the story line, may have been suggested by the Danish film made in South Africa, *Dilemma.* Cesare Zavattini's *Mysteries of Rome* (shot by a dozen camermen—none of them introduced to each other, I'd hazard) was a glib mixture of the French process with left-over attitudes from early *neorealismo,* in the creation of which Zavattini himself was once the glorious pioneer. Why at this stage (either of his life or of his career) Zavattini

should suppose there's anything novel or even diverting in the *voyeur* tactics his cameramen employed to surprise lovers on the banks of the Tiber or to interview whores and stripteasers is the only "mystery" purveyed by his film. I was fairly bored by Chris Marker's interminable vignettes of the everyday, but by contrast with those of Zavattini they were various and often lyrical. The Rome-in-a-day film showed us a city in which there is no intellectual activity, no responsible private life with vivid content, nobody performing fruitful work, no theater, no music above the jukebox level, no art galleries, no feeling of history except in a gratuitous shot of Santa Maria della Pace by night—as who should say, "That's the lousy past, labeled FOR TOURISTS ONLY." Perhaps I'm being naive. Most people in the know here were ready to assure me that Zavattini's emphasis on the poor, the outlaw, the sick, and the exploited was neither an outcome of the limited view nor an expression of Christian charity; it was a piece of calculated political opportunism.

Louis Malle's film, *Le Feu Follet* (literally *Fatuous Fire*, which may present something of a challenge to foreign distributors) * was in one respect affiliated with *cinéma vérité:* it employed the concerto form (one soul moving through an exterior world in which it can find no solace) but far more purposively than Enrico's *La Belle Vie*, for instance. Malle has taken some curious directions since he came up for air some years ago from Cousteau's *The Silent World*— he was one of its principal cinematographers—and I've always followed him with confidence, even through the terminal footage of *The Lovers* and of *Private Life;* for when he's in control of his material throughout a film, there's not a more intelligent director in the Paris School. *Le Feu Follet* is under control: a skillfully modulated film on a perilously morbid subject—the last hours of a dying alcoholic, as he persuades himself that none of the solutions arrived at by his friends are valid for him. What Malle has, and many of his younger contemporaries with Balzacian ambitions are in need of, is a *precise* sense of the social milieu engaged at any moment. The others either ignore half of society (usually the polite half, not because it's less viable but because it takes more subtlety to discover in it what is cinematically effective)—or believe they're capturing a wealth of significance by dropping in for five minutes to borrow a cup of sugar. Furthermore, Malle's fluency in this case doesn't run away from the inceptive point of view; the film is unfailingly guided

---

*Footnote 1971. Idiomatically, it means *will o' the wisp.* The American title was *My Life Is Mine.*

by a controlling consciousness—and I mean Malle's, primarily, not the protagonist's. Now, this is exactly what the extreme members of the *vérité* group want to reject, in the belief that they're freeing themselves from a limiting convention. Their own method is the more limited, however, since it sacrifices discrimination for multiplicity. At best it makes gains in energy, and that's unarguably the principle through which the film medium is renewed. But energy in itself will never invest a film with distinguishing value; only insight, under control, will do that.

An incidentally exciting failure at the festival, pertinent to the subject I'm touching lightly, was Kurosawa's *High and Low* (I believe that's the American-release title). Here was a film loaded with energy and certainly not lacking in insight; but at some point in the conception, or perhaps during production, Kurosawa tried to say too many things and in too many different ways. The first third of the film, theatrically if not cinematically expert, raised an ethical problem, which might well have occupied the whole film. Abruptly he solved the problem, and then came a fascinating section of pure detective story, no less masterful than Hitchcock at his old best. After a flight-and-pursuit climax wherein the teeming life of Tokyo was more sensuously present than Paris has been in any New Wave film I know of, Kurosawa changed tone again for a final and terrifying confrontation with a nihilist criminal, as if he were trying to warn us of the insensate hatred at the core of our expanding city of mass-man.

Between the acts. The press conference can be a diverting escapade. The unawarded performer in this comedy at the 24th, *designato in concorso,* was an American girl from Trieste, required to translate Italian questions for a director who could handle only French—or vice versa—then translate the answers and often, to be obliging, ask if anyone needed a further translation of both question and answer into English—or Swahili. Remember this at your feasts when you coldly read a stupefying utterance purported to have issued from the mouth of an artist justifying his existence before the Venice tribunal. . . . Not that stupefying utterances weren't uttered. I'll vouch for Joseph Losey's because I had no difficulty in understanding him. His syntax, I mean. Some paradoxical undertone of his argument eluded me, leaving me baffled and shaken as if I had just seen his film. In fact I had. Losey, defending the catastrophe which some few of us insisted had overtaken that film (*The Servant*) at about the two-thirds mark, first tried the Robbe-Grillet strategy of implying that the ambiguity was too sacred to be defined except by the individual observer. (The movie is you, dear reader, *you*.) Soon he was protesting that he had made a very *moral* film and I don't think any of us was ruffled by that admission. But in response to I-didn't-hear-what controversial question (everyone talking simultaneously), there he was, asking bitterly (I thought he was going to cry), "Do you know what it's *like* to be a *servant?*"— which, Lord love us, was the first inkling any of us had that "the servant," depicted in the film as a fairly unmitigated rotter, was secretly Mr. Losey's hero! . . . This was *not* my favorite moment. Too painful. I preferred the inscrutability of the Japanese delegate who, upon being asked by an Austrian fellow viewer why the four fisher folk (in Kaneto Shindo's *The Man*), dying of starvation in a drifting, rudderless boat, didn't try to fish, replied with impeccable seriousness: "If they had done so, the film would have had a radically different ending."

Conclusions. Not general conclusions; I've already incorporated those. Here I want to pay brief attention to those films at the 24th I'm likely to recall favorably hereafter. . . . I'm no unqualified believer in a Golden Age of the Silents, yet I'll concede that there was more cinematic art in the retrospectives than in the parallel program. To my taste for wonder, the greatest film shown during the festival was *Salt for Svaneti,* made in the wilds of the Caucasus by M. Kalatozov, 1929–1930. The substance of this magnificent documentary poem was the fantastic ritualism employed by a feudal community in response to a weird phenomenon of nature that threatened its existence.* (Present-day Russia was represented *in concorso* by two characteristically boring products of the Soviet, which has eliminated the backward ceremonies of life and death available to Kalatozov. I'll not belabor the irony.) . . . If I now took up space for restating the familiar genius of Buster Keaton or for praising the unfamiliar genius of the no less ingratiating Max Linder, I'd have to sacrifice indispensable paragraphs of tribute to a handful of contemporary film-makers who deserved more tribute than they collected.

Neither *Le Feu Follet* (mentioned previously) nor *Billy Liar* is in desperate need of recommendation. Malle's film received the Special Prize, and the popularity of *Billy Liar* was already proven

---

*I'd like to acknowledge my debt to Jay Leyda's *Kino* for having alerted me to the probability that this film would be a momentous discovery. So far as I know, it was heretofore unseen by any Western audience.

in pre-festival release. I was gratified to see that Schlesinger, who re-created the Beastly Life with such uncompromising fidelity in *A Kind of Loving* that the reflection was as unbearable as the image, is not averse to a more oblique interpretation of the same subject—and with no loss of asperity. *Billy Liar* is inventive, extremely funny, and intensely painful.

Il Demonio, an *opera prima* of Brunello Rondi, was the only Italian film I found enthralling. Preceded by a scholarly testimonial to its veracity, it purported to reenact the "recent" persecution, in a Lucanian village, of a young woman (no doubt less attractive by far than Daliah Lavi) under the stress of an erotic obsession and hallucinations. The villagers' methods of exorcising her "devils" included rape, setting fire to her family's house, and stoning her from the precincts. She was finally stabbed to death, after ecstatic sexual consummation, by the object of her desire, the man whom she had succeeded in demoniacally luring from his connubial bed at midnight. The film was dismissed from serious consideration by non-Italians, who didn't believe that the events depicted could have taken place, and by Italians (to judge from many derisive outbreaks in the audience), who were nervously afraid that they might have. It would be interesting to see *Il Demonio* in Naples, for instance, where the presentness of the past is more familiar to all and where the audience would not be inclined to treat as a joke the less violent curiosities of the film, such as the rural wedding ceremony. I'm not troubled by the possibility that Rondi's film was a "fiction." The here-and-now boys tell us that a primary function of film is to show us how people relate to each other. One way they've related, time out of mind, is by expelling from their midst, with barbarous initiations, those who fail to stay put in the common dimension. I was persuaded by the film; I admired its tautly edited treatment of horror, the intensive photographic style, the sparing use of cogent music.

I liked the two Spanish entries. Juan Antonio Bardem contributed a melancholy chronicle of a long-alienated, middle-aging couple in a stagnant town, infused momentarily with a breath of life brought to them by a visiting French nightclub dancer (played by Corinne Marchand—*Cleo*). The breath stirs them without relieving them: they indulge futile hopes of escape, they expose each other to embittered recriminations. The dancer leaves, alone; their life resumes as before. Hence the title: *Nunca Pasa Nada.* If this sensitive, constrained "chamber music" hadn't the kind of defining power which

Antonioni or Bergman has bestowed on comparable situations, it was all the same a noteworthy essay on the saddest subject there is: illumination glimpsed too late. The other Spanish item was a comedy, *El Verdugo*. Luis Berlanga's preceding films have been rather labored, and too broadly acted by their principals. The improved tone exhibited in this one can safely be attributed to Italian participation; the leading player was Nino Manfredi, one of Italy's finest comics in the unobtrusive mode, and Ennio Flaiano was credited among the writers. The scenario entertains a highly sardonic premise: that the only way José Luis can support his Carmen in marriage *and* in a new apartment is to accept promotion from burying people to killing them. In short, he must exchange his respectable but commonplace job of undertaker's assistant for the prestige post of official executioner, which will be left open upon the retirement of his father-in-law. In the last brilliant scene, while José's first client, a condemned man, marches with stoical unconcern to his death, the executioner himself has to be dragged, half-fainting, supported by four guards, cajoled and soothed, on his way to the site of his new operations. "It's always like this the first time." "You won't feel a thing, it's all over very speedily." I heard at least one cloud-cuckoo member of the press dismiss the imputation that there might be any political overtones to this film.

The Golden Fern (*Zlate Kapradi*—Czechoslovakia) was easily the most beautiful film shown in competition at the 24th, and I hope I'm never so up to date as to regard beauty as a disqualifying attribute. Jiri Weiss, having read a fairy tale to his infant daughter, was moved to combine it with imagined aspects of life under the imperial regime of the Habsburgs. The resulting combination is caviar to the pragmatists. (It's worthwhile to note here, for reasons which will shortly disclose themselves, that the tale is by a contemporary Czech writer, Jan Drda, who once wrote resistance-movement scenarios.) Here's the fable in outline: A young shepherd, pressed into army service against the Turks, vows never to forget his hamadryad wife, whom he had invoked from the forest by stealing a magic fern. Lesanka, the wife—named *Sylvanie* in the French subtitles— weaves an enchanted shirt for him, and with the help of this talisman he is rapidly promoted for his bravery in battle. Thereby he comes to the lethal notice of the general's daughter (a handsome Medusa reminiscent, especially in her preference for horses, of Strindberg's Miss Julie). For her, and secretly, but with the understanding that her influence will release him to his waiting Lesanka

(Daphne? Eurydice? Penelope?), the shepherd-officer accomplishes two impossible tasks—the theft of a horse and of a necklace from the camp of the Grand Vizier. By then he has transferred his devotion to the new arbitress of his fortunes; before attempting his third mission, the theft of the Vizier's nightingale, he discards the protective shirt. He gets the nightingale, but his escape miscarries. Discovered by his officers as he lies wounded, in the Turkish costume he has donned for disguise, he is sentenced for treason, and in the unyielding presence of the general's daughter he is drummed and saber whipped from the regiment (one of many superbly edited crescendoes in the film). What's left of him gets back to his woodland home. In the closing sequence, as the camera rises slowly to the treetops, we hear him calling in vain for his Lesanka, who has been reclaimed forever by the resentful spirits of the forest.

Those in the festival audience deprived of their prose evidently paid scant attention to the poetry with which they were asked to put up instead and were therefore no reliable witnesses to a flexibility of style that consistently enhanced every facet of the subject. The nature scenes—now real, now refracted—distilled the ancient sense of magic in forests and flowered pastures; the hero's escapades at the Vizier's camp were shot and edited with a summarizing fairy-tale economy that rightly suspended one's disbelief, yet with sufficient logic of selected detail to satisfy a degree of probability. In the absence of any other laurels for the film, Dana Smutna (the general's daughter) might have been honored, at least—if only for just *being!* Her performance was a lesson in perfect tempering: the power never insisted on, the disdain never too explicit, the promise never premature. (Apropos of nothing save the inane connective tissue of things, I find that Smutna means *sad.*) ... Not surprisingly, I was informed that the style of this film was too traditional—by which I'm to understand it wasn't shot *à la* Godard or Resnais or Rouch? More grievously, it wasn't "relevant." ... God give me patience, relevant to *what?* How many among us have not been near whipped to death for discarding their shirts to catch nightingales for the general's daughter?

1963

The Italian Film:
Left Hand, Right Hand

What's happening to Italy today is as neatly exemplified by Dino Risi's film *The Easy Life* as by any recent export from Cinecittà. The original title is to the point: *Il Sorpasso* (*Overtaken on the Road*). For Italians—enough of them to confer on this breezy film the suggestion of a parable—have been overtaken, forever. Bruno, an extrovert of unbridled proportions, is at the wheel, with a musical horn, and he's out for mindless pleasure. Roberto, in the film a "shy" law student (not a conception to have taxed anyone's ingenuity), hearing the siren voice of the claxon, is seduced into accompanying Bruno on a twenty-four-hour journey to Samarra. By turns frightened, confused, annoyed, envious, and thrilled, Roberto—the unwilling passenger—is finally, by his own consent, sucked into the rage for acceleration—"*Drive faster,* Bruno!"—and, as a consequence, destroyed. The film is effective rather than definitive; its "implication" has no concealed nuances and can be swallowed whole without rumination. Taken strictly as a narrative, it would have been even more effective if the fatal trajectory had not been broken for so long a social detour. As it is, the detour, revelatory but expendable, breaks the tension necessary to the last crescendo. Risi never quite regains his initial beat of premonition, the gathering sense of a pulsating joy-drive into disaster. When the disbelieved-in moment does arrive, it has the shattered rhythm of an anticlimax.

So it seemed to me. For reasons of another kind *Il Sorpasso* missed fire in Italy, if one of the more profitable films of last year can fairly be described as having missed fire. However, I presume that Risi had *tried* to point a grave object lesson, with enough skill to bring this off within the convention of tragicomic suspense. In which case I don't know whether to assert that the Italian audience (at large) was 'way ahead of him or 'way behind him! On that audience, in any case, the pathos of Roberto's fate was lost, and with it what we must believe was the directive point of the film. Italians who thronged to see *Il Sorpasso,* again and again, didn't give a hang *what* happened to Roberto! They loved Bruno! Bruno is what every back-street and back-province Italian wants to be: a high-speed versatile egomaniac, always at the wheel and never at a loss, a cynosure at the ping-pong table, on the dance floor, in a speed boat, and on a diving board. Bruno is in fact a prototype, by way of Via Veneto, of what our old friend Sheldon once defined as the *somatotonic,* which, as embodiment of a mass ideal, seems to outnumber and outlast all other envied categories of man in our time. And there is some justice in the mob's adulation of Bruno. He has vitality on his side, the kind that shows, and Roberto hasn't. Bruno, the film version, is equipped with the advertised weapons of success—an unending supply of adrenalin, histrionic talent, unanswerable comebacks, inexhaustible cash, and *women* on whom to spend it. We're overfamiliar with him. Risi and his script-writers didn't invent him. But with the help of Vittorio Gassman, who played Bruno with untiring adroitness and something murderously close to fascination, they projected an irresistible variant at a strategic Italian moment, at the hour of boom (relative, of course), on a day of reckoning with the inevitable affirmation mass Italy was bound to make, when given half a chance to become as badly civilized as the examples we have provided—and with malevolent resources of its own.

The sequel, on the business front, is relevant. Delighted with the outcry for Barabbas, the producers of *Il Sorpasso* promptly retained the scenarists, rehired the same leading actors (Gassman and Jean-

Louis Trintignant), and secured the clumsy services of a director unknown to me (or to anyone, I think), Mauro Morassi. The sacrificial anecdote was again attempted under the title *Il Successo*. Having no heart for it, the script-writers put their minds on it; Gassman worked twice as hard with a character half as plausible and not at all personable, and the result was a crudely packaged and fraudulent reprise, offering the bait of Gassman-as-heel together with an unconvincing moral doom by which he is supposedly overtaken. For all I know, this movie was as lucrative as its predecessor. Gassman has already been featured in two more films (one directed by Risi) that further obscure or denature whatever critical asperity had been originally intended by *Il Sorpasso*, while preserving without equivocation the ingratiating force of Bruno-More-or-Less. And I'm certain that many more of those melodic claxons have been sold in Italy in the last six months than ever before.

That commercial film-makers should exploit as an emulative figure of fun the very character they had set up as a feigned object of their moral disapproval will shock none but the exaggeratedly naive. Such opportunism all but constitutes the history of the large-scale film industry. That Italy is unrivaled today in all the venal directions of film production and promotion will be news only to the out-of-touch who still equate the Italian film with a handful of *neo-realismo* masterpieces and the unpopular art of Antonioni. Rome is the world's co-production capital for an annual half-hundred of those costume brawls attributed, by remote euphemism, to "historical sources." Cinecitta has no competitor in the calculated dissemination of the perverse and the pornographic, whether ineptly camouflaged as anthropological field excursions (encouraged by *Mondo Cane,* I and II—"Nothing inhuman is alien to me") or offered without guile for what most of it is, barrel scrapings, internationally accumulated: *Forbidden Cities, Forbidden Sex, Neon Night Life,* I and II: *Around the World in Ninety Nights,* and *The Nude Look by Night.*

Nonetheless, if we insist dreamily on taking the long, long view of *all* film production, in the belief that only the exceptional movie justifies the whole prodigiously vulgar undertaking, Italian films continue to engage our divided attention. After you've agreed that the Italian film-making scene displays all the idiotic and corrupt practices common to Hollywood, that scapegoat with the highest smell, you have yet to account for, or simply to rejoice in, the fact that whereas year after year nothing—*virtually nothing*—comes out of America or, for that matter, out of West Germany's thriving industry, Italy somehow breeds and maintains a De Sica, a Fellini, an Antonioni, a Monicelli, a De Seta, to say nothing of many others who perennially invite our confidence that "this time" they will fully recover the spirit of a past promise. (I think of, for example, Rossellini, Visconti, Lattuada, Zampa.)

This phenomenon is truly a cause for amazement, and it's the essential subject of my remarks here, which I want to illustrate by scanning the work of some Italian directors who have emerged as Names during the last five years. In their work there is especially noticeable the double burden which the Italian film director typically supports. (I have reference, naturally, to the typically worthwhile director, not to the full-time merchants.) In addition to the supply-and-demand pressures that assail men of good intention anywhere, the Italian, with notable exceptions, takes a long time to trust himself. He is easily swerved from his personal power—by a pet actress whom he allows to distort his subject matter, by the reproaches of his friends, by political resentment (his own or that of the press), by a seemingly authoritative style just created in Paris, by clamorous appeals to be more class-conscious or less, more Italian or more international. It's not the case that he doesn't let his left hand know what his right hand is doing (no political pun intended); he is only too aware of what *each* hand is doing, and tries obligingly to grow a *third* hand! He has the devil of a time trying to keep his eye on the *object,* which he's almost afraid to acknowledge unashamedly as the *art* of the film. (This is all implicit in Fellini's *8½,* but for the present I think the subject of that film has been sufficiently adumbrated. I'm after less articulated examples of the predicament.) I've a strong feeling that the confusion is an extension of the Italian social scene. The artist's conditioned background in Italy operates against the ruthlessness of individual dedication: the family table, the gregarious street and café life, the plaza as forum, the stand-up *espresso* bar; these institutions and their like are basic to the *public* orientation of the Italian. They nourish his ego, they supply his texture of reference—and they frequently prolong his weaning. As a result (the film is again my illustration), you can never be quite sure, when faced with a catastrophic failure of judgment from a director you had built up respect for, if he has sold himself out or, regrettably, sold himself short, in an effort to appease someone or other, someone with an impressively loud voice, who has persuaded him to betray what he

can do best and instead do something else held to be more significant, fashionable, or whatever.

When Damiano Damiani, for instance, entered film-making four
years ago with two crime stories of authentic moral content, *The
Lipstick* and *The Hired Killer,* I thought of him as a welcome arrival who had not securely won a style to enhance his subject. If I
were to judge him by his current film, alone—*La Noia* (*The Empty
Canvas*), a travesty of Moravia's novel so complete that any debate
over it would be futile—I'd say, rather, that it wasn't so much style
as rudimentary taste and intelligence that were eluding him. *La
Noia* is not only one of the most badly motivated films of the Italian
year, it is one of the most poorly executed. Now, I don't *know* if
Damiani was actually caught in the machine and was maneuvered
into making this film against his own wishes, or if he deluded himself, to some prodding, that the Moravia world of not-very-cine-
matic social rancor and masochism was just his forte. If a director
makes the wrong choice of material for himself or has something
unnegotiable (like Horst Buchholtz, especially) thrust upon him,
I'm not too surprised if he loses many of his bearings. But I'm
mystified when he seems totally to have forgotten, between one
movie and the next, what a motion picture camera is used for.

Mauro Bolognini inspired me with a misgiving almost as grave.
With *Il Bell' Antonio* he seemed to have assimilated the French
effects he had previously depended on to serve him not wisely and
too heavily and made a film magnificently energetic, commanding,
and compassionate, rich with local accent and saturated with a kind
of baroque anger. Successively he lost himself again, for the sake of
décor or for that of the literary facsimile—in *La Viaccia, Senilità,
Agostino.* In the last named you can see the whole art of film editing
and structure falling apart in his hands, a spectacle the more astonishing by contrast with his recovery of the art in *La Corruzione,* released this year and quickly snubbed by the Italian press. I'd not
strenuously contest the snubbing if I believed the special grounds
for it justified the dismissal of the film's remaining merit. Italian
critics evidently saw no further merit after they had sneered at
Bolognini's adaptation of a subject thoroughly staked out by the
French; since the treatment was manifestly derived from Fellini
and Antonioni, it was easier to include this in the sneer than to examine the film more closely.

A young man fresh from divinity school is prepared to turn his
back on the affluent world he is heir to (his father is a successful

publisher) before even testing its positive pleasures. His father (played by Alain Cuny with finely tempered cynicism) gives the boy a trial run of the worldly life, in the foreshortened course of which, and with the collaboration of his father's mistress, the young vulnerable learns that for most people corruption is something they live comfortably with. The consequence of rejecting corruption, while remaining within sight and reach of its advantages, is tormented isolation. The film's ending—incidentally a *tour de force*—leaves the youth hesitating between retreat (into the Church?) and the world, mainly accounted for by his father's blandly manipulated environment and the sin of having been seduced by the father's secretary. I've taken liberties with the summary, but the issue is almost that glib and you'll need no overediting from me to question many oversimplifications in this film. But if you can manage to take these aspects of the matter in your stride, I think you'll be rewarded by some of the most sophisticated film style of the season. Certainly the Antonioni influence is prevalent, especially in the long central sequence on the publisher's yacht (the sinister islands, the spatial undertones of the music, the duration of the bold facial closeups). Must I point out that there *is* such a thing as fruitful borrowing? Bolognini makes these elements his own; they are reminiscent of another movie but you never doubt that you're in this one! Follow closely the suicide sequence at the publisher's office, characteristic of the film's flawed skill. The timing of the tragedy is awkwardly invoked; allow it poetic license, however, and you can appreciate the brilliance of the montage which follows (watch from the moment father and son clink glasses, through to the agitated scene outside the building, shot from the inside staircase, when the publisher slaps his son away from the sight of the body). This is a model interlude of movie narration: how to achieve maximum tension with the fewest number of cuts. . . . For Bolognini's inconsistent progress I have an undocumented explanation. I think that he feels he should disapprove of the rich on principle, and the rich are the chief begetters of that opulence which Bolognini has so marked a talent for re-creating as cinematic atmosphere. The tension between his flair for décor and his moral attitude toward it is at the troubled source of his work. If he ever resolves his lover's quarrel in subjects as personal for him as he made *Il Bell' Antonio* he'll outfilm Fellini, with less expenditure of effort.

One tenth of Bolognini's art would be useful to Francesco Rosi, who has become a darling of the left and a nag to the fearful by the force of his single-mindedness alone. Rosi's subject has always been combat, usually in a borderland where the working-class milieu and that of the racketeer overlap. More often than not, his stories have been transcriptions of actuality, increasingly slanted toward an explicit political stand, as in *Salvatore Giuliano* and *Hands on the City*. Indecision is not Rosi's problem. He knows what he's doing (i.e., politically), and I see no reason for doubting the sincerity of his commitment. I simply find all his films quickly forgettable because he hasn't the root of the film artist in him. An exponent of the political film more rewarding to follow (so far) is Carlo Lizzani. His background to some very crisp melodrama has been fascism and World Word II (in *The Hunchback* and *Trial at Verona*); he has a weakness for compound plots and an excessive number of violent climaxes, which at least signifies his passion for making an indelible impression. How judiciously he can pursue that ambition within his present historical ambience remains to be seen. Florestano Vancini has a comparably puzzling future. His film, *La Banda Casaroli*, based on the brief pathetic career of three provincial bank robbers in 1950, is almost the classic Italian example of not knowing when you've sung it. Up to the point where two of the Casaroli boys are slaughtered in a car that won't start, in an empty piazza (as harrowing a climax as I can recall from any hoodlum film), Vancini was making the best action film of the year; better than that, he was creating at the same time a social study of Italian small-city mores which showed up all of Rosi's effort as even more cumbersome. Then came the recoil: twenty minutes' worth of gratuitous vespers. It was like watching someone create a living creature and then, in a fit of revulsion, drive nails into the newly beating heart.

A few years ago, when it was mandatory for someone in every country to try his hand at the anti-film film, Ugo Gregoretti and Pier Paolo Pasolini, each in his own synthetic way, did duty for Italy. Gregoretti's first film, *The New Angels,* a form of *cinéma vérité* which had already been done better (but not a great deal better) by Jean-Luc Godard, Chris Marker, and others in Paris, was quite as boring an imitation of a New Wave studio joke as any I had seen from Poland, Denmark, Finland, or Manhattan. It had *verve,* I suppose, but perhaps I wasn't in the mood for verve when its social inspiration was so patently imported. Last year Gregoretti reached farther, and as unavailingly, afield than Paris, but even with *The New Angels* to warn me I was quite unprepared for his

55

paralyzingly uncomical essay at science-fiction, called *Omicron*.
The reason I mention Gregoretti at all is that I have since seen him
in person (i.e., on Italian television) and all by himself he is an
astonishingly funny man. I am left with the deduction that he is perhaps avoiding his single destined subject—out of modesty. As for
Pasolini, a visitor from literature who has been too readily encouraged to believe that he's precisely what the motion picture has been
waiting for, I am primarily astounded by the persistent opinion that
he is profound as well as bizarre. Not only was I made uncomfortable by the affectations of his *Accatone,* I was repelled by his
willful identification therein of the criminal, the poor, the Christian,
and the androgynous. What is good enough for Dostoievsky is not
necessarily viable in Italian *avant garde* film. This season Pasolini
has reverted to the most orthodox neo-realism topic of the forties
(prostitute trying to conceal her profession from her son), at the
same time retaining sundry "progressive" touches, consisting notably of disparities between the musical score employed and the
scenes it accompanies (a trick stolen from the French and which he
had utilized in the earlier film!) and much very questionable theological symbolism—certainly questionable as being *avant garde.*
Mamma Roma is the title of this embroilment, and not all of Anna
Magnani's undying resources can for long give credibility to its com-
pulsively masochist treatment.

Mario Monicelli has earned popularity and respect without quite
being regarded as an "important" director. None of his films has
been either great or sensational. He hasn't made a comedy as profoundly artful as *Miracle in Milan* or *The White Sheik,* nor as
wildly amusing as *Divorce—Italian Style.* He has simply discovered
a fusion of social naturalism and wit and he's intelligent enough to
let that suffice him until he's ready to give it greater scope. Each of
his films is better than the one preceding, in a special way hard to
define but probably summed up in the tone of his latest of full-
length, *I Compagni* (U.S. title, *The Organizer;* he has contributed
a single episode to *High Infidelity,* which I haven't seen). In *The
Organizer,* as he did in *La Grande Guerra* four years ago, Monicelli
re-creates a milieu of our medium-distant past, a past far enough
away to yield nostalgia, near enough to be a brutal reminder. And
he re-creates it as a *joke*—a lighthearted joke, not a wry one; he in-
vests biting social realism with comic observation (it never appears
to be invention) and he brings this off better than anyone I've seen
attempt it. Moreover, he does this within the orthodox (not to say

stale) framework of the classic Soviet strike film of the twenties and early thirties. All the ingredients and most of the characters re-appear for Monicelli's rehearsal of a Turin spinning-mill strike at the turn of the century: a "reasonable" leader pitted against a hot-headed one; a widow who carries on after her stalwart husband is killed in a fray; a prostitute of exemplary loyalty to the cause of the strikers (and of incredible beauty in the social context). Plot-wise, in fact, Monicelli's principal point of variance from the model (*cf.* Piscator's *Revolt of the Fishermen,* 1935) is his use of a Socialist professor as the brainy lever of the resistance.

If the clichés remain, at least nominally, why are they accept-able? Because they're conspicuous only in retrospect. Because in Monicelli's film (this is true of all his later work) every moment is *alive.* He has a feeling, above all, for scenic vivacity; even in the most restful or most conversational scene something is always flick-ering, moving, lighting up with expression. His timing is nearly perfect, his direction of little bits of human business is pertinently incidental, and he never permits a character, once established, to flatten out into a mere repetition of a key idiosyncrasy. Mastro-ianni's characterization of the Socialist, for which I assume we can give a degree of credit to Monicelli, is built on surprise motifs. Ab-sent-minded and generally timorous, the professor is never wholly as ineffectual as he seems at such moments as when you discover him in bed with his mittens on. He's a dedicated man, not a senti-mental one; he lives inside his own operational planning, and his love is an idea, no matter how the workers may flatter themselves that they are the sole objects of his solicitation. Withal he is capable of lashing out violently, not from heroism so much as from irritation at being disturbed in his concentrations.

The movie critics of the Italian press selected, as their three best Italian films in 1963, Fellini's *8½,* Visconti's *The Leopard,* and Rosi's *Hands on the City*—as craven a choice as you'd ex-pect in any country at this level of estimation. There's probably no argument against the Fellini film, and the Cannes and Venice festival juries had ratified the other two for them. There's a double margin of safety here, since Visconti and Rosi are widely known as "communists," and you never know when you might need a friend at court. I still have a rhetorical question. If period portraiture and leftist sympathies are in truth an appealing combination, why not *The Organizer,* a creative hour and a half of movie-making, rather than *The Leopard,* which ran for well over two hours, and in which I don't remember—there was so much window dressing—more than one cinematic idea? (The one is not vital enough to merit recapitulation.)

Beyond this (the critics' main choices), though I read avidly through all the supplementary mentions—best décor, best supporting actors and actresses, best special camera work (you know the routine)—I found no listing whatever of the single Italian film of the year I'll most want to see again five years from now, let's say, assuming it hasn't by then been buried forever. This is *La Mano sul Fucile* (*Hand on the Gun*), the first film of twenty-eight-year-old Luigi Turolla. None of my moviegoing acquaintances in Rome had heard of the film when I discovered it on the third-time-around programs. The setting of Turolla's film, photographed by Carlo Bellero, is the high escarpment and glacial meadows of the Lombardy Alps in 1944. A Partisan group is trying to reach a designated clearing where a supply parachute will be dropped. A Fascist patrol is trying to stop them. Owing to the nature of the terrain—a vertical wilderness, above treeline, with sparse patches of melting snow field—an open contest is impossible or suicidal. The men, on both sides, dig in, snipe when they can, reconnoiter stealthily, move swiftly at lethal risk under cover of dark or of a sudden flurry of mountain mist. On both sides they spend a long time waiting, a short ambushed moment dying.

As one explanation of the film's unenthusiastic reception, it was suggested to me that the civil aspect of Italy's war—when Italian openly fought Italian—is a relatively tender area for debate or drama. I beg to disbelieve, in view of the syndicated histories and biographies of the Fascist era which are constantly appearing in popular Italian magazines. I'm sure the reason is to be sought in the character of the film itself, not in its subject. Italian audiences can take internecine war movies, but not if these are as unadulterated as Turolla's. They love *Four Days in Naples,* which is essentially *kitsch.* A host of lovable characters, including a small boy (taken from the real life-and-death situation), are labeled at the outset so that you know precisely which will be the ones you'll see die in generously heroic fashion. Furthermore, the identity of friend and foe—Neapolitan and German, local insurgent and Fascist—is never in doubt. And the whole film proceeds in a scarcely relieved din of shooting, operatic screaming, and the amplified musical score of

Carlo Rustichelli.* Turolla made the mistake, from the audience viewpoint, of filming a political action without political emphasis. *Hand on the Gun* is a crisis situation, too late for political argument. In that last Alpine oubliette where two dozen men have become composite creatures—part man, part rifle, part rock-rooted bush— only survival has value, and the means to survival are details, most of which yield a limited degree of personality: a blurred shape seen through a telescopic sight (man or wind-shaken boulder?) ; the last cigarette, or less than half, dry-nursed on a cracked lip; the last cartridge, fondled between thumb and finger. In a superbly photographed rest period, the camera moves slowly from one man to another, hesitating at a face staring at the sky, at another talking softly, on hands clutching rifle barrels or toying with the distance mechanism, on a boot, or the inside of a discarded helmet. After a barely perceptible dissolve midway, Turolla slyly moves us from the Partisan camp to that of the Fascists. Men are equalized by the terms of their existence, a comment also made at the end of the film with unprecedented sardonic inspiration; it is the more unprecedented in Italian film because it is made without a single word.

Hand on the Gun is too pure a film for the Italian audience to accept with reciprocity. I saw the film three times in outlying Rome cinemas and each time the Brunos of the audience were unable to control their boredom or impatience with Turolla's careful pace and dogged but poetic handling of his austere subject. It may be argued that the Italian audience does not entirely consist of Brunos. It does not—yet at any social or temperamental level a subtle film-watcher in Italy is rare. The sensibility of the Italian film- or theater-goer has been opera-conditioned, if indeed it doesn't derive more directly from his social life where, equally, there appears to be no such thing as a significant silence or an unexplained cadence. Italians hate silence; in the theater, as in life, something audible must be going on at every moment—if not action, then talk—which is why they are baffled by Antonioni in Italy, no matter what other rationaliza-

*The substitution of musically aroused for film-created emotion is still the besetting vice of Italian movie-making. Rustichelli, as facile a hack as an Elizabethan balladmonger, is the favorite of Italian directors who have only half done their job on film. No doubt he is also imposed on directors who don't need him or can use him in moderation. Rustichelli scored both *I Compagni* and *La Mano sul Fucile*. Monicelli knows best how to exploit him, Turolla knows how to control him. I suspect that if Turolla had had the authority of experience in the industry he would have curtailed the music track more drastically. Rustichelli's hurdy-gurdy theme is the only instance of excess statement in Turolla's film.

tions they produce; and this is why, after two years, a minority of them are just beginning to appreciate De Seta's film *The Bandits of Orgosolo,* acclaimed everywhere else in Europe. In short, the average Italian knows so little how to *look at* a movie, it must be counted as a miracle that a handful of Italians knows how to *make* movies!

1964

The Wilderness Art
of Arne Sucksdorff

The first image is that of bubbles in dark water, suggesting the primordial source. Then the camera sidles slowly over the shadowed frozen floor of northern forest. The lonely steeple of a remote village church comes into view; simultaneously we hear the first strains of a devotional *fantasia* by Bach. The camera resumes its stealthy glide—through dissolving shots so swift we barely note them, back into the inhuman night and a grove of immobile trees. An ermine—sleek, beautiful, and nervous, feeding on his kill—is startled by the rattling of a nearby owl. He slips away apprehensively as moonlight suddenly brightens the woodland arena and a fox appears on the scene. While the shadows stir, the newcomer eats the remains of the ermine's plunder, watched by the owl (seen in closeup) from his observation branch. For a moment the wind rises and the owl blinks mildly. The distant chords of Bach from the church organ are more distinctly heard. On the border of the forest a white hare lopes across the crystal beds of snow. A lighted house, alien and safe, frames the background. Wind rustles in bone-dry leaves, and the inscrutable owl answers with another hoot—of derision or warning, who can tell? The hare runs, as if pursued by the camera, the ermine peers cautiously from the hole into which he has dropped for shelter, the configurations of Bach die out almost imperceptibly, and a piercing scream tears the sylvan silence of the night. The ermine quivers, the owl peers into the barricade of shadows cast by birch and pine, with curiosity or resigned knowledge. The fox eats the hare. Abruptly stirring himself, the owl soars to the moonlit feast, perching himself ominously on a low branch close to the gourmandizing fox. Precariously, a few tremulous inches to a movement, the ermine slithers to a safe witness point, flinching and crouching as he hears another outburst of murderous screams. The fox has now fled. The owl gorges on what's left of the hare. . . . One more change of scene: furrowed, snow-topped fields and the lighted house. The Bach *fantasia,* released from its fearful *pianissimo,* now swells in crescendo as the film ends.

This is the substance of a nine-minute film made by Arne Sucksdorff in 1948—*En Kluven Varld (A Divided World)*; it is doubtful whether in the history of the short subject a more potent statement has been made with greater economy. Certainly within the category of nature film, if one is content with such a definition, it is a peerless achievement. Sensational documentary records of wild life, if not precisely commonplaces in the motion picture, have been retrieved by a considerable number of naturalists-with-camera. Yet there is no corpus of film documentary that can rival, *in kind,* the quality of a dozen short films made by Sucksdorff, for the most part in Sweden, between 1943 and 1950.

The genius of Sucksdorff lies in something more than his acute nature-knowledge, though without that he would scarcely be the Sucksdorff whose work we know. When Edgar Degas told the poet Mallarmé that he too was interested in writing poems but had difficulty in finding ideas for them, Mallarmé reproved him by declaring that a poem was written not with ideas but with words. Degas no doubt appreciated the distinction, since he was constantly having to rebuke literary people in similar terms. Frederic Amiel had written of painting as "a reflection of the soul," whereupon Degas had retorted, "We painters do not use such affected language! Painting is a reflection of my eyesight." We feel sure that the protests both of Mallarmé and of Degas were defensive: they knew very well that there was much more to poetry than words and melody and more to painting than an eye for the plastic. Nonetheless, ideas or states of soul are of no use to a poet who has no ear or to a painter who lacks the eye and hand.

Comparably, you might say a movie is not made with ideas but with *images in fluid sequence.* To be sure, the most memorable poems are those in which idea and language have most completely fused, and a great painting is one in which—by means it seems impertinent to call technical—a subject has been so defined as to make it almost unnecessary for any other painter to attempt it. And the films of Sucksdorff are likewise most telling when the striking images of which they are normally composed relate indivisibly to their controlling theme. This should go without saying: is it not the prescription for any film worthy to be called art? All the same, in the special area of film documentary one cannot overemphasize the truism that an eye for data, however meticulous, is insufficient for conferring that enduring resonance by which we know we are in the presence of a film-maker gifted with more than intelligence and sound observation. What distinguishes the short films of Sucksdorff (together with his first feature-length film, *The Great Adventure*) from all other films, short or long, which they seem to resemble, is the element for which we have probably no better word than *vision.*

The whole of a sequence in the best of these films is always greater than the sum of its parts. True, we may in retrospect recall only single, fabulous images: the sabbath stillness of broken roots shadowing a veil of snow; the shriveled larva of a dragonfly against the veins of a leaf, like a Gothic cadaver on a cross; sunlight exalting the vapor of a waterfall plunging over cinder-black rocks; the close-up antlers of a reindeer which, glimpsed in isolation, might be the branches of some cruel unknown tree from the deserts of the East; icicles, pendulous and fugitive, dissolving as you watch from crystal fingers to freshets; whirlpools of a pond in chiaroscuro, momentarily static, their surface patterns suggesting the plumes of a peacock or a veined cross section of marble. Now, it is not impossible that the seeming uniqueness of these frames could be matched, if you jogged your memory, from films not made by Sucksdorff. At least it's probable, and by what standard will you decide in Sucksdorff's favor? The criterion is as subtle as that employed in discriminating the timbre of a violin; moreover, you must "hear" Sucksdorff's instrument, too—which is to say you must receive those images *in motion.* In Sucksdorff's art every image is what it appears to be, yet has at the same time the force of a metaphor. By super-sentient instinct he seems to have penetrated to the core of phenomena and there aroused vibrations that give the mere "pictures" an occult value, but one suspects that the determining factor is just that quality of vision to which I have alluded.

Comparisons may, from time to time, be thought invidious; nevertheless, it is all but inevitable to compare Sucksdorff's films with those of Robert Flaherty, the more so since their subjects have often run parallel. Flaherty was an empiricist. He filmed admirable narrative records of men in nature. He never rose from this accomplishment to a definition of man-in-nature. Though a skilled craftsman, with all his fidelity to the epic character of occupational ritual (as in *Nanook of the North* or *Man of Aran*) or to its lyric parentheses (as in *Louisiana Story*), Flaherty never really felt beyond the motions of man to the universal situation of man—i.e., to man seen not simply as *contesting* nature but as an uneasy *component of* nature. In Flaherty's films, man is the sum of the work he does; in Sucksdorff's, he is the mystery of the web he inhabits. Of course, the nominal subjects of Flaherty were infrequently identical with those of Sucksdorff, but *Louisiana Story,* for instance, can fairly be compared with *The Great Adventure* (both are experiences, predicated from a juvenile point of vantage, in discovering the nature and limit of a particular environment). I do not hesitate to pronounce Sucksdorff's film as infinitely more sensitive, inventive, and penetrating; surely no one would maintain that these superlatives derive from superior photographic equipment! And this is not to deprecate Flaherty's personal achievement; his essential approach was different in kind from Sucksdorff's. Using analogous material, the two film-makers evolved qualitatively different expressions. Their films, seen in contrast, constitute the distinction between documentary and vision, between plastic prose and poetry.

The pragmatist will argue that notwithstanding these suspiciously metaphysical inferences a camera is a precision instrument and that Arne Sucksdorff is not a hamadryad. He is mortal; he is a technician; he has, presumably, a budget to meet; he is faced with an inordinately difficult task, that of filming the unpredictable content of nature in flux: birds, beasts, fish, insects, and the migratory currents of the air. To the practical mind the *how* of Sucksdorff is more important than the *why*. Just how, in the name of reality, does he get the shots we see, assembled and ruthlessly edited, as poetry? Watching Sucksdorff's pursuit of a hare or fox through the nocturnal wastes of a Swedish wilderness, it must dawn on one, sooner or later, that since it was impossible for him to have followed a wild animal with smoothly tracking camera in the orderly sequence you have witnessed, and since to have matched up shots of a number of animals of the same family to get this one interlude would have taken seasons of his time, there is bound to be a more plausible answer. Just so. Mark Van Doren once said of Shakespeare's plays that they must have been easy to write—else they would have been impossible!

Sucksdorff's films could not have been easy to make. So it seems, at any rate, to my unpracticed sense of the matter. The *how* can in various instances be explained, yet I'm not convinced that the explanation is in decent ratio to the result. For *The Divided World,* Sucksdorff staked out an area of forest within which he had noted—during how many weeks or months I don't know—the habitual routes taken at night by such creatures as the hare and the ermine. Thereafter he set up his camera "nest" along those routes, to photograph the animals from a variety of emplacements and, of course, under fairly predictable conditions of weather and degrees of moonlight. Simply to expound this much is to open up marvels of patience, timing, cinematic know-how, and, before these, the bred knowledge of one attuned beyond the ordinary to the manless world of the underbrush. The secret of learning the wilderness life is as easy to declare as it is rare in cultivation: you must learn to sit still. He who would not only overtake but reveal—with a camera or any other instrument—the furtive doings of the natural world must have the patience of a fisherman, the cunning of a hunter, and the perceptions of a poet.

And time *is* of the essence, since luck is fickle. While shooting *Vinden fran Västen* (*Wind from the West*), 1942, Sucksdorff spent two weeks suspended daily in a camera cage below a shelf of rock, high above a Lapland valley, in order to get a perfect closeup of a confronted, angry eagle—with the light just this way and no other, and a cloud in the background of just the desired form. If you deduced from that example the number of shots in even a twenty-minute film, each taking two weeks to secure, you'd arrive at a perplexing ratio and begin to ask yourself, "Exactly how old is Sucksdorff?" Naturally, this intrepid man could not afford very often to spend a fortnight snaring one image, but his ratio of shots taken to shots edited for the final print is customarily high: for *A Divided World,* in meters, about thirty to one. (The produced film contains roughly a hundred shots.) It took Sucksdorff a summer—i.e., about three months—to make *Trut* (*The Gull*), 1944, a 500-meter film that runs eighteen minutes, and about the same length of time for *A Divided World*, which is half as long in viewing time. *The Great Adventure*, completed in 1952 (running time, an hour and half), took two years of shooting and editing.

Time is merely one of numerous unpredictables when the object of movie-making is nature in the raw. On some few occasions Sucksdorff has resorted to employing animals partly domesticated. At least once this had damaging consequences for a luckless assistant. *Skuggor över Snön* (*Shadows over Snow*), 1946, a characteristic Sucksdorff anecdote in which a predator of the wilderness lives to prey again, required a bear as leading antagonist. A presumably tamed bear was enlisted for most of the necessary close-in shooting. Notoriously, of all wild beasts that lend themselves artfully to man's trusting hand, a bear is the most unreliable. This one suddenly reverted, attacking a Lapp who was trying to appease him. The animal had to be shot, which created inestimable difficulties for Sucksdorff, since he had to fake what should have been the climactic moment of the film. The Lapp's difficulties were graver, however; his arm was so badly mauled it had to be amputated.

Such is the nature of the hazards undertaken by one film-maker in his quest for authenticity. The example given may be thought of as a regrettable illustration of calculated risk; it was all in the day's work, so to speak. The expense of spirit is something else, probably never surmised by the innocent spectator who, refreshed by encountering a ten-minute vignette of Sucksdorff on an otherwise undistinguished program, is unaware that these pastorals with sometimes ominous undertones were wrung from an inner life almost as tormented as that of Ingmar Bergman. The converging sources of so elemental an action as *A Divided World*, for example, quite apart from problems of execution, were extraordinarily complex. To give some hint of them it is necessary to review, in larger outline, the biography of the man who made the films.

Arne Sucksdorff's formative years were importantly qualified by three conditions. He was born in 1917 to a wealthy family; he was brought up in the country (in the vicinity of Södertälje, southwest of Stockholm); he was early exposed to (or it may be expressed that he was early imposed on by) his father's absorbed concern with institutional religion, specifically with the doctrines of the evangelical Oxford Group, for which he was an influential spokesman in Stockholm. Wealth gave Sucksdorff independent leisure in which to follow his bent—which, even in his youth, was an amateur's fine addiction to the still camera (his earliest triumph was the capture of a first prize in a national photography contest) —and later on it was useful to defray production costs if his producers happened to be reluctant. The importance of the countryside nurture is obvious, but the intensity with which Sucksdorff dedicated himself to its spell and to its implicit challenge can only be understood by reference to the third condition—his father's religious propensities, against which he reacted vehemently. The belief held by the Oxford Group that aggressive impulses could be eliminated by the grace of God, attracted by right thinking and daily prayer, was not visibly encouraged by the spectacle of nature—presumptively under God's mercy also—in which survival depends on superior strength, superior cunning, or even superior cowardice.

Thereby, for the young Sucksdorff, a dialectic was set up that later was to serve the antipodal forces which so often characterized his film motifs: on the one hand, Stockholm and his father's theological involvements; on the other, the central Sweden forest and farmland. Town and country, irreconcilable: the ameliorative constructions of the mind, expressed in creeds for which he felt no sympathy, posed against the natural life that sharpened all city-nourished contradictions. When Sucksdorff began to produce films, these were the disparities he sought, not always explicitly, to convey. Even the film *Uppbrott* (*Breakup*), 1948, which appears to be a sport in the Sucksdorff filmography, was directly motivated by this conflict. On his reluctant way to Stockholm he used to see settlements of gypsies temporarily housed near the highway. Much later he made this film, dealing entirely with the breakup of just such an encampment and the gypsies' removal to another clime. It's a sensuous, classically built episode, abounding in juxtaposed rhythms and shock cutting, quite out of Sucksdorff's personal style (it was photographed by Martin Bodin), but it's doubly interesting when you realize that for him it expressed yearning, the migratory instinct, the passion for escape. *Människor i Stad* (*Rhythm of a City*), 1947, sponsored as a promotional feature, is a film of buried motifs. Taken at face value (except by members of an official Swedish organization, who were shocked by its disparagement of the capital!), it appears to be a lyrical tribute to Stockholm, with an elbow nudge here and there. This was not Sucksdorff's aim. The prize-winning "documentary" was designed to propound his *antipathy* toward city life, together with minor concessions to its incidental poetry. (The title of this film has been misleadingly translated, for it should be *Man in the City*.)

What Sucksdorff began to distill, at first in a minor key, when he made his first wilderness films during the early years of the war, was a prevalent theme in modern thought: the broken balance of man and nature, more particularly the dilemma of intellectual man seeking a consistent answer. As Sir Charles Sherrington has pointed out in *Man on His Nature,* perhaps more objectively than any writer of our time, man can only justify himself as a genus by discrediting himself as the member of a species. When he consults the evidence of evolution by which he has presumably been shaped and motivated, he finds only a blind, inclement will to live, in ethical contradistinction to the avowed benevolence which he claims as the dominant principle of *human* existence. All natural life, if you look closely enough, is a battleground for survival, with few mitigations and no merciful interventions. Sucksdorff had been living with this truth all his waking days. World War II and German philosophy (not Sherrington) brought it within closeup. His response was initially indirect; his premonitions were concealed behind the vital communion of his eye with the less disheartening overtures to life and death. These earlier films announce the subject but usually leave it on a note of felicity.

En Sommarsaga (*A Summer's Tale*)`, 1943, the sketch in which Sucksdorff's style was first unmistakably projected, features a baby fox which is as yet insufficiently equipped to be the devourer it would wish to be; the gist of the situation is largely his comic failure to act aggressively. *The Gull,* referred to above, is a beautiful, if fairly stark, chapter in the life cycle of a colony of birds on the island of Karlsö in the Baltic. They gather food, hatch their young, are invaded by a larger and more bullying species of gull, and urge their infants to launch themselves from rocky heights into the ocean below at the risk of being dashed to pieces on jutting boulders. The cycle has a "happy ending": a marooned chick, threatened by a giant foe, flounders valiantly through the air to land in safety on the buoyant waters. In *Wind from the West,* as also in *Den Drömda Dalen* (*Valley of Dreams*), 1948, a child seeks to escape (actually or through fantasy) from the rational to the instinctual life by fleeing to a grandiose territory of mountain plateau. Both films conclude with his (or her) return to the circle of community obligations. In *Gryning* *(Dawn)*, 1945, man is expressly depicted as a wanton intruder, an irresponsible hunter who kills for the sport of killing and heedlessly breaks the living boughs in his path. Yet as he sights along his gun at a deer and its fawn, some instinct of mercy, or shadow of a prohibition, restrains him. The film ends with the deer feeding contentedly, in respite for the time being.

A Divided World is the concentrate of these and other films; *The Great Adventure* is an amplification of them. The former, perhaps the most consciously conceived of all Sucksdorff's parables, followed a period of intense self-searching and of anxiety over the fate of man at large. Two world wars had done nothing to alleviate the pessimistic inferences drawn by many thinkers from the discrepancies of Darwinism or those of revealed religion. Given to brooding over nineteenth-century German philosophy, Sucksdorff's forebodings were if anything accentuated by the literature of Karl R. E. von Hartmann,* midway between Schopenhauer and Freud with its author's contention that civilized man, unable to reconcile the claims of Eros and Death, would desperately invoke, by violence, the peace of nonexistence. This unconsoling probability, together with prevailing concerns of a personal nature, inspired the mood of *A Divided World*. Still, the precise treatment might not have come to mind if Sucksdorff had not just then seen a short film made by Gösta Roosling, called *Christmas Morn*.

Roosling is now better known as a cinematographer of more famous films by others (e.g., Sjöberg's *Road to Heaven*). During the forties, however, he pioneered, for Swedish film, the short subject with little or no spoken narration. *Christmas Morn* is his masterwork in the genre, composed from the details of a service in a rural church surrounded by acres of deep snow and sparse clumps of woodland. People arrive by sleigh, with lighted torches, for it is as dark as midnight. Roosling then builds a selective montage as the prayers, organ responses, hymns, and sermon proceed. Close-up shots of the altar screen, hymnal numbers, organ pipes, the triumphal crucifix, members of the congregation or of the choir are crosscut with snow-covered tombstones marking the shrouded graves in the churchyard. As the people leave, daylight slowly waxes; one candle on a grave remains alight, flickering in the grey dawn; branches weighted with snow, like summer blossoms, are embraced in closeup. It is a perfect miniature of movie language,

---

*Karl Robert Eduard von Hartmann (1842–1906): *Philosophy of the Unconscious*, 1869; *The Religion of the Future*, 1886; *Philosophy of the Beautiful*, 1887.

edited with decorum and a sure touch for progression of effect. And it was just what Sucksdorff needed.

A Divided World is, among other things, an answer to *Christmas Morn,* a denial of the safe life neatly separated from the unacknowledged struggle for existence. Even so, it is not the answer as Sucksdorff first pictured it in his mind. Originally he planned to duplicate Roosling's setting, up to a point, by crosscutting from a church congregation—snug, safe, beatific—to the battle being waged in the forest underworld. Contingency, in the form of an electrician's strike, radically modified this contrapuntal, and less subtle, handling. Sucksdorff was unable to shoot the interiors he needed and his remaining schedule would not accommodate delay. Thus in the film he did make—while the wilderness, rather than a passive contour blanketed by snow, became a harsh microcosm of life endowed with fang and claw—the lighted church is no longer the initiating subject. Instead it is an extremely dubious, if focal, element of the total drama. Ermine kills bird and fox kills hare (perhaps next time the ermine as well) ; an owl, on this occasion, outfoxes all of them. The lighted church and the lighted house, seen only in middle distance, are not meant to convey solely the superior complacency of man, removed from an internecine world. That world—of owl and fox and the others—*also* exemplifies the world of man. The lighted buildings and the Bach are the precarious weapons of his mind and heart. . . . This compound subject may be too heavy a burden for some filmgoers to support within so restricted a dimension; it is only fair to report that such was Sucksdorff's revised intention.

Det Stora Äventyret (*The Great Adventure*), released in 1955, is an epic yet less disturbing essay in defining the limits beyond which human consciousness has no power over the neutral scheme of things. The theme is neither so mordantly outlined nor so nakedly revealed as in *A Divided World;* for one reason, it is narrated with the sensibility of two children (the young sons of Sucksdorff) in the foreground and therefore never rises to the pitch of troubled consciousness reached by the compact sensate drama of the short film. Sucksdorff once called it "an allegory with a documentary perspective," which overstates and reduces it at the same time. Directly allegorical it is not, and "documentary perspective," a good craft description, falls hopelessly short of defining the breathtaking montage from which the film accumulates its intricate and boundless beauty. The four seasons, the four winds, night and day, earth and sky, the hunters and the hunted, mating and death, innocence and knowledge: the old, old subjects, scented in the living scene and orchestrated in a symphony of cinematic wonder unsurpassed.

Anders, aged ten, and Kjell, six, live the Sucksdorff way, nerve-rooted in the life of forest and lake-border, learning to listen, watch, sense, and react like any fox, owl, or sandpiper. They capture an otter, cherish it as a pet through the winter, only to see it escape, with no symptoms of regret, when spring comes, to its native element. In the wake of their disappointment and of the panorama of change and death which they have witnessed, the boys learn that the wilderness is more than a playground for man; that there are, in conscious fact, two worlds, not one; that however far we succeed in entering that other world and even in modifying its phenomena locally, we can only inhabit it by renouncing our own identity. At the last, each world claims its own. A naive revelation, to be sure, when paraphrased out of the context—but so to all of us is the first shock of birth, of love, or of defeat. Yet I do feel that this aspect of the film is recited rather too explicitly. A six- or even a ten-year-old could not be expected to imply such acuity; at least not unless he were himself a natural creature of the wilderness. (In this sense, the native boy in *The Flute and the Arrow* would have been a more expressive vehicle for the primal insight if the theme of that film had required him to be so.)

The didactic residue of *The Great Adventure* is probably the last thing anyone recalls. As usual, but in ampler terms than ever before, it is the poetry of the matter that overpowers, the summation of Sucksdorff's astonishing empathy. Everything is photographed as if from inside, not vis-à-vis, the other world. The camera *becomes* the creature it observes: a wounded vixen struggling to escape leaden death, turning over convulsively and seeing the sky as a last paroxysm of light, a hunted otter fleeing, belly pressed, through a canebrake, a flock of migrating fowl for whom the terraqueous land below is as impersonally sighted as it would be by a questing bombardier. Owls sitting erect on the limb of a dead tree stare with amazement at slipstreams inscribed like knots in the air, stretching their necks to a climax of quaking, global-eyed apprehension. As the earth turns within its veering orbit, Sucksdorff registers the advance and transition of each season with a laconic purity of images—a mackerel heaven and a bare bough for November, stalks like black arrows in the snow for December. Winter is the supremely magical season when blinding or filtered light on snow totally transforms every vista, near and far, into a more artistically harmonized landscape. Otters fish through the ice, a lynx prowls, a rabbit sits up alertly like a creature in a Lewis Carroll dream. One shot—through the snow-padded forest—of the alarm clock which the boys set with their trap creates an underworld cavern out of Hans Christian Andersen. Light and shadow, the fabulous Oriental patterns formed by a harvest moon reflected in the lake, ribs of a turned-up rowboat, a lattice of shimmering leaves, and always the life of *sound*—frogs, owls, chickens panicked by a fox, the metallic challenge of the wood grouse, cries of migratory cranes: all this is the web, the rhythm, and the magnificently inhuman continuity of the great adventure.

Sucksdorff must have realized that with this film he was concluding the wilderness phase of his larger subject, the harmony and discord of man-in-nature. After *The Great Adventure* he had no thematic material left to justify another fable with a Northern setting. He found none, at least. These films of his first active decade are so related one to the other by theme and image that they tend to come together in the mind as a single indivisible impression. By comparison, the films he has subsequently produced display no such unity. A clue to the faltering transitions of Sucksdorff's later work can be found in two items, unfalteringly executed, made on his first visit to India during 1950–1951, preceding *The Great Adventure* but not in general release until some time later. In these two short films, linked only by their common motif of water, he was already transplanting and modifying what we might call his Nordic subject—the transitory or imperiled relationship of man to his organic home.

Indisk By (Indian Village) is directly concerned with the ecological basis of man's struggle: the appalling effects of drouth on the life of a back-delta community. About a half-hour in length, it's a masterful documentary, emphasizing with all Sucksdorff's power of cumulative statement the devastation caused in a relatively limited area by the inexorable withholding of one vital source. Whether he is focusing on hopelessly exposed roots shriveling above a morass of drying mud, on a native's close-up glistening profile as his mouth gluts water from a jug, or on a legion of squatting vultures scouring the bones of stricken cattle, he is alike mesmerized by his picture-sense. The result is infinitely more vivid than a hundred existing films of the same length reporting the same generic subject. *Vinden och Floden* (*Wind and the River*) is a sinuously beautiful essay in undiluted motion and sound: images of a journey down a river, without any accompanying narration, as untroubled by a meaning beyond their own fugitive vitality as an impromptu by Schubert. The film is not much longer than *A Divided World* (with some 150 images) and no less perfect, but it is linear rather than contrapuntal and has no extrinsic comment to make. It simply puts you into the heart of a serpentine, fluvial rhythm, watching the banks of a river—the world of flute players, waving women, children, and animals—slipping by irrecoverably, the way life does even as you begin to accept the current of it.

The reconciliation of the expressive possibilities in these two short subjects from India may well stand as the animating problem behind all Sucksdorff's film-making. If it is possible to make so artificial a distinction, he is, as an eye, attracted by the potency of images. As a man in society, he is moved deeply by the spectacle of suffering in any form. While *The Flute and the Arrow* (1957) and *The Boy in the Tree* (1961), both full-length works, are, properly speaking, beyond the subject of this essay, they do comment on it; they suggest the nature of the creative impasse with which today Sucksdorff is struggling. In *The Flute and the Arrow,* although there were some lovely allegretto moments filled with dance and the rhythm of turning wheels and many exotic shots of Indian jungle life, Sucksdorff was no longer stalking his subject; he was standing in front of it and photographing it. *The Boy in the Tree,* filmed in Sweden, is beautifully *felt,* but as a human situation it is fairly preposterous. Neither film is an adequate bridge from the loss of innocence to a mature acceptance of the loss. For the moment, Sucksdorff remains entrenched in the romantic's position, unable to surrender the obsessive theme of eternal division between man and his environment. He has reached the limits where elegy awaits analysis or transcendence.*   1964

Footnote 1971. I should like to record here the invaluable assistance provided me by Bertil Lauritzen (formerly production chief of the Swedish Institute Film School) when I was preparing this essay. At that hour Sucksdorff himself was out of the country, and Mr. Lauritzen, who is probably more responsible for encouraging Sucksdorff's early production than his modesty will permit him to acknowledge, fed me details of Sucksdorff's personal background and his filming strategies from a memory that was both unfaltering and impressively articulate.

The final paragraph of this essay was added to the original in order to provide a transition for an extended discussion of Sucksdorff in a projected history of Swedish film which I later abandoned.

Some Obiter Dicta
on Recent French Films

New Wave? Old Wave? It's all the same ocean.
Claude Chabrol

The principal error in so much confused writing on the subject of the French New Wave is the notion that some twenty-five young directors who have emerged in the past eight years have been going in twenty-five directions, each separate from the other, all radically opposed to the method of any director established before 1958. The assumption will not survive a closer scrutiny. Since the majority of critics (by which I probably mean the jackals who sustain film festival jargon) would be helpless without the assumption, they can scarcely be expected to challenge it—had they the perception for so doing. What should seem obvious to any filmgoer who is old enough to have a memory is that the similarities between this generation of film-makers in France and the preceding ones are more numerous than the discrepancies. However exuberant, experimental, informal, or even disorderly the new contingent has insisted on being, with whatever degree of seriousness its members have tried out audacities of narration and cutting, it has been working for the most part in what might be called the classical tradition of French cinema. This is to say that the new young men have rarely abandoned the intellectual schemata available to them and they have seldom operated outside the milieux of their predecessors. There is a visible link that unites *Le Garçon Sauvage* (1951) and *Les Quatre Cents Coups* (1951), even to the oceanic brink-of-freedom note on which both films end; *Les Cousins* (1959) recalls (as do a score of films, internationally) Jean Renoir's *La Règle du Jeu* (1939); *Les Dimanches de Ville d'Avray* (*Sundays and Cybèle,* 1962) is reminiscent, poetically, of *Poil de Carotte* (c. 1932); the tone of René Clair, from away back, is implicit in the films of Doniol-Valcroze, Philippe de Broca, or Pierre Kast; *Last Year in Marienbad* is directly traceable to Cocteau's *La Belle et La Bête* (1946) —as well as to Sjöberg's *Miss Julie*—and by way of Cocteau to *The Fall of the House of Usher* (1929); and Jacques Demy has explicitly acknowledged (in *Lola,* 1961) his debt to the art of Max Ophuls (Ophuls was Alsatian, trained by Reinhardt, but made his best films in France). To add a Chinese box to this nest, Marcel Ophuls, son of the late master, is also a member of the new dispensation.

The keynote of the New Wave is not anarchic, though all efforts to assert artistic individuality are likely to have anarchic features. The movement has been, rather, a spirited *reprisal* of an abiding continuity, and within that continuity few newcomers can be said to have worked alone and unrelated. They have been fully and gratefully aware not only of the precedent over their shoulder but also of each other: they observe each other's films; they deride each other (a form of flattery); they steal from each other; they sometimes vulgarize what they steal, but as often they improve on it. (Factionally, they may be said to sleep with each other; within circles that hail each other in passing, you will note the same cinematographers, writers, designers, and actors.) All the while they operate from common cultural presuppositions and this above all gives their films, collectively, that unity of temper which is really their most distinguishing virtue. There can be no fruitful duplication of the French New Wave elsewhere, for you can't transplant a cultural assumption, and all attempts to do so, in this case, have produced embarrassingly empty results. As a Frenchman, the filmmaker of today, like his elder contemporaries, sees life as logical, which is not to say he doesn't (therefore) see it as terrible, just as the Italian feels life as lyrical, which isn't to say he doesn't experience it also as a nightmare (*8½* is here the consummate expression). The poverty of most Anglo-American films is (among other factors) the result of there being behind them no implicit life-feeling (which informs a rhythm as well as a philosophy). They never express, with any artistry, an inborn collective principle that goes deeper than the subject of the hour-and-a-half; their view-point, when you can isolate one, is always and only social—at a categorical level. They may, therefore (i.e., English films), develop ingratiating characterizations or (in the American film) a degree of soured wit and feckless energy, but they never acquire form from the perception by which they were conceived; they cannot define the cultural gamut within the shape and span of a single situation. The short way of saying this is to declare that our films are not made by poets.

I want to illustrate the range and the rich interdependence of French film-making with four films, three of them current, one from 1960. My justification for introducing a five-year-old film is my belief that among the critic's obligations is the salvaging of neglected films before they go softly into that dark night, a fate that appears to be overtaking François Leterrier's *Les Mauvais Coups*. But a primary question, because the answer is interesting: Who is François Leterrier? In 1956 he had no connection, to my knowledge, with film or any aspect of theater, when, as a philosophy student, he was chosen by Robert Bresson, who detests professional actors, to assume the dominating role in *Un Condamné à Mort s'est Echappé*. By what means he was seduced from asking questions about phenomena to making imaginative constructs of them, I am not informed; I know only that soon afterward he was an assistant to Louis Malle and that by 1960 he had learned enough, if that's an adequate predication, to make *Les Mauvais Coups*. This was a peak year in French film releases, New Wave variety and others. Among notable productions were Malle's *Zazie in the Metro*, Michel Drach's *Amalie*, Clouzot's *La Vérité*, Godard's *Breathless*, Truffaut's *Shoot the Piano Player*, Chabrol's *Les Bonnes Femmes*, Clément's *Plein Soleil (Purple Noon)*, Doniol-Valcroze's *L'Eau à la Bouche*, François Reichenbach's *L'Amérique Insolite*, and Jacques Becker's swan song, *Le Trou* (now in the U.S. under the title *The Night Watch*). In my opinion only Becker's film and the Reichenbach "documentary" are, for evident reasons, more impressive than *Les Mauvais Coups*: no other film of that year, from France, and few since, can safely be nominated as a finer example of craftmanship subtly elaborated. Therein, perhaps, lies the reason for its obscurity.

The term New Wave became attached to special categories of film —those that featured obvious visual and temporal dislocations or those, on the other hand, that were as close as possible to unedited reportage (*cinéma vérité*). This sophomoric classification has successfully condemned to oblivion many sensitive films of the period in many countries—among them Leterrier's, which is no more New Wave than a sonata by Chopin.

Subject and setting are as old as French film; more to the point, they're as old as the French novel. Here is the chateau in the woods where countless women from Stendhal's Ernestine to Mauriac's Thérèse Desqueyroux have been bored to extinction or have murdered (or tried to murder) their husbands and lovers.* The only important difference in the contemporary version related by Leterrier is the proximity of a casino and of a daily bottle of Johnny Walker, both permissible for the woman. It is not a saving difference. The antagonists, called Milan and Roberte, are self-doomed: he is an ex-champion of the automobile-racing world, voluntarily shackled to Roberte, whom he had ceased to love before he married her (from compassion). We learn, drop by dialogue drop, accumulating as gradually as the rain that closes down over the melancholy countryside, that a friend and racing companion of Milan had committed suicide on the track, for love of Roberte, ten years before. She, in the perverse fashion of her kind (woman), has been ever since drinking herself into the age she deeply fears and driving daily nails into Milan to see how many he can bear and still stand up (or lie down?) like a man. When a young schoolteacher arrives in the village, Roberte sees another weapon with which to goad Milan to the brink, by which she's actually horrified. Eaten by jealousy and fear even as she does so, Roberte proceeds to beautify the girl in her own former image—the better, she thinks, to get her into her husband's bed. The weapon backfires with admirable precision. Milan does fall in love with the girl, but this only propels him into shaking off ten years of lethargy, writing a contract to drive again, and leaving for Italy—alone. Long servitude to a lethal

---

*In 1962, Georges Franju made a movie from Part I of Mauriac's novel, and you could well believe he had photographed the same oak trees that figured in Leterrier's film. With all respect to Franju, I think his film is inferior to Leterrier's: the editing is more uncertain, the transitions are more "theatrically" contrived. Since writing the above, I have seen *Diary of a Chambermaid*, manipulated, with acrid skill, from an earlier-period novel of Octave Mirbeau, wherein the "same" setting, but with utterly charmless interiors, has become a *mise en scène* for the further scatology of Luis Buñuel.

woman burns too much heart out of a man for him to believe he has enough left to risk on another. The girl is consoled, as they always are in such matters, by a dull young man lurking in the background. Roberte, having achieved the rejection she dreaded more than anything in the world, and deprived of her daily diet of torture, commits suicide by driving herself into a lake. In the counterautomotive last shot, the husband, in Modena, receives the news impassively as he straps on his helmet before taking his first test run into "freedom."

The style of Leterrier's film suggests to me that he learned structure from Malle and restraint from Bresson. He made a better film than any so far made by his masters; he is never so dry as Bresson and he's more musically indolent than Malle. He shares, with many of his contemporaries, the one conspicuous advantage they have over such veterans as Renoir, Delannoy, Autant-Lara, or Cayatte; they are less sententious than their elders. Leterrier handles symbolic motifs with graceful indirection; he assimilates "literary" textures with no loss of film values.* The opening sequence, so disingenuously played out by husband and wife, duck shooting at dawn, supplies all the undertones necessary to prepare you for the mortal combat which will occupy the rest of the narrative. You don't get the full gravity in one discharge, either. Complete alienation is not the daily condition of such a relationship: even between handcuffed souls love is as routine a habit as hate. So there are exchanges, almost tender, and disarming questions about the evening arrangements, little sparks of spite you're not quite sure were intended, all interjected between the sudden leveling of a gun, the mid-air collapse and spiraling descent of a dead bird—and at one moment Milan forcibly quiets Roberte (in one of those vain attempts one makes to ward off the irrevocable) by holding her attention to the neutral wonder of a pale sunrise sifting over the wet fields and the glum oaks. . . . And before getting far into the film you are forced to acknowledge how utterly right Simone Signoret is and how disastrous it would have been if Jeanne Moreau had played Roberte. I think most of us have by now come to similar conclusions about

---

*The script is by Roger Vailland, from his own novel. In the same year, Vailland co-wrote the screen version of *Les Liaisons Dangereuses* (a related subject) for Roger Vadim's direction. A comparison of these two films would suffice, if other evidence were wanting, to illustrate Vadim's essential vulgarity. . . . Since *Les Mauvais Coups*, Leterrier has made two other films: *Un Roi sans Divertissement* (1963) and *La Mer Promise* (1966). I have not seen them; they seem not to have been widely distributed.

La Moreau: that with all her skill, which consists importantly in her instinct for variable degrees of *energy* (Signoret, by contrast, has a relatively unvarying pace), she has become, between one film and the next, simply unbearable to look at in closeup, since her consistently wanton expression is limited to roles where that is the required characteristic. Whereas the slowly impending effect of Roberte is devastating just because Signoret is not at once and prevailingly a bitch. As in all other films we've seen her in, she is unbelievably authentic with every move or preparation for one: the way she smokes without handling the cigarette, the art with which she manipulates domestic things—lipsticks, purses, knives, bottle openers—the way she reviews all possibilities in her eyes before she says the one (damning or irrelevant) thing. And there's an interlude at the casino that seems to have been designed for her to show everything she knows about non-acting.

Avec Des Si . . . (1964) is seemingly as different from Leterrier's film in subject and method as two movies can be, yet Leterrier and Claude Lelouch speak the same language—French. Lelouch may have a great future ahead of him: he's a troublemaker. Three short documentaries from his hand have all been doused by the censors; one other feature film he has shown only to his friends (I don't know why; perhaps there's a connective reason). So far as we're concerned, then, *Avec Des Si* is his first film. (The title is untranslatable: my heavy approximation would be *Not Without Reservations*.) I'd say he was closer kin to Reichenbach than to any contemporary whose work I have seen, for his film gets most of its fun and all of its dire point from its dialectical view of the big nasty crowd that constitutes present-day society, then shakes us with the unwelcome revelation of how tainted each of us is by that crowd's perspective. I can't adequately explain this remark if you haven't seen the film, since to do so would betray a strategy of which you have to be ignorant until then. Suffice it to explain that the film is structured as a special kind of suspense story. As substantially as I can narrate the action, we are accompanying a man on a drive through the French landscape to an unrevealed destination, and a third or more of the movie is taken up with establishing him in counterpoint with the distant swarmy world, by way of the car's radio, as he drives. The major motif of the broadcasts is the pursuit of an escaped prisoner, jailed for a sex crime, and the effect on us of the national news bulletins, particulars of which are *visualized* and abruptly crosscut with the foreground business of the man driving, eating, resting, and so on, is a growing conviction that, balanced against the general depravity of man at large, a sex maniac seems no more culpable (a reading, under the aspect of black humor, that recalls William Bolitho's appalling subterranean theme in *Murder for Profit*). By the time our lone driver has picked up a girl at a country tavern and resumed his journey, with the police in pursuit, across a now snow-covered landscape, we are prepared for the consequence of our deductions. In short, this is a "gimmick" film, and there's this to be said strongly in its favor: the mechanical area of the gimmick—the radio news visualization—is more amusing in itself than Godard's jump-cutting and moreover *functions* in the development of the narrative (though I can't say that Lelouch, in his enthusiasm, doesn't overwork the device). The classic French unity is preserved. Once more there is that familiar double measure, the constriction followed by the release: the claustrophobia of the car and the inane scope of world-wide Man; the figure on the beach breathing freedom near the beginning of the film, the man on the lighthouse pier at the end. All in all, I think Lelouch comes near to what he claims to have attempted: the confrontation of the world with the life of one man. But what endears the film to me more than its forensics is its sheer poetry, the feeling for weather and movement and liberating space that Lelouch sustains while up to his deviltry. (For those who savor the technics of the business, *Avec Des Si* is alive with illustrations of how to use a zoom lens with maximum effect for plausible reasons.)

Umbrellas of Cherbourg (1964) could also, I guess, be classified as a novelty film, albeit a prose summary would seem to refute the possibility of there being anything novel about it at all. Genevieve, who works in her mother's umbrella shop, loves Guy, a gas station employee. When Guy is drafted into the Algerian war she is sure she'll die without him. After five months, during which either he hasn't written or his letters have miscarried, she (pregnant) accepts a rich suitor, Michel, who in fact seemed on the verge of being her mother's suitor. Guy returns and after a wild sulk appeases himself with his aunt's nurse, who has waited for him more unrelentingly than Genevieve. On a snowy Christmas Eve (yes, indeed!) four years later, Genevieve, now a rich widow, stops her limousine at a gas station *owned* by Guy. Time rolls back, momentarily, as they try to say something nostalgic and relevant to each other; however, since Guy is happy with his fate, which includes a child of his own (decoyed into the snowflaked closing tableau), there is nothing to be said.

I can put myself in your place. If anyone recited the above to me I'd promptly say, "Yes, I've seen it." If he then protested that it was in color, I'd be likely to growl softly, "So what?" If he further insisted that the dialogue *was not spoken but sung, throughout,* I would close the subject with the icy observation that I had had it. . . . But Jacques Demy and Bernard Evein (responsible for the décors) have refuted our inferences with art: there's no more recherché way of putting it. Unlike Reginald Gardiner, who could imitate wallpaper vocally, I haven't the talent for explaining, in prose, *why* Demy's combination of singing and of exquisitely nuanced color transforms the timeless geometrical banality of human relationships into enchantment that misses, by a hair, the pitfalls of archness. If I say that the film, by these means, is situated in another dimension, I don't mean to imply metaphysics. I simply mean that like *The Importance of Being Earnest,* for example, the pleasure is *artificial*—it is artifice, concerned approximately with daily life, yet as remote from it as a ballet. To approach this experience with any other expectation would be disastrous to your appreciating its quality. Demy has insisted that for him film is form—and only form. Whether or not he's guilty of making a false conceptual distinction is not so important as his being entitled to judgment in his own terms. His film is an exercise in style, like Agnes Varda's *Cleo.* Some critics heavily deprecated Miss Varda's effort in the mistaken belief that she believed she was creating a tragedy, whereas obviously, I should think, *Cleo* used mock tragedy as a subterfuge for a loving excursion into milieu. To be sure, *Umbrellas* is not everyone's fun. If you can only spend time on films that trouble the soul, stay away. But I would suppose it to have appeal for all those who enjoy, or claim to enjoy, the art of Vermeer, of Matisse, or of Vuillard. It is definitely one way of making film. Godard's is a way of un-making it.

Umbrellas won not only the Louis Delluc prize but also the Grand Prize at Cannes, where, on the same occasion, François Truffaut's *La Peau Douce* was first shown last year. This must have put Truffaut's nose out of joint, a chastening rebuff. I have had for some time the conviction that Truffaut is probably a "born" movie-maker, and I've wished he'd more quickly accept the inevitable and stop doing beastly things—like encouraging Godard, organizing claques against Antonioni, saying cute things for the press, and assisting the sinister apotheosis of "Tubby" Hitchcock, who became cinematic lard ages ago. *La Peau Douce* is welcome assurance, at least, that Truffaut is not bogging down in, or being blown away on, his own powers of virtuosity. The lightning bugs who jitter in festival corridors have been sputtering like dampened wicks, unable to "place" this film in Truffaut's "development." Should they relate it to *The 400 Blows* or to *Shoot the Piano Player,* or should they assign it to outer darkness because there's no felt spray from the Wave on it—because it's a backtracking to "traditional" film-making, not central to, crucial for, or representative of the new generation of which Truffaut himself, who wrote the script of *Breathless,* et cetera? . . . God forbid they should cease this vain bibble-babble and just acknowledge *La Peau Douce* as a damn good film, rich with social inflection, supple as the work of Ophuls.

The ill-chosen title (*The Soft Skin*) conceals a baleful subject. This is one of those time machines the French put into motion so expertly. Life is a mechanism: some people survive and prosper in it, some are crushed before their hour, some can step out of the mechanism and back into it again without being missed and be carried on, with no further hindrance, to a ripe and disappointed age. Once in a while, even for the opulent and the heretofore lucky, the timing seriously and unaccountably miscarries: then—POOM! the whole thing blows up in the unsuspecting face. *La Peau Douce* is a suspense story, but you don't know it is if you can't *feel* throughout that you're waiting for something (I mean something more than the sexual resolution) with every take, every episode, every erotic or intellectual divertissement; that the purring dynamics, the propulsive strategies of the comings and goings, the synchronized operations of airplanes and automobiles and elevators, the departures from an unsuspecting wife, the perfunctory kissing of the children, the hasty conferences and assignations in hotels and motels, the pearls cast on the subject of Allegret's film about Gide, the ludicrous evasions of an importunate admirer in Rheims: that all this, much of it the tangled web of a triangle, that ancient bloody triangle, veils the brute fact that life is overtaking a man—a very nice, shyly smiling man whom, as the film ends, you're beginning to love, maybe, because he's really too foolish, in a way you know, to be unconcerned about, too pure at heart to be reprobated, yet too knowing to be pitied. . . . This is Jean Desailly; you wouldn't believe he could play any other part if you hadn't seen him as a chief of detectives, all softly beaming face, a resolute walk, and a heart of tungsten. The girl is Françoise Dorleac, and I suppose she has charm—she's more piquant than Miss Stewart, who occupied the same position in Leterrier's triangle—but three weeks after seeing the film I can't remember what she looks like. The *actress* in the film is Nelly Benedetti (wife), perfectly in control, not one bit anxious to show you any more than her perfunctory self until provoked (though her contours are unmistakable), knowing to the second how long to coast, where the accents fall in a scene, how to hoard, when—and how!—to explode, refulgent and final like a shower of Roman candles.

And I suppose that all the coy attention to silent-film comedy and gangster films that Truffaut indulges may be explicable as the clown side of the recognition he pays to the patently malevolent role that timing plays in the destiny of a man. For at the eleventh hour in *La Peau Douce* the irrevocable doesn't have to be. The girl knows what world the man belongs in better than he does, and why it's not hers; all the man has to do is choke it down and strap himself back into the machine, with one more regressive dream to befuddle himself with in whatever spare time he has earned with his fame. . . . If only his wife hadn't chosen that moment in which to send his suit to the cleaners; if only he had had the change with which to make those two telephone calls consecutively! A coincidence: that demonic plaything of logic, supposed not to be logical—or is it supposed not to be artistic? When art employs coincidence, we call it unnatural, yet a coincidence in life we see as a crowning jest from art. . . .   1965

Films from the Perimeter

In fifty years there will be no lost tribes, no vanishing clans, no unspoiled agricultural peoples, no autonomous Andean Indians or oceanic islanders weaving cloth and dancing to invoke the approval of unseen powers. Today every film that embodies ethnic values has won a territory against the near future, when human variety will be a phenomenon which only students of anthropology or history will be permitted to recall.

Pour la Suite du Monde is such a film, though I hasten to add that it does not come under the heading of *exotica*. Produced for the Canadian Film Board, it concerns the relatively uneventful lives of a fishing community, located somewhere in the terraqueous reaches of the St. Lawrence, known as L'Isle-aux-Coudres. A few years ago the inhabitants of this island were offered $500 by an American aquarium for a large white tuna, to be delivered alive. Since tuna fishing was a tradition long since abandoned by the village, the economic proposition involved them in months of debate, speculation, research, and finally preparation. Overlapping this period two young French Canadians, Pierre Perrault and Michel Brault, spent a year and a half making the film. In so doing they defined the daily life of a rural community as, on film, no one has ever done to my recollection. Twenty years ago Georges Rouquier set himself a comparable task and spent about the same length of time with a peasant family in the heart of France. The product was *Farrébique* (1946), to my sense one of the more boring among many earnestly made films on which the term "classic" has been bestowed by surveyors of film history (Visconti's *La Terra Trema* is another). And it's useless to argue that the life of the St. Lawrence islanders is more susceptible to cinema than that of Rouquier's farmers. You find poetry in the fact, as the admirable Grierson used to insist, yet I'm not sure he didn't understate the importance of there being a poet on hand to find it. But roots he never undervalued. Perrault and Brault have roots in French film-making, and Perrault has roots in the island (he's married to a native of Coudres) : they were thus, perhaps, less self-conscious than Rouquier in their scrutiny.

This much and little more I know about the directors. What more there is to know can be inferred from the film itself, wherein the moments that do not directly contribute to the decoy subject (the trapping of the tuna) are just those through which the film lives. If you try following the scenario as a straight-line chronology you will miss what's really shaping up: what the people believe, of what their daily elations consist, how they work, how they divert themselves. In all this, as a life-way, there's nothing spectacular. The villagers of L'Isle-aux-Coudres look as if they'd been left by the tide. No doubt their ancestors were. To the disengaged eye, their immediate surroundings are no different from those of a hundred back-country places one has been in and couldn't get out of quickly enough—whether they were in Oregon, Central Sweden, or Bavaria. With a difference that's especially striking when compared with Rouquier's microcosm in *Farrébique:* these people are happy. As I recall, the peasants in the earlier film did little more than grunt at each other as they sat down to their potato soup, and there was no music in their lives save a once-a-month jig in a bare tavern, whereat the men danced joylessly with each other. In Coudres, life is relationship and exchange and it moves to the artless accompaniment of fife, fiddle, and concertina. The oldest generation quote from the Bible and harangue their juniors from the logbook of Jacques Cartier; the younger ancients dispute them and cheerfully insult each other in a peculiar patois of French probably surviving from the Renaissance period. They are, in short, expressive: they're provincial in the purest sense but they are not lacking in articulate philosophies, and a trace of civilization—i.e., of the civil—lingers in their smiles and in their gestures.

Perrault's method is basically that of *cinéma vérité* but he's not impeded by it; unlike Jean Rouch he is not at pains to let the subject film itself. For yards of time he may confront some old gaffer still full of life juices and Gallic gesticulations while he talks and talks and talks. Then abruptly, as if the camera had independently protested and run away to pick flowers, he cuts from the argument or whatever it may be, into the more pointless and artistic flourishes of existence, often retaining a musical rhythm from the scene deserted, as he follows a jog-trotting timber sled or a bouncing rowboat. The trajectory is almost diametrically distinct from that of Vittorio De Seta, who, intent on similar material, plunges into a group action already in crescendo, sustains a driving pace without looking to right or left, then terminates the whole thing just before it all settles down and levels out. The settling down and leveling out is part of Perrault's music. This is a difficult mode of composition, achieved principally, I would guess, during the editing stage, and this entails, of necessity, the shooting of much more material than you have running time for. A fact film, especially, since it can't be shaped in advance, must get back from its edited footage the life it intermittently recorded, but with fresh relationships. If report is correct, Perrault's ratio—about three to one—was not exceptionally high; the more to his credit that the resulting continuity feels inevitable without seeming calculated.

Nobody Waved Goodbye is quite another matter. This is quite another Canada, where a tuna fish, far from being as eventful in community history as a flood or a crime, is merely something that comes in a tin. *Pour la Suite du Monde* isn't really about Canada; it's about L'Isle-aux-Coudres. Perrault wants to show you something; Don Owen, an English Canadian, wants to tell you something. He wants to tell you what you already know, but he tells you with such a disingenuous, bright-eyed method, for the most part, that you don't at all mind listening. What he has to say, through the story of a mutinous adolescent, too intelligent too soon, is that urban Canada, no less than any other progressive country where the nerve has been removed and the cavity root-packed, is bored to extinction by the materialism it has willed—and defensively complacent about its boredom. The film owes so much to those high-minded American TV dramas we've been seeing on sundry social problems—drily reasonable and unhistrionic, with all sides having their innings—that it comes as a pleasurable shock to realize that the probable model was *The 400 Blows,* with all the crucial differences which, apart from the central fact that Peter Kastner is older (yet newer) than Pierre Leaudy, may as well be accounted for by the distance between Paris and Toronto.

In any case, the pattern is almost identical. Peter, like Pierre alienated from his family (and in this case from his girl), is led to the brink of crime—not so much from neglect, however, as from his impatient disgust with the only social aspirations offered him as desirable. Apparently Owen let his actors improvise their dialogue, after giving them the situation, and this is a hazard over which a director can damn well struggle without my sympathy. I could have done with two-thirds less dialogue and far fewer closeups, not only of Mother, whose voice was too authentically desiccated for my shell-like ear to withstand, but also of Peter's "girl," who deserved to be abandoned for not having once combed her hair. To be sure, Owen rescued some wonderfully disarming moments from this unaffected treatment, but since he had too much conscience to remain dependent on reality unadorned, his film increasingly became an uncertain compromise between the lifelike and the suavely cinematic. Even so, underneath the public prosecutor message of *Nobody Waved Goodbye,* "It's easier to steal than to think constructively," there drums the unanswerable—"It's better to steal than to be a stalled ox," and this is an unexpected motif to emerge from the long tradition of tedium maintained by Canadian Film Board documentary. Owen and others with whom he is associated herald a new outlook from that brand-new sector of film-making in which heretofore Norman Maclaren has been the single bright anomaly. I might mention in passing that Owen has even more confidence when out of this world, if I may judge from an engrossing short film he made called simply *Universe* (except for some streaming nebulae, it had an all-star cast?). I don't know how astronomers rate its contribution to the field, but as film poetry it's superlative.

Set it down in the good book: everything else being equal (an economic foundation and a visual tradition), countries with the highest proportion of cultural lag make the most vivid films. Japan, for instance—where timeless occupations linger in fact and where atrocious historical codes survive as subjects for art because their kinetic power is irresistible. For some years I have treasured among my favorite documentaries a half-hour film made in a mountain wilderness that observed, with fitting reverence, a season in the life of an old man (the last of his breed) who catches and trains falcons (for whose use I have no idea). And recently I have seen *Seppuku* (or *Hara-kiri*), a generously full-length film which I found sympathetic for some of the same reasons. It also celebrates a vanished dedication—insofar as we are speaking of the physical subject, self-disemboweling, one that is not likely to arouse nostalgia in anyone known to me. The essential terms of the film are familiar to us: death before dishonor or, rather, death to wipe out an attributed dishonor. Hanshiro, a *ronin* who has been discarded in the shuffle that has established a new shogunate, must die by hara-kiri if he is refused service as a samurai. Two and a half hours of relentlessly inhibited narration are occupied with a foregone conclusion. Since it is disclosed, or alleged, that his son-in-law died disgracefully, Hanshiro (played with something like demonic self-possession by Tatsuya Nakadai) is on hand not only to perform the definitive act himself but to recite the unspeakable truth of the matter concealed by his "host."

Such subjects in Japanese film give every sign of surviving the most violent social changes. To what extent they are relished for their ethical content by the Japanese themselves, only an informed witness (Donald Richie, for example) would know. For us (meaning those who share my impaled consent to the genre) the appeal is that of style, which means much more than the salient formality of the settings and the theatrical vehemence of the action. Style here is the outward expression of the concept that man is authentic to the degree that he accepts the circumstances of his fate and vindicates the cruelty of them by undergoing the rituals ordained for transcending their futility. That this is the very opposite of a "modern" attitude, East or West today, has obviously not diminished its fascination for a sizable number of people who are surely as averse as I (more they couldn't be) to the notion of cold steel voluntarily planted in the belly. The beauty of the samurai tradition, like others of its historical kind, lay in its artful simplicity: the unshakable laws of conduct were the moral equivalents of the ceremonious prescriptions for debate and for dueling; like these they derived their force of character from the tension that constrained them. We might describe the whole tradition as an unusually dynamic expression of what we call classicism—while everything is known, thematic variations are infinitely possible.

Much of this compact alliance of tensions has been preserved in Masaki Kobayashi's direction of *Seppuku*. The pace is calculated to extract every ounce of suspense; the flashbacks and supplementary actions are timed with sadistic precision to interfere with the forthright development of the main event. As a whole it is more successful in these terms, and has a more expressionist accent, than Kurosawa's *The Throne of Blood, Sanjuro,* and *Yojimbo*. No small part of the conviction is assisted by the fact that early in the film we are made to witness the actual hara-kiri (or as much of it as can be contrived and most of us can bear) of a previous victim. As in the *Forty-Seven Ronin,* which has been filmed a half-dozen times, the whole pent-up force is released with orgiastic ferocity in the last fifteen minutes of film, a dependable convention that taxes the inventive wits of the director. . . . Among unexpected consequences of my seeing this film, I found that it reduced to virtual nonsense a favorite aphorism from the late Aldous Huxley: "One culture gives us the pyramids, another the Escorial, a third, Forest Lawn. But the act of dying remains always and everywhere identical." If Mr. Huxley now inhabits a world where time is more plastic than even he supposed, he may be in a position to submit this conclusion to a number of fellow shades. And somewhere there must be a samurai who died trying to gouge his insides out with a bamboo sword because he had sold his own more effective weapon.

The act of dying, in all its variety, is a subject too omnipresent, in any case, to be repudiated by film-makers. And death by violence is as universal a language as love. Surprisingly, a group of Cuban films I saw not long ago was comparatively temperate if you consider the normally high saturation in bloodshed of movies made in Latin America, whether in Brazil, Argentina, or Mexico. From four programs of Cuban film I can't indulge a rage for prophecy. I'm not even sure there's anything of great cinematic moment going on today. I hope there may be, for the reasons I set down earlier. All I know is that the Castro regime has been supporting film production and has imported European cinematographers to instruct the first Cuban contingent. The advantage of a revolution, to the film-maker who shares its goals, is self-evident: it gives him basic physical situations, ideological simplicities, quickly reducible choices. It faces life with death, and this is a *sine qua non* of drama. Two of these films, both multi-episodic, dealt with allegedly factual material gleaned from the last days of the Batista regime: *Stories of the Revolution* and *Cuba 58.* They centered on such questions as: Should you exploit a bourgeois girl friend by asking her to conceal hand grenades in her skirt so that you can blow up a building in the name of the revolution? If a guerrilla comrade is dying in the jungle, do you stop him from blowing out his own insides with a gun? What happens to cops when the regime they have been serving with willing brutality is overthrown? The execution of these and some short documentary items was predictably uneven, but all in all there was an unmistakable tang of sincerity that led one to feel encouraged about the possibility of a new film-making frontier. Yet our hopes are understandably discolored by skepticism. The very notion of Castro sponsoring films dedicated to liberty seems a dirty joke to most of us, but the irony has wider application. All regimes instigated by revolution administer the kiss of death. After the first vital flurry of approved subjects, the film-maker (novelist or whoever) is faced with the problem of analytically expressing the resumed life instead of recapitulating the hour of glorious upheaval. Then if he suggests that individual problems remain, which the state hasn't solved and which can't even be shared by the new community, the knife comes down. We have seen the effects of this conditioning in Soviet Russia and, with variable degrees, in every satellite country. Our interest in Polish film producers, sustained through many disappointments, is sharpened by our sympathy with their desperate hunt to find unequivocal subject matter in the grey environment of a post-revolution society.

Yugoslavia is signed, sealed, and delivered. I went to see *Skopje 63* on the not-unfounded assumption that since it was the record of a tragedy—the razing of a town by earthquake—essential emotions would be visibly revealed: the emotions of survival, in which shock, gratitude, and grief are blended. I escaped unscathed. Despite the numerous closeups of wreckage, the wailing, the stunned faces, the soup lines, the rigging of tents for the temporary housing of the survivors while a cloudburst harried their already tormented lives—despite all this I felt as deeply untouched, if as decently sympathetic, as one does during a newsreel when you're trying to suffer vicariously for the victims of a mine disaster, ten seconds after leaving the Paris mannequins revolving like lighthouses for an overhead shot to show off the season's new hats. When I told some friends of mine that the film had left me unmoved, their look asked me plainly, "What did you expect? Blood?" I suppose I did, in a manner of speaking. I expected something authentic, and what is more authentic than sorrow? But to deduce it is not enough; I can't be expected to make my own movie from the hints of a movie someone else didn't make. The fact is that we have long since passed the stage when any full-length documentary is bewitching because it's "real." We do expect something close to art; we demand the results of an inquisitorial eye, we are accustomed to electrifying closeups and adroit editing, we wait for the unpredictable reactions of people caught off guard. To exploit disaster effectively—and if that wasn't the point here, what was it?—takes more than reverence. I am convinced that if Perrault, Vittorio De Seta, or Frederic Rosi (who managed that fabulous re-creation of the Spanish Civil War, *To Die in Madrid*) had been assigned to the ruins of Skopje, any one of them would have brought back a potently disturbing film.

However, the failure (as I see it) of *Skopje 63* can't simply be accounted for by alleging insensitivity to the director. The insufficiency was guaranteed by the conditions of Yugoslav film-making. According to a report published a few years back by Donald Richie (in *Film Quarterly*), the procedure of getting a scenario accepted and produced is comparable to that of labor-management negotiations in certain countries we're familiar with. The recommendation is passed on from one People's Committee to another. Naturally the writer shares the common assumptions or his script would never get beyond the first committee. This is no doubt considered a democratic process, and therein lies the clue to what happened at Skopje —and to what didn't happen. They made a movie and submitted its content to arbitration. The film begins with its director introducing to the people the footage he shot—presumably the film one is seeing thereafter; it ends with his soliciting a referendum from the audience. Do they approve? Do they have any complaints? Have they suggestions to make? I don't dispute the right of people to have their privacy respected (a paradoxical sentiment in countries where everyone is owned by everyone else anyway), but if that was really the issue why try to make a movie in the first place? The belief that you can create film by the same method with which you settle a strike is one of the exemplary stupidities of the socialist mind.

In other countries, besides those collectivized, film-makers often have to beat their thickets to flush a subject, the difference being that if they find one their chances of expressing it are not so hopeless; their problems are likely to be temperamental rather than political. The Swedish, with no social ferment, little ethnic variety, no photogenic minorities, and no moment of national danger to recall, are forced to dig deeply into what exigent conflicts they have, or to look for trouble elsewhere. This is why Swedish films mostly seem so *willed,* so gratuitously intent on finding pain or working up joy. There's little point in begging this question; that's the way they make film and if it's the hard way it can't be said not to yield results. Against the films of Bo Widerberg and Mai Zetterling, which have most caught international attention this year—films that to my sense illustrate strenuously this primacy of the will—I'd like to urge a different example of Swedish film art, the more gratifying for its breakaway from the vitreous pictorialism and from the cold bite of anxiety that dominate the Swedish cinema. Arne Sucksdorff's film, *My Home Is Copacabana,* is one of the purest victories won by poetry from sociology that I've seen in some time. Growing organically from Sucksdorff's deepening intimacy with a handful (among thousands) of Rio de Janeiro's homeless boys—they live by their wild wits, always within fearful distance of the law—and made in the teeth of seriously interfering conditions, it is so inconceivably balanced between what I know to be actual and what appears to be too alive to be "true" that long after seeing it I was in a mood of delight shot through with disbelief. This is a work of quite extraordinary veracity, astoundingly free from special pleading and from the easy ingratiations of dialectic. It sings all the way, soaring above the prose of implicit misery like the dancing kite with which the film opens. But that kite is tethered to the guiding hand of one small boy, a creature of infinite jest and unquenchable vitality. Sucksdorff (with his camera always attentive and rarely at rest) never deserts that boy and his three co-urchins as they play, fight, beg, shoe-shine, steal, and above all fantasize. He worked with these youngsters for eight months before he ever focused a lens on them. The "trained spontaneity" he elicited by so doing, in order to reenact their plucky, desperate, and instinctively histrionic lives, is a miracle of effort concealed. Most remarkably, he never takes up an attitude toward them and never stops to stress what is sufficiently obvious— the big, luxurious, indifferent city waiting to certify them as criminals and grind them up. Rio is always there, far below the scrappy, picturesque heights where the boys live (in an aloof wasteland of tropical scrub and vulture-tended garbage) or curving away into a scenic fugue of beach and massed luxury hotels.

Always the craftsman—his editing of the film is as nimble as his cinematography—Sucksdorff has regained the unfaltering instinct that made him a master of the animal and bird world in the films he produced between 1943 and 1953. The fundamental purity of that instinct, informing every passage of *My Home Is Copacabana,* is expressed with final and subtle authority in his ending of the film. Misfortune is surrendering one of the boys to voluntary captivity, and at this concentratedly painful moment Sucksdorff's decision to keep the scene at distance, observed from above, is as inspired in its own way as Truffaut's in his, when he brought his equivocal young fugitive into commanding closeup.   1965

The Verge and After:
Film by 1966

Whoever is creative in a truly original sense . . . aims at being self-sufficient; whoever indulges in the bizarre seeks to impress his contemporaries or to amaze them.
Max Friedländer, *On Art and Connoisseurship*

The party's over. . . . Another phase of film history, in many ways the most creative, is drawing to a close, accompanied by a jump-cut bang and a pornographic whimper. Consistent with the cycles that prevail in the public arts, the masters of the last decade have been in turn extolled, exploited, excoriated, and finally expropriated. What makes the spectacle doubly painful is to note how often the elect have themselves lost nerve and dignity, producing travesties of their own work in obedience to the querulous onslaught which infallibly followed the first wave of pseudo-intellectual adulation from the gaggle of geese that yearly troubles the air over Cannes, over Berlin, over Venice, over San Sebastián, and over Karlovy-Vary.

If we look back to some of the outstanding films released between 1957 and 1964, no *revenant* with a lapsed party-membership card, a volume of Paul Rotha at his beck, and a picture of Garbo next to his mother's over the bed can persuade us that there was only one

Golden Age (in a mere fifty years of film-making) or that it had more to offer the mature mind and the exacting eye. Reconsider the following, *made in Europe alone,* and ask the jealous archivist how many movies of the Silent Era or of any period before the fifties have exposed the human muddle more searchingly, with such a range of idiom: from Sweden, *The Magician, The Virgin Spring, Winter Light;* from Italy, *L'Avventura, La Notte, Labbra Rosse, Bandits of Orgosolo, Fellini 8½, Il Posto;* from France, *Le Beau Serge (The Friends), The 400 Blows, Le Trou (The Night Watch), Les Mauvais Coups, Un Coeur Gros Comme Ça, Jules et Jim, Sundays and Cybèle;* from Poland, *True End of the Great War* and *Knife in the Water;* from Soviet Russia, *Lady with a Dog;* from Greece, *A Matter of Dignity;* from Spain, *Viridiana;* from Hungary, *The Lark.*

An arbitrary selection, of course, perhaps even highly personal; it comprises films which have never acquired the doubtful status of being *en vogue,* as well as many that stand precisely for what we mean when we talk of a new wave, a new refinement, a new liberation. What they have in common, regardless of genre and of whether the immediate subject is elemental or sophisticated, is a kind of authenticity which used to be labeled *adult* (still is, in areas where filmgoers haven't grown up to it—and never will) and resources of style for conveying the values of quite diverse experiences. Remarkably, the best films of Bergman, of Antonioni, of Chabrol and Truffaut (and of numerous Frenchmen not named here), of Cacoyannis and of Leopoldo Torre-Nilsson (not listed above) have cultivated a growing tendency since the late war to provide a starved minority with film subject matter distilled from civilized sources of reference. These films have been distinguished by a rare quality of exposition—sentient, especially, in the realm of the unspoken—heretofore restricted to literature, without containing a foot that would have been more effective *as* literature. Thematic music has been drastically reformed or banished, actors have had tyrannical demands made on them to *feel* so that they'll look as if they're capable of thought. The irony is sharp. At the hour when the New Agglutinate is feverishly diligent, blurring all distinctions of class, capacity, sex, color, and nationality, and just when small, remote countries are haggling or plotting to efface themselves in an international supermarket, film-makers have at last learned, with some consistency, to disclose the telltale nuances of creed and behavior that make people interesting to one another at all.

For compound reasons, this newfound land of subtle possibilities has already been placed out of bounds or vandalized. We can better understand how and why if we relate what is happening now to what was promised in the fifties. As of today, Bergman and Antonioni are in purely defensive positions; Cacoyannis has done the unspeakable thing, proving (with *Zorba The Greek*) that he could stoop to the level of Jules Dassin; Polish film-makers have thoroughly tapped their one potent subject, the war within the War, and are looking for an *avant garde* to join outside their borders; Buñuel, a flourishing but impaired veteran, having made the definitive version of his bitter fables (one would suppose) in *Viridiana*, carries on vindictively, with seasonal reversions to anti-clericalism, exposés of the ruling classes (no longer ruling), and the fate of would-be saints in our time, for all the world like a literature professor I once knew whose main diversion, at fifty-odd, was to protest his rebellious virility by telling obscene stories to the nuns who attended his summer courses! The élite of the young Frenchmen have barely had a chance to establish themselves before being relegated by freezing funds and by the force-fed preference for Godardism. Chabrol has never recovered the classical definition of his first films. Resnais can scarcely ring further changes on an abstract mode which was, in any case, a revival of procedures thirty years old—and he's wisely not trying. Truffaut will survive, invincibly—or I'll never drink sack again. A dozen of them will survive creatively if they rob banks or implore Malraux to save them from the salt mines of the industrial documentary or the public shame of Anglo-American co-production. This leaves—among the master composers alluded to—Leopoldo Torre-Nilsson and Fellini. I haven't seen the last few films of Torre-Nilsson; on the basis of those I have seen I feel more confident of his future sanity than that of any director who came to prominence within the last fifteen years. So far as I've been able to verify, he hasn't been paralyzed by a monomaniac style, he has made no concessions to the liberals' good-housekeeping label, he hasn't begged us to look at his wounds, he hasn't wept or snarled because there is no God or because he's no longer breast-fed, and he hasn't closed a film with an immobilized frame (I hope I'm correct here). His settings—the colonial palaces, law courts, cafés, and spider-webbed attics of Buenos Aires—are indelible. Ruthless and picturesque, his films have been about responsibilities and they have usually taken place, morally, at the nexus of private dream and public importunity. So, in another way, have Fellini's. Unrivaled by anyone save

Kurosawa for sheer velocity and virtuosity, Fellini remains, if nothing else, the supreme epic mannerist. For how long his centripetal subject matter and his disingenuous self-regard can be kept alive by his ravishing energy I would make no attempt to predict. This would appear largely to depend on how many members of his family he can transfigure before being consumed in a blaze of vulgarity. Since he has the ingratiating notion that we are *all* members of his family (a triumph of Italian solipsism rather than of Catholic Christendom), he may have many more Roman candles to ignite. (I write this before the arrival of *Giulietta 9½*, trembling at every advance report.)

Of the three directors who have notably made film by schooling its means, rather than by amplifying them—Bresson, Antonioni, Bergman—the last named has shown the greatest staying power. Bresson, to whose monkish art Antonioni paid close heed twenty years ago, is now too much in love with God to cherish the finer points of cinema. Bergman hates Him with sufficient ambivalence to honor Him with a rival perfection. Antonioni mopes. . . . In 1958 Bergman was receiving a degree of rapt attention never before accorded a film director of such high-minded originality. Always too convenient a vehicle for critics hunting an esoteric thesis—in the French spirit, they hope—Bergman has offered other film-makers nothing to recapitulate except his forbidding integrity. He has taken some silly detours, even recently (such as *Not to Speak of All Those Women*), he has made embarrassingly defiant gestures and taken his subjects into polar wastes where few care to follow; yet his later work, seen as a whole, is incredibly disciplined, purged of all but the irreducible elements of theme, character, and setting, un-upholstered by auxiliary effects, optical or musical. Defiance hardens; it tends to encourage a man's most stubbornly held principles which, in an artist, may not be his purest. Film directors are terribly at the mercy of outside demands, which makes it inordinately difficult for them to be self-dedicated and diffident at the same time. Buñuel, Antonioni, Cacoyannis, and Fellini have all fatally reacted to their audience (i.e., to the hecklers) instead of abiding by their own consciences. Bergman has reacted negatively; making no attempts to comply or reform, he has simply retreated, and this strategy has certainly contributed to the austerity of his work. The question remains: how many more films about three people in a box canyon of the mind can we be expected to anticipate with pleasure? . . . Where Bergman *has* been used, grossly, is in the area of his compulsive sexual candor, which, in fact, assuming the need for being so visually explicit (I think this is the least important prerogative acquired by film producers), he has personally handled with extraordinary adroitness. Other Swedish film directors, however, share neither his justification nor his skill; yet, undeterred after *The Virgin Spring* and again following *The Silence,* they have more than abused his precedent, supplying us *ad nauseam* with panting simulations of orgasm, and explorations of every borderline activity they can hound the censor into releasing. As a Swedish problem, this is less significant than formerly; almost everywhere in the West, as well as in Japan, sex is simply another of the great forces devaluated by mass culture.*

Ansiktet (*The Magician*) occupies, in Bergman's chronology, a comparable position to that of *8½* in Fellini's, but when Bergman's film was premiered, Fellini was initiating his most grandiose mutation with *La Dolce Vita*. Almost before the film was edited, those who were privy to what had been going on in Rome were rushing to film a wilder party than the terminal one of Fellini's Morality. I don't know who is considered to hold that pointless record. I'd contend that the only grand orgy on film with as integral a function within its provoking subject is the terrible climax of *Viridiana,* and it's quite unlikely that Buñuel needed Fellini's inspiration for that. Altogether, Fellini has been too protean for anyone else glibly to adapt. His zestful commitment to life (be it ever so humble, fatuous, or corrupt, Fellini will find melody in it) is as inimitable as his sentimentality and his bent for allegory. Furthermore, the paraphrasable content of his later films does not lend itself to congenial reproduction. Fellini's treatment is everything, his message a modest ingredient. *8½,* for instance, can only be partitioned by egomaniacs with far less charm than Mastroianni-Fellini and with none of the author's expressionist poetry. That film does lend itself to crude simplification, no doubt of it. Removed from the immediate dazzle of the kaleidoscope and one's ready acknowledgment of the sad disparity between effort and achievement, you may be tempted to ask yourself if a director involved in large-scale movie-

---

*The pattern of Japanese film-making closely parallels that of the West—a hubbub of genuine experiment and calculated sensationalism, violent exhibits of suppressed panic and sexual belligerence and, at the still center, a few figures going their own temperate way. . . . The best of the *shomingeki* films, from the early fifties (made by Naruse, Gosho, and the late Ozu), rely on a form of understatement which suggests Antonioni but which, in sociological reference, is closer to the work of Ermanno Olmi.

making—especially, as depicted, one with such indiscriminate taste in women—is quite the ideal analogue for the Jasperian thesis that man is his situation!

Antonioni is the exemplary victim of unreserved admiration, excessive abuse, and—it must be confessed—of his own single-track fixation. When he transposed the dying strains of *La Dolce Vita* into reverberations that seemed to arise from the heart of an unembodied but distinctly felt doom, the result was a dimension of film language which should have been inviolable. Nothing is sacred. A periphery of apes clad as apostles has been making Antonioni-films galore, i.e., shooting sequences in which one or two lonely-of-course, alienated-of-course, dreamy individuals take an interminable length of time to answer a question or cross a room or, by the fact of their being juxtaposed with a leafless tree, a bank façade, or a sheet of water, are intended to suggest profoundly existential cramps. Unhappily, Antonioni is now doing little more than that himself, and the philistines who never understood what he was doing in the first place are bleating, "We told you so." Antonioni perfected a formalistic style which he was unable to rescue from mannerism, principally because he couldn't infuse it with creative variations of his single theme. He has an Italian gift (an eye for the scenic), but he is alarmingly devoid of an Italian resource: he is humorless. When a reporter asked him why he always used the same woman in his films, his reply was no less naive than the question: "I didn't think I had!" There's more than a touch of Savonarola in his makeup, and Italian critics, for whom all issues are political, have played on that nerve, shaking his confidence that there is nothing more important to be than a poet. The strain evident in *The Eclipse* is a rupture in *Red Desert*, where he has restated, feebly, the design of *Cronaca di un Amore* (1950) and, in part, of *Le Amiche* (1955): the socially displaced woman and the indecisive man, vaguely associated with the world of work. But *Red Desert*, a beautiful but damned silly movie, could as well be entitled *Red Herring*, since there is in it no adequate perspective, among the many tentatively advanced, from which to interpret what one is seeing. And this is not comparable to the cold, anagrammatic ingenuity of *Marienbad;* it denotes the confusion in Antonioni's mind as to what he's doing, what he's saying —which film he is re-making. Is one supposed to take seriously Monica's view of her surround—if so, why, since she's a psychoneurotic character? If not, whose? The lover has none (he hates all places), and the husband sees only the pragmatic content of things. The flirtation with "socialism" is a characteristic Italian gratuity these days (shake the hand which may yet feed you) —the rest is iridescent décor, and electronically contrived sound where there used to be ominous silence. . . . The wheel has come full circle. Antonioni's tacit subject, first announced in the short film he made about street sweepers (*Nettezza Urbana,* 1948) is the nature of the space that man inhabits. In the episode of the Princess Soraya film directed by him there remains only space—loaded with another great emptiness, the unbelievably inexpressive features of that woman. We needn't be too shocked by Antonioni's participation in this fraudulent advertising feature; he has done commercial stints before (co-direction of *The Tempest* and *Sign of the Gladiator,* in 1958, both uncredited) . It's known as singing for one's supper. All the same, it's a great pity, for no director has made a purer contribution to film art.

Purity is rarely transmissible and seldom for long attracts the young, who rightly prefer spontaneity. Several young Frenchmen have managed both qualities and thereby confounded the eager in their train. The movement in France proved the most fertile source of an inventiveness which could be filched without obligation to employ it as artfully. Henceforth the credentials for fashionable film-making—besides a handful of ephebes acting out "problems," preferably half-dressed—were the inclusion of leapfrog editing, accelerated sequences reminiscent of the silents, and—indispensable! —the frozen frame. The intellectual locutions of Alain Resnais were more difficult to negotiate at feature length. Lately a young Czech, Jan Nemec, has achieved a conscientious duplication of the Resnais ellipsis, and there's a conspiracy afoot to declare *Diamonds of the Night* (1964) the most important film since you were Hiroshima and I was Nevers. I admire Resnais' craftmanship; I happen not to appreciate his theory. To my sense, the Czech film fails for the reason that it's sponsored by that theory. Nemec takes his point of departure—and I do mean departure—from two adolescents fleeing a prison-camp train. Since you're presented at once with two seemingly tangible boys in an historical context, brutally familiar to all, you expect them to show some identity, development, *breadth*. Within ten minutes you realize they are tokens only and that their flight will never be resolved, will be shuttle-cut only, for an hour and longer, between a present indicative and what might be past, future, or just hallucination. You are left with the cold comfort of watching a cinematic *process* and, as in *Hiroshima* and *Marienbad,* cheated of an emotional investment. At least the film was earnestly intended and anxiously edited with an eye to beauty and terror (as a fifteen-minute short it might have been commendable), which is more than can be said for the products of Jean-Luc Godard and his followers.

Godard has been a godsend to those who want to make film unimpeded by fine workmanship or preconceptions of the statement they're making. *Breathless* was a sardonic exercise that delighted the border-intellectual lowbrows who were the subjects of the film's passive attack: fringers, sufficiently in the know to sense their limited capacity for life, who retaliate by fleeing to a dead end of mental seediness and aimless convulsions of flippant protest. The film's calculated slapdash, the staccato elisions of the cutting tempo, the tease allusions to Humphrey Bogart, William Faulkner, Dylan Thomas, and the rest, the drawn-out nervous monotony of the bedroom scene, disproportionate to the total running time, were fitting correlates of the morally spastic world conceived in Truffaut's story outline. Thereafter Godard was on his own. If he has persisted, in at least ten films since, to utilize much the same treatment, on principle, we must conclude either that he believes the whole world—or those areas in which he has played the clown—is as amoral, impotent, and disjunctive as the criminal-bohemian one for which he first devised the method, or that his negative technique has no creative connection with his point of view. That he has a point of view is debatable; unarguably he has no scale of values. A will to translate any subject into a protracted stutter, that's what he has, and an itch for culture that urges him to flatter the collegians and other coteries with a spasmodic slipstream of literary references. His technical recipe—formula would be too complex a term—is pervertedly simple and consequently sadistic. When in doubt, commit every solecism formerly eliminated by trial and error in film-making; fix the camera immovably while two characters talk interminably; flout anticipation by cutting within a scene or from a scene at the least judicious moment; disdain amenities of lighting and any thought of balancing textures or sound levels of diverse episodes; choose the least esthetic of optional compositions, as well as the roughest of your "takes"—and drain every gag unmercifully. This patently destructive principle reveals the desperation of a barren yet egocentric movie-maker as surely as action painting, pop art, and happenings have reflected creative bankruptcy in those fields, together with the same reflexive contempt for an audience foolish enough to insist on a structure of meaning. The derisive content, such as it is, of Godard's films is as critically ineffectual as that of Buñuel's is getting to be.

Indeed, there's more than a hint, in *Les Carabiniers* and in *Bande à Part,* of the anti-films made by Buñuel in the thirties. The distinctions are of course considerable. Buñuel's attacks on cultural contradiction have usually been organized around an identifiable nucleus of images—pertaining to sex and death—whereas Godard has no organizing power and has discovered no lucid category of images, largely because the butt of his bad jokes is film itself. Contrary to the received idea that he has enlarged the possibilities of cinema, the opposite view may be taken. Film is not his medium. There is no fluent scenic art in Godard's movies; they take place nowhere and are neither interestingly real nor satisfyingly abstract. All action is dissipated into fragments or arrested in static sessions of talk, uneasily situated between the proffered context of the film and the equivocal process of film-making—a debased amalgam of Pirandello and Fellini. The revue sketch may be the proper place for his whimsies. . . . Certain bystanders have tried to account for Godard's anomalous role in French film by the fact that his origins are Swiss. He's a born offsider, that's for certain; the gauche redundancy of his humor and his antagonism toward form and the reality principle alike are quite un-French. Yet I'd be no readier to blame him on Switzerland than on Pierre Braunberger, who first backed him financially, on Truffaut and Chabrol, who assisted with the script and production of *Breathless,* or on Jean Cocteau, who initiated the journalistic farrago by announcing that this film was the most important in ten years. The French, I believe, are too fickle to support Godard's loveless precocity much further. In the lagging countries his example, if widely followed, could only hasten another breakdown of the values by which cinema is best articulated. These are essentially musical values, and every important film-maker always has sought to maintain them, each according to his personal rhythm.

For the time being, however, Godardism is all the rage, fanned by critics and endorsed by juries. Richard Lester, the Beatle-browed American who made *The Knack* by combining the most frantic ingredients of Mack Sennett and New Wave, is obviously a stepson of Godard at the mechanical level. Lester contends, in the teeth of his own film, that anyone intelligent can make a movie. Perhaps he was misquoted and actually said, "anyone of limited intelligence." Giving him the benefit of the doubt, we'll continue to believe that any film worth seeing twice is made not with intelligence but with imagination. Anyone *can* make a film if he's content to follow his most irresponsible promptings and to play games in the cutting room. I found *The Knack* adolescent in the worst way and idiotically mirthless. By comparison with Germi's *Divorce—Italian Style,* an expression of vitally comic disorder, Lester's film is merely an outbreak of juvenile delinquency. The influential gentry at Cannes last year were of Mr. Lester's party. By awarding his film the top prize, they gave notice that *The Knack* was creative movie-making and that Rosi's bullfight film, Ichikawa's *Tokyo '64,* and Sucksdorff's *My Home Is Copacabana* were not. Similarly in Berlin, two months later: there was never any serious question as to whether or not the Golden Bear should go to Godard's "science-fiction" essay, *Alphaville.* Since Eddie Constantine, the star, was on hand to deliver Godard's personal message, "Love can triumph over modern life"— with the help of Lemmy Caution—the jury was no doubt relieved at being able simultaneously to placate the plebes and reassure the keepers of the flame.

There was a film from Sweden shown in Berlin on this occasion, which I'd not otherwise give space to, that so perfectly sums up the wild intramural parasitism of the last few years it would seem to have been designed as an object lesson. The subject, so to speak, of *Love '65* (Bo Widerberg's third film) is lifted blatantly from Fellini's *8½* (jaded film director looking for a new dimension) ; the surface style from Antonioni; the dialogue from Godard (at least I know of no other as loaded with laborious mental effort, shop talk, and name dropping) ; the sexual encounters from Bergman or Roger Vadim (you could fool me there) ; the musical treatment from Cocteau-Bresson-Reichenbach-Pasolini; the final frame from Truffaut. Somewhere in this shrewd synthesis Ben Carruthers makes a bewildered appearance as Ben Carruthers, come to Sweden to act in a movie, evidently playing the part originally intended for Anita Ekberg—and why not, if everyone is to be interchangeable?— which gives Widerberg (i.e., the director *in* the film) a chance to affirm his social democracy by sparing a few kind words for *Shadows* and sending his regards to the producers thereof. I like to think of this film as *2½* but *Love '65* serves Widerberg's purpose well, I'm sure. He's building up to his magnum opus, four years hence, and don't you believe that propriety will restrain him from calling it *Love '69*.* By that time he may be out of date; within a year we can expect to see coprophilia on film and to be called reactionary if we demur. Widerberg is prepared for any eventuality. In the film under sanitary inspection here, he includes, besides a conventional bare-bosom closeup or two, a conversation between two women squatting to urinate, and an exchange in which the dimension-hungry director holds forth on the cinematic *raison d'être* of Antonioni, while lying in post-coital embrace with his friend's wife—on the floor.

And wherefore could I not pronounce "Amen"?   1966

**Footnote 1971.* I identified the trend, if not the directors, correctly. Widerberg switched to social accusation, and Jorn Donner made a film called *'69*. It was about love.

Three Film-makers
Revisit Themselves

Artists do not stem from their childhood, but from their conflict with the mature achievements of other artists; not from their own formless world, but from their struggle with the forms which others have imposed on life. . . .

André Malraux, *Psychology of Art*

Intended as an anti-Freudian missile, Malraux's dictum is in one sense profoundly self-evident: a work of art is achieved with a form-creating talent, not through the exercise of sensibility alone. Since sensibility is not autonomous, however—it must always be exercised by *someone*—the argument is circular. It has often been said that if a given artist had not been unduly affected by his childhood, he wouldn't have become an artist at all; at least he would not have become the artist we know. We are never in a position to re-conduct the experiment; hence we argue against supposition, which is to say against nothing. The question is as unanswerable by Malraux as by anyone. But rich connections between the personal experience and "the forms imposed by life" (not necessarily art forms) are in many instances discernible, and fascinating for their own sake. . . .

Kurosawa, Bergman, Fellini—three creative film-makers: the extent to which they recapitulate the shocks, the hungers, the perspectives of their earlier years is sufficiently remarkable to make

Malraux's observation academic. Of the three, Kurosawa's cinema is the least transparent. What we learn of the man, by way of Donald Richie's compendious study of his work,* we may well find confirmed in the films—*confirmed*, not exploited. We never feel, in the diverse films of Kurosawa, that proximity (often uncomfortable) of the director's ego to which Bergman and Fellini have progressively exposed us. Here ethnic sanctions are powerfully effective. The culture, as much as the child, is father to the man. Akira Kurosawa was the son of an army officer of the samurai class, whose specialty was rigorous physical education. The boy, though not without prowess, was delicate; he lacked, or suppressed, the belligerent instincts. When he went to middle school, he consistently received a zero in military training. At the same time he studied the fine arts, with liberal encouragement from his father. His elder brother—from whom, incidentally, he received his first lessons in cinematic appreciation—was disowned by the father for living with his paramour; one day he left for the mountains, where he committed suicide. Kurosawa was then eighteen or thereabouts. One need not have been trained in Vienna to relish the sequel: the boy who was on the sidelines of competitive sport and who hated military exercises became the greatest film exponent of, among other things, physical combat. The youth whose brother was victim and celebrant of an inflexible code grew to be the man who now says that his films have perhaps a common theme, the question "Why can't people be happier together?"—a wholly inadequate and quite touchingly modest rubric with which to account for *Rashomon* or *Living* or even *High and Low*. Closer to what we ourselves value in his best work—besides, of course, its always inordinate virtuosity —is his tribute to the novels of Dostoievsky, Tolstoi, and Turgenev, which show us the "undersurface" of things. "To be an artist means to search for, find and look at these things; to be an artist means never to avert one's eyes."

In fact Kurosawa confines himself in many films to the surface of things, but his touch on that surface is always incisive and resounding—and one can usually hear the clanking reminder of mortality behind the flapping banners or beyond the sound of thudding arrows. Yet I have a strong feeling that Kurosawa undervalues the samurai in himself; I think Richie, perhaps to oblige, undervalues it, too. His abrupt involvements with social dialectic—in the few

---

The Films of Akira Kurosawa, University of California Press.

films I have viewed to which this description fits—seem to me compulsive, as if he were reminding himself of an obligation; even, it might be, convincing himself that these are the honored subjects of Western narrative art. I could be wrong, since my deductions are in part arrived at through Richie's synopses of the Kurosawa I haven't seen: *The Brave Sleep Well,* for example, or the recent *Red Beard,* of whose merits Richie's verbose praise does not, in advance, convince me.

Fellini grew up bewildered. This is the abiding impression we get from the sum of his marvelous monkey-colored answers to the questions of Tullio Kezich in the "long interview."* We may infer what we're *not* told, from our knowledge of jungle Italy: the smothering family, the piety, the lack of elbow room. But listen to this man on movies:

> My first memory of a film goes back to *Maciste all'Inferno,* I think.
>
> I was in my father's arms, the house was packed, it was hot, and they kept spraying an antiseptic that grated the throat and dazed me. In that slightly opiate atmosphere I remember the yellowish images on the screen of all kinds of people in Hell. Then I remember shots of priests in a large room with wooden benches, black-and-white shots of churches, Assisi, Orvieto. . . . I was always thrilled by the shows that preceded a movie, as by a circus. For me a movie house is a room bubbling with noises and odors; chestnuts, the urine of children, that feeling of the end of the world, of disaster. The confusion that comes before the stage show—the musicians arriving in the pit, the voice of the comedian, the sounds of the girls behind the curtains. Then the people who go out the fire exit in the winter, into an alley, made children again by the cold; someone hums a tune from the picture, people laugh. . . .

All Fellini's movie-making—the best and the worst of it—is in that paragraph. The delights, no less than the tediums, of his cinema derive from the evocative power of his memory, his ability to evoke and to chide the growing pains of consciousness, the long, abject folly of growing up, the pathos of the unresolved life, the pursuit of baubles. Like most Italians he can also charm the teeth out of your mouth with simulated candor.

> I'm still a little ill at ease because I have a complex about being a little schoolboy—intimidated but somewhat naughty; I'm

---

***Juliet of the Spirits,* by Federico Fellini, edited by Tullio Kezich, translated from the Italian by Howard Greenfeld, Orion Press. The screenplay of that tawdry film takes up two-thirds of the book. Publication was justified by the first third, "The Long Interview."

not mentally free of this. You remember the producer we went to see today. I'm ready to tear that kind of man to pieces when it comes to work. However, that man, apart from work, makes me uneasy, makes me feel profoundly inferior. In front of him I again become a boy, placed under paternal authority, whether it be threatening or benevolent.

The corollary follows, as in Bergman's case:

Every time I feel that people have confidence in me I am satisfied. It flatters me even when I feel it shows up my shortcomings.

Bergman's case is indeed so well known, in rumor form at least, as to have earned a rest. Yet Vilgot Sjöman's journal of *Winter Light** reports some electrically revealing moments when Bergman consents to speak freely on matters traumatic. On one occasion he tells Sjöman that when he was a boy he was punished, in the fashion of the day, by being ignored, or, when extreme measures were called for, by being shut up in a closet.† To this day he admits to a degree of claustrophobia and acknowledges, as well, that nothing more quickly infuriates him than someone's turning away when he asks him a question. Sjöman aptly points out that the subject of Bergman's last three films has been God's silence. . . . Since authority problems relate to security problems, it is worth noting, on the way, that none of these men feels comfortable beyond his ken. To my knowledge, Kurosawa has never left Japan, Fellini is unpleasantly disturbed by foreign travel—"in the great maternal womb of Rome . . . I feel I can enjoy even fear"—and Bergman says that when Esther, in *The Silence,* looks fearfully out of the hotel window at the city of Timoka, that's how he felt on his first visit to Paris in 1949. I asked him once if he could imagine making films in any other country. He all but shuddered.

Bergman's two favorite film-makers are Kurosawa and Fellini; Fellini's, Kurosawa and Bergman. Bergman owns a print of *Rashomon* which he must have viewed by now at least twenty-five times.

L 136: Dagbok med Ingmar Bergman by Vilgot Sjöman, Stockholm: P. A. Norstedt and Sons, 1963. The title, which suggests a submarine, signifies the SF production number of *Winter Light.* This is a day-by-day journal kept by Sjöman throughout every stage of the film—preparation of script, shooting, mixing, press reception (i.e., in Sweden!) . Evidently the book has remained untranslated, except for a chapter, on the assumption that it would interest only "specialists"— the like of me.

†Herbert Hendin (in *Suicide in Scandinavia,* State Hospitals Press, Utica, New York, 1962) has called attention to the importance for Swedish relationships of the strategy *tiga ihjal,* to kill with silence. In somewhat Thurberian fashion, Hendin explains: "This tendency to control anger through detachment tends [*sic*] to result in a general dampening of affectivity and interference with the ability to sustain interest in a relationship. . . ."

I doubt that he's enthralled by its message of moral relativism so much as he is by its sheer visual declamation, the variable energy, the blend of savage realism and the supernatural—the dark wood, the voice from the dead, the forest heat of the day, and the torrents of black rain. Sjöman quotes his brief praise of *La Dolce Vita:* not a word of its socially ramifying scrutiny; for Bergman it's a "baroque tapestry." (A revolutionary judgment in Sweden, where *baroque* is a term of condescension!) Fellini returns the compliment in kind. "I've never met Bergman but I feel close to him through his films. He is a conjuror—half witch and half showman. I also like his tricks, the spectacle made from nothing. . . ." And of Kurosawa: "Watching *Rashomon* or *Seven Samurai* I become a boy again; I feel an unqualified admiration."

Whatever opinions of these films we may hold ourselves, it is surely refreshing to encounter, in this age of stilled enthusiasm and utilitarian cant, an approach to art that hails its ancient privilege. Bergman and Fellini agree with Flaubert that "the highest achievement of art is to do what nature does—fill us with wonderment." At this point we might be tempted to concede that the most discerning apostle of genius is another genius. Amplify the cross references, however, and the spell is broken. We do not learn from Richie what opinion Kurosawa holds of either Bergman or Fellini; the European director he most admires (the only one he takes occasion to mention) is Antonioni. Now, it might be supposed that Bergman would be the first to divine Antonioni's somewhat parallel gifts; yet, when he saw a sequence from *L'Avventura* five years ago on television, he dismissed the Italian as being of no importance. Sjöman asked him if he thought he could fairly judge the film on a sequence only. Yes, Bergman thought so. Subsequently he saw *La Notte* and was more impressed. Nonetheless, when last year Antonioni visited Stockholm, as a morose advertisement of his newly opened film, *Deserto Rosso,* and as a guest of the Film Institute, Bergman saw to it that he was unconscionably busy in the cutting room. Antonioni, on his part, made only perfunctory inquiries on the availability of Ingmar. It would make a rich sequence in a movie—two tomcats cautiously circling each other in the frozen North. Nor is there any finer harmony between Luis Buñuel and our Nordic friend. Toward Bergman the Spaniard shows all the fine scorn reserved for renegades from the Devil's party. (Time was when Bergman used to sign all scripts and letters with a drawing of a forked demon.) Interviewed on the subject (in London, I think) while Sjöman's record was in progress, Buñuel owned to a failing admiration for the Swede, who was now "wasting himself on wholly uninteresting questions. What does he ask in every film? God, the Devil and the Good—does God exist?—one simply can't be bothered with such things! He can only sell this quasi-philosophy to a decadent public. Typically, he has succeeded with it in America. Americans, those gringos, are interested in such stuff." Perhaps in retaliation—Sjö-man does not date the continuity here—Bergman, after watching the Last Supper episode of *Viridiana* on TV (again, a sequence only), pronounced the film "singularly tasteless and puerile."

In some quarters there will be dancing in the streets if I empha-size the shared aversion of Kurosawa, Fellini, and Bergman toward film critics. Kurosawa contents himself with saying, "I've never read a critic who didn't put false meanings into my work." (One can al-ways shrug, "Well, those *Japanese* critics!") Fellini is routed by the very name and nature of the critical process. On the downward path from his princely affection for *Rashomon* and *The Magician,* we note that he was "moved to tears" by *City Lights* and finds John Ford's *The Informer* "unforgettable." The truth is that Fellini finds too much of the wrong thing unforgettable.

> I don't measure adjectives when I find something I like, nor does my enthusiasm cool off with critical considerations. For me criticism is a kind of masochism. Why re-evaluate some-thing that has moved you, water it down, control it, kill it?

The dear man's misapprehension of our noble craft needs no labored refutation in these pages. And the consequences of his will-to-innocence may be seen in every tasteless meter of *Juliet of the Spirits.* In his most confidently temperamental moments, Fellini has expressed better than anyone the central catastrophe of European life, which Ortega y Gasset once defined as "the fatal divorce of culture from spontaneity." The Juliet film shows him corrupted by culture, abandoned by spontaneity. And the failure is nearly total; one scene, the Miracle play in the convent school, suggests what was lost. Otherwise the fun is unfunny, the psychology worse than elementary, the invention puerile—and there isn't a character pres-ent who isn't a clown or a freak.

> . . . there is a time when I feel the screenplay isn't sufficient. . . . Then I open my office. I call in people; I have hundreds of faces pass before me. It's a kind of ceremony to create an atmo-sphere, one of many and certainly not the most important. When I'm in my office, the door opens and an old man comes

in, a little girl, someone who wants to sell a watch, a countess, a fat man. I see a hundred in order to get two for the film. . . .

This time he saw a thousand to get a hundred. Perhaps he has reached the hour when he can only *talk* a good film—and that, to be sure, is an unmixed blessing. Insofar as we're paying attention to the first sixty-four pages that constitute the Introduction and "The Long Interview," the Kezich-Fellini book is the only one of the three that empowered my subject which may be profitably read as literature. I don't agree with a word of Kezich's support of *Juliet,* but I find him a pleasure to hear—just a Good European whose intelligence is indistinguishable from his culture. How far his editing is responsible for the pith of Fellini's phrasing I can't say, nor do I know, in turn, how much of the happy result is the contribution of Howard Greenfeld, who rendered the Italian into some of the most graceful, nervy English I've read for some time. Fellini on dreams, on actors, on screenings for distributors, on color (results notwithstanding), on balloons, and on marriage in Italy: these paragraphs belong to the best I know among those on art uttered by the artist— van Gogh's letters, Renoir revisited by his son, Degas explaining why to paint ballet dancers is not a romantic occupation, Arthur Schnabel expressing with tireless variety his disdain of audiences.

Sjöman's *L 136* is exempt from literary standards. The task of getting down as precisely as possible what was said, on and off the cuff, during a job of shooting, over the lunchroom table, or driving to location from the studio, can scarcely be expected to produce a sustained effect of deathless conversation (the less so as everyday Swedish is a language for ravens). One theme is unalterably clear. Bergman sees critics everywhere, like flying saucers. Relaxing after work by screening Albert Lamorisse's *The Red Balloon,* he decides with murderous glee that the film is a parable of the artist and his critics (not a half-bad interpretation). When *Through a Glass Darkly* has its premiere, he growls "Typical!" because *L'Avventura* has been reviewed on the Culture Page of a certain Stockholm newspaper while his own film occupies the entertainment columns. He complains that probably none of the critics who are holding forth on the subject of his theology have read a single word of Luther's Little Catechism, reads a wild analysis of his work in a weekly picture-magazine by a so-called professor and spits on the page, and, even though half his mind is already occupied with his next film, *The Silence,* he is already brewing his vengeance on all critics in an outline which became the dreadful Opus 26, known as

Not to Speak of All Those Women. Finally, he and his Boswell assemble the Stockholm press notices of *Winter Light* and deal the
reviewers red or black marks accordingly.

Fully to appreciate this phenomenon you must be willing to go
halfway (much further than any Swedish reviewer) with the author
of *Suicide in Scandinavia.* Hendin defined "performance anxiety"
as the Swedish male's most characteristic hazard; it follows that
adverse criticism of performance (or even insufficient praise) will
be another turn of the screw. Moreover, Bergman has intensive jus-
tifications within the generic pattern. A small, nasty Establishment
of academic Sweden has never acknowledged Bergman's evolution
from poor playwright to great film-maker—and it never will! An
outsider might find it difficult to imagine the unsleeping malice,
each toward another, by which Swedes, within competitive circles,
are quite commonly animated. On Bergman's side, no requital
seems to be sufficient. Independence, authority, and international
respect are powerless against the germinal outrage; in his father's
house he has been stood in the closet.

"I have sometimes said, and I think honestly, that when a film is
finished, it would be the same for me even if it never came out."
Thus Fellini. Obviously, Bergman could not share his indifference
on this score; to suffer from "performance anxiety" implies that you
expect judgment from others as rigorous as your own. For Bergman,
the premiere constitutes the first stage in his trial by ice. Furthermore, despite appearances to the contrary, Bergman is very much
a part of the working world. The austerity of his late films represents the puzzling out of a personal syllogism, not an authentic retreat from society. He lives theater, either making it or seeing it,
though he made it plain in his ungracious speech when offered the
Erasmus Foundation prize for cultural achievement (together with
Chaplin), that personal artistic satisfaction is inadequate. Art is insignificant in our time, he protested. "By insignificant I mean that
art no longer has the power and possibility to influence the development of our lives." Presumably it influenced *his* development, but
he can't forgive history for not having sustained the artist as a law-
giver (assuming that he ever was). Fellini, while haunted by a
comparable sadness, puts it with greater tact. "I am bothered by a
kind of nostalgia for a more complete morality."

For whatever reasons of culture or innate spontaneity, Kurosawa
emerges as the most self-possessed personality. Richie, rather
quaintly, describes him as a "philosopher." Kurosawa appears to

hold a few simple convictions which, darkened as they may be by the flux of things, are as rooted, as serene, and almost as old as Fuji-yama. Misgivings allowed for, his subject is man as hero (to complement Bergman's man as sinner and Fellini's man as fool). He, too, hopes that art may be educative—he wants his films to be ethically influential with the younger generations—but he doesn't stew over the probability that they won't be. Of the three directors, he alone is wholly contained in his art. Bergman and Fellini sometimes talk as if they were; their performances deny the self-sufficiency. We might wish them the stoicism on which Kurosawa takes his stand, if we could delude ourselves that with it they could have made the films whereby we celebrate them:

> I am a director . . . that is all. I know myself well enough to know that if I ever lost my passion for films, then I myself would be lost. *Film is what I am about.*

The italics are mine.   1966

International Film:
Tensions and Pretensions

We must credit François Truffaut with at least a suppressed anxiety for the future of human liberties; otherwise we cannot explain his wanting to make a movie of *Fahrenheit 451*. To be sure, he may have needed an excuse for playing with fire engines or for indulging his peculiar fidelity to that deck steward among the diabolists, Alfred Hitchcock. In either case, Ray Bradbury's novel was far from the inevitable choice. We may think of that novel as *kitsch,* a world removed from the canny presentiments of Orwell's *1984;* nonetheless it is *kitsch* in a good cause: it touches the life-and-death ideas; it is sufficiently persuasive to make us look out of the window to see if the expected glacier has arrived at the end of the street. And oddly enough, it is more cinematic than Truffaut's film; the images on the screen—except for Oskar Werner's playing of Montag—are inadequate to the suggestions provoked by many pages of the book. Truffaut reduced the terror and provided nothing sanguinary in its stead. As science-fiction the film is uninventive (the least of my complaints). As a suspense story it is hampered at the outset by more serious moral stakes, and mocked when all is over by a "camp" curtain call, entirely out of keeping with the nightmare we have agreed to believe in up to that moment. Incomprehensibly, Truffaut devaluated Bradbury's effects at every level. A world in which books are hunted out and burned for fear of the ideas and associative emotions they give rise to is a world with its back already broken, a penal colony awaiting final extinction (which, in the novel, takes place). The society shown us by Truffaut, however, seems merely circumscribed, despite dark hints of constant surveillance; while nobody must read a book, it is yet possible for reading societies to survive illicitly and for anyone to talk as fearlessly (if as stiltedly) as the lamb-eyed ingenue played with understandable remoteness by Julie Christie. In the book, when Montag desperately tries to arouse buried human responses from a trio of bourgeois housewives, he reads from Matthew Arnold's poem, "Dover Beach"; in the film, from *David Copperfield!* Bradbury has a talkative spokesman named Faber who makes it clear that books were wonderful not so much for their expression of precepts or cosmic ideas as for the eloquence with which they had conserved the contingent values, the texture and sight of familiar things, the irreducible sentiments evoked by a million fabulous objects in nature or created by social man. Faber is eliminated in the movie and has not been replaced by the camera. Never for a single moment in this imperiled world does Truffaut dwell on the flight of a bird, a blade of grass, a packet of old letters, a dripping tap, tea leaves in a cup, the sound of distant bells. He is so intent on the single *gimmick,* the destruction and recovery of books, that he fails to endow his characters with primary sensuous equipment. (Montag's attempt to reclaim his wife from sexual frigidity is not developed—perhaps it was just as well.) To a degree, the hazard was built in: once you have insisted on stepping through the looking glass, you have lost touch with your controllable milieu. Bradbury's novel was set in a nebulous America of the future. Truffaut wanted to make the film in England (with an Austrian hero) and his natural frame of reference is French. The result is not strange enough—just a middle-class Everyland under a reign of terror whose agents are audibly British. One noticeably bizarre preference emerges from this uneasy alliance. Truffaut tries hard to be representative when choosing the titles for all those books burning in *montage,* but it seemed to me that an inordinate number of them were twentieth-century French, and I'm hanged if the accumulated wisdom of the human mind is very acutely inferred by the bric-a-brac of Jean Cocteau and the autobiography of Salvador Dali. . . . The end of civilization doesn't arrive in Truffaut's version. Instead, the hero and that girl escape, all too easily, to an idyllic woodland (England—and it isn't even raining!) where an unmolested colony of omnivorous readers are committing their favorite books to memory for the benefit of posterity, confident that there will *be* a posterity. I should be gratified, I suppose, by the evidence that Truffaut is not a thoroughly frightened man. Yet it would have increased the tension of his film if he were. I'm prepared to see the destruction of mankind played as a savage farce (*cf. Dr. Strangelove*), since so final an event may as well be laughed at (our final gallantry), but the prospect of humanity living mindlessly and insensibly forever, in a setting that resembles the sleeping suburbs of Stockholm, does not, to my way of thinking, lend itself to frivolous treatment.

Truffaut can still draw on a fund of good intentions, which may be why his film has been accepted with more generosity than not; I think we all agree that the thoughtful young man who made *The 400 Blows* and the bright young man who made *Jules and Jim* is securely on the side of the angels. No such benefit of the doubt can be extended to those Swedish directors responsible for a half-dozen or more films made within the last three years, now being distributed to the "art" cinemas of the world. Whatever causes may be finally assigned to the essential impotence of these films, errors of love are not among them. Swedish film, with the honorable exceptions I am always eager to single out, is loveless and is every bit as remote from credible daily life today or yesterday as *Fahrenheit 451* or any lesser science-fiction fantasy. Donner's *Here Begins Adventure,* Sjöman's *My Sister, My Love,* Mai Zetterling's *Loving Couples* and *Night Games,* Abramson's *The Serpent,* Halldoff's *The Myth,* Mattsson's *Nightmare* and *The Murderer*—among these (whether promoted as works of art or merely commercial entertainments) it might be difficult to decide which is the most preposterous (i.e., the least authentically motivated). Mai Zetterling's *Night Games* has strong competition from the Sjöman and Abramson films for the title of Most Indecent, but it has no rival as the most reminiscent job of them all. There is scarcely a sequence that doesn't remind one (uncomfortably) of Fellini's *8½* and *Juliet of the Spirits,* of Buñuel's *The Destroying Angel,* of Bergman's *The Silence,* and of Miss Zetterling's previous effort, which was in turn an anthology of effects from all the best Swedish films of the last fifteen years. Even more anxiously than in the earlier film, Mai Zetterling makes it clear in *Night Games* that she is never going to forgive God for having made her a woman and for not supplying her with a rotting upper-class family. To repair the latter deficiency she has invented one—very poorly. Her sexually impotent hero is a country gentleman (of a sort), very nasty to women, who discovers with the help of encircling flashbacks—the movie-maker's dynamic substitute for the static couch—that the *real* source of his affliction (now, you won't tell anyone who hasn't seen the movie, will you?) is that he was sexually fixated *on his mother!* The ending is in a classic mode, too—that of the pyromanic ritual. The enlightened victim sets fire to his villa, gives away his possessions, and rolls happily on the ground with his mistress—potent, if homeless. I confess that I was tempted to construe this as a political touch, an injunction from the Social Democrats: "Let's burn up the past and copulate in the snow!" . . . I have implied that the film was derivative. I overlooked Miss Zetterling's two conspicuous contributions to fearless film-making: a publicly conducted *accouchement* and a steady glimpse of a naked boy with an erection. To a *New York Times* interviewer Miss Zetterling complained, "Some people seem to have thought this film was erotic."

As unlikely as it may seem, a judgment by Matthew Arnold on the prose of Macaulay is an accurate description of many Swedish films: "the external characteristic being a hard metallic movement with nothing of the soft play of life, and the internal characteristic being a perpetual resemblance of hitting the right nail on the head without the reality." One usually exempts the films of Ingmar Bergman from the generic character of the Swedish cinema. But I wonder how far *Persona* can be said to transcend it? To the extent that Bergman *is* an artist, of perennial powers, and the others, at their best, simply craftsmen? That should serve as a primary distinction. The chances are that a Bergman film will be worth attending, even if it incidentally exasperates, because the man himself is consistently driven by a force, a something, he doesn't understand, and the films he makes are often marvelous clarifications of what, at the moment, through a particular film, he has managed to understand. I can't make this claim for *Persona*. His intentions, if I have even half understood them, strike me as being unprofitable, his execution of them aggravating in the extreme.

Somewhere at the still center of *Persona* —if you can overtake it, undistracted by the whirligig *montage* of the Paris school to which he has now cravenly conceded—there is a suggestively analytic depiction of what we might call the nuclear fission of a soul. What we at first believe we are seeing is a case of transference: a nurse takes on her patient's traumatic burden and is soon in worse case than the patient. That this level of interpretation will not serve is confirmed by the increasing instability of the closeups; the faces are conjoined like those of lovers or of blind twins in a womb; they waver, they divide, they half-merge, they fuse. We then revise our conception to accept the probability that there is only *one* woman involved here; the other is the *persona* (the mask or the projected antagonist) of the first. Elisabet Vogler, an actress suffering from a breakdown which appears to have rendered her speechless, has contrived a fantasy figure, the nurse Alma (= soul) in order to tell herself the otherwise unwelcome truth about the radically histrionic basis of her existence. She learns the truth, and presumably carries on (by assimilating it or concealing it we never know), while Alma, completely voided, takes flight in a state of incoherence. It is almost equally plausible to read the clues in reverse order. Alma has conjured an invalid toward whom she can assume an adoptive, superior pose; when her mechanism of self-aggrandizement breaks down, her complacency is fatally disturbed in a crisis of self-exposure.*

I might have been impressed by Bergman's table tennis had he been content with the double gambit which was already more than enough to assimilate. However, with special assistance from the interjected bits and pieces, many from Bergman's films, that disrupt the equivocal contest (film igniting, studio sounds, glimpses of the camera, documentary shots of butchery and war), the struggle between Elisabet and Alma is ostensibly being heightened (perhaps mocked) by the universal discord. At the same time, a quasi-Pirandello comment is being offered on the absurdity of art (i.e., moviemaking) as a paradigm of life. Furthermore, the guiding threads in this labyrinth can most readily be grasped by those with a swift recall of the director's earlier films. When Alma confronts Elisabet Vogler in the hospital with her failure to substitute the reality of theater for the simulations of life and when, at the beach house, she discovers, by reading the diary, how dispassionately she is being

---

*Footnote 1971. Those who read *Cinema Borealis* will realize that later I arrived at a more decisive interpretation of the Alma-Elisabet relationship.

observed by her patient, the filmgoer who remembers that Vogler was the name given to the artist figure (also publicly mute) in *The Magician* is likely to be the first to recognize the super-subject of *Persona:* the predatory nature of the artist, who can survive only by feeding on the tribulations of others.

For me, the sophistry of the message is not dispelled by the complexity of the treatment. As a good Lutheran, Bergman seems peculiarly obedient to a text of St. Jerome: "The proper business of a monk is not to instruct but to mourn." For some years now, Bergman has been mourning on two counts: because God is silent and because the art of film-making has not satisfied his thirst for salvation. Both demands are theologically outrageous and philosophically absurd. I learn from Mircea Eliade that certain African tribes are also puzzled by their belief in a *deus absconditus;* they meet the situation by periodically sacrificing a white cock. As to the notion that art is inadequate for expressing the accumulated misery of human existence, this could come only from a mind in which all perspective is undergoing attrition. Who has ever supposed that art has such potency? While this and other familiar obsessions introduced into the film are personal to Bergman, they are not unconnected with a rootedly disingenuous habit of the Swedish mind, the pose of refusing to acknowledge a law of ecology: that all life feeds on other life. We begin by feeding on our mothers (and I wouldn't have it any other way). You can see how the national disbelief supports the issue of neutrality, though, can't you? And you will note how it accounts for the temper of the Swedish film. Immaculate surface, maculate content. Genuinely creative aggression is converted into sadomasochism. Nine out of ten Swedish films are animated by "failure of communication," untransfigured sex, suicide, violent death, incest, or insanity.

The tenth does arrive, praise the hidden God! This year it was Jan Troell's *Here Is Your Life,* appearing in mid-winter like a warm river irresistibly breaking through the ice. With a single giant stride Troell has overtaken the three modern masters of the Swedish film —Sjöberg, Sucksdorff, and Bergman. He's in their debt, of course, he has learned their territory; but he has been looking almost as steadily in the direction of France. (One sequence is bodily lifted from Truffaut's *Jules and Jim.*) These are idiomatic borrowings only; in the sweep of the film (it's nearly three hours long) they are subordinated—the *feeling* is refreshingly personal. What is more, it conveys affection, a rare virtue in these latitudes. Troell is an original, in the only way possible: he has returned to the source. *Here Is Your Life* (the very title is a challenge) must seem to be a counsel of desperation to those film-makers who believe that the road to internationalism runs through Carthage. Troell has not snubbed his own experience, the only authentic material he has to grow on. He has adapted two novels of an autobiographical work written by Eyvind Johnson in the thirties which exemplify a pioneer Swedish subject—the self-discovery, within regional limits, of an adolescent boy during the World War I years. Young Olof takes on a succession of rough-and-humble jobs. He experiences the rigors and the rewards of hard-collar capitalism; he is seduced by the promise (as in a glass darkly) of doctrinaire Marxism; he learns something of the lineaments of love—no less from a carnival-queen hussy than from tearful, floppy-hatted farm girls. His bucolic education takes place on a small stage, a province of northern Sweden, given epic dimensions by Troell's respect for the subjective value of every transition in the boy's environment. At the end of the film, Olof is following the railroad track—alone with his barely injured innocence—footing it southward across a pelagic waste of snow, headed for the city and the perils of maturity.

Here Is Your Life is creative provincialism. Troell has not hesitated to embrace the parent rituals, neither shuddering nor weeping. In his own habitat, where the whine of the sawmill and the cry of the curlew have not been struck from the calendar, he is doing what Fellini did in *I Vitelloni*, what Truffaut did in *The 400 Blows* —and Kurosawa in *Stray Dog*: he is discovering the common denominator for whatever worlds thereafter he may find provocation for exploring. Critics make it easy for themselves by classifying every good cinematographer as a poet. Troell photographed and edited his own film (he's thirty-five and this is his first feature-length work) ; his poetry is visible enough in a dozen dazzling sequences, color as well as black and white, but his master gift is perhaps his unfaltering balance of the workaday detail with the cadence in which a life-illumination is being concentrated, even as it vanishes into the flux: the death of a friend, the ill memories of old age, the fuss and feathers of lovemaking, the shock of acquiring personal authority. Troell is as weather-wise as Sucksdorff and as intent on undertones as Bergman can be (in *The Virgin Spring*, for example) . Films based obediently on narratives that impel their heroes from A to Z, opening sociological doors on the way, are usually interminable and homiletic. You find yourself counting the landings as you follow. There is no prose footage in *Here Is Your Life;* no encounter is a mere linkage to move the story from one place to the next. Every image has its due value and every sequence the rhythm and duration which seem proper to it. Everything is *movie* and all of it has the charm of impressionism: a social context analyzed by an eye unusually alive to the vibrations of the transitory. If I have ignored the many actors without whom the film wouldn't have been what it is, that's high praise actually. They are all perfect, coming and going as if they'd never heard of making a movie, doing what comes naturally.

Sweden has found its Troell. France has its Reichenbach, its Bourguignon, and its Truffaut (errors of commission allowed for). A few years back Italy had De Seta and Olmi, at present in abeyance—but Italy is always fertile. England has no Troell; only the Beatles and some rancidly articulate TV programs. One overhears much talk on the BBC about the contemporary British renaissance in cinema, which usually turns out to mean all those promising young men making false alarums when they mean nothing but a May game (*Darling, Alfie, Morgan, Georgy Girl, et al.*). I suppose the "English" film of the year was Antonioni's *Blow-Up,* in which he transported his customary dialectic between people and their décor to the shabbiest purlieus of London, with the usual meticulous preparation for a second coming which never takes place, and, as ever, parsimonious hints of social disparities and metaphysical jests. As poetry, it's all texture, no core, and I'd have been more delighted, sequence by sequence, if I shared Antonioni's predilection for fuchsia (and the East End voice). Since the old master can't plot, he has this time used someone else's story, which takes an unconvincing final turn toward the equivocation of physics. If Antonioni (following the author?) is merely saying that the eye sees what it wants to see (a mini-truth—the eye is culturally conditioned), the body under the tree is far too palpable—in any case a strenuous way to illustrate the point. For the rest, his guard is down; he treats with fashion-photo affection the phenomena in which he once found cause for tears. *Blow-Up* is like the latest copy of *Vogue*. It commandeth the eye but sticketh not in the memory.

Germany is barren. Once in five years there's a German film worth importing. Last year, by rumor, there were two, of which, up to now, I've seen one, *Young Törless,* which received a special prize from the critics at Cannes. From some of the critics, I should say. Before Kenneth Tynan returned to a job he performs better (I trust), he delivered from Cannes, via *The Observer,* a number of last testaments to his uselessness as a film spotter. Among them was the spiteful opinion that Volker Schlöndorff's film—which suggests that tyranny would not flourish if no victims offered themselves— was merely a belated apologia for the Third Reich.

Now, Tynan was in as informed a position as anyone to know that the novel from which Schlöndorff had composed his manuscript was written by Robert Musil in 1907, that of all Central European writers of the time Musil is probably the last who could be accused of proto-Nazism, that furthermore the adaptation of his book today could scarcely reflect the desire of anyone associated with the film to rationalize the late events, the less so as one of the co-producers was the French director Louis Malle. It seems to me that to make such a film requires more than ordinary courage, for the reflective nature of the problem expressed in it is too subtle to escape misunderstanding, a danger to which Tynan, for one, promptly exposed himself. My acquaintance with the literature of Musil is far from extensive. I assume that this novel represents a transitional, ruminating phase in his art, an exercise in nostalgia and a brooding reexamination of man's obligations to his fellows. The situation is thoroughly interrogative. At an Austrian cadets' training school, a plump and unprepossessing boy named Basini is brutally handled by a kangaroo court of his schoolmates, ostensibly because he has stolen money from one of them, certainly because he is disliked for his toadying manners. (There is more than a suggestion that he has not unwillingly served the sexual vice of a ringleader.) Törless, diffident and intellectual (acted gravely by Mattieu Carrière, who looks like a pre-Raphaelite angel), knows exactly what has transpired; he is a confidant of the bullies, he has taken a scholarly interest, you might say, in the phenomenon of Basini. When the students go wild and hang Basini by his heels in the gymnasium, the authorities, who then discover the extent of the persecution, want to know why young Törless, the model pupil, the paragon of sagacity and poise, had turned on his heel instead of reporting the whole dirty business to the masters. Törless explains, in effect, that there were too many ambiguities involved for him to choose right and wrong categorically. *In fact* the victim *was* a thief, and a coward as well; moreover, when Törless had sympathetically asked Basini how he felt at being humiliated and tortured, the wretched boy had blankly explained that he didn't know how he felt—he experienced nothing! On this note, with Törless returning home, the film ends.

A precarious offering to motion picture audiences, this; the subject is not one over which most people are inclined to temporize. They prefer to have their loyalties underlined for them, and they're by no means prepared to consider a certain kind of vulnerability as among the deadly sins. This is a very muted film, altogether. Conventionally photographed and sedately paced, it implies the setting for a period within the confines of a single institution. I wish I could give it unreserved praise, but the occasional music of Hans Werner Henze, one of those calculatedly unmelodic achievements of our advanced mode, irritated me no end, for it seemed to chill the air and was quite out of harmony with the time and tone of the story.

Since there have been more than a few hints, following the cry of "sentimental!" at Venice in 1965, that Akira Kurosawa will soon go the way of De Sica in the estimate of critics everywhere who are seized by a rage for optical novelty, this may well be my last chance to insist, with any hope of a hearing, that *Red Beard* is an overpowering experience. I recognize that fewer people all the time go to films wishing to be overpowered. Soon I'll have nobody to talk to. . . . When I first read a synopsis in praise of *Red Beard* (in *Japanese Quarterly*) I couldn't imagine why the author was enthralled. I can see now how difficult a film it is to write about if you expect to observe the proprieties of criticism. To analyze *Red Beard* with a view to impressing the academic filmgoer (thematic parallels, shot relationships, distribution of closeups, and the like) or those who must be appealed to on sociological grounds (exposure of medieval conditions in a Tokugawa-period clinic) is in either direction bound to fall short of the mark. Kurosawa's art is principally the sum of his conviction. By now we can take for granted that he knows how to achieve the intensity at which he is aiming—esthetic distance is not his ideal—and where to place the viewer whom he hopes to subjugate. I was subjugated by this film. A detached appraisal of it, two months after the event, is something I am unable to deliver.

Because, in truth, I felt myself being submerged during the running time of *Red Beard,* I tried desperately to keep my critical distance, but I was unequal to the resolve. I wanted to resist the nagging logic and the driving agony of the film, to quarrel with it, become bored by it, condescend toward it—just as one does when assailed by life itself. And after every bout of fidgeting, sighing, and protesting under my breath, after every obstinate refusal to yield my sentiments any further, I was forced to give in and to return (fascinated) to the fray, to the importunate suffering, the hopelessness, the pity, and the stench. Kurosawa's power over me was comparable to that of the doctor, Red Beard, over the reluctant interne, Yasumoto. I felt restrained against my own will to live under iron-clad restrictions among the sick and the mad in a cold, bare cluster of frame buildings, as uninviting as so many rabbit hutches, in a cold, grubby, eternally cloud-wet landscape. (Nineteenth-century Japan? I might as well have been on the moon.) Like Yasumoto, I didn't *have* to stay; I had been tricked by my idiotic respect for the categorical imperative. And I doubt that others are as unaffected by this film as they may claim unless they are simply incapable of sustaining a three-hour movie with any capacity for attention (it's usually a problem for me; I demand a cigarette break). I suspect that the normal strategy of the filmgoer who finds himself at the mercy of an emotion too painful to bear is to retreat beyond the peripheries of compassion or anger. By what means he manages to do this, I don't know. I don't think I really want to know.

That's the moral subject of the film, at any rate, as clearly as I can articulate it—Yasumoto's struggle against what fate and Red Beard have quietly decided. He is nearly assassinated by a mad nymphomaniac, he listens to stories of unbearable misfortune, he faints during an operation (perfectly macabre scene!), he is given a nearly half-witted child, Otoyo, to restore to life, wants to be quit of that obligation but manages to fulfill it (with Red Beard rescuing him at the lowest depth), only to discover when he is finally free to leave this infernal outpost that he no longer wants to, for his only freedom consists in doing what he must. When I left the cinema, after *Red Beard,* I knew that for some months any film that aimed at less would seem unworthy of my attendance. . . . To the suggestion that the film has its shortcomings I am not immune. I have not been entirely bereft of judgment. There were perhaps too many parenthetical stories in the first half; Red Beard vanquishing the defenders of the brothel with judo was merely a handout to the *aficionado* of *The Seven Samurai;* the arrival of a small, unfortunate boy whom the girl, Otoyo, can cherish in her turn was too neat by far; life seldom provides such timely diversions from misery. Even so, these were incongruities I noted with half a mind. Kurosawa's foundation is firm. By comparison with *Red Beard,* the artful nihilism of the new Japanese cinema—judging by the productions

I have seen—as well as the finicky pessimism of such a film as *Persona* are luxuries of the spirit. Suffering is an absolute value, not to be impugned by democratic hedonism nor bewailed by accusing a God in hiding. Kurosawa's best films, and this is one of them, do what serious art has always done when engaged with the human condition. They challenge us to live authentically.   1967

Poetry, Politics,
and Pornography

A friend to whom I had delivered the opinion that *Persona* was at bottom fraudulent wrote me in reply that he had accepted fraud as a common denominator of Bergman's recent films and now viewed them simply as good or bad theater. To what extent theater can be fraudulent and remain "good" may well be a matter for the individual's discrimination. Yet I wonder if most educated people today don't accept fraud, unwittingly, as a common denominator of all the public arts. Toward film they tend to adopt the attitude that the medium is not to be taken seriously. From the point of view of the grave, very little is to be taken seriously. While we pretend to wakefulness, the expressible content of life may not so whimsically be dismissed. Since a film is neither a philosophic proposition nor, commonly, a political manifesto, most filmgoers find it tiresome to consider whether or not it "makes sense"; hence a widening gap prevails between the moving images that seduce and the implications that stupefy. And the gap is further widened precisely by those whose obligation is to bridge it, whose function should consist in saying what a work of art is good for—the film critics. In magazines for the film buff, writers are all too numerous who support the imaginative poverty of the new mindless cinema with a cant of their own. That they're not confined to such journals can be tested by consulting the pages of the international press. A characteristic sample of what I have in mind is a statement made by the *Times* (London) film critic in defense of Godard's *Made in U.S.A.*:

> If, instead of trying to decipher its political significance, if any, we said it was a film "about" the relationship between a shot of a cold white wall with "Liberté" scrawled across it in blue and the immediately succeeding shot of Anna Karina against a burning yellow door which fills the entire frame, we should probably be much nearer the mark.

Which mark, Mr. Taylor? (Prithee, let's talk fustian a little and gull them!) If audience sensibilities were not so uncertainly lodged between the barbarian and the chic-at-heart, few films given votes of confidence lately would survive any more serious analysis than the foregoing. The "advanced cinema" audience has been brainwashed by film journalists who follow the bent of their cousins, the art critics: when the object yields no pleasure, invent some, or resign yourself to having no professional justification. The result is self-evident. The more frivolous the film, the better chance it has to win a film festival award and the higher the price paid for its distribution rights. I have no objection to a film which is nothing but color, movement, and music—for ten minutes. If I'm going to spend two hours with people represented as having stakes in the world, I want finer delights for my emotional investment. Even frivolity has its logic (in art). I think it's important to decide if a film-maker intended frivolity or if he simply landed there because his thoughts were muddled. And I firmly believe that if we suppose his film to have political significance, we should by all means try to decipher it; this touches us where we live—if not today, hereafter.

Claude Lelouch's *A Man and A Woman,* which has been running forever in the capitals, is a comparatively innocuous example of the new escapism—all style, speed, and tease. Lelouch had one eye on the *Magnum* annual, one ear cocked toward Godard. There's nothing he can't execute cinematically; he can even simulate the rim of the profound. I recall most vividly the racially refined faces of Jean-Louis Trintignant and Anouk Aimée, during a wind-ruffled interlude on a ferryboat, saying nothing, hands making tentative advances toward an intimacy not yet acknowledged. Expecting something fateful from the inceptive dialogue about previous marriages, violent death, and the preference for saving a dog rather than a Rembrandt from a fire, I was duly attentive. Yet nothing, after all, was conjunctive. In this love story of an auto racer and a script girl who improbably talk like a book—a book for the Left Bank—there are no insights, only photoflashes. Lelouch had a subject for his first film, *Avec Des Si*—the irony of mistaken continuity (within the film). He tried something like it again with his next, *The Girl and the Guns*—tried too hard. If advance reports may be relied on, his fourth film will duplicate the method—if it is a method—of *A Man and A Woman,* which is to say that it makes elaborate plans for a journey with no destination. At present Lelouch's nervous energy is in excess of his sense of reality and he's in danger of being governed by the tour de force, like Orson Welles and Roman Polanski.* For this reason it is not reassuring to hear that he has been collaborating with the High Camp sector (Godard, Varda, Resnais) on a film about Vietnam (not made there, and anti-American—of course).

Of Alexander Kluge's *Abschied von Gestern* (*Anita G.*)—called *Yesterday Girl* in England—there seems to be a widely insinuated notion that the film is a contribution to political criticism. The notion is as arch as the title of the film and provocation for it is not hard to discover. Kluge put his sister in the leading role of Anita G., identifying her as Jewish, as who should say, "If you don't like my sister you don't like Jews, and if you don't like my movie, which is funny and anti-German, you're not a liberal." The gudgeons at Venice in 1966 swallowed Kluge's hook and gave him the grand prize. A special award from the Italians went to Alexandra, his sister. What the film says for Jews or against *Wirtschaftswunder*

Postscript 1971. I should like to qualify this remark. With *Repulsion,* 1965, and *Cul de Sac,* 1966, Polanski had not yet learned how to be a professional spook: in these films the blood and wickedness seemed gratuitous. But he admirably transmuted his preoccupation with the lunatic border of things in his Dracula parody of 1967, *The Fearless Vampire Killers* (or, in the U.S., *Your Teeth in My Neck,* a Jerry Lewis title) —actually a work of scenic art, designed with macabre beauty, very funny, and, by Polanski himself, acted with what I'd call impassive charm. As for *Rosemary's Baby,* 1969, while I'm not easily frighted with false fire, I think this is one of the most hair-curdling films I've ever seen: extraordinarily well cast, besides (Mia Farrow unnerved me) , and with a brilliantly contrived sound score. Mr. Polanski has a disquieting sense of evil. I shall not dwell on the cost. . . . My mention of Orson Welles was not adventitious. I believe the two men have one problem in common: uprooted from his own culture, each must find subject matter far from home to sustain his formidable talent.

Germany is for its defenders to expound. What we see is Miss Anita G., jail bait from the Eastern Zone, with the brains of a shrimp, proto-criminal instincts, and a will of butter, aimlessly casing West Germany for a berth or a job, convinced all the while that she's worthier and wiser than anyone. Social reality never gets a hearing in this film; every male adult—doctor, lawyer, *polizei* chief—is depicted as a blockhead. At one stage in her cyclic journey between jails, Anita G. attends college to no point and jumps her hotel because she can't pay her bill (why would a college student be living in a hotel?); at another we're supposed to believe she could stagger miles down a main highway bearing a loaded suitcase, without being offered a lift! All interior scenes are crudely lighted, clumsily staged, and when Kluge senses that his narrative is fatally going to pieces he fills the breach with those silent-film speedups done to death by Richard Lester, if not by Chris Marker *et al.* ten years ago. This film is trash, launched through moral blackmail as a herald of the new German cinema. There is no new German cinema—yet. There is only a handful of anti-German Germans making amateur movies.

As for Miss Kluge's performance, I suppose it was as credible as the incredible continuity permitted. Further than that compliment I'm not prepared to go. Perhaps an aging member of the Venice jury was. We live in the Age of Lolita—which was again corroborated at Cannes this spring when the Best Actress prize was bestowed on Pia Degermark, the seventeen-year-old nothing co-starred with Thommy Berggren (a little older and, if anything, nothinger) in Bo Widerberg's *Elvira Madigan*. What of the film itself, if one can separate it from the only inhabitants that supply its *raison d'être?* The historical source from which it was prettified demanded a more subtle conception by far. Lieutenant Sparre, in actuality, was something of a tomcat before he met Elvira, the tightrope walker. A Don Juan from the Swedish landed gentry who, in the cause of true love, repudiates his class, deserts his regiment, and throws away his life—his life *and Elvira's:* there's the real story, there's where the dog lies buried! Or in any case this is one potent suggestion held out by the material; there must be many more. What Widerberg chose to express was nothing dangerous, only the dying fall. He settled for a prolonged, rainbow-hued picnic in the woods of Denmark, with no suggestion that Sparre was a flabby egoist who was killing the thing he loved. After an hour and a half of puppy babble and pussy fret, we learn nothing, nothing whatever, about these star-crossed ephebes except that they were stupid enough to reach the brink of starvation and perish.

The French, themselves flatterers of the first rank, were overjoyed with this iridescent idyll. Seemingly, Widerberg had followed the strategy of Agnes Varda's boorish pastorale, *Le Bonheur,* by enlisting Mozart to provide whatever emotional lift might have been otherwise wanting. To give Widerberg his due, he had recognized the film-saving powers of baroque music (Vivaldi) some years before. Widerberg is a smart weathercock. Back in '65 when he was trying to crowd Antonioni with that silly sex-on-the-floor film I reviewed in these pages, he was simultaneously giving public lectures urging the welfare state to ratify the sexual emancipation of fifteen-year-old girls by equipping them with the requisite safety devices. Then he felt the wind shift, if only in his own mind; his preface to *Elvira Madigan* announces that free love is indefensible—if for no other reason, it is not conducive to survival. But that was in another country, and besides, the wench is dead. . . . Widerberg knows how to play close to the appearance of the real thing. Should he ever discover wherein his integrity lies, he might just become a poet.

Vilgot Sjöman never will. His unacknowledged legislation will flow in other channels—toward what end is dismayingly predictable. . . . One of those touring Americans whose interest in Sweden is frankly directed to below the belt line greeted me with stars in his eyes after previewing Sjöman's latest release (and I do mean release), *I Am Curious.* When I pressed him to relate what had stoked his visible wonder, all he could come up with was "a fabulous backtracking shot" of a couple fornicating on the balustrade of the Royal Palace in Stockholm. In truth, perhaps no other sequence of the film would better stand for the whole. The whole that I saw, which is but a half. Sjöman took nearly two years to assemble this alleged documentary persiflage of life under social democracy. Unable to reduce his total film mileage to negotiable limits, he was permitted by Sandrews to cut two feature-length films from the accumulated stock. (*I Am Curious, Yellow* and *I Am Curious, Blue.* Perhaps I should remind the reader that blue and yellow are the colors of the Swedish flag.) The content of the first half is quite enough for anyone with as fastidious a stomach as mine. Such fun as may accrue from on-the-spot answers by the public and the politicians to the question, for example, "Do you think we have a class society in Sweden?" is not inexhaustible. Actually, the questionnaires and the crosscut editing of advertising messages and political slogans comprise a stalking-horse for the preferred pastime of the odious young female, porcine and violent, who conducts the survey. She is obsessed by the fifty-seven (?) positions of sexual intercourse, most of which we are not allowed to take on trust, for she is unsparingly photographed with her beefy sparring partner, often inter-cut with closeups of the genial caterpillar himself—Vilgot Sjöman, leering and avuncular. Before the copulating marathon is run, the tramp shoots and castrates her stud in a fantasy episode which is hopefully linked to her rebellion against Father, a slob who has done nothing useful since fighting against Franco. Suck whatever sense you can from this trifling with Freud and political action. *I Am Curious* (hereafter to be thought of as *I Am Spurious*) is the sewer toward which Swedish film, in certain hands, has been heading for some time. Taken together with *Elvira Madigan,* with which at first glance it would appear to have no affinity, it suggests the plight of a society, deficient in the culture that would alone dignify its isolation, steadily substituting non-commitment for authentic living, at every level. Sex, so goes the rumor, is its sole resource; logically enough, a failing one. *Elvira Madigan* and *I Am Curious.* Sentimentality and pornography are the polar consequences of impotence: the former, all ideal extension without human contingency; the latter, the forked radish thing-in-itself, devoid of any ideal development to distinguish it from the coupling of rabbits. The net result, in either case, as Widerberg and Sjöman were impelled to reveal, is murder.

By contrast, Luis Buñuel's invitation to the *voyeur, Belle de Jour,* is merely nasty-minded. In a Thurber fairy tale the Golux declares, "I had high hopes of being evil when I was two, but in my youth I came upon a firefly burning in a spider's web. I saved the victim's life." "The firefly's?" "No, the spider's. The blinking arsonist had set the web on fire." . . . This is Buñuel's predicament; he never knows where his worst interests lie. *Belle de Jour* exploits a puritan solution: gloat over Catherine Deneuve in her panties, then punish her for the provocation—and make the form of the punishment, which includes smearing, as salacious as the spectacle you have approvingly witnessed. (What women derive from these films is too ambiguous a speculation to be tackled here.) The clinical veracity upheld for this film is a straw grasped by those who need sanction to relish the tawdry situation: that of a married bourgeois somnambulist who works by day in a brothel, since only humiliation has power to assure her she's alive. Quite unconvincingly conveyed, however. And another prize winner (Venice, '67), Buñuel's sad valediction: in thirty-eight years of film-making, his occasional genius has been mainly employed to extend the limits of our nausea. Judged within cinematic bounds, *Belle de Jour* is shoddy stuff. The color is vile, the editing is harsh; spreading the dénouement throughout the film is gratuitous and an impediment to whatever suspense might have been conjured from this paltry and profane enterprise. All the actors save Francisco Rabal (whose role *couldn't* have been designed for this film!) seemed put upon and resentful. Miss Deneuve joins the long procession of females who have managed to ambulate through a two-hour movie wearing a single expression—nay, wearing none.

After 10,000 years (give or take a few thousand) of standing upright rationally, mankind still looks to the pelvic area of the opposite sex for its *axis mundi* and is universally unable to coax a pleasure principle from the orientation. Japan, relieved of its suppression overnight by Western conquest and enlightenment (the truth about the human animal?) wakes with a cry of rage, finding itself unattractively naked and unequipped for the freedom of spirit that should have ensued from the overthrow of conduct. Films that claim to reflect the contemporary Japanese attitude seem to be of two kinds, both hateful. On the one hand, there is the cold curiosity of, e.g., Shinoda's *With Beauty and Sorrow*, 1965 (in which two lesbians destroy the man who threatens their commitment to each other), or Teshigahara's impeccably structured fables (*The Case*, 1962; *Woman of the Dunes*, 1964; *The Face of Another*, 1966). The stylistic equivalents for these films in the West would be Antonioni at his most static moments and Alain Resnais at his most cryptic. On the other, there is the latent hysteria of *The Amourist*, 1966, directed by Shohei Imamura: black humor at its inkiest, somewhat turgid from the indignation that from time to time boils over. Imamura's anti-hero is a grubby little photo-pornographer, dominated by the conviction that he is an unappreciated benefactor of humanity. In view of the fact that he despises the mankind he serves and, though virtually impotent, is not aloof from the promptings to which he contemptuously caters, his argument lacks persuasion. His domain is a water-side jungle where he lives on a boat and alternatively sweats to satisfy the concupiscent widow he lives with and to seduce her fifteen-year-old daughter. Eventually the widow dies, demented; the girl becomes a tart; her brother expects to bribe himself through the university exam. To mend all, the pornographer invents a life-size doll which, with no personality problems, will purvey sex like a machine, hence bringing man freedom from sexual disquietude. The poor wretch's devotion to this creature prevents his patenting the invention for market; at the end of the film, the dock-side boat unmoors itself and floats out of the harbor, bearing him and his ersatz Venus toward a receding horizon of oceanic ecstasy. . . . If the scrabbling, simian behavior of the characters doesn't alienate you instantly or soon thereafter, you may find a sort of insane consistency in this film, not altogether irrelevant to the collective descent into hell on which Japanese life, in common with ours, appears to have embarked. "I think we have thrown Japan morally backwards a thousand years; she is going to adopt our vices (which are much too large for her)." That observation was made by Lafcadio Hearn—in 1893.

If much of the cultural dropout (that terrible conception) in the West has been taking place in one of the principal citadels, England, it may yet be from England that the most vocal retort to the consequences will come. *Privilege,* 1967, the first full-length film of Peter Watkins, is a case in point, happily free from the stammering montage of today's pop style in movie-making and addressed directly, scornfully, and with stunning color effects, to the pop subject —with a difference. I regret not being able to discuss it further but I prefer to spend my remaining wordage on *Accident,* one of the two or three superlative films I've seen among the 130 to which I subjected myself during the year. Joseph Losey is the American film-maker who has been helping the English to fight their class struggle, in such films as *The Criminal, Eva, The Servant, King and Country.* I had not previously been convinced of his merit by those who were in fact merely endorsing his aims. A certain theatricalism as well as an ill-concealed personal testiness impaired many moments in his earlier work. *Accident,* again with the assistance of Harold Pinter, is the sensitive, authentic film predicted by his more discerning supporters. It suggests that Losey has come to acquire respect for at least the setting and ambience of a vestigial tradition, without surrendering his sense of the evil that haunts the remembering oak and the storied cloister. Few films have had a more portentous beginning: the quiet Oxford house, the accelerating roar and crash of the automobile, the long quiet broken only by a far-off dog in the night; Bogarde rescuing the numbed girl from the wreck; the police inquiry, a constable apologizing for his cough, Bogarde momentarily breaking down into a stutter and a facial twitch. By now we are in the midst of life and expect heartbreaking deeds. They

come to pass, retroactively (the parabolic form is beautifully utilized) and always politely, a tragedy with National Hunt rules—
never confess, with one ill-placed remark, that the issue is lethal.
Three men—two and a boy—unconsciously desire death by way of
the customary oblivion: an inscrutable girl, probably just blank,
who wants nothing except perhaps the lineaments of gratified desire.
The two men are dons, both restive under the yoke of the years and
of marriage too long endured. The one (Stanley Baker) is a scant-
born gentleman, a productive hack, and a fumbling wolf; the other
(Bogarde) is a scholar with civil courage who has schooled himself to greater decency than his passions dictate. The boy is just a
Yang looking for his Yin, a cheerful killer from the lordly classes,
all surface candor and physical confidence. Bogarde contains himself; the others share the girl. Was the boy driving or was she, at the
fatal hour? You never know; you assume—else why does she leave
Oxford? No matter; the youth asks for death and gets it, being priv-
ileged. The men die a little more; they're used to dying and they
keep stiff upper lips. The girl (from Vienna, we're told, but it's not
likely) steps on the boy's face, Bogarde saves hers, and what does
she learn? That fair wenches cannot want favors while the world
is so full of amorous fools. In the small dark hours between the
"accident" and the birth of his son, Bogarde's gratuitous desire is
consummated.

If the lingering camera, spying out shadows and listening for
night-jars, restates Antonioni, the general temper is closer to the
understatement of Ford's novel, *The Good Soldier* ("This is the
saddest story." . . .) . Here youth has its poor innings and "drops out"
speedily. Sweet Thames continues to flow softly, nurturing the
lawns beneath the feet of bloody-minded man, and insatiable mortality has the last cry.   1967

London Film Chronicle:
Variation on a
Personal Theme

The essential reason for my not being able to live in my native country permanently is my inability to confront, without pain, the changes which are overwhelming it: the grossly erupting skyline of London; the dying villages replaced by a neo-urban contempt for the organically created settlements; the leaden drift toward socialism; the stilted efforts of intellectuals to be liberal by standing on their own necks; the frightening, if admirable, good humor with which everyone is prepared to tighten his belt again, stand in line, and act the deferred life in obedience to one more political promise; and the brittle indifference toward historically grounded sentiment expressed by the not-exactly-young and, it would seem, not-exactly-educated who represent the influential forces. Nowhere more than in England do I feel as if I were on a great ocean liner going down with all lights blazing, while every passenger repeats, over his penultimate whisky and soda, "And a jolly good thing, too!" It's distressing to watch a decent people liquidating itself—sadness behind their eyes but the chin still dauntless. Set me down almost anywhere in north continental Europe and I'm happy. But in England, as rationally as I try to conquer the feeling, I remain melancholy beneath whatever positive pleasure of the hour I may be receiving. In Ulm, Nuremberg, Bremen, or Rotterdam I am *intellectually* aware of comparable changes in the climate and precisely familiar with the literal damage suffered between 1940 and 1945. But I am not personally identified with the consequences. On native soil, where a genuine foreigner accepts any phenomenon as an exotic and reassuring instance of the eternal England he has gleaned from Wordsworth, Dickens, or Winston Churchill, I have just memory enough for shocks of recognition, insufficient to feel confidently related. I have lived for too long in too many other places; when in England I entertain assumptions for which I have no sanction from a living status and I soon feel like Peter Schlemiel—the man who cast no shadow.

My notes tell me that I was deeply shaken by Peter Watkins' first film, *The War Game:*

> It is unlikely that anyone else will succeed in compressing the end of the world into fifty more disturbing minutes of film . . . the blighted human face, children and animals singed, maimed, denaturalized in a matter of seconds, the impinging smaller terrors, the tyrannical grief of people you thought you hated yesterday. . . . If the moral nature of scientific man has brought us to this—death by fire or, worse, by slow voiding of the body liquid and erosion of the bone—better to die now. . . . London still stood when I came from the theatre. Invulnerability is the greatest of our illusions.

High praise, no doubt, for the immediacy of Watkins' film; yet some months later I feel no compulsion to recommend *The War Game* as the greatest story ever anticipated. More than one critic has been tempted to believe that a film which acutely treats the most important subject of our time—for which subject has priority over our fear of total extinction?—must necessarily be the most important film of our time. The logic of the heart deceives them. Disaster is always affective to the quick imagination. Turn on the radio, pick up the newspaper, put your ear to the ground; you'll have your fill of terror, if you insist. *What's the meaning of all song? Let all things pass away.* But the human mind is protected from paralyzing inconsequence by a recuperative mechanism which fanatics mistakenly call indifference. We've always thought the world was going to end: when we fell out of love, when the first sirens sounded, when we lay dying in a hospital bed. One day it will. Until then, we gain no greater glory than by *living,* as gratefully (and as gracefully) as we are able. *Try to be one of those on whom nothing is lost.* As for *The War Game,* to be quite honest, I have all but forgotten it, so soon after my quaking response to it in London—which neither invalidates the film as a compelling documentary nor removes for a minute the dire possibility it prophesies. Watkins' method is almost too effectively impersonal, the brilliant simulation of crucial actuality as if caught in the flying present by a TV crew. But a newsreel, because it's *true,* has no such durable hold on the imagination as a work of art.

All the same, two films by Peter Watkins helped to intensify the probably morbid gratitude with which, even under daily rain, I re-experienced that city where so many monuments to eloquence and courage have been preserved and where, after the worst has been said of him, your man on the street is civil and self-disciplined to a degree unmatched, I am convinced, elsewhere. I had to ask myself, upon seeing *Privilege* for the second time: could the people I saw around me in the pubs, the undergrounds, and the museums be herded into the abject condition Watkins obviously feared when he made that film? Were they self-disciplined or docile? Had they been so conditioned to queuing up—for postwar rations, buses, cinema tickets—that they could be forced to stand in that ultimate queue where the most substantial liberties are surrendered? I didn't believe they could. Conceivably I didn't *want* to believe so. Of course, the first weakness of that film, as of all such, is that we are required to accept the premise, the *fait accompli.* We are asked to infer an international crisis so terrible as to break the English nerve. It has never before been broken—not to the root. But a breed is dying out and the new breed hasn't been tested. I'd like to pin my faith on the native kindness and on the preponderance of intelligence over imagination (a virtue in life, a hindrance in art) that distinguishes British empiricism. Against panic in the bowels and pressure from the pimps, however, kindness and intelligence may have no more weight than the barking of a dog. . . . This time around, *Privilege* seemed most cogent when it pegged the social flunkeys, cross-biters, and panders—Levantine or Protestant—who run show business and who, Watkins imagines, may be running England, before 1984 is in sight, with the alarmed assistance of a fearful coalition establishment.

The two "British" films of the past year which have most sugges-tively rendered a sense of the English past, *A Man for All Seasons* and *Accident* (the latter by indirection, for I don't believe Harold Pinter gives a damn for the English past) , have been directed by foreigners. (Zinnemann is Viennese, by way of Hollywood; Losey is American.) I revisited *A Man for All Seasons* with special affection: quite simply, it is riches for the eye and ear. (And suspect by the purist, for it's lifted from a play and what would it be without the spoken language of the original—especially as spoken by Paul Sco-field?) Before all, it has a subject, one so irreducible as to appear archaic in the window dressing of today's cinema: a man's con-science—*that charming, conversable, infinite thing, the intensest thing we know.* Zinnemann translated Robert Bolt's discursive trag-edy into the moving, often radiant, likeness of an age when the lyric and the ax shared the same domain, when the language and the architecture of men went far to minimize the cruelty with which they lived. I find that I'm on relative grounds, however. Anglo-Americans and/or Catholics may be counted on to enjoy this film; elsewhere, and the more so where the English tongue can't be savored, boredom sets in. More than one Swede, for example, told me that he thought Sir Thomas "foolish." Foolish because he was Old Church, no doubt, and sixteenth-century casuistry is irrelevant to "our problems." Where security is the sole value, I suppose that a man who prefers to die rather than acknowledge a butcher with an itch for a new bedfellow as supreme head of the realm under Christ must indeed appear foolish! A question remains: would they have been as bored by a film about Martin Luther?

One of the two period films made by Englishmen which in Novem-ber had newly arrived on the London screens was Richard Burton's embarrassment (to me, if not to him) , Marlowe's *Dr. Faustus.* This bewildering movie was impetuously undertaken (that it could have been engendered in cold blood I'll never believe) on the basis of a staged experiment by the Oxford Theatre Society, in which the visit-ing celebrity had a vested interest. Instead of leaving well enough alone (benefit of doubt given) , Burton made a film, retaining him-self in the title role and adding to the depressingly camp perform-ances of the students a lab-full of cinematic trickery, gauche sound effects, meretricious color—and his wife. If Burton had shown the film first to a dependable chum, he might have been told, "Quite interesting, old boy, but you're not going to release the damn thing to the public, are you?" I should prefer to assume that Burton would then have had sufficient self-respect to get the point. Since he did in fact release the damn thing, one is led to credit him with a pathetic wish to protest that if he were not so susceptible to the Hollywood-International *dolce vita* he might have become our leading rhetorical actor. In *Dr. Faustus* the formerly rich elocution is perfunctory and the camera inconsiderately magnifies a bloated face and an absent eye. Less tolerable than this: because Marlowe's play is a better argument than any by Shakespeare for Lamb's objection to staging Elizabethan drama—it takes place only in the ear—special genius was called for (which in Burton's case he has not got) to invent credible settings. Those attempted suggest a TV complex for Dr. Jekyll's laboratory, sufficiently mobile for simultaneous invasion by sound and camera units. Marlowe's space-time is bounded in a nutshell. Roman Polanski's designer was infinitely more inspired when planning the delightfully inane scenography of *The Fearless Vampire Killers*. *Dr. Faustus* is hereby included with the classic errors of film-making: with, for instance, Sergei Yutkevich's *Othello,* the Orson Welles *Macbeth* (not *his Othello* which was, whatever else, supreme film art), and Gustaf Gründgens' version of the Goethe *Faust* he had previously staged in Hamburg. Nor is the Burton film redeemed, I am not reluctant to add, by the presence of Elizabeth Taylor in several stages of undress as the immortal Helen. Mercifully, she is not called upon to speak. For one appearance she is held together with gold dust, for another by what looked like an overall clay pack. However encased, she is, of course, imperturbable. When Burton-Faustus asked, "Is this the face that launched a thousand ships?" I was quite prepared to lead the audience in a choral rejoinder—"Not bloody likely!"

John Schlesinger has affirmed the steady indifference of British film-makers to the tradition of their nature poetry in the very act of trying to mend the indifference with a stereoscopic, giant-screen production of *Far from the Madding Crowd*. He has brought forth a blockbuster, which may not be entirely to his discredit if you consider that any more suitable director than he might well be defeated by the plain fact that Thomas Hardy wrote novels with all the structural elements of a blockbuster. They had a great deal more. They had nobility of theme (the failing struggle of thought to transcend instinct) and they had at their best a live-oak tenure in the soil; a sentient, if stoical, response to the moods of weather and season which, among other things, one waits for in vain during the tedious passage of Schlesinger's movie. A female writer in *Vogue* described Nicholas Roeg's photography as "exquisite." I can see that with the new tide of color we shall get as many unfounded judgments on that property of film as we've ever had on acting or on the "real subject." Far from being exquisite, Roeg's camera work is conventional. The first sight of the sky in this film should convince anyone but a mole that he has little better to expect thereafter than views to reward the easily glutted tourist. No such sky ever existed. Schlesinger and Roeg have assembled an attractive facsimile of England in the age of the shire, the sheepwalk, Kersey cloth, and the resident landlord, but we never hear stirrings in the grass or sense the earth turning as the wind wears down stones, bevels the Downs, and deforms the gesture of a tree. To film Hardy without this sense is like conducting Sibelius without hearing wolves in the distance. (To be fair, who with such a sense would have freedom to express it on an MGM high-budget schedule?)

Once, the film comes truly alive and close to the underskin of Hardy: when Sergeant Troy "woos" Bathsheba by showing off his saber ritual in a cleft of hills denuded of any other human trace. Schlesinger here captures the spirit and the topography of an authentic Hardy moment, the vital impassivity of nature mocking egoistic concerns: treeless mounds rumble away oceanically; the silly, skillful man, a child and cad, demonstrates to a frozen, fascinated female the cut and thrust, the feint, the parry, the charge, the razor-sharp kill. Terence Stamp is largely responsible for the concentrated interest of this scene; he was born to play Sergeant Troy —which is, I fear, no compliment. When all is done, any conviction that animates this film, wherein every shot is given equal value with the next, comes from the actors (just as in the Hardy novels, this one included, we are held by our curiosity about the characters, while outraged by the situations they get themselves into). I said the actors; I mean the *men:* besides Stamp, Peter Finch and Alan Bates, each playing a suitor endowed with an unreasonable degree of forbearance. I don't know what Julie Christie (Bathsheba) was doing in this film. But then, bless her, I don't know what she's doing in any film. As the big-sister girl of Billy Liar she was briefly the apt thing. As a lady farmer of early Victorian England she is no more feasible than she was as an international whore in *Darling.* Always I have the feeling that she missed her vocation by saying no to that job as an airline hostess.

England is suffering, more perhaps than any European country, for having failed to educate—or at least to *accommodate*—its urban lower classes. Since the days of Hardy's novel and the industrial revolution, there has existed a static mass that resists all but economic change, a mass amenable to organization but utterly incurious otherwise. Proud of its own inertia, it wages class warfare passively by refusing all higher interests on the grounds that they're the property of a higher class. As the upper levels, economically supported, break down, the art of being English becomes to a large extent histrionic—for it consists, to begin with, in maintaining a style consonant with the social level one is born to; failing that, with the level from which one has fallen or to which one aspires. To be *without* a social level is nominally not to exist! From this perspective, the "Mods" are *reactionary;* contemporary only in their lingo, they represent a kind of underground Restoration, with nothing to restore but their lack of identity. They have rejected their grandfathers as well as their fathers and returned, sartorially at least, to the era of the Four Georges, in the pitiful hope that a change of costume will confer a change of rank. Many who fail to rise in the English social scale and cannot live at the level to which circumstance or education has restricted them form a lunatic fringe on which they survive by self-delusion. Taking up an antisocial position, they secretly harbor social pretensions.

The old, indigent woman in Bryan Forbes's marvelous film, *The Whisperers,* converts her lifetime of servitude into one of authority; her deadbeat, cadging husband, a ferret in the social landscape, insists on the pose of a respectable man down on his luck. Bryan Forbes made *The Whisperers* with production money raised by two young Americans and personally supplied the bleak scenario (from a novel by R. Nicholson) that recounts the daily paranoid existence of old Mrs. Ross, who, long since deserted by her husband and son, lives (in appalling poverty) by the grace of Social Assistance, to which she writes politely condescending letters explaining that as soon as her estate is settled she will no longer need the back of their hand. She hears conspiratorial whispers in the pipes, in the water taps, behind the walls, outside the windows. They are the only company she has and all the company she needs, the only whisperers to whom she can talk back without incurring the troublesome responses of a reality her mind refuses to face. By strict standards she is mad. Yet there's a fine edge to her madness; it supplies her with a performance, large as one way of life, which most people have agreed to indulge. An Assistance official who alone has taken a personal, guardian interest in this old ruin knows that in truth she spent her years as a domestic in the homes of the well-to-do: hence her refinement of diction, her marchioness deportment, her innocence of the relationship between cause and effect, her genuinely fatigued civility when exposed to logic, to verbal abuse, or physical violence. . . . For two-thirds of the film Dame Edith Evans carries nearly the whole expressive burden, meeting triumphantly that difficult challenge to the vanity of an actress—appearing to forget all she ever knew about acting. During the last third she is assisted, superbly, by Eric Portman as Archie, the recreant husband imposed on her, with every good intention and no good result, by Social Assistance. Forbes sustains the tone of his depressing subject with such frugal accuracy that I expect the film will be a financial disaster. Some masterpieces of naturalism are too successfully conveyed for anyone to assimilate with more pleasure than pain. *Umberto D* took five years to reach New York; exhibitors believed it would drive people out of the cinema. And I was never able to persuade anyone to see *The True End of the Great War* (Kawalerowicz, Poland) after outlining the content for them. (I should keep my big mouth shut.)

The England of Forbes's film is that of the industrial Midlands, once on a time covered by forest but long ago given over to "the dark Satanic mills," grimy, red-brick homes, grey chapels of the Dissenting Sects, rubbishy side streets, and draughty pubs—the back lots of a great society. There are acres of living ugliness in beautiful England which no sane man can excuse and no hopeful man can expect to see greatly improved. A talent for theater the English have in abundance; the talent for building seems to have been lost in them forever. 1967

I've Been Reading These
Film Critics*

All claret would be port if it could.
Old Saying

Fifteen years after attending my first *avant garde* film program, at Cinema 16, I find that the New American Cinema holds no surprises for me: neither the films themselves (those I sampled at a series recently presented in Stockholm) nor an anthology of the same title, edited by Gregory Battcock, comprising a number of heady, as well as visceral, manifestos by practitioners of, and apologists for, the Deviated Art. Here, in the audience as in the book, are the same faces and the same sounds as of yore. At the screenings you can't tell the males from the females—the smell of unwashed hair knows no gender; in the book the women express themselves somewhat more politely: while they approve of four-letter thinking, they don't

---

*The New American Cinema, edited by Gregory Battcock, E. P. Dutton, $1.75. *Film Makers on Film Making*, edited by Harry M. Geduld, Indiana University Press, $6.95. *Jean-Luc Godard*, by Richard Roud, Doubleday, $2.95. *Film, the Creative Process*, by John Howard Lawson, Hill & Wang, $7.95. *Movie Man*, by David Thomson, Stein & Day, $6.95. *Man and the Movies*, edited by W. R. Robinson, Louisiana State University Press, $7.95.

employ the words. Jonas Mekas tells us that *avant garde* artists "are trying to bring some beauty into a world of horror." His own films and those of such fellow travelers as Carl Linder, Jack Smith, Kenneth Anger, and the Kuchar brothers would appear, rather, to be bringing more horror into a world of beauty. Harry Geduld's collection of personal statements by pioneers and masters of the craft—Vertov, Von Stroheim, Cocteau, Welles, Antonioni, Satyajit Ray, *et al.*—confronts you at last with the lone invective of Kenneth Anger, which might better have been printed on toilet paper. But Battcock's selections provide one with less relief from the scatology, the self-regard, the special jargon, and the obsession with *equipment* that alike typify the eternal amateur. I was delighted to find, by way of contrast, "Art Today and the Film," in which essay Rudolf Arnheim suggests that the living fantasy of the undersea realm in Jacques-Yves Cousteau's *World Without Sun* cancels most attempts by film-makers to produce clinically based fantasy in the studio.

Gregory Battcock is crazy like a fox. Ostensibly permitting negative opinions, he safeguards his text with an opening admonition by Jack Smith: "Film critics are writers, and they are hostile and uneasy in the presence of a visual phenomenon." I like that touch—*visual phenomenon!* Does Smith mean I'm hostile and uneasy in the presence of a sunset? Let me quote Orson Welles—he's always fun —from an interview republished in Geduld.

> . . . you always overstress the value of images. You judge films in the first place by their visual impact instead of looking for content. This is a great disservice to the cinema. It is like judging a novel only by the quality of its prose. I was guilty of the same sin when I first started writing about the cinema. It was the experience of film-making that changed my outlook.

Smith's insolent contention is of course a menace feebly posted by Battcock to inhibit any disparagement of New Cinema, such as Dwight Macdonald's, which he might have too liberally included. He warns the reader, in fact, that "Mr. Macdonald approaches these films with what may be considered conventional critical apparatus. . . ." But suppose the films had been approached with an *un*-conventional critical apparatus and the writer thereof had nonetheless taken a dim view of Battcock's stable. What, then, would have been Battcock's plea? We may never know. He declares further, "A Mekas film that Mr. Macdonald does not concern himself with here is *The Brig,* one of the outstanding productions of the new film movement." Naturally, if Mr. Macdonald *had* "concerned himself" with this film, he would have been bound to agree with Battcock! *Pravda.* There is one booby trap remaining in this sentence—the *new* film movement. Normally, our partisans of the New honor nothing older than six months. The founders of the aggregate known as the New American Cinema have been trying to impose themselves for nearly twenty years. Pat to their purpose comes Susan Sontag; her pontifications celebrate the permissiveness on which alone their demands for attention hang.

> The best works among those that are called Pop Art intend, precisely, that we abandon the old task of always either approving or disapproving of what is depicted in art or, by extension, experienced in life. (This is why those who dismiss Pop Art as a symptom of a new conformism, a cult of acceptance of the artifacts of mass civilisation, are being obtuse.)

The quotation is from Miss Sontag's apology for Smith's film, *Flaming Creatures* (an intra- and inter-sexual orgy), first published in 1964. Please note that whereas many of the underground-cinema spokesmen (especially those devoted to abstract forms or "techno-structured" methods) are busy repudiating any connection between art and life, Miss Sontag is, on the contrary, relating them, "by extension." The contradiction, as well as the propaganda intended to resolve it, is implicit in the disturbed sexual and/or political nature of the independents, a phenomenon acknowledged by indirection in Annette Michelson's lecture at Lincoln Center, September, 1966, "Film and the Radical Aspiration"—now published in the Battcock anthology. Miss Michelson's hi-fi existentialist prose, employed in defense of Godard's *Alphaville*, is worth analyzing, since it reveals, when the wrappings have been removed, a message which may be central to understanding the sources that link the political left to the mystique of the New Cinema.

> *Alphaville* is an anxious meditation, in the form of a suspense story, on the agony and death of love, liberty and language in a society which is trapped in the self-perpetuating dialectic of technical progress. It is about feeling in deep freeze. Now, to argue or contest the validity of that idea as a theme of discourse seems to me somewhat questionable in itself, but to attack the "story" except insofar as it served as a support for a cinematic structure was, above all, to betray insensitivity to the film's central "statement."

To begin with, "anxious meditation" is an odd way of defining Godard's high-speed, staccato, science-fiction fable. But let that pass: *who* has been arguing or contesting "the validity of that idea" which she believes to be Godard's subject? She doesn't say, having just previously noted that the film had been greeted the season before with "critical malaise"—only that. Is she referring to a specific criticism or is she synthesizing a number of reviews? No matter: it goes without saying that to attack a given theme in itself might well be "somewhat questionable." But Miss Michelson is nervous; she hastens to announce the gravity of Godard's theme, in case there were critics remaining who hadn't quite construed the film in her terms. Further, *who* attacked the story except as it *supported* a cinematic structure? (Doesn't a structure usually support a story? Not in Paris? *Nous avons changé tout cela!*) Why are story and statement in quotation marks? . . .

> The progress or plot of *Alphaville* is, therefore, the passage from one revelation to another; its peripeties are perceptions, structured by the pace and tension of a detective story, of "finding truth." In the face of this, the accusations of "triviality" or "pretentiousness" became embarrassingly irrelevant. The film "states" its concern with the creation of a morphology; the concentration is on pace, tension, weight, and syntactic coherence through narration—narration being in this instance a form of "relating" in the fullest possible sense of the word: a manner of creating *relational* strategies through *telling.*

The progress or plot is a passage from one revelation to another: yes, isn't this usually the case? I'm hanged if I know what the rest of the sentence means except that quite simply the nature of the events that take place in *Alphaville* is disclosed during the course of the action. In the second of these sentences it now appears that words are put in quotation marks when, among other reasons, they are insufficiently subtle to explain the arcana of the Godard film. *Relational* and *telling,* however, are in italics. Will they do? we ask hopefully. When, by the way, is a strategy *not* relational?

Miss Michelson's relational strategy is obvious enough, when the seventh veil has been dropped. Anyone unprepared to believe that *Alphaville* adds anything to *1984* (even to *Fahrenheit 451*) , anyone reluctant to accept a cheap hood and a frozen Danish pastry as adequate emblems of love, liberty, and language (Lemmy Caution's language?) , anyone, furthermore, who thinks to complain of the absence, in *Alphaville,* of such "square" ingredients as thought, passion, psychological plausibility, and interesting protagonists—this anyone is going to be intimidated by Miss Michelson into swallowing, instead, *morphology, pace, tension, weight,* and *syntactical coherence* (coherent syntax in a Godard film? That'll be the day!) .

Alain Robbe-Grillet has asked us to look at the world surrounding us "with entirely unprejudiced eyes." (Sounds to me like Francis Bacon's blank tablet mind all over again.) Susan Sontag demands that we experience art and life without approval or disapproval. Miss Michelson expects us to embrace Godard steadily and embrace him whole; to entertain reservations would prove us to be "embarrassingly irrelevant" and would "betray [our] insensitivity." The ideal audience for these people would be babies and dogs—or the population of Alphaville.

Godard, like the New American Cinema (and Caesar's wife) is above suspicion. And his apostles will always insist on the last word. If I were to suggest that *Alphaville* appears to owe a great deal, if not enough, to Orson Welles's *The Trial* (even to the casting of Akim Tamiroff in a part similar to the one he played in the earlier film) and if I were to add that the hero of Godard's *Pierrot le Fou,* which followed *Alphaville,* blows himself up, just as K. does in Welles's version of Kafka, with the same reference to the atomic bomb intended—I feel sure that Richard Roud, if not Miss Michelson, would exclaim, "Yes! Wasn't that clever of Godard!" Roud gives a comical demonstration of this technique in his study of Godard, repeatedly working to ingratiate himself with his subject and with the possibly skeptical reader at the same time. Absurdly, he is reduced to calling attention to Godard's solecisms in order to conceal them! (A prevailing custom may be partly responsible. In all books on a single film director I've lately read, the rule is never to acknowledge that your chosen daddy was ever fallible, ever made a poor film, ever helped himself to another's inspiration, ever missed the boat, ever fell flat on his face. No other field of inquiry so consistently demands of a critic that he say nothing but the best.)

Except the political field, to be sure. Something more than sales psychology accounts for critics like Miss Michelson riding shotgun for Godard, Robbe-Grillet, and N.A.C. The ill-concealed desire to stop our mouths and neutralize our discrimination is a common symptom of insecurity; self-confidence never attempts moral blackmail. Among the principal sources for such insecurity, Miss Michelson confesses to the political, in a paragraph too long to quote in full here (p. 93, Battcock). The essence of her explanation is that the process of dissociation which, in extreme form, characterizes contemporary art is a consequence of Trotsky's expulsion and the counterrevolution of Stalin. "European cinema, and European art as a whole, abandoned a certain totality of aspiration. . . . Politically oriented art at its best became a chronicle of absence, of negation, an analysis of dissociation and, in the best modernist tradition, *a formal statement of the impossibility of discourse.*" (The italics are not mine.) Had you dreamed it? Modern art is the ash of old political fires. The Manhattan Underground and the Marienbad-Godard axis are fragments shored against the ruin of Trotskyism. When the world proletarian revolution never took place, the disappointed ones, down to their children's children, refused to play with the other little boys and girls. But never ceased to make faces in order to get attention.*

There may be something to it, in the context handled here, although my personally preferred point of departure would be closer to Freud than to Marx. Suggestive, all the same—and it clarifies something I've brooded over. Why did John Howard Lawson, patently a Marxist and an activist, with no patience whatever for works of art that do not prepare the way for social revolution, accept *Last Year in Marienbad*—on the grounds that it reflected the disintegration of bourgeois values—while ignoring, for example, Leopoldo Torre-Nilsson and sniffing suspiciously at Bergman and Antonioni? I thought at first he feared not being *au courant* at the hour his book was ready for publication. I see now that there were reasons more binding. *Film, the Creative Process,* indeed! It is subtitled "The Search for an Audio-Visual Language and Structure," which wouldn't fool my cat with his eyes stitched up. The hidden persuader peers through the dedication, "To the Association of Film Makers of the U.S.S.R. . . . ." Prefaced by a friendly nod from Jay Leyda (birds of a feather defect together), Lawson thereafter cleaves an unerring line between his sheep and his goats. He expresses concern at the failure of the French New Wave to produce any new "image of man"; respecting certain affiliations, however,

---

*These words were written before the shameful events of May 18, when Jean-Luc Godard, François Truffaut, and other sansculottes sabotaged the Cannes Film Festival. It is interesting to note, as an example of Godard's "anxious meditation," that on this occasion he defended (against Roman Polanski) not Trotskyism or even Marxism—but *Stalinism!*

Footnote 1971. I was far from suggesting that the Cannes Film Festival was so sacrosanct as not to need drastic overhauling, but reforms of festivals should be carried out beforehand, not while they are in progress. Obviously this was an act of immediate opportunism and political hysteria, in anticipation of "the Revolution." With characteristic disregard for anything save their own fanaticism, the instigators left visitors to their own resources. The festival broke up, with a transportation strike paralyzing the country, and many foreigners were obliged to take taxis to the Italian or Swiss border.

he concedes generously that the impulse was, in part, "an attempt to define the human dilemma resulting from the breakdown of bourgeois values." (Pardon my thumb, but in, for instance, *The 400 Blows*, the dilemma would seem to have been the consequence of bourgeois values remaining all too intact, assuming you construe bourgeois values negatively.) "He [the artist] must be prescient concerning the hidden forces that shape people's lives." If he only meant that, I'd break bread with him: but woe and damnation to the artist who might find that the hidden force was not a capitalistic-bourgeois value or, alternatively, the working-class struggle. Dubious of *L'Avventura,* he finally refuses it absolution because of "the preordained weakness of its characters which cuts them off from reality." (Preordained? That's not even a good Marxist criticism of the film.) *Los Olvidados* is a "virulent and ironic indictment of bourgeois values," despite there not being a character from the bourgeoisie in the film except those socially constructive chaps who run the rehabilitation home. And Lawson's single-sentence summary of *Divorce—Italian Style* states that it "is brutal in its mockery of church and law." He *doesn't* say that the Germi film is funny.

Between the East Berlin mind, tight as a clenched fist, and that of the obscurantist, our life of reason goes in peril. I browse through David Thomson's pages and find this sort of thing (not exceptional; I could have easily selected a dozen such):

> The valid personal contribution Vitti makes in her walk through the hotel at the end of *L'Avventura* and her experience of the airport in *L'Eclisse* lead on to an epistemological consciousness that is always rejected by the director's reversion to a simply anecdotal level, even though the ethos of his films has overcome so simple an interpretation of life.

Anyone sufficiently reckless to publish language of this order should at least seek to sanction his practise by introducing his book with that jewel of Marshall McLuhan, "Clear prose indicates the absence of thought." And adopting this standard, W. R. Robinson's anthology is also a thoughtful book, for it includes many, many strophes quite as baggy as Thomson's. The contributors are a diverse lot, united by their appetite for movies (bad ones, especially) and by having, at one time or another, passed by the University of Florida. In the main, they are academically placed; a few are doing the world's work, in the television and film studios—and very defensive about it, too. The readable pieces in the book are the less daring: affectionate and fairly cautious studies of the Huston-Bogart films

(Alan Downer), of *Tom Jones,* novel and film (Martin C. Battestin), of Visconti's *Vaghe Stelle dell'Orsa* (Walter Korte), of Antonioni (Jonathan Baumbach). Leslie Fiedler, vitally out of place, casts a golden eye at the self-pity cult of Hollywood writers. Nathan A. Scott, Jr., explains, lucidly enough, why he is beguiled by "The New Mystique of L'Actuelle"; in my view, he too readily mistakes a Parisian phenomenon for "a new concept of reality."

The wide-screen exhibits in this volume are as alarming as they are incredible. W. R. Robinson pretends to believe that "The overall pressure of the essays is an insistent demand that the movies are and can be something more than rhetoric, a sincere, trustworthy vision committed to nothing but the truth, talking honestly and with heartfelt passion." Some of his boys didn't get this message clearly, for they insist, at length and in Gevacolor, that they *don't want* movies to be "something more than rhetoric." They adore rhetoric; they've been breast-fed on it, they've grown up facing the television screen and Frankenstein at the drive-in. The commercial poisons of the age have taken hold of them—forever. Judging by these pages, not to say thousands of others in print on the same subject, a generation of teachers whose job is to instruct the young in clear thinking and exact writing has abdicated from a task that secretly bores it. These men can no longer tell *kitsch* from the real thing, nor trash from entertainment, and they're working hard to obliterate the surviving distinctions. Enfranchised by semantic fads and 120 units of disbelief in anything that can't be taken to bed or accelerated, they have joined their students' revolt against themselves.

R. H. W. Dillard, for example, accepts the horror film as "a part of the great imaginative tradition of art . . . and as such it shares an aesthetic approach to life with works of literature as varied as Spenser and Kafka, Poe and Lewis Carroll." At the close of his rhapsody he identifies himself, in a passage which must be read in context to be believed, with the Frankenstein monster, then climbs to this cadenza:

> The horror film is not the sum of art but it is art. . . . Its demons are the demons of our hearts; it teaches us to recognize them well, but also to contend with them with reason and belief, not to despair, to know the strength of love and life within that very heart wherein they dwell.

If you want to know how he got from the first quote to the last, you have thirty-six pages to answer your curiosity. Some of Fred Chap-

pell's "Twenty-Six Propositions about Skin Flicks" justify poetic
license; they are nonetheless ill founded on a distortion of the word
cheap, confusing it with *sordid* and, by this dislocation of sense,
bringing *Anna Karenina* and *Madame Bovary* into line with the
pornography he is archly defending. A good try but a poor joke.
Richard Peck ("Films, Television and Tennis") makes his living
from television and is hence determined to kiss the hand he cannot
sever. "Television is the characteristic art form of the 1960s." . . . "*I
Spy* and *Dr. Kildare* reach and affect more people, more benefi-
cially, than any feature film ever made." (*Yeah?* What about *The
Sound of Music?*) O. B. Hardison is a master of that Hitchcock-
teasing prose which has become S. O. P. since Claude Chabrol and
François Truffaut approved the quasi-Freudian cockney muse for
highbrow treatment.

> One is reminded of James Joyce and Stephen Dedalus, and the
> contrast as well as the parallel is illuminating. Stephen left Ire-
> land to forge the uncreated consciousness of his race, while
> Alfred left the grocer's shop for a medium that has as its self-
> imposed goal the easing of the race's already created and very
> uncomfortable sub-conscious.

W. R. Robinson himself, the pace setter for these hucksters of the
Word, attains perhaps the greatest altitude. Marilyn Monroe

> has gained immortality. She has been released, as has the
> moviemaker and the viewer and, indeed, man's mind every-
> where, to dance in the imagination's heaven. . . .
>
> Out of the darkness and chaos of the theater beams a light; out
> of nothingness is generated brilliant form, existence suspended
> somewhere between the extremes of total darkness and total
> light. [And on the Seventh day He rested and saw that it was
> good!]. . . .
>
> Unburdening us of the hunger for and anxiety about meaning,
> the free movie teaches us that to be is enough; existence needs
> no justification.

Mr. Robinson, meet Miss Sontag.   1968

Children and Fools

Ole Dole Doff* is a damned silly title for a movie, even in Swedish. Our equivalent would be *Eeny Meeny Miney Mo* (which is no improvement) and the subject of the story (from a novel by Clas Engström, *The Island Sinks*) is the ordeal of an elementary school teacher, Mårtensson, under daily saturation bombing from the little bastards in his charge. A howling nightmare opens the film: a class-room-full of juvenile monsters facing *us,* the teacher—cold eyed, defiant, beyond appeal—drumming with their desk lids in unison, unreachable as only the insane or a congregation of hostile kids can be. At this hour of history, the sequence is an unhinging predicate. Here is the hive of the near future, one is bound to reflect. In seven

---

*Jan Troell's second feature-length film, awarded the Golden Bear at the eighteenth International Film Festival, Berlin 1968. His first film, *Here Is Your Life* (see pp. 298–300) , has not yet, as I write this footnote, been released by the American distributor. For the English-language market, I suggested replacing Ole-Dole-Eeny-Meeny with *Rebel Behind the Desk* (it cuts two ways) .

years, Mårtensson's pubescent mob, trailing clouds of glory (what?), will be storming administration buildings and planting red flags on opera houses—unless, which is more likely, the exertions of their present seniors go so far as to invoke a counter-tyranny, in which case you'll see a decade of collegiate suppression comparable to Russia's under Nicholas I. Actually, by comparison with the delinquency pictured in such films as *The Blackboard Jungle*, the Swedish version is this side civility. Until the end of the film, these babies do nothing more violent than pelting Mårtensson with snowballs. Their war is waged with familiar weapons: daily resistance and baboonery. Mårtensson has been whipped to a standstill, in class and at home, and here the film suffers, I think, from its own honesty. For it is not, when all is said and seen, an indictment of permissive educational theory, as its producer and author announced; it's an uncommonly painful closeup (amplified by Troell's success in preventing Per Oscarsson from acting) of a man destroying himself because he's sentimental. He can't reconcile his wistful vision of what children might be with what, in effect, the brats in his homeroom mainly are—and it's clear that they're partly what they are because he's but half a man; we have to take on trust that he was ever more. His predicament, in any case, which he tries to rationalize by seeing the children's side (a vague conviction that they're created by the "system"—yet he's a unit of the system, is he not?), involves his becoming impotent with his wife, since in the very idea of procreation he finds so little cause for carolings. She, fretful beast, waits just so long and not a breakfast longer, then leaves him to sweat out his vigils and his nine o'clocks on his own.

I'm sure that at the first screening (under informal conditions, with long discussions between reels) I was eager to be impressed. I respond crucially to Troell's marveling attention to the life in fugitive things, people, and places. He has a special feeling for those suspended seconds when one is forcibly diverted from overpowering anxiousness by the wonder of simply being alive—noting the weather-wise tree, the bird dancing for a crumb, the violin arpeggio down the street with which an unschooled simpleton is trying to breach heaven. His shooting and editing of the film were alike drastic: he used a 16mm. camera (we see a blown-up print, which means modified definition of the image); he frequently concealed the details of a scene from the children who were to participate, in hope of catching authentic reactions; he cut the film disharmonically, to emphasize the confounding zone where reality and hallucination merge. On second viewing, in the impersonal milieu of a cinema, I found that this jagged, documentary way of seizing the neuralgic moment vexed my concentration. Objectively considered, there was a more serious defect, as I hinted above. Mårtensson is in a false relationship to life; his real problem is not the one we're invited to believe in—and I couldn't help thinking that any "foreigner" might reasonably ask the damaging question: Why doesn't he find a more suitable job? (Another aspect of the situation a non-Swedish audience may construe to be false is the cool desertion of the teacher by his wife. There, the author was not stacking his cards against Mårtensson. Swedish wives and husbands do not customarily turn to each other for consolation when under stress of personal grief. On neither side would consolation be expected.) Still, we're closer here by far to life of some order than we are with Bergman's *Vargtimmen* released the same winter. Since I shall have to try dealing solemnly with that film in my book on Bergman, I shall only remark now that I am unaffectedly amazed by anyone having taken it seriously. Who's afraid of Ingmar's wolf?

As if designed for contrast, there's a film of André Cayatte in circulation, also about the near extinction of a teacher victimized by his pupils (vixens only)—*Les Risques du Métier* (*Occupational Risks*) . And with the long tracking shot that initiates the disaster—a girl about fourteen sobbing as she runs through the narrow streets of a provincial town—we may well settle back, knowing Cayatte, murmuring to ourselves, "Let us endure an hour and see injustice done," yet we experience no such intravenous shock of reality as Troell administers. What we see thereafter is theater, plausibly mounted and juridically certified—but constructed from the outside. The teacher in the Cayatte film is not a sponge filled with vinegar, that's the root of his trouble; he's too attractive for safety; as the action gets under way he is accused in rapid succession of having molested two girls in his class. Before he can assimilate the all but comic enormity of these accusations, a third child testifies against him, whereupon the bourgeois community rises to crush him with that most vindictive instrument fashioned by Western man— French law. Nothing more finely distinguishes the tone of this film, at its best, from that of *Ole Dole Doff* than the relationships of the adults to each other and to their children. The Swedish parents are on the periphery, stony and diffident. The French are concerned; where they're not cruel out of fear they're decently inquisitive. Moreover, the teacher (Jacques Brel, who combines force with charm) fights back, supported by his intensely sympathetic wife (played with lady-like confidence by Emmanuele Riva). It is in fact she who wittily points out that if he were a father (they are child-less) he would not be eligible as a Don Juan in the fantasies of the children; nor would his guilt be assumed so readily by the citizens of the town. Being female, and beset, she has her own hour of un-certainty when the evidence seems too ponderous to be wholly fic-tion. But she rallies, and it's she who applies to the conspiratorial girls the psychological pressure that eventually frees her husband from the ruinous prospect of imprisonment and professional disgrace.

All this has the somewhat dry interest of a well-briefed detective story. One praises Cayatte for the sobriety that leads him to suppose that intelligence is enough. But it is not. He has something to say—that's bracing—but most of the time one feels he could say it as well in a novel or on stage. His films are seldom as effective as their intel-lectual design suggests. This one suffers by comparison not only with *Ole Dole Doff* (Troell's method does at least establish a felt psychic combat between Mårtensson and his choir of prosecutors) but also with *Term of Trial,* made in England a few years ago (with Olivier and Signoret); it is strangely less sensual than the English film and terminates with no such subtly outrageous irony. Cayatte is characteristically indifferent to movie-making as an art. Most of this film is shot with confrontation sequences linked by cutbacks that merely illustrate what has already been verbally summarized. No doubt someone in the studio mistakenly tried to renovate his approach. "*Quand même, monsieur,* one no longer makes cinema in this mode! You must fracture the time sequence in some captivating way." So Cayatte tried fracture, gratuitously, and included a few frozen shots just to show that he could keep up with the "tradition" established yesterday by those then under thirty. Hour of the wolf, indeed? Hour of the sheep!

In *Mouchette* (novel by Bernanos, film by Bresson) the balance is redressed—or should I say that the imbalance is perpetuated?: a *child* is sacrificed. Mouchette, a village girl in her early teens, is everyone's scapegoat for no mundane reasons researched by the film, though it's an acute insight on the part of Bernanos (I assume) that whether or not Mouchette was once a blameless vessel she can now hold her own in spitefulness. Persecution has a way of shaping its victims so that they become indistinguishable from their persecu-tors. Mouchette's father clouts her, the boys shout dirty words at her, the music teacher humiliates her, the girls shun her (she retaliates with rocks and imprecations), the shopkeeper, an elderly woman, appears to have obscene reasons for giving her coffee, and Arsène, an epileptic, violates her—if not entirely against her inclinations. Penelope Huston once summarized the Bresson world in a paragraph which would be difficult to match. Part of her conclusion was that Bresson takes his characters "on a series of spiritual journeys without signposts. . . . Driving himself, his characters, his audience, he imposes his view of where man stands in relation to God: a Bresson film is an exercise of will in which the only victory is surrender." I think the key word here is *imposes,* for it is notable that those who claim to love God so jealously (Bernanos, Bresson, Greene, Bergman) cannot permit man to get the better of Him; in their zeal they normally contrive a world over which He could not possibly be thought to preside!

If I had never before seen a Bresson film, I might have been moved deeply by *Mouchette* (it is one of the purest and most integrated films of the last year or so). My consent was considerably diminished by my awareness that I was seeing an all-too-familiar rehearsal of Bresson's increasing determination to leave no stone unturned that has a toad beneath it. Paradoxically, his style has become more flexible while his metaphors remain limited. After the Joan of Arc film he must have realized that he might just as well compose a movie of still shots (as Chris Marker did in that tiresome experiment, *The Terrace*). With *Au Hasard, Balthazar,* he displayed a new resiliency. I enjoyed that film: the sensitivity to setting, the social complexity within the rural compound, the shifting élites of moral depravity, even the donkey as an epitome of passive suffering. *Mouchette* is no less supple, visually, but the animal motifs are obtrusive and frequently irrelevant. Arsène snaring a bird during the opening footage is clue sufficient to the fate of Mouchette; but you can't with any sense of reality go on to employ the shooting of rabbits as a symbol of universal voracity if you're depicting a region where rabbit is a basic source of food! This is not the first time that I've had the suspicion, when watching a film of this derivation, by Bresson or not, that what I'm witnessing is not so much the inhumanity of man as, quite simply, the inhumanity of certain French provincials.

A touch of inhumanity would have been sanguine relief in the pseudo-Fragonard surroundings of *Benjamin*. For the benefit of anyone who finds good clean fun in psychoanalyzing the critic, I'll confess that I left the theater after *Benjamin* mumbling, "Don't make love, make war!" This is the sort of French product that brings out all the Anglo-Saxon in me. It would appear to have been sponsored by Air France to entice aging American lesbians and British teen-agers to chateaus on the Loire. Michel (of course) Deville is the director. I know nothing of him, but I'll risk the conviction that he spends much of his time dreaming he's a girl's bicycle seat. His film is "about" an eighteenth-century teen-ager sent to a country estate, roughly the size of Versailles, in order to advance his sexual education. There he is forever being stripped, bathed, and caressed by a backstairs sorority of giggling cocottes (none of whom stirred my Adam); concurrently, an aging but potent goat is incomprehen-sibly in hot pursuit of an animated marshmallow (Catherine Deneuve). Since the boy (Pierre Clementi) was represented as toothsome, the man (Michel Piccoli) as irresistible, and the marsh-mallow as eminently desirable, I was personally left with nobody to whom I could attach my credulity. I detest Clementi more than any juvenile in European film (saving only Thommy Berggren, per-haps), and I was embarrassed by Michel Piccoli's attempting what I would probably accept without discomfort from Vittorio De Sica, who is perhaps fifteen years older than Piccoli. Ostensibly I was seeing a comedy but I was never tempted by mirth. Nor have I a steeled antipathy to rococo; the Watteaus in Berlin, *Vierzehnheiligen,* the suites of Couperin armored with harpsi-chords are prominent in my anthology of select experiences. I am simply not aroused by peekaboo pornography at the cinema, no matter in which century it avowedly takes place. I've had to face the fact, brought home to me by the movies, that some of my best friends are voyeurs. I remain unamused by actors and actresses who fumble at each other's buttons and ribbons and proceed to lick, sniff, and nuzzle while the emotionally starved spectator pets his invisible neighbor or stuffs chocolate into his mouth with nervously sweating hands. This film is the sort of thing Clemenceau had in mind, I suppose, when he told the French—"Your end will be deli-cious—and prolonged: it will be like cutting your veins in a bathtub full of milk." I was beguiled into seeing *Benjamin* by a finespun description of it signed "Genêt" in *The New Yorker.* No doubt her acquaintance with French thought, mores, and pastimes is more ex-tensive and intimate than I expect, or want, mine ever to be. In this case, I'll make bold to observe, she confused a *peu de chose* with a *pièce de résistance.*

Jeu de Massacre illustrates the distinction pungently. Alain Jessua, who made *La Vie à l'Envers (Life Upside Down)* is nurturing a subject—do not say exploiting, the participle would be too crude—for which he appears to have a unique competence and over which he exercises perfect control: the salvation and the catastrophe of dreams. This, his second film, is balanced to a dram between the unlikely and the just conceivable; intellectual tact, to say nothing of sheer art, prevents the solemnity of the implication from spoiling the fun. Pierre, a writer and serial cartoonist running out of ideas (and funds), encounters a half-loony young rich man, Michel (Pierre and Michel again—you see what I mean), who feeds him with quite incredible tales of adventure in Vietnam, of expeditions to exotic islands, of women by the bushel who plague him with their ardors. Little by little, after first yawning it through, the writer becomes interested in re-creating this mythomaniac as a character in a serial, an enterprise decisively encouraged when Pierre and his wife are invited by Michel and his attractive mother to make themselves at home in a Swiss villa, where Pierre and Michel can refuel each other, as it were, and the two women can dote when they're not bathing or playing tennis. The *ménage à quatre* is established; the laws of attraction and reaction begin their insidious work. Michel's runaway fancy spurs Pierre to wilder inventions, and incidentally blinds him to Michel's growing fondness for his wife; Michel is stimulated to real-life escapades in simulation of his other self. As the overlapping accelerates he tries to rob a bank (owned by his mother, as it happens), imperils the lives of a lakeside bathing colony by driving a motor launch at top speed, robs a jewelry shop, and kidnaps Pierre's wife. Finally, in a burst of irrepressible consistency, he acts out a suicide attempt and goes through the indisputable first motions of murder. At which point, Pierre is called upon to conceive a quick-witted, sedative conclusion. Each balance wheel in this lovely, comic mechanism is disturbed; none is finally impaired. Danger looms but keeps its distance, like an unseen beast snuffing behind the window-pane. Pierre's wife is half enthralled by Michel's whirlwind abduction of her; Pierre himself is on the verge of infatuation with Michel's mother; everyone recovers. . . . When we're in good humor about the French mind, Jessua is part of what we mean: wit and classical poise seriously at work in the realm of the more than faintly absurd.

François Truffaut should be making films of this quality. That he is not may be attributed to a variety of reasons I haven't the authority to nominate. One source is clear, however. Against our loyal expectations, Truffaut is in no haste to grow up as Truffaut; he's waiting for the day when he can get Alfred Hitchcock's heart, by transplantation. I like thrillers when a master of their rigid art is sensible as well as intricate and hair-raising. If against the clamor of my superego I am to find myself in breathless sympathy with bad people in sticky situations (commonly the mainspring of good thrillers) I demand at least a veneer of plausibility in the sequence of things and a show of respect for what goes on inside the characters while so much that is preposterous is going on outside. Hitchcock is no longer the model for such requirements: his grasp of abnormal psychology is that of a parvenu; his indifference to articulate plotting reflects a small boy's impatience with the finer points of the necessary fiction by which grownups justify their existence. Truffaut seems to be falling heir to Hitchcock's negative proclivities; else why should he have recourse to *The Bride Wore Black* (from a silly novel by Cornell Woolrich) which gauchely embodies them, when, in his own language, there is all of Simenon to warn him and, for that matter, the paragon of French ingenuity among contemporary films of this coat, Louis Malle's *Ascenseur à L'Echafaud* (*Frantic*, 1958), more sophisticated and more inexorable than any Operation Hitchcock I've seen for twenty years?

Against that standard, and against the standard Truffaut himself maintained in *La Peau Douce*, which had the form of a suspense story, it is doubly baffling to imagine how he could work on such a script as *The Bride Wore Black*—week after week of repeated takes —without being mortified by its stupidity. This idiotic yarn of a mysterious woman intent on killing five designated men who don't even know her is not alleviated by a shadow of the could-happen. Against all unwritten rules of the game, we are informed of the woman's motive after the third killing, which not only dispels the mystery but exposes the feebleness of the plot. (After this, it is out-and-out rubbish.) The only excuse for the premature revelation would be to switch our sympathy from the men to the woman, which, in turn, would depend on our being as spellbound by this apparition in white as the men improbably appear to be. But Jeanne Moreau is really quite confoundedly ugly; she looks as if she'd been saved from drowning but not quickly enough to erase the expression of horror stamped on her features! . . . To be sure, there are moments in this film—uncomfy glimpses of the domestic subterfuges by which two of the men (one a bachelor living in a hotel, the other a married suburbanite) convince themselves that they're alive to some point—that suggest what Truffaut might undertake with the comedy of sour manners if, as we have insinuated, he could get introduced to himself again.

The best Truffaut film made *outside* France I've recently seen is a Yugoslavian movie, *Rondo*. I trust this does not sound as if I were slighting the talents of its director, Zvanimir Berkovic; it is intended to express my surprise, in view of the black-humored art I've otherwise seen from his country, at the carefully modulated tone of this perfect comedy (ultimately sad) about two friends who—in an unacknowledged sort of way—play chess for the wife of one of them. Since it seems unlikely that any English-language film distributor is going to pick this film up (the release date is 1966) it may be gratuitous of me further to exploit an appreciation you may never be able to share, or to contest. Yet in truth I can tell you no more without divulging the unpredictable resolution toward which every nuance of the film is beautifully and ineluctably directed. Just keep the title and director in mind—the former is the easier assignment! If you liked *Jules and Jim* and Polanski's *Knife in the Water,* this is your film.   1968

War Games:
Work in Progress

Here is such patchery, such juggling, and such knavery! . . .
a good quarrel to draw emulous factions and bleed to death
upon . . .
                              Thersites, in *Troilus and Cressida*

We are today more than ever being submitted to moral blackmail
by film-makers who advance their fears or their whimpering pug-
nacity as radical social criticism. We should guard ourselves against
tolerating these false Dmitris. . . . An object lesson for me was my
too trustful reception of the films of Peter Watkins. *The War Game*
was, I do believe, conceived by Watkins in a genuine and pardonable state of terror. I should not wish to retract the strong impression it made on me when I first saw it. On the subject of *Privilege*,
I had certain misgivings which I suppressed when I briefly discussed it. I was ready to believe that because he hated hateful
things Mr. Watkins had an abiding affection for things that were
lovable—an assumption long on generosity if poor in logic. When
I saw *The Battle of Culloden*, made by Watkins for the TV, my
misgivings increased. Very like *The War Game* in method (i.e.,
treated as if a TV interviewer had been present in eighteenth-
century Scotland), the film suggested, on the part of Mr. Watkins,

a compulsion to go a-hunting for doom in the past if he could not, at the moment, find a better equivalent in the present or in the immediate future. He appeared, on the dark face of it, to be demanding compassion for those who die in senseless battles (and God knows the deaths of the Scottish infantry at Culloden were senseless); yet an intuition, which I might not easily be able to objectify in a given sequence or line of the film, convinced me that his animosity (in this context, toward the military over-class at the time of Culloden) was far in excess of any pacifistic motives. Last September, Mr. Watkins arrived in Stockholm to shoot *The Gladiators,* which, like *The War Game* and *Privilege,* will have its setting in a future as brutal as the past—that segment of the past, at any rate, chosen by Mr. Watkins to stand trial. At his press conference, into which I nosed from professional curiosity, my worst fears were confirmed.

Rarely have I heard such a rush of ill-conceived and paranoid remarks as Mr. Watkins volunteered within the half hour which embraced the limits of my attention. Without inviting anyone present to the courtesy of quizzing him first (the usual procedure), Mr. Watkins launched himself into a tirade which he hadn't managed to work off or talk out in England. First and last his grievances were inspired by the BBC for their having refused his film, *The War Game*, as a suitable diversion for their captive audience. He supposed that Swedish television would be equally obdurate, then hastened to add that of course he knew nothing yet about Sweden, except that a Swedish company was backing his film. This kind of lunge and recovery was characteristic of his style of address thereafter. He had soon evoked a conspiratorial cloud that never assumed precisely discernible shape; from time to time it was much like a whale and very like a weasel. I'm not now certain in which order he delivered his lugubrious insinuations and his toil-and-trouble prophecies, since order was not a specialty of his discourse. Early he declared that of course nobody could assume to predict the future (though doing so, cinematically, is a responsibility he has now taken on, himself, three times)! Five minutes later he was quoting statistics purporting to have scheduled a world famine to arrive in ten years; he was quite indignant that nobody was worried about it. Everyone, he asserted wildly, was sunk in apathy; not only were they unimpressed by the prospect of famine, they were also indifferent to the equal probability of their extinction in nuclear warfare, before famine could do its worst. I don't know what stoical company Mr. Watkins keeps in England, but I couldn't help wondering how on earth he could describe as apathy what had been violently taking place everywhere in 1968. He plunged on, with a parenthetical tribute to "the students" who in Paris had been trying to reenact the Revolution (presumably *they* were exempt from charges of apathy). As there had been at least five factions of these students, each at ideological cross-purpose with another, this reference was as comprehensive as, and no more apposite than, his tiresomely sneering allusions to "the status quo," "the machine," "the system," and "the establishment." . . . *Which* system? Which status quo? The system of capitalistic interests, which makes it possible for him to produce films and have them distributed when the BBC is reluctant? The status quo represented by the audience members for whose survival he professes to fear? The establishment: things as they are (or were when we looked out yesterday), or an interlocking board of directors somewhere? We learned, in any case, that this machine or system was a sinister thing and would go on forever; in the next breath he was assuring us that we'd be blown off the earth shortly. England was becoming more *Right* every day (he has news for Prime Minister Wilson) and one concluded from his tone that for some perverse reason this *Right* didn't *care* whether it was exterminated by nuclear warfare with all the others who are not *Right* but who'd rather be right than be alive and be *Right!* . . . You can scarcely appreciate the flavor of this fanatically delivered nonsense without an image of Mr. Watkins standing there—young, chalk faced, burning eyed, tight as a clove hitch. I was reminded vividly of Illidge in Huxley's *Point Counter Point*.

Paul Valéry warned us some time ago that since the world takes the shape of the mind imprinted on it, the modern world, created in the mental image of modern man—inventive, unstable, vindictive, and absurd—will become increasingly unforeseeable as it assumes the form of our minds' disorder. Mr. Watkins' mind is symptomatic; it is committed to total disorder, to disaffection, and to a most unmanly panic. Happily, the films he makes are not yet as confused as his formulated opinions. *The Gladiators* may well turn out to be an enthralling film*, and so long as Watkins makes it easy for himself by confining his subject to that of fantasy, with a dash of bitters, or to the abuses of the past, he may fulfill his promise as a distinctly talented director. If he expects to be persuasive in the

---

*It did not.

forum, however, his talent will not suffice for the absence in him of common sense, humor, and a modicum of respect for the spoken language he has inherited.

Yes—well! We know by now, don't we? that it's possible for a man to put together striking pictures in a narrative sequence, yet not have a responsible intellectual conception in his head. And that's no matter if he's not trying to instruct us in love and death or good government. Unfortunately, we are just now besieged by young (for the most part) film-makers who have nothing to express but their hysteria and their contempt for nearly everything that fails to allay it. Jean-Luc Godard has taught a generation how to deceive critics into believing that if a film is *against* something, it doesn't matter how badly it is made. It can even be made well, if they insist! His own latest, *Weekend,* was inevitable. Even as before, a wishful, grinding thought inside Godard was presented as if it were the voice of society: if the machine doesn't run fluidly, destroy it. Young Godard will soon be old hat but he is leaving a scattered lineage in every film-making capital, including those of the Eastern bloc. Alexander Kluge and Richard Lester are of his party; both of them have acquired the false prestige of political artfulness and social acuity. Lester, I'm told, is funny; I don't find him so. And when he stops jump-cutting, horsing around, and history baiting, he's as unsurprisingly devoid of serious ideas as Godard himself. Witness *Petulia,* an empty, meretricious film about empty meretricious people. Lionel Rogosin is cousin to the Godard sect, though he preceded its appearance. He discovered *cinéma vérité,* so to speak, which Jean Rouch and his friends later claimed as their invention. There's little enough in it to lay claim to. Rogosin's first two films, made respectively in Manhattan and Johannesburg and dealing respectively with the daily life of alcoholic derelicts and the sub-social life of exploited Negro mine workers, were easily the most boring films of 1954 and 1959—respectively. They revealed ignorance masquerading as theory: the implicit belief that reality in art is of the same stuff as that reality which can be witnessed around you, with no intervention from mind. By 1964 Rogosin was in England, learning to put his mind on his art, but I fear it was too late. While *Good Times, Wonderful Times* (a bouncy title, stolen from a German postwar film) did at least have the benefit of a reasonably competent photographer and an alert cutting-room staff, this was insufficient to lend the film *moral* coherence. The procedure was the subject: it consisted of establishing a London cocktail party (which had the air of being the real thing), then inter-cutting, from remote sectors of our troubled globe, a montage of crisis: Koreans, Africans, and Vietnamese killing and being killed, suffering hunger, disease, torture. Meanwhile the cocktail party, to which we intermittently return, rattles on, the implication being that everyone present (except members of the film crew, who did not, I wager, refuse the cocktails) was fatuous and irrelevant because he wasn't dying in the Congo, dragging his arse through a paddy field, or demonstrating in Trafalgar Square. One suspects that the purity of the accents being recorded was an integral element of Mr. Rogosin's nebulous accusation.

At any hour in history, equipped with a movie camera, you could assemble a profusion of villainous contrasts for an illustration of this kind, but what exactly would it illustrate? Always there is somebody dying while someone else enjoys the fullness of life (or does it dirt); always while one creature is trapped in the fact, another is idling away his hours, in corruption or in innocence. We eat; others starve; and sometimes the reverse. We rot as others prosper. People like Rogosin (there are *thousands* of him in our time but they don't all make movies) find it inconceivable that existence is contradictory. They presume to identify themselves with the poor, the oppressed, and the outlaw, not because they want to make his concrete problem theirs but because they themselves are poor in resources, oppressed by incomprehension, and self-outlawed by the conceit in their self-pity. Rogosin's film plays with juxtapositions, deceitfully or ignorantly offered as significant contradictions. Someone is to blame, he hints darkly, but he doesn't know whom, and his failure to find the short answer irritates him. He as well as Watkins and Kluge and Lester and ever so many others are demanding applause which they haven't artistically earned; they supply us with scapegoats we don't want and expect to be credited with sagacity. Characteristic of them all is their inability to create an image of decent man, personal to *them,* discovered in the subtleties of daily contacts and social collisions.

That moral imprecision is not a hazard limited to the New Left and the Young Wave (or vice versa) is fully evident in Ingmar Bergman's *Shame,* which also fails to pay its own way, trading instead with the public coin of chronic fear and of pity for the beleaguered neutral—pity that costs nothing, since the situation glibly (if with fine craftmanship) evoking it is marked "Payment Deferred." The summarizing inference of the film—that there is nothing to choose between one antagonist and the other—may be a plausible negation when you have provided neither with cinematic definition. Given the time and the place in which this movie was made, however, together with the man who made it, such a conclusion smells to heaven of moral ignominy. . . . The title of the film couldn't be more just.

Anticipation of the worst, too long sustained, is demoralizing. Our great fear is that our behavior under stress—of sickness and siege, of war and the other violations—will not support the illusions of courage on which our superegos feed. (Hence the Swedish critics' acceptance, without a dissenting murmur, of Jan's rapid and unresisting degradation, in *Shame*.) Peter Collinson has recently contributed two essays on the devaluation of man which add to the ambiguities suggested by the films I have noted above. *A Long Day's Dying*, about three British paratroopers trying to break through a German encirclement, is in one sense an alternative rendering of Watkins' *The Battle of Culloden* and Lester's *How I Won the War*. Both Watkins and Lester would like to think that war is largely a game contrived and maintained by the military profession for their own aggrandizement. I suspect that Collinson, who seems tougher minded than many of his contemporaries, might acknowledge an equally cold truism: that he is alive today, even as you and I—free to take the air, listen to Schubert, and make or look at movies—because others died for us in wars that our side won before we were born. *A Long Day's Dying* suffers from the problem of reconciling the fact of heroism with the dirty, unheroic cunning required to survive the last ditch. Since Collinson wanted to assure us that his hero, trained to the hilt in all the commando strategies, does not actually relish killing (which is fairly incredible; he would have otherwise been washed out long before arriving at this oubliette), he supplies him with an off-screen inner voice, touched with poetry. While the picture continuity, as ruthless as any I can recall, captures the close-up dodges of murderous combat, this mellifluous prose, floating from the sound track, tends to vitiate the reality (and is, besides, somewhat incongruous with the "pop" face of David Hemming). "I'm a pacifist!" screams the hero's thought as he hurls a deadly grenade. This is closer to parody than to pathos. The esthetic insecurity in itself is not my point (the film is compelling, even so) ; it reflects an interesting irresolution of attitude, even more suggestive when you see *A Long Day's Dying* with Collinson's first film, *The Penthouse,* in mind.

Adapted from a play, acted and directed with such conviction that we are hounded into giving its quasi-infernal content more value than it deserves, *The Penthouse* introduced us to a loving couple, a Mr. Average and his mistress, imprisoned in their flat-with-a-view by two criminal perverts with deceptively nance accents, ready knives, and an infinite capacity for finding the soft places in the guts of their intimidated captives. The creeps tie the man of the house to a chair and proceed to fill his mistress with booze until she abandons her inhibitions and eagerly, wantonly, goes to bed with her captors. After some hours of sadistic trifling, the marauders take their leave, having forced the trussed-up male to the ultimate humiliation (on pain of their return) of swearing never to disclose that anything at all has happened to him. Since the limp victim has his own sweating fright to live down and his woman's concupiscence to cover up, he willingly consents to the vow of silence. . . . A social parable, then: the poor man's *Rashomon?* If we go along with the nasty argument, the generic female of our time is a tart; all she needs to prove it is an ample dosage of gin. And our representative male animal is an invertebrate with nothing inside him but sponge cake. There remain the smilers with the knives, who have what it takes to endure the battles of the Bulge. Perhaps I identify Mr. Collinson too closely with the author of *The Penthouse,* but he did make a film of it, did he not?—and I scarcely suppose he did so with a gun placed at his temple by the producer. Questions about the nature of his commitments do impose themselves. I would say that his future as a film-maker is in doubt and I would add that it is a reasonable doubt. We cannot help wondering—as we do when faced with so many films today that importune our attention to the crucial worries—whether his inquests of domestic cannibalism and of man under fire are moved by pity, nausea, or a species of cruel delight.

"History is a nightmare from which I am trying to awake," mused Stephen Dedalus. Our contemporary artists, in every medium, have taken him altogether literally. The resulting dilemma is only more visible in the movies. What do we do when we awaken, *without history*—which is to say, with a view of it as nightmare, merely—and with a present condition in which we find no more vital diversion than pornography, as unconsoling a game as war?   1969

Film Chronicle: Notes on the Compulsive Revolution

> Do we not have a society in which we see the attrition of law
> and national wisdom and general craft? Do we not have an age
> anti-intellectual and violent, in which there is felt a kind of
> total responsibility to total disorder? Who looks ahead except
> to a panacea or a millennium which is interchangeable with an
> invoked anarchy, whether in the world or in the individual per-
> sonality? Do we not above all each day wonderfully improve our
> chances of misunderstanding each other? . . .
>
> R. P. Blackmur, "A Burden for Critics," 1948

I have long entertained the suspicion, which I have tried to conceal
behind a mask of professional courtesy (not altogether successfully,
I am given to understand), that the film director is the affluent ape
in the jungle of modern art. Since I have not read Wolfgang Köhler
for some years, I can't recall if he claimed that the ape typically suffered from loneliness. The film director does, that's for sure. He
can't bear not to be doing what all the other little beasts are doing:
hunting someone else's fleas, wearing women's hats, swinging from
tree to tree just to prove his equality with the gibbon, masturbating
for the audience as a reminder of the "reality" which its vaunted
evolution in vain attempts to deny. Everybody (in these circles)
wants to get into the act—the same act. About seven years ago, nine
out of every ten films, long or short, ended with an immobile shot,
Kodak-as-you-go, and usually included a sequence of jump-cutting
in space and much chronology-shuffling in time. A few years later
came the libidinal revolution: we were emancipated; in no time at

all we were permitted not only to hear but to see the vocabulary of copulation in all its diversity, not excluding sodomy, fellatio, or cunnilingus. That's as far as my exposure has taken me but I'm not deluded that there's relief in sight. "The worst is not yet, while we can say, 'This is the worst.'" Unmercifully, these phases have not passed, one after the other; they have overlapped and are now interlocked with the fad of being politically subversive. The paradigmatic film of the day is one in which what happens when is never self-evident; only the blame for it is simple to locate. Epilepsy at the cutting table is not enough; one must protest about something, and the most available something is the whole system of check and balance which has provided this frenzy of permissiveness to begin with.

CHARLEY

Remember it, from the backward reaches of 1968? A lovable moron upgraded by scientific experiment? A fantasy with a grim touch of probability and an ambience of pathos: that was the tone required. But social accusation had become chic; the producers, groping for the Oscar, must incorporate social accusation. When Charley faces a panel of biologists and shrinkers to display his intellectual progress, he launches abruptly into a denunciation of the social drift as he has learned to see it, with his newly conditioned eyes: more computerization, more hate, more wars, more education by TV; the familiar charges and by no means impertinent, but nothing heretofore in the pragmatic nature of Charley's observations has prepared us for this outburst. Whenever we'd seen him, he was memorizing equations with no pain and amorously pursuing Claire Bloom in the green belts of Cambridge. When did he have time to speculate darkly on the accelerating contradictions of man? And how do they concern *his* success story except—and his discovery was crudely planted—as a form of suspicion that he has been tampered with for the prestige of science and might better have been content with a low IQ in the first place? The confusions in this film were prodigal and basic. Before the compulsive attack on the organization man was inserted, the development of Charley's do-it-yourself capacity had been run in parallel with America's coming of age, assisted by copious references to the War of Independence and by guided tours of memorials to that event in Boston and vicinity. One might suppose that emergence from a state of imbecility was not the most fortunate analogy for the productive growth of the nation! Or should we have inferred that America, like Charley, was animate solely by virtue of a technological shot in the arm and would shortly regress to a sub-social level of proficiency? . . . Too many cooks is my guess, trying simultaneously to butter up the progressives, the institutional patriots, the pre-med faculty, the dropouts, and the Academy of Motion Picture Arts and Sciences.

THE LOVES OF ISADORA

According to the film, Isadora Duncan the person, whatever contribution she made to modern dance (the nature of that contribution is still unclear to me), was obviously an idiot who euphemized her concupiscence, her greed, and her benevolent egoism with yards of Greek hymatian and a flow of milked-from-Shelley gush about truth, beauty, and revolution. As in many films, the convoluted montage is made to do duty as interpretation; yet it seems clear that Karel Reisz could not have intended to glorify her (to celebrate her, that's something else, and to use her as a mouthpiece for his flirtation with Moscow), but it is equally clear that critics (male or female) who are in love with Vanessa Redgrave take the apparition she portrays (splendidly) with some degree of seriousness—no doubt because Reisz has supplied her with an erotic gamut to go with the times (our times) and heaps of *style nouveau* and Loire chateau décors in which to exercise it; for a surprising number of people Sybaris is still the capital of the Life in Art. So it was for Isadora; hence she could afford radicalism, like a movie director. "All artists are revolutionary," she rants, comprehending nothing about revolution, politics, or the cavernous mind of man. (A pre-Raphaelite hippie, that's the term I'm groping for.) The Boston episode is a large handful of Reisz, a front behind which Isadora may shout his message at the audience (in the cinema). Following a riot that empties the theater, "We Americans used to be wild!" she pleads. *"Don't let them tame you!"* I have news for Mr. Reisz. There is no danger.

Z.

That's a film title: of that daring revolutionary number which took a prize (excuse my yawn) at Cannes last year, made in Paris by a Greek letter fraternity in which Yves Montand, Jean-Louis Trintignant, and Jacques Perrin were conspicuous. If the Cause wouldn't bring them to the box office, the cast would. As a guarantee of authenticity, the director was Greek and Irene Papas played Zetta's grieving wife (unfortunately, her sustained silence was too patently a device for avoiding the language barrier to be wholly convincing). Regarding the political issue: there may well be times in history when every member of a regime you despise is a pig by any human definition; there is never a time when the opposition is totally composed of genially subversive heroes. In any case, it makes for crude drama to assume so and certainly makes it easy for the script-writer, the director, the sales division, and those who went to the movie to fan the hate they had already documented. There's some incidental, ferocious action in the film and a number of weird bit players who were diverting in themselves; all told, though, I found the ordinating conduct of things unreal. The director was facetiously eager to evoke predictable responses. And as much as I do like Jacques Perrin and Trintignant I don't buy them as Greeks. The reporter, clad in summer whites, who smiles sweetly and pushes the hair off his forehead: this must be the silliest conception since Paul Henreid, also wearing an immaculate linen suit, sauntered through Casablanca as a leader of the French underground. Montand, who walks like a waiter, I couldn't accept, either, as the inscrutable "Z" who is reputed to have survived a lethal clout on the head and to be hibernating somewhere, like Barbarossa, until the hour when, summoned by his followers, he will be resurrected and lead to victory all those good people who will live democratically ever after, playing *Never on Sunday* for liberal tourists.

IF (We're up to two letters in the title!)

Lindsay Anderson, whose best work in the past (*O Dreamland*, a short, and *This Sporting Life*) had seemingly been motivated by pity, now joins with his many countrymen in the area of social cinema who are more than anything else guided by class hatred. It was whispered to me that the black-and-white scenes in this film, about a dreamed revolt in an English preparatory school, were fantasy, and those in color, reality; however, I could make out no sense from following this clue, nor could I find any consistency by reversing the description. I think that the device, together with his subtitles like chapter heads (tiredly reminiscent of the French Old Wave), was direct evidence of Anderson's uncertainty. He wanted to make a straight I-hate-England film and at the same time needed to pay his respects to the sophisticated knacks which are all the go. I don't know what to say about the conditions imputed to the school represented in *If*. When I was in an English boarding school in the twenties, cruelty to "fags" had been outlawed years gone by—as a consequence, we were all taught, of Thomas Hughes's reforming novel, *Tom Brown's Schooldays*. If such a school as Anderson depicts does survive, it is scarcely typical, which of course does not exempt it from attack, though it does invalidate it for the more sweeping purpose Anderson had in mind.

I thought the first half, more or less, was funny, exact, and nasty in the way of Evelyn Waugh's *Decline and Fall*—the barbarous rites, the articulate hostility, the dreary poetics of homosexual yearning. I could all but smell the urinals. The more Anderson underlined, the more incoherent he became. By now we've seen so many oblivious headmasters, sunset colonels, snobbish prefects, and pneumatic matrons (Alec Guinness has played most of them) that it takes a great deal more invention than Anderson displayed to get a laugh or a corroborative sneer from me. To shift from this level of wincing to dreams of mowing down with a machine gun the whole social brigade alleged to condone brutality (simply not true) is to move from justifiable indignation to hysteria and terrorism. (Even Peter Watkins thought Anderson had gone too far!) They loved it at the Cannes Festival, though. And the comment made to me by an approving Swedish female may, for all I know, typify the universal reception. Looking me straight in the eye, she said brightly, "It certainly makes one understand why the English are so arrogant and stupid." I consoled myself with the belief that she had Mr. Lindsay Anderson in mind.

ÅDALEN 31

Naturally, the Swedes, those born nonparticipants, would be foremost in asserting how vexed they are by social injustice, the more so if its victims are a thousand miles away or have been a long time dead. Bo Widerberg has been scouring Sweden to find something about which he can be outraged and make a documentary. He found something last year—the huffing and puffing that took place at Bostad when the South Africans were invited to play tennis and were then uninvited by a demonstration and the police tried to maintain order. You don't want to know the details—this is small-town stuff. The disturbance in Ådalen, 1931, was about as important in the annals of labor-and-capital strife. The program was classical: a strike was called, the company called up strikebreakers from Stockholm, the Ådalen workers dumped them into the harbor, then marched in protest; they were blocked by a small cavalry contingent, threw rocks at the riders (this was omitted in the film), and the rattled military opened fire. Five workers were killed, two by ricocheting bullets.

While we can agree that tragedy is not governed by quantitative measure, we can insist that in movie-making the important thing is whether or not something vital was made of an encounter and, further, if we experience more than meets the eye. Something pretty was made of Ådalen, let's say that; there was more nostalgia than grapes of wrath. Symbols and antitheses abound, in the manner of the silent Soviet and UFA films; lilac and guns, sunshine and shadow, pregnancy and death. Every working-class character is pure and rural; the "capitalists" are epitomized in one round-table scene—all cigars, indifference, and telephones. The mother of the girl with whom the working-class lad is in love introduces him to the art of Renoir, so that Widerberg can point up his effort to reproduce Renoir scenically, even to the plump-cheeked girl with her hair tied back. When Mother takes the girl to an abortionist rather than have plebeian blood in the family (I find this incredible) and the boy's father is shot by the Cossacks, Renoir can then be rejected as an upper-class possession. (You can't say Widerberg's reach doesn't exceed his grasp. He'll go to Heaven.) There are furlongs of domestic chores, sex, and dancing, all of which made time pass slowly and seemed strangely fake-pastoral to me. A revolutionary film? Lord love the man, he's a paper tiger. He filmed a collision and only the physical climax was at all effective—the long line of marchers in the spring sunlight, the mounted men more fearful than fearsome, the rearing, reluctant horses. Of the real, intricate, and rooted enmities that prepare such an incident there is no consciousness. Widerberg scowls and growls, like the urchins in those *Small Fry* cartoons of Steig, trying to scare hell out of each other, never realizing that his pink-and-blue films repudiate his grimaces. At the end of this one, his child (one is in every film he makes, like Alfred Hitchcock in his)—there's this child, blowing soapbubbles in the garden. Life goes on sort of thing. This says it for Widerberg: a soapbubble dreaming it's an angry man.

EASY RIDER

Like most American films, it is easier to enjoy if you don't question what certain of my friends would call its *moralische Bedeutung,* which I take to be the conviction that in the U.S.A. Dionysus is doomed to be destroyed by Apollo. I would have been more impressed (I *was* impressed by the confidence, the style, and the fluency) if I had not to accept the narcotic peddler, the lush, and the problem child* as symbols of a defeated will to insurgence. Bill, the longhair junky, replies to the whore who endearingly calls him a freak, "I never thought of myself as a freak." In truth he is a freak: he is so calculatedly, he works at it, his idiom is contrived to screen out all other linguistic responses, he dresses freak; the sickest thing about him generically is that he doesn't believe he can be described generically, yet there's a mob of him who share his coded vocabulary, his narcissism, his sloppy morality—and his smell. Sidekick Captain America, played with warm cool by Peter Fonda (true son of his adept father) is the eternal American innocent (Natty Bumppo burned out young, Billy Budd as a pusher) who combines infinite kindness toward a world he never made, and will never begin to understand, with a heedless affection for the gummy side of the law. And the charm with which Jack Nicholson plays the young Texas lawyer who toasts D. H. Lawrence, dons a football helmet, and drops out into violent death need not blind us to the fact that we're being offered that infantile American alternative— "Either I'm made null and void by Daddy or I take to the bottle and the road." Mind in America cannot be brought to initiate civilized alternatives; the drift is always out and down, a direction in which space itself conspires. So it is entirely fitting that these cycling junkies should speed their appointed highway to extinction across the ravishing, mindless plateau of the Southwest, America's Egdon Heath—volcanic plugs, mesas that look like altars for gods who never showed up. (I lived in that country for years and could never decide whether it looked more like the end of everything or the dawn of everything.) The post-frontier neurosis—"Lie to us! Dance us back our tribal morn!"—receives perhaps unintentional travesty in that scene among the hippies of Sacred Mountain, wearing the

---

*Someone in the authoritative profession, whose name now escapes me, was quoted in a recent issue of *Encounter* to the effect that we are witnessing a revolution by the first generation that was picked up when it cried.

shreds of whatever cultural memory they condescend to retain: Ikhnaton, Mary Magdalene, Francis of Assisi, Wild Bill Hickok. Left to itself, the erased mind is powerless: refusing the rational content of its culture, it is driven to supplying itself from the beachheads of Camp or the imagery of drug-induced hallucinations. And if Jung is right about the racial subconsciousness, not there can it escape the eternal return of someone else's cultural storage.

THE IDIOT (BBC)

In a review of Dostoievsky's notebooks for *The Idiot* (*The New Yorker*, October 5, 1968), Harold Rosenberg described Myshkin as, among other things, "the original of those who seek to persuade through self-renunciation [like the] flower children of the 1960's convinced of the perfidiousness of the adult mind." Mr. Rosenberg's essay is brilliant, but I found this single comparison quite incomprehensible. Myshkin was an aristocrat with a thirst for purity, heightened unnaturally by epilepsy, who, insofar as he felt a social allegiance, was wistfully in bond to the flagging established order. Remember the conclusion of his prophetic tirade at Aglaya's party: "You think that I was afraid for the *others,* that I am *their* advocate, a democrat, an upholder of equality?" (He laughs hysterically) . . . "I am afraid for you, for all of you, and for all of us. For I am a prince of ancient lineage myself, and I'm sitting among princes. I am saying this to save you all, so as to prevent our class from vanishing for nothing into utter darkness. . . ."* Dostoievsky has been claimed by many factions; perhaps with more justification, from their perspective, by the anti-liberals in pre-Hitler Germany than by the present generation of juveniles which, whether or not it's aware of the fact, is suffering from the invertebrate liberalism of the last forty years and more closely resembles the creature against whom Dostoievsky posted his most profound warning: in a word, Smerdiakov. For do we not see this Smerdiakov everywhere today? Smerdiakov again confronting Ivan, and whining: "Everything is permissible! *You taught me that!*"

I was fortunate to see, soon after reading Rosenberg, a fabulous production of *The Idiot* from BBC television, an experience I owe to that "harmonizing pluralism" of our system, held in such con-

---

*My quotations are from the David Magarshack translation of *The Idiot* (Penguin Books).

tempt by Herbert Marcuse, "where the most contradictory works and truths peacefully coexist in indifference." I'd like to say a few words about the occasion here because this was a film creation of a rare, dedicated order in these days when most films for the cinema are made by nervous whores and are about Goths. The adaptation by Leo Lehman (he's Polish, actually) was presented in five episodes of about fifty minutes each, and after every one I was left shaken, if enriched, and, I'll freely confess, lachrymose. Here was simply that deep, exciting revelation which film can be when its content is at the same time rich in social texture, unsparing in its compassion, and ruthless in its reminder that, to be sure, the unexamined life is *not* worth living. The direction (Alan Bridges) was masterfully baroque—by which I mean that the rhythms and the metaphysical suspense seemed always threatening to burst the limits of the space and duration to which they were confined. The actors were marvelous, above all David Buck as Myshkin and Anthony Bate as Rogozhin. (All these names were unfamiliar to me.*) But the ruling hero of this enterprise was Leo Lehman, the scenarist. Recall that fantastic party when Nastasya is supposed to accept Ganya's proposal; Myshkin is there and Rogozhin arrives drunk, loaded with money, expecting to buy Nastasya; the rooms are swirling with social crosscurrents, rash confessions, naked spite. After a tormenting crescendo, during which Nastasya has resolved to marry Myshkin, thrown Rogozhin's money in the fire to test the cupidity of Ganya, who faints after this ordeal—and a world of subordinate reminiscences and plots has intervened—she, Nastasya, suddenly rushes from the party and from everybody, forever, dragging with her—Rogozhin! Pausing at the door to survey the devastation she has left behind, she throws over her shoulder, by way of self-explanation, the line, "There *are* such people!" . . . I screamed with delight: "That great Dostoievsky! What an amazing line! And how inspired of Lehman to leave it in the script!" He was more inspired than I then knew, for upon returning later to the novel I discovered that Nastasya said no such thing. She should have done, but she didn't.

---

*That English actors have an inexplicable talent for interpreting Russian characters was established by the Redgrave-Olivier production of *Uncle Vanya* (among the great theater experiences of my lifetime) and confirmed by the recent film version of *The Sea Gull*, even though *as a film* it was bad, bad, bad— Sidney Lumet discovered no interesting cinematic form for the original play; the actors, however, were, in their feeling, authentically reminiscent, intensely personal, and disturbing.

One instance more of Lehman's creative adaptation. When Myshkin tries to elaborate his feelings about capital punishment for the Yepanchin girls, their thoughts are obviously on another subject. They all but dismiss his gravity by chirping, "Yes, well, now tell us how you were in love." He hesitates, then replies, "I have not been in love. I—was happy in a different way." Now, in the novel, this extraordinary statement is a preface to his long chronicle of the girl, Marie, whom he had defended from persecution in a Swiss village. Since Lehman could no easier include this narrative than many others in the book, it had to go. But miraculously he left that mysterious remark in the continuity, and there it beautifully hung, incandescent and unexplained, much more like an inconclusion of Chekov, teasing one for days thereafter with its haunting ambiguity . . . "I was happy in a different way."   1969

Films from Hungary
and Brazil

Miklos Jancso, Hungarian, makes film of men going about their work. Their work is slaughter. What endows his art with its macabre distinction is the un-vulgar curiosity with which he observes their grave, professional pursuit of this occupation. If from time to time we did not witness, often with blank amazement, the precise consequences of their actions (as they crumple up or spin under the impact of bullets), we might well wonder what strange, serious game these men are playing, out there in the middle of a savanna nowhere, marching back and forth, galloping up and down, lining each other up, interrogating and informing, sorting themselves into squads, unsorting themselves, getting into feverish huddles, and standing helplessly against walls. Hungarian prisoners and their Austrian captors (c. 1868), packed into a compound on a plain lonely as the ocean, remind us oddly of other occasions when, to a spectator, there is something altogether absurd in the oblivious solemnity with which the participants in a busy-busy act comport themselves: a meeting of rival labor unions, for example, at which it is to be decided whether or not they will accept a construction job from a cartel with notorious political affiliations; or the preliminary stages of a film to be shot on location, when local talent is being assigned to the cavalry unit or considered for speaking parts. In Jancso's contest, however, the reward is somewhat more crucial than the domination of CIO delegates by those of the AFL, or a stand-in job for someone who is content not to be photographed if he has day-long opportunity for apple-polishing the assistant director and smelling the leading actress. The issue here (I am describing *The Round-Up,* 1965) of all the backing and filling, the pike trailing and secret sessions, the inquisitions and the betrayals is nothing less than a lease on life. (Although few, in the end, procure it.) The primary object, if anything so categorical can be defined in a Jancso action, is to find someone in this pen of outlaws and peasants who can identify a former resistance leader named Sandor who may or may not be among them, who may or may not be known to them as Sandor, who may or may not be alive, even. Hence the bargaining, the cross-examinations, the escorting of prisoners from one cell to another, to an exercise yard, or to a sun-blessed wall against which they are targets in relief are all about nothing or about something so nebulous that it serves only as a means for the officers, time heavy on their hands, to refine their already considerable skill at eliciting confessions without drawing blood.

The Red and the White (1967) is a much richer film, if equally dispassionate; the engagements are more deadly, the rhythms and counter-rhythms more sharply syncopated—of men on horseback and other men on foot fleeing them, of pursuers tramping confidently up wooden staircases and across bridges, the pursued running, like sheep without collies, around fatal enclosures. The political situation which informs these rhythms is an interlude, so to speak, during the post-Revolution battles of Reds and Whites, involving the desertion of numerous Hungarians to the cause of the Bolsheviks, to preserve their own future liberty. I can't believe Jancso is not fully aware of the irony he is supporting. Naturally the film (co-produced by *Mafilm,* Budapest, and *Mosfilm,* Moskva) is intended to glorify the solidarity of peoples' republics; its nominal subject is the systematic elimination of Red resistance in the area of battle Jancso has chosen (somewhere around the upper Volga). A skirmish opens the film, Cossacks chasing winded Reds across a river to the other bank. When the head Cossack overtakes one of his fugitives he demands to know his nationality: "Are you Russki, Austrian—what are you?" On being told the man is Magyar, he orders him back into the river. "Go on, get into the river," he tells him, indifferently. The Hungarian runs with dispatch into the river, which is, after all, the escape route. The Cossack shoots him unerringly, as he reaches waist-deep water. Efficient. No exposed corpse, no time out for burial. Much of the burden in this film is the White Russian complaint: "This is not your war! Why don't you go back where you came from?"

The required partisan slant in *The Red and the White* gives little encouragement save to the single-minded (I almost wrote the *simple-minded*). Death comes too quickly and casually for us to decide what our feelings about it *ought* to be, and on both sides there are moments of equal reluctance to kill as well as moments of shocking ruthlessness. I couldn't have cared less how many Reds or Whites *as such* were done to death; in a film—at least in Jancso's film—one's sympathy is involved *at the moment*. Are they actually going to execute this stalwart if bewildered young man with all that serviceable muscle packed around his shoulder blades? Not that you are concerned because he's a Red, but because he's flesh. Are you pleased now to see the Cossack who shot the Magyar and was about to have a girl raped on a windy hill in his turn told to remove his boots and pray? Not actually. You share his surprise and you can't help admiring his scornful grunt and the way he stands before the leveled rifles, as if posing for his photo, one hand on hip, chin tilted disdainfully in the air. When they shoot he does a little skip, like a puppet crudely animated by an inexperienced operator.

This thoughtful White Russian staff captain who alone never wears a hat, as if he likes the caress of the breeze in his hair, and walks, hands clasped behind, like an idle country priest: a courteous man whom we want to like. We *do* like him. But what horror might he not now be preparing as, on his orders, his jaunty adjutant herds a group of nurses from the outpost hospital far into the woods to the accompaniment of the military band? There, in a clearing among the spectral birches—he invites them to waltz with each other; just waltz! "You have the music, no? *Valz, valz!*"—he snaps his fingers impatiently. So they waltz with each other, self-consciously to be sure. Some don't know how, or they're embarrassed, or they don't want to, or they're frozen with fright. Two of them do very well: very well indeed. Is the staff captain delighted? This has been arranged for his pleasure, after all, or was it for that of the women or for the onlooking men? We never learn. His face doesn't alter its habitually puckered expression. The wind ruffles his hair. He nods to the adjutant. This gallant snaps his fingers again. "You may go home now." And the ladies melt away among the palings of the ivory birches. . . . Later the staff captain finds it necessary to threaten a few of these females with death unless they identify the active Reds among their casualties. To his regret they are not cooperative; he finds them very difficult. Sighing, he gives them a chance to change their minds. "Go away, stand over there," he tells one of them solicitously. "This is nothing for *you* to see." Lying on the ground are ten half-stripped male patients from the hospital. They are shot dead as they lie there rigidly staring at the sky. Perhaps some of them were already dead; two scissor upward in reflex, the others remain as horizontal as before. Out of nowhere, on the other side of the river, a troop of riderless horses comes over the hill, stirring dust; where are the riders? As the staff captain studies the situation appraisingly, not yet suspicious, the bullets of the enemy strike him. He has barely time to complain before hitting the ground, his face puckered more than usually, hands to his midriff as though an intensely sour apple had just reached his intestinal tract.

Jancso's camera runs parallel with his action, you might say. When you most expect and fear that it will confront you with a horror you don't want to face, it keeps its distance; sometimes it paces like a caged leopard kept from the kill by a barrier against which it rubs in vain; it stares hungrily over the heads of those interposing mortals, who make such strange noises, at a something beyond—not quite identifiable but surely edible. When a man is told to jump into a stream from a low platform and, as he goes under, an officer drives a long fish-gaff through him, Jancso is not eager to crowd in and see the damage. We watch the episode from a hundred feet away, groaning with relief at his comparative tact. I can think of no director since Jacques Becker (unless it be the Buñuel of *Viridiana*) who makes us so quake with the thought of what his camera might next reveal, but in Jancso's case does not—not directly and never with relish. Jancso's interest is not sadistic. I am not at all sure it is compassionate. Did Leonardo feel compassion when he accompanied men to their death to sketch the expression on their faces? Jancso's immediate aim is the creative arrangement of incongruities, in the shadow of death; the pity and the wonder arise from the spectacle of men who earnestly believe that they kill what they are killing or earn what they are dying for. If Jancso were not so resolutely on the perimeter of driving emotions, I should be tempted to call him the Kurosawa of Eastern Europe. He shares Kurosawa's sense of bodily momentum, his feeling for space in a shot, either to exalt or to reduce the value of figures isolated in it; he likes to balance a spare composition against a crowded one or, for instance, to track vis-à-vis a troop of charging cavalry as the shifting lie of the land bends their formation, making them race diagonally up the wide screen, lower right to upper left, then sharply down, the dynamic flow switching its direction from a climb to a plunge. He cuts very seldom within a sequence limited to a confined area. The continuity in which the Cossack prepares the girl for rape, only to be forestalled by his superior officer cantering into the scene, is conducted with one steadily observing and discreetly gliding gaze.

A highly rational acquaintance (Nordic) accompanied me to one showing of *The Red and the White*. He was impressed, with reservations. It was all so surreal, he thought; there were things, he said vaguely—motivations, customs, military details—which did not satisfy his sense of logic. I finally told him: "Slavs and Magyars, and you expect logic! You want egg in your beer!" Effects of the kind managed by Jancso were described by Tolstoi as "making it strange," as if this were an exercise you could choose to indulge or not, a calculated option of the literary intelligence. At any moment I can personally note, in the world of event, the bizarre collisions noted by Jancso. But I do not see the world that way all the time! There is evidence for concluding that men of one culture make consistently different selections from reality than men of another culture. I believe that Jancso arrived at his mode of perception, beyond the circumstance that he is an *artist* (whose job is to organize incongruities) because he was born at the other end of the Danube. I suggest that the whole theater of action in which the East European mind pursues its destiny might be called "making it strange."

At the Berlin Film Festival in 1965 I saw among the trade showings (of films intended for commercial appraisal) the last two-thirds of a wild, weird film from Brazil, *Black God, White Devil,* and a film from, of all places, Colombia, entitled *Voice of Anxiety:* dry, powerful, relentless. When I reported to many of my should-I-say colleagues that the two best films I had seen at this festival were from

South America, in a trade show, they looked at me as if I were working to be exclusive, showing off—making it strange! The sequel
followed, as I expected. I've been through this before. (You think
I like film critics any better than Bergman does?) Less than a year
later, *Cahiers du Cinéma* took up South American films and published interviews with Glauber Rocha (director of *Black God,
White Devil*). Now, three years after, the critics who never went
near the trade shows, and *never* discover anyone before being clued
in by the French, are scolding exhibitors because they don't buy
Brazilian films, and museum film societies are trying to interest
avant garde members in South American film, to fill the gap left by
the successive vogues of Bergman, Antonioni, and Jean-Luc
Godard. Glauber Rocha is the favorite and I suspect that he will not
be as easy to sell as some of the previous objects of bohemian admiration. The appeal of his films is allegedly in their covert incite-
ment to revolution. Their treatment, from the little I know of it, will
scarcely recommend Rocha to northern Marxists or their dropout
cohorts. The Catholic ethos, to say nothing of the bloodthirstiness
and the Portuguese baroque trimmings, is not a proclivity of your
typical Anglo-American film critic who, when he's not Jewish, is
Protestant or sniffily secular. I am not yet willing to accept Rocha
as the leading light of the "New Brazilian Film," since I've seen less
than one of his works and I recall with disgust the French directors
of the early sixties who were ignored and possibly stopped in their
tracks by critics who thought and looked at film *factionally*.* I'm
not prepared to write conclusive summaries of the Brazilian film
movement. I'm feeling my way. As evidence, I add here notations
on two films from Brazil which, if far from superlative, may be
exemplary.

The Time and Hour of Augusto Matraga (1966), directed by
Roberto Santos. This, I gather, may be the type of cliché South
American film, seriously dedicated but wanting in talent. I say
South American because, long before *The Bandit* (1951) established, I believe, a mode of Brazilian sardonic melodrama, I had
seen not a few films from Argentina with similar ingredients (probably the sources are in the literature) : the excessive cruelty, de-

---

*Since writing this article I have seen Glauber Rocha's *Antonio-das-Mortes*,
which shared the Director's Prize and received the *Prix International des Critiques Cinéma et Télévision* at Cannes, 1969. I would describe the direction, the
editing, and the acting as alike villainously incompetent and the film as a whole
unflaggingly loathsome.

picted with no mitigation or remorse from the director, who clearly delighted in re-creating it at length and up close; the alternating stiff-backed pride and the howling abandon of men taunted to out-bursts of horrible revenge; the simple power distinctions—those who ride horseback, those who ride mules, those who walk; the Chaucerian archetypes: the *padron,* the priest, the peon, the bandit, the vituperative whore, the withered, maternal crone; the framing of an action as ballad in order to lend it distance, give it poetry, stress its legendary aspect to cheat the political censor (this may be a recent twist, developed by Rocha) ; the burning hatred of Church prerogative and counsel but the retention of a Catholic superstruc-ture, fatalistic and ultimately redemptive. Augusto, in the Santos film, pays for his earlier arrogance as tyrant and chief stud of a vil-lage by being broken and branded at the behest of the *padron* he opposes (a scene so juicily prolonged that I vowed to rub vinegar into my wounds when I got home) ; after a desperate struggle he attains quietude and a species of Christian resignation. But the old Adam—or the old Augusto—erupts with outraged pride, prompting him to join a band of outlaws, thereby invoking an end more appro-priate to his temper; for he dies gloriously, in defense of a boy the bandits have picked as hostage and marked out for killing in a church. I was left with the impression of a lesser work by Verdi, cross-fertilized by a samurai legend!

The Priest and the Girl (1966) . Direction and manuscript by Joaquim Pedro de Andrade. Ninety minutes running time, which seemed like one hundred and fifty and recalled Carl-Theodore Dreyer at his most heedless, mistaking the interminable for the lei-surely. Or Robert Bresson at *his* worst, he who loves God more than montage. Yet moments come alive: violent, sensual, inventive. I think you've been here before. Anatole France and Ambrose Bierce, among oh-so-many others, have told the tale. A young priest arrives in a primitive community to replace a priest who has died; he is tempted by a girl who so decisively scatters his forces that he readily believes she is an emissary of the devil. There is a certain ambiguity, never, thank Heaven, dispelled, in the nature of the girl's sexual relationship with the dead priest (when he was alive, I mean) , with her elderly guardian, and with a creepy storekeeper. However committed her relationships may have been, she is passion-ately certain she has not been "loved." Predictably she inflames the newcomer, who "rescues" her from the village, believing his inten-tions are chaste. But in flight across the wasteland he succumbs to her beauty, loathes himself thereafter like Paphnutius, rushes back to the village and the church he has betrayed, she following, where he has to fight off the indignant villagers and again flee, with his forbidden and ever-ripening fruit clinging to him like a lovely leech. They take shelter in a cave and here the film ends, ancient women from the village trying to burn them out—or are they exorcising them?

I don't know. Is it *kitsch* or is it not? The situation gathers a lot of conviction for itself, after its pedestrian opening scenes, chiefly because Paulo José is utterly believable as the mulish, harassed priest and Helena Ignez is the most persuasive rebuke to celibacy I've seen for nigh twenty years, palpably bewitching, with her young amplitude, heavy eyelids, earthy hands, and long Raphael-esque neck. (I am dedicating my next bull to her.) There is one particularly impressive piece of cinema, probably suggested by *Woman of the Dunes*, when she sits stark maddeningly naked in the desert. The camera frames her face and shoulders, *primo piano*, tendrils of corn-silk hair blowing into the lens. After which, a curve of shoulder and naked back—pure draftsmanship. The priest, in profile, kisses her arm; past reason haunted, he drops to his feast; the camera remains, above it all, just focusing the melody of her face. Beautifully done: nothing Swedish here.   1969

PARENTHESES FOR REVIEWS NEVER WRITTEN

Through the years one accumulates notebooks, filled with notations made in the dark or expanded later to nourish memory. Sometimes, at home, one writes the thing out, just to maintain the sense of shape or to see if one has the makings of an article. Perhaps you use the occasion for a soliloquy on a more general subject. Again, you may believe that you'll write a "definitive study" when you've seen all this director's films. Time passes, and you don't see them all and at some point you no longer care. In any case, you write more than there's demand for or that you would care to print.

From scores of such notebooks I have extracted a few examples, in the hope that their immediacy of expression, even when tactless, may interest the reader as much as an essay more thoughtfully brushed and combed. I have been guided in my selection by the wish to be consistent with my international coverage, by the desirability of alluding to films *relatively* available to the reader (but I'm never sure), and by the degree to which I have regretted not having had the chance to comment on certain movies or their directors.

I have tried to leave the comments as nearly as possible in their notebook state, but a tyrannical ear has forced me in many cases to renovate prepositions and adjectives and to provide transitional paragraphs where otherwise the connections would have remained a private business. Substantially, however, these pages are as they were conceived at the impulsive moment.

Knife in the Water
(Poland)

A diabolically sagacious film. This young Polanski has an unveiled view of what men and women think they're all about. . . . Man and wife, too close for too long (one assumes), are in fierce division, driving toward an unhappy weekend together in the great outdoors. They pick up an insolent, handsome young hitchhiker, obviously an egocentric bore. To spite his wife, the man invites the youngster to accompany them for a weekend on their sailboat. He invites into his life the very factor which will expose his insecurity, though he unconsciously utilizes the boy in order to impress his wife with his own male prowess and though at first, and largely, it is the youth who is exposed.

The hitchhiker can do nothing useful on board; he is not even interested, since the ceremony of sailing a boat relegates the value of his self-conceit. He can do nothing that isn't easy to do. For fun he can shinny up the mast like a monkey, but when a process has an object it's no fun. A landlubber with no curiosity about any other element (little enough he has about the earth he treads), he is quickly disillusioned: if to sail a boat means that you have to work at it, use your head (and watch where you lift it), study the sky, handle the sail, feel the rudder and the tide that moves you, and even—this really explodes his patience—get off and lug the craft by hand through a shallow channel—he has already had more than enough; he's bored.

Train a new instinct—for what? Discover that beauty is sometimes a by-product of function? Not for him. He wants nothing that isn't a reflection of himself; his ego is exemplified by the switchblade knife he sports, which might be useful on a boat if he knew how to use it for anything save showing off. It is no good in the water, which is where it finally arrives, swept there impatiently by the elder. When he loses the knife, he loses all proof of his manhood . . . except the thing itself!

A definition of strengths. All three are tested: the capable family man, the quiet bitch, the good-for-nothing. The man is masterful; he knows the ropes, i.e., he knows the world over which he has command. Yet he childishly envies the expert knife-dance which the boy executes, back and forth between his outspread fingers, the facile sex allurement. Expressing his scorn beyond the limits of self-confidence, the man succeeds in pushing his wife into the orbit of the boy's appeal. Women like strength until they are threatened by it; then they must reassure themselves that they have a weapon worth two of ours.

When the boy dives overboard for his knife and fails to surface again, the man, in a panic, swims to shore for help, ordering his wife, meanwhile, to sail the boat after him. The boy has not drowned; he has concealed himself behind the buoy and upon the husband's departure he climbs back on board. It takes no time at all for him and the wife to recognize each other. . . . Afterward she takes the boat in, dropping the youth off at another pier. A distraught husband meets her, explaining that he hasn't raised help and must report the incident to the police. Coolly she tells him that the boy is alive and adds, "He made me unfaithful with you." Her man rounds on her contemptuously at saying such a stupid thing, even in jest. "Very well," she says, firmly and obediently. "I promise never to say such a foolish thing ever again."

From time immemorial, whatever the worth of the man, his possession of the woman has been determined by her freedom for drifting leeward. She tolerates the husband-figure, yearns for the lover:

thus only can she renew herself, for her identity has no great value without male attention. In this film she is a cipher: quiet, competent, mockingly cool behind the mask of her sunglasses, more dignified than either man, since she is not being called upon to assert a talent which is in doubt. The importance she concedes to any man, she can destroy in an hour, if he dares to forget that it *is* a concession.

That all this takes place on a boat, traditionally a female by appellation, is a fine coincidence of inspiration. The man can handle the boat, but not the woman. The hitchhiker can show off a flashy maneuver but he tires quickly; he's a fair-weather sailor. Proudly he opposes walking to sailing, but his walking depends on his being picked up by others; he gets nowhere without their consent. Of course, if to overthrow the pillar of society by laying another man's wife is an achievement, he "gets somewhere." The eternal Don Juan exists to deprecate the stability of the Commendatore, yet in himself he is less than autonomous, used as a seducer while congratulating himself on his seduction of others.

All the husband's assurance, his social position, and his navigational ability are powerless against the titillating appeal of a young man with a handsome body; the pathos of the situation is that this should inevitably *concern* him. . . . The dénouement is beautifully ambiguous, for this is not a trial by water in the spirit of that other Pole, but a comedic variant. The husband's elimination of boy and knife brings him no relief; he has invoked the betrayal he thought, inside, he wanted, in order to put his wife in a vulnerable position. But she doesn't accept the exposure as such, and he can't face the truth of the issue which he has himself initiated. He doesn't really want her to prove she *could* betray him.

So there they sit, in the car; she has said what she had to say; he is suddenly irresolute. If he believes that the young man is safe ashore, he has to believe that his wife has cheated. If he doesn't want to believe that, he must go to the police and seriously report a drowning at the risk of making a fool of himself. The camera backs away from the car. The film ends, leaving the man's dilemma unresolved. 1963

Harsh Awakenings
(Argentina)

A reviewer in *New Statesman and Nation* recently delivered what appears to be the more common attitude toward the films of Leopoldo Torre-Nilsson: that their director "picks such tiny subjects to be black and aloof about." The statement was precious as well as inaccurate. Certainly the reviewer in question could not have seen *Fin de Fiesta* (1959), which has as ample a subject as anyone demanding social orientation might wish for. *Fin de Fiesta* is about the education of a young man, Adolfo, whose elderly uncle (I think that was the relationship; I saw it without titles) is the country's dictator, ruling his roost by coolly murdering his opposition when it gets too troublesome. Adolfo grows up in relative ignorance of the extent to which Braseras is personally culpable, and he is kept from learning the worst by his friend and mentor, Guastavino, the old man's most reliable henchman. While deploring the boy's youthful idealism, Guastavino does his best to save Adolfo from the consequences of political disillusion, diverting his questions when they encounter groups of blindfolded men on the estate or limousines which have clearly been demonstrating that they're bulletproof. Meanwhile the boy grows up in the way of a spoiled scion. We learn something of the social and sexual ramifications of his class: he conducts a sporadic and inconclusive relationship with a girl, Mariana, but at the same time seduces country girls in chicken coops.

In one richly specified tour of the city, his protector, Guastavino, tells the youth something of his own footless origins (orphaned early, he was illiterate until he was sixteen, earned a living opening car doors for the wealthy), and takes him to see his French-speaking mistress, with whom he can scarcely converse; in fact he needs Adolfo to translate his insults so that she has no chance of misunderstanding him! In a violent street battle with an opposition group, Guastavino is wounded. Adolfo bites the bullet out of his flesh, performing the act of blood-brotherhood which thereafter helps restore the boy's awakening to political self-consciousness. Braseras attends the funeral of a man he was responsible for murdering; when Adolfo asks pointed questions with this inference in mind, Braseras packs him off to a Jesuit school. Subsequently, Guastavino reaches *his* limit; he objects to a killing ordered by Braseras, whereupon the old man, sensing that his lieutenant is growing a mind of his own, has him shadowed and shot down in the street.

Adolfo divines the truth and openly accuses Braseras at a garden party. The outraged man has a heart attack, from which he never recovers. The tide now begins to turn; as he lies dying, the opposition party is emboldened, launching an investigation which effectually discredits the Braseras regime. Here is one of many instances in the film when Torre-Nilsson stands by the psychology of the situation as it culturally exists—something few American or European directors are able to do and something which is apparently incomprehensible to our critics at large. The boy is, after all, kin to the old man, and his feelings are ambivalent as the tyrant is hastened to his death. Since he has been raised with the assumptions of the ruling class and has at least some of its finer principles, he stands by dutifully, attending to the old man's affairs until the end. In recoil, as it were, from his frustrated aggression, upon meeting Mariana again he resolves to take her by force. In one of those violent Torre-Nilsson scenes in which desire is inseparable from infliction, the youth throws her to the ground in the woods. Discovering that she is no longer virgin, he abuses her. I submit that no director in the

North would damage his political hero's profile by attributing to him this double sexual standard. The morality is by no means limited to Argentina, but it is evidently a predominant one in Latin-American and Mediterranean countries. (A magnificently comic treatment of this dualism was the Pietro Germi film, *Seduced and Abandoned.*) Insofar as this morality is there widely condoned by custom, I think I know no one in my own world who would not regard it as barbaric. I suspect that Torre-Nilsson so regards it, but that is the custom with which he is dealing and I think criticism has been extremely feeble when it has confused the issue by implying that he is indifferent. . . . Adolfo does not ultimately reject Mariana. When he decides to renounce his political heritage, he realizes that her future allegiance to him is of more value than his bigoted ego, and clasp-handed they walk into the future, with the winds of change too literally blowing down the Braseras posters—the only visual cliché in a splendid film.

If pragmatic criticism had an ounce of the political wisdom its authors imply, or an ounce of the humane curiosity which should play a major role in political interpretation, it would perceive that the films of Torre-Nilsson (I'm judging by the five I've seen) are dispassionate analyses of the way sexual and political mores relate to each other in Argentine society. The equivalence is not absolute—that's the subtlety that embarrasses the critic, I suppose: i.e., liberal politics do not indicate a liberal view of sexual transactions. In *The House of the Angel,* an extraordinarily faithful period piece, the man who seduces the sequestered girl in a fit of passion, inspired by the possibility of his death in a duel, and then, surviving the duel, ignores the girl thereafter—this man is a political idealist, the "hero" of the story.

I don't know how Torre-Nilsson's films would average out if I saw the dozen (I think) he has made. He makes no great claims himself for his earliest efforts; he speaks with a decent candor when nailed by naive interviewers at Cannes. If he has made no single film as distinguished as the greatest of the Big Three (Fellini, Bergman, Antonioni), he is markedly more intelligent than any of these men. . . . His films might all be called *Harsh Awakening.* They are usually about the individual finding his shape (or, if the individual is female, failing to do so and being buried for life). They are about honor in a peculiarly Spanish way which we do not always understand, and they transpire in a labyrinth of evil which seems to be the effluvium of a society determined to maintain itself in a colonial vacuum—with values and vices alike left over from the colonizers, which it wants passionately to preserve. If anyone believes that these films (largely from the novels and scenarios of Beatriz Guido, the director's wife) are Gothic exaggerations, I can only say he has not had the opportunity I have had—in place of going to Argentina —of listening, appalled, to a young lady from that country, now undergoing psychiatry, whose relationships have been as radically damaged as anyone's I've heard of, arising from an Argentinian childhood (in our mid-century) the character of which would match the cruelty of that in any Dickens novel—if that's your paradigm—you've ever read.

Experto credo. But I do not offer such testimony to settle disputes about Torre-Nilsson's film art. Fidelity to life, while parenthetically important, is not the sole measure by which we receive a movie. Torre-Nilsson tells a good story, intricate and often horrible; his milieu should interest us because it is unfamiliar; the people in his films are attractive to look at; the camera style he employs, as he tries to find a baroque of his own, is alternatively sensuous and jagged, contending against the original influence of Alf Sjöberg.

To balance the negative quotation I used when introducing these remarks, here is Isobel Quigley's summary of the Torre-Nilsson world in her review of *Hand in the Trap* (*The Spectator,* May 28, 1965), itself a perfect example of the insight toward which criticism should always strive:

> . . . he seems to know all there is to know about the pressure of looks exchanged, eyebrows raised, social politeness and what now seems social absurdity, ramming down the explosive forces of fear, shame and sex. There must be few places left where his world still exists and fewer artists who dare to say it does, and to use its values.

1965

My First Love
(Japan)

The conventions of art take small heed of philosophy. And one of the conventions toward which I am specially incredulous is the not infrequent predication that numerous elderly citizens in this world, advancing toward their already discernible graves, indulge themselves ruefully with poignant flashbacks dominated by girls they loved and lost when they were sixteen. If a man has not acquired sense enough to rid himself of erotic regrets when he is pushing four-score years, he has lived in vain, and, by the canons of one eschatological sect with which in my time I have brushed elbows, he is doomed to be reincarnated—times out of mind—in order to suffer from the self-same disability until he has become wise enough to mend it.

I was revisited by this premise upon skeptically approaching a Japanese item, directed by Keisuke Kinoshita, called *My First Love* (1955) in which, once again, I was asked to sit on my disbelief and close the lid while I watch an old gentleman, who looked about one hundred years older than Victor Sjöström in *Wild Strawberries,* recapitulate the ailment so dear to the illusions of those who write fiction and film scenarios. This is not my favorite genre of Japanese film. It is not my favorite genre of film from anywhere. Imagine my astonishment (and remorse) when, within fifteen minutes, I am thoroughly captivated and quite convinced that I am seeing one of the most beautiful-to-look-at films ever made and that, having swallowed the *assumption* of the film story, which was, after all, only a device to enforce the sentiment, I am seeing some uncommonly authentic moments of human suffering, photographed—which is to say, directed—with an uncanny perception not only of the natural world, so gloriously indifferent to our pain while it minds its own business, nurturing clouds and plum trees—but also of the minutely registered way in which people (Japanese people, at any rate) react to grief.

At the beginning, Masao (octogenarian, as I said) is being poled up a river to the valley of his boyhood where (in the Japanese 1880's, I suppose) he had loved his cousin Tamiko briefly and achingly, before she was ordered to marry another and died after a miscarriage, having cried herself to death for Masao, who, away at school, was unaware of the tragedy. Landscape and subject are twin: lush, alluvial land lying at the feet of mountains where clouds forever bunch above or form veils or descend within touch, you'd say, and pad every view with a soft texture like the brush of a fox. The whole film is framed in ovals like nineteenth-century portrait photos; the milky borders of the oval give an ephemeral feeling to every shot. Sentimental? No doubt of it—but exquisite.

In an early sequence, the boy and girl go to pick cotton in a field distant from home. Most of the sequence is wordless but undulant with motion: a light wind teases the stalks of corn, the feathered grass, the daisies, the wild camellias. Aware that sly things have been said about them, the two kids never engage their feelings directly: he compares her to a camellia, she him to a gentian, they smile at the broken sunlight, they pick their cotton; their glances, each at the other, are eloquent, but neither here nor in any scene they share is there a kiss or even a handclasp. At the end of their return journey one suggests to the other that people will talk about them, and the other asks, "Why? We have done nothing wrong." At the very moment the camera escapes to long-shot and shows them walking along a ridge; the clouds, formerly far aloft, have abruptly banked from sky to earth, obscure and ominous. A contingency of the weather, unintended? Knowing something of the way films are made, I doubt it. You don't order a "premonitory cloud" from the property department, but you can shoot a film when you're fairly certain that you'll have the cooperation of God, or cirrocumulus. Still, I've seen few outdoor sequences which so seemed not to have been shot in cold blood, with a calculated schedule and a rabble of grips and lugs and clapper boys and script girls in attendance!

Later . . . Tamiko, in the presence of her father, mother, sister, and grandmother, consents formally to marry the timber merchant. She is at the moment removing a tray-full of impedimenta from the meal, a duty which covers her alarm and her complete misery. As she walks away, she is arrested by the question which must once and for all test her consent to a life she doesn't want. Her back is toward us and remains so in this brief scene. She stops; the camera moves from the floor upward, catching one betraying movement of her foot as if a hot flow of rebellion, only half quelled there, disturbed the member's poise before it ran, stiffening, up her back. She controls forever the agony she is going to experience, she recovers, she turns her head into profile and with the requisite smile of submission says *hai* (*yes*, I assume) before resuming her interrupted departure with the tray. I don't know when I've seen anything so utterly kinetic as this electrifying response, performed with such immense economy.

A similar moment: Masao is home for Christmas, with the world gone under in the snow. He is seated at table (in a boxed-off area of a larger room) with his father and sister—the customary family stance: nobody says anything not packed in ice. Bluntly, without transition and without sympathy, his father tells him that Tamiko is dead. The camera position shifts from its middle distance into the group as the boy becomes rigid, exercising the social control of centuries; then it retreats again to frame the three of them. The father savagely shovels rice into his mouth to cover his indiscretion; Masao goes on with his meal, impassively; the sister says something plaintively and the father spits some words of rebuke in reply. At last Masao breaks, and the camera cuts in again as the boy abandons his post of grownup and rushes from the house to sob alone.

The last leavetaking, between the boy and his sister, on the street —public but isolated, snow in the air and in the mind; they talk and they say nothing. Everything is said, nothing is verbalized, the suppression here being characteristically, if not uniquely, Japanese, since it depicts an eternal failing: that we do not or cannot say the one kind, deep thing that would melt the iron in our throat or ease the heart of another.

What can one say of such a film? That it was worth the doing. The degree to which sentiment includes or repels us is probably a personal matter. Most people fail to make distinctions; if they are touched at all by an experience they call it sentimental, whereas I am inclined to believe that sentimentality arises from esthetic ignorance (either in the artist or the viewer), the exploitation of a feeling for its own sake, with scant regard for its context. No question: Kinoshita *imposes* nostalgia on the texture of his film—something Ozu, for instance, never does. Yet at the end of Ozu's *Tokyo Monogatari* the girl speaks a last sententious word, declaring that she is not going to live like her elders, and I am immediately made conscious of the message. The truth of Kinoshita's situation was essentially developed from an historical formation and from the powerlessness of individuals to transcend it. His framing device tried my credulity; the precision with which he explored the human frustration I found remarkable. It may be that while I am offended by the didactic I can sometimes accept a corresponding excess of beauty. . . .   1966

Thoughts After Attending Another Film Society Buñuel Series

"The horror of that moment," exclaimed the King, in *Through the Looking-Glass*, "I shall never, *never* forget!"

"You will, though," the Queen said, "if you don't make a memorandum of it."

Buñuel keeps memoranda.

In the lives of some men there are inceptive pursuits simply too fitting for belief. When we read that Luis Buñuel studied *entomology* at school, our first reaction is, "You're making it up!" I don't remember who said of whom that whenever he saw a butterfly he thought of wheels. Buñuel's wheels have spikes in them.

Buñuel has announced (frequently!) that his films are meant to convince people they don't live in the best of all possible worlds. Great God, how ingenuous can you be? Does he not realize that people who believe they do never go to a Buñuel film? But in any case, how can he be so *sure?* Did he ever live in a better one? If so, why did he not remain there? It would have been bad for his art?

Times have certainly changed since I discovered Buñuel for myself and was more than once snootily accused, when claiming that *Los Olvidados* was among the great movies, of being a sadist. Today one of the signs of being NOW is to approve, with no reservations, of the entire Buñuel menagerie. (Literally: Buñuel's films are, more than anyone's, zoologically laden—cockroaches, scorpions, praying mantises, dogs, oxen, and monkeys.) And I note that Buñuel is a compulsive preference of just those who disapprove of Jacopetti. Yet do not Jacopetti and Buñuel share a single illusion?—that if you accumulate enough evidence of men's depravity you will have thereby defined man as depraved? Buñuel's historical sense is somewhat keener, if no more merciful, than that of the Italian. Jacopetti appears to have no interest whatever in why certain ethnic or social groups behave in ways that outrage *us,* who are paragons of rational conduct. Buñuel implies no distinctions. To him all of us are more or less like those villagers in an Italian hill region, photographed by Jacopetti, who, following a custom the source of which they have long ago forgotten, assemble annually and butt their heads against an oaken door until the whole male population of the community is streaming with blood and self-congratulation.

I used to wonder what consistency lay behind the invariable lineup of favorites among quasi-left critics. Those who enjoy Buñuel *en lump* always claim to enjoy with equivalent relish silent-slapstick comedy, Alfred Hitchcock, Jean-Luc Godard, and Joseph Losey. Sometimes, somehow Robert Bresson gets into that gallery, which betrays the provenance of this heritage in the area of *Cahiers du Cinéma.* I think the route was confirmed by way of John Russell Taylor, who in 1964 put together *Cinema Eye, Cinema Ear* under the immediate influence of the Parisian arbiters. One can see the underlying logic: except for Bresson, who is admitted to the club on snob-appeal grounds (he's an *auteur!*) , this *légion étrangère* appeals to the leveling syndrome. Laurel and Hardy, with their degrading masochism, drain off the aggressions conveyed more obliquely by the others: Hitchcock, the corpulent bourgeois, dreaming of the bombs he'd like to have thrown; Godard, the café talker, dreaming of the revolutions he'd like to incite; Losey, a sort of American-expatriate Buñuel, with more spite than imagination (a hero to the clique because, allegedly, he was a political ejectee).

Buñuel, a tormented soul who, through the language of surrealist anger, reveals himself *au fond* as a humanitarian guided by excruciating pity—this is the view commonly entertained by critics who need a rationalization for the pleasure Buñuel gives them. Buñuel is adopted, conspicuously, by pseudo-Christian intellectuals who have never suffered a day in their lives, who have never been exposed to "the people" except when forced to ride a subway or to attend a movie which isn't privately screened. For reasons of personal insecurity, no doubt, they like to hint that they consider their days parasitical and worthless. One such character I know is fond of declaring that what Buñuel (or Bergman or Pasolini, depending on who is odd-man-in) is *really* saying in a given context is "We are all executioners; we are all victims." (Ever since Cayatte named a film *Nous Sommes Tous les Assassins,* this has been a slogan of the liberal entente.) The chap I have in mind went straight from a choice university into "culture journalism" without turning a hair or a hand; he has never been seriously inconvenienced by economic want or occupational frustration; he drapes his rump in expensive flannel; he takes a taxi to cross the street if it's raining. Of what, I wonder, does he conceive himself to be a victim? As for being an executioner, he wouldn't have the guts to kill and bake a hedgehog if he and his wife were starving.

"By their audiences shall ye know them them" is probably too harsh a judgment for any film director to survive. No man should be held wholly responsible for those who adore him. The typical Buñuel audience is, however, suggestive. Everywhere the composition of it is pretty much the same, whether at the Palais de Chaillot, at MMA in New York, at ABF in Stockholm, or in a basement of a commercial cinema where Sunday morning "art films" are offered, in Rome as in München. How, by now, do we name them? As "internal exiles," that euphemism of Czeslaw Milosz for *dropouts* (his have more laudable motives)? As Anabaptists? Like Donkin, in Conrad's *Nigger of the Narcissus,* they are dresssed in everyone else's cast-off clothes. Unable to establish their own habitation of mind, they derive all their identity and most of their joy—if such mirthless consent to Buñuel's prevalent scatology can be called joy—from witnessing the degradation of others, the more so if the others are of a hypothetically ruling order which they hate in inverse ratio to their acquaintance with it. They are always prepared to jeer before anything jeerable has appeared on the screen; they can be counted upon to applaud Buñuel's crudest gambits and his most shopworn metaphors. They constitute the smuggest audience I know, save for those who swarm to Eisenstein revivals. Frequently it's the same audience. Koestler once wrote of such gatherings, "a collection of neurotic Cinderellas who wanted to overthrow a society in which nobody asked them to dance."

I don't know whether idealism or timidity inspires Buñuel's compulsive talent for depicting cruelty, but I suspect there is little genuine compassion involved. If we concede that *L'Âge d'Or* was a furiously inventive response to the fractional existence of modern man, whose instincts have been cut off and perverted by Society (the Rousseau formulation), it is surely remarkable that Buñuel has never thereafter abandoned for long his fascination with the amputee. He is firmly identified with the objects of his loathing, since there is an insufficient distance between, for instance, *Los Olvidados*, arising from rancorous moral indignation, and a so-called parody like the Archibaldo Cruz film. Significantly, the only film with which he was importantly associated during his long servitude in Hollywood was an item, *The Beast with Five Fingers*. I recall it rather vividly, for it featured a single dismembered hand which, removed from the body of its owner, a concert pianist, insisted, like a demented crab or the heliotropic segment of a centipede, in remaining "alive"—in this case for the purpose of playing the piano arrangement of Bach's *Chaconne!* I witnessed this spectacle with sharply divided emotions; actually the film introduced me to that particular Bach arrangement, which is marvelous, and the hand, if you could contemplate it without a qualm, was in itself beautiful: it was, I believe, the hand of the actor Victor Francen. But normally I know nothing more loathsome, in art as in life, than a member removed from the organic whole to which it should be attached. (Someone with a better clinical background than mine might be interested in Bergman's comparable obsession with cut-off members, during the fifties especially. I'm a little afraid of the obvious deduction.) In any case, one can scarcely take lightly in Buñuel's films the prevalence of the foot-fetish, obsessional leg washing, impotence, blindmen, hunks of quivering meat. At his best, these images work as symbols, but I'm sure he can't make a film without them, and, like holy relics, their redundant presence has been drooled over by his apostles, who, like all other apostles, find sacred each expiration of the Master. I am sometimes led to believe that ninety-five out of every hundred "film people" lost their daddies (if not their mummies) when very young. Once they have discovered a director who has made two or three films with which they are *d'accord*, they adopt him as their liege lord; their life occupation then becomes a jealous defense of every celluloid foot he has absent-mindedly exposed (pun intended). There used to be a Griffith nut running loose in America. Every time some other film pioneer was praised, he would rise to scream, *"Griffith did it first!"* If you praised Griffith, he'd write a letter to your editor or publisher anyway, because you had praised him for the wrong reasons.

One of the most irrelevant descriptions of Buñuel's method has appeared recently in the *Times Literary Supplement*. A. Alvarez, the author, has stepped boldly into the trap that awaits all literary critics who, writing about film, tell themselves, "I must remember to say something about his use of the camera."

> . . . the art of a master like Buñuel lies in his being not only original but also utterly unobtrusive. He simply uses his camera to look at people, plainly, patiently, mostly in mid-shot, without tricks or illusions or expectations. Like a man whose gift of silence makes other people talk more and more anxiously, Buñuel's camera waits for the characters to reveal themselves— their obsessions, their perversions, their corruptions. The director, meanwhile, defines nothing, he remains detached, accepting, sardonic. . . .

This is truly incredible. I don't understand how Alvarez would suppose he could substantiate such an interpretation beyond a few arbitrarily chosen sequences. *Nothing is further from the facts.* Allowing for the Pirandellian conceit (which we all indulge) of film characters being autonomous, I would say that what Alvarez is postulating, if you except the sardonic attitude, could only be applied to De Sica: not even to Bergman, but not at all to Buñuel. Without, for the moment, going back to *Un Chien Andalou* and *L'Âge d'Or*, totally expressionist, surreal films, hence involving a completely arbitrary selection of events and an importunate employment of camera ("tricks, illusions, expectations"), we can dispute Alvarez' claim by reference to any of the more famous or notorious touches in Buñuel's films we care to pick out. We need to recall only, for example: the stunted population of Las Hurdes in

Land Without Bread (shot by Buñuel with hand-held camera), in which certain of the inhabitants were photographed with their feet calculatedly placed in the foreground, to be reminiscent of the Velásquez foreshortening (this was the region from whence dwarfs were recruited for the Philippean court); the hair-bristling scene, among many, in *Los Olvidados,* when Pedro's mother floats across the room in water-treading slow motion with a raw steak in her hand, which is snatched from her son's grasp by the hideous Jaibo, appearing nightmarishly from under the bed; or the exchange of lust-in-the-eye between that same Jaibo and the mother as she washes her legs, followed by a cut to the blindman's performing monkey; or the final scene, when the boy's body is dumped incontinently from a barrow into the trash pit, with the camera at low angle, which then swivels to the lone, dust-laden tree, an image of choked life. Is this the approach of a director who "defines nothing'"? Remember the interplay that opens *El,* the recurrently focusing glances of the church usher at the *feet* of the communicants—for it is by way of this fixation that he becomes interested and, for them both, disastrously implicated with the woman. Or take one (*the* one) overwhelming example from *Viridiana*: the Last Supper orgy—the whole mounting scene, inexorably timed to the music and the derisive dancing, a faultless selection of shots, each from the most telling perspective, to create a maximum of outrage within a measured unit of frames. Buñuel's camera never waits for his characters to reveal themselves! He moves in and reveals. This is what it means *to be Buñuel!* He has a creatively prejudiced point of view; he has preselected his characters precisely because they have obsessions, perversions, and corruptions to reveal; he would not else be interested in them. At his greatest, which may be less often than his admirers suppose, his camera *analyzes,* it *prosecutes*—it *crunches!*

Only *The Destroying Angel,* perhaps, or an indifferent exercise like *Mexican Bus Ride* or *Robinson Crusoe* might qualify, negatively, for Alvarez' illustration. If by "detached" we mean that a minimum of camera movement has been initiated, this is certainly true of *The Destroying Angel,* and it is one of the reasons, to my sense, that the film is tedious. The work was adapted from a play: ergo, the confined setting and the rigorous acting-out of the point we have already caught in fifteen minutes. The film has an excess of pan-shots of characters not in motion, one of the most artificial film devices and the hardest to handle with any conviction. For the rest, the material is of course set up for Buñuel's most rabid admirers; it enables Buñuel to conspire against his characters.

If *Viridiana* is, in my opinion, the greatest justification of Buñuel's twisted smile, *Robinson Crusoe* is perhaps the test by which he most seriously failed, or which at least defined very clearly the substance of his bias—that he finds it easier to sneer than to think. It demonstrated how innocent his mind is of any conception about unhomogenized man. With this subject, one might have asked, how could you miss? Only one actor to keep track of and a completely swept field for your projection of what—given certain cultural predispositions—Man is all about when he's totally alone, naked to the elements. Crusoe as given, whom you don't wholly have to accept, was of course a rational, pious man, product of Good Queen Anne and the Age of Reason, an instrument of propaganda for Defoe's belief that all you need on a desert island besides a bucket of nails is a mercantile soul and a carpenter's talent. From there you can go anywhere. Buñuel went nowhere. There were no surprises in this film, no invention.

Here is a man, Crusoe, with nothing between himself and annihilation but his hands. We never see Crusoe's hands in this film. And the crucial revelation, when he comes upon another *footprint*—never did an important moment from literature get transcribed so poorly, because (in my reading of the possibilities) Buñuel never prepared us by, for example, concentrating on Crusoe's *feet* from his witness point until we are so hypnotized by them that just when we have given up anticipating another foot this is just the moment when its outline would appear. Funny how un-sensuous Buñuel really is: feet as fetish objects he can animate, but a foot which does nothing more sinister than announce a human presence he cannot handle. Likewise the juncture at which Crusoe is suddenly aroused by the woman's dress he salvaged in the sea chest, which now, stirred by random breezes, is invested by his fancy with a woman's body. This, you'd suppose, is where Buñuel would excel, the more so as it was his inspiration. Feel the possibilities: the tropical evening, the oceanic loneliness, the plants breathing, the devastations of memory visiting a predominantly physical man—the unbidden but palpable shape of lust, hardest of all our inclinations to divert. How in the name of Satan did Buñuel miss? The episode is dead, completely dead. Buñuel has said that he didn't like the story but he was interested in the character. I don't see how you can divorce them from each other; the book is the situation, the situation is the man. I said before that there was only one actor to keep track of. But a single actor implies perfect casting to begin with, and the deficiency began there, I suppose. How did he ever pick that Irish ham who'd never be able to spit a curve in the wind without a soft-focus lens on him?

Beyond this solecism, Buñuel has no basic view of man. In society Buñuel is quizzical, alert to every distortion of character—alert, one might say, only to distortion. Place him in a universe of parrots, sand, stars, and a wind that bloweth where it listeth and he doesn't know how to watch lonesomeness, how to wait, hear, observe, inhale at a different rate. Crusoe was a man intent on remaining civilized. I don't think Buñuel cared. Man is interesting to Buñuel when he is a victim, when he is maimed, when he is reacting to the vices of society. A healthy man he cannot envisage, a man plagued by the absence of people is evidently nothing poignant to him. Many critics have labored to give Buñuel credit for the ending, at least, where Crusoe is presumed to have graduated from white mastery to shared fellowship with Man Friday. I didn't think this aspect materially differed from that in Defoe. And I must say that the more consciously Christian Buñuel tries to appear, the more boring he becomes. *Nazarin,* apart from being just a clumsily made movie, rests on an assumption I find very difficult to accept: that a failed imitator of Christ is a tragic figure rather than a foolish one. Someone should remind Buñuel of Nietzsche's remark: there was only one Christian and he died on a cross.

If a director is great who has made two great movies (give him three, I'll not argue too hotly), Buñuel is a great director. He is not a master, for this title implies that the artist so named is in perfect control of his medium even when he is doing a commercial chore or is not too taken with his immediate subject. This is simply not true of Buñuel; he has made bad movies and he has made many just average ones, flavored by "Buñuel moments," some of them silly. Consider *Susana, La Ilusion Viaja en Tranvia, El Rio y la Muerte, Cela s'Appelle l'Aurore, The Young One,* or *La Fiévre Monte El Pão.* His films, from one to the next, are technically uneven; many are indifferently turned. Their most ingratiating quality, I would say, is their bisulfate humor; the least, their "philosophy." Buñuel has spent a lifetime railing against an imperfect world, which is a waste of time. He was hurt when young, is my guess, and like Bergman is too conceited to assimilate the hurt. Which is why, to the anarchists among us, he's the village saint: they pretend being fired by injustice; in truth they despise excellence and are proud of having rejected all possibility of a world in which fastidiousness is a value. Buñuel's *voyeurism* satisfies their need for disenchantment. The joke is on them, however; they don't see themselves in *Viridiana*. Buñuel, like Stendhal in this respect, is a Jacobin in the drawing room, a Bourbon on the street. As many of his films assault the predatory poor as they do the predatory rich, and for his most memorable villains, as sometimes for his scapegoats, he "Employs the Handicapped."

You can lie awake at night and hear his lip curl. His natural ancestor, in film, was Erich von Stroheim, who hated all his characters (except those he played himself) ; that was the secret of his charm. And like Buñuel, one feels, von Stroheim kept a diary in which, under THINGS TO DO TODAY, he wrote, "Remember to be nauseated."

If the good society came into existence tomorrow, Antonioni just might be one of its adornments. Behind his morose and glossy nihilism, he suggests a vision of order. Buñuel would be rattled by the arrival of Utopia; he would be compelled to renounce it, for its advent would put him out of business. Like Bergman, again—amusing how much they distrust each other, how much in common they have. The one is nostalgic for the Devil, the other for God, and their occasional sociology is a fraud. W. H. Auden has noted that most artists are way ahead of Marx; for them the state "withered away" as soon as they were conscious. From time to time Buñuel projects, feebly, the outlines of social amelioration (in *Los Olvidados* with the social workers, and in *Cela s'Appelle l'Aurore* and *El Río y la Muerte*) , yet one cannot imagine Buñuel finding one of those single-party Swedens, like Algeria or Cuba, an adequate compensation for his hostility toward all factions. That is why he continues tirelessly to assert the same negations, a more vital occupation for him than to wake up, one dismaying dawn, to find himself contented. Ingmar Bergman, too: he grew up in a "social democracy," entirely irrelevant to his formation or his needs; only the puritan roots of his country made any lasting impression on his outlook. He wants to suffer, as Buñuel wants to be revolted. If you listen to him instead of looking at his films, he might appear to favor a Christian society (of a kind unrecognizable by T. S. Eliot, that's for sure) . Wistfully, enviously, he has evoked a vision, comparable to that of Henry Adams, in which he yearns to have been one of those anonymous builders of the Gothic cathedral. Luckily for his reference, Adams picked Chartres: an historical accident has so far concealed from us the principal architects of that particular cathedral. But we know who erected most of the historically important churches, and scholarship may discover for us tomorrow the master builder of Chartres. But to the point: is it conceivable that in any age Bergman would be gratified with anonymity? He is not propelled by community, or by adoration, but by revenge. . . . Two supremely disobedient minds. In the fifteenth century, Bergman would have been a recreant monk, preaching hellfire and a Second Coming for the elect. Buñuel would have been a thief—a rhyming thief, like Villon. They would have met at a crossroads. Bergman would have been burned at the stake. Buñuel would have been hanged by his thumbs.

1967

Some American Films:
A Modest Proposal

Confronted with the problem of evaluating contemporary American films, I have come to the conclusion that the best are those in which the solemnities of high-minded film criticism have been flatly ignored. American film critics (while not alone in this tendency, they're in a better position than others to know what they're about) have an uneasy itch for Significance: probably a heritage from the country's theocratic origins, combined with the pragmatic inclination to respect in art only what is socially useful. They want Hollywood film-makers to handle important problems and incendiary issues. For many years Hollywood has been trying to oblige and it should be by now self-evident that in proportion to the effort expended in that direction the results are mortifyingly inadequate. The authentic American film is one in which the writer, to say nothing of the director, has been free to remain totally immune to the Idea—like Huck Finn refusing to be civilized by his aunt—and to concentrate on the anecdote. When he labors to extend his reference, when he snubs the unity of his limitations, when he strains to be universal or, less expansively, tries to be "relevant" to whichever camp of social uplift makes him quail, he is sure to contrive an embarrassment.

Since this is so persistently the case, it seems to me that critical wisdom would consist in settling for less, in the confidence of thereby getting more—I mean more of the real thing—and in calling attention to the proven merits of American film, which are largely empirical, instead of applauding (or, alternatively, disdaining) the feverish attempts of worried California executives to say something resonant and definitive about Race Relations, The Generation Gap, The American Commitment, or some other capitalized issue better debated on the floor of the House or in the columns of qualified social observers.

Nobody who is not hopelessly naive can conclude that *In the Heat of the Night* makes a fearlessly radical statement about the problem of racial discrimination in the American South. But let's not lose our heads; it *is* related to the problem. The film is a melodrama, adapted from a play and directed with uncommon assurance (by Norman Jewison), with an essentially cinematic art of noting ugly tremors below the joshing level of crossroads humor provided by the dialogue. The plot pattern is that of a western, which in turn is rooted in nineteenth-century American literature (reread your Mark Twain and your Bret Harte), the old "town-tamer" situation: a stranger rides into the community and nobody wants him until they decide he's just the man to settle their local disturbance; he settles it, against odds and against the deeper inclinations of the townfolk; he rides away, with their grudging thanks.

The novelty here is that the stranger is a Northern-based Negro arriving in a Southern town—furthermore, a skilled detective (Poitier). There is wit in this conception; both the Negro and the sheriff (Steiger) who takes him on to solve a murder are alert to the abrasive joke they've agreed to play: a Negro needed by a paunchy poor-white; a cop chasing the criminal and hearing the hounds at his own back, compelled to run down the guilty and to run against time, in order to save his own skin together with that of an innocent victim; compelled also by gratification born of hate: once, with his guard down, the Negro betrays himself with a flicker of resentment, eager token of the lust to kill. Squeals the sheriff in delighted recognition: "Why, you're jes' like us!"

The resolution of this fable is less than credible, no doubt: our sheriff not only putting the detective on the northbound train but also carrying his suitcase deferentially. In reality, if we may so speak, Poitier would have been low-man shortly after pinning the tail on the right donkey. Hence certain of my fellow critics rejected the film altogether: it didn't tell the truth, the whole truth, and nothing but. The rage for veracity can be a form of blindness. Until that last lame scene, the shifting grounds of hostility and communion between two representatives of law had been acted out with no falsification, in a yokel setting where the governing smell is that of paranoia. The night episode when Poitier and Steiger relax over a beer—deceptively at ease each with the other until Poitier expresses *sympathy* and evokes from Steiger the atavistic dread which boils over into snarling hatred—is as accurately shot and paced as in any comparable scene of Antonioni. In this sequence, something comes alive, deeper than one South confronting another, which is the sum of ages: man's compulsive need for man and his equally compulsive fear of being touched. We survive by opposition; we define ourselves by what we conceal. Mutual exposure is a nocturnal luxury, the margin of poetic license we permit ourselves in a world of prose.

Of the two principals in the film, Steiger has the richer opportunity (but of course he's intrinsically the better actor), since the sheriff has a regional flavor absent from the man who went north, and Steiger wears the part as if it were flesh of his bones—shrewdness and vanity co-existing with a buried temptation to be just, and a sour secret knowledge that single-handedly (poor tool of whatever law prevails) he's holding back the jungle. One day, when his shoulder muscles slacken, he'll be a decrepit lion in the path, and every jackal of the area will help pull him down (he'll wind up as a night watchman in the railroad yards).

In Cold Blood should have been a near-great movie. To my conception it missed by miles. By comparison with *Bonnie and Clyde,* this is stock stuff, but even when comparing it with *In the Heat of the Night,* it seems to have suffered from its greater freedom of opportunity. Jewison's film had a relatively confined setting and a focused confrontation—theater, you might say. With the Capote novel for a shooting script, as it were, Brooks had space to move around in—all outdoors—and stretches of time to incorporate with flashbacks. But every director has to find his own unity of effect; where Brooks failed, principally, was in his martext desire to say more than the narrative would express if he had restricted himself to the irreducibly unbearable fact at the center: the wanton murder of a family, totally unknown to them, by two psychopathic bandits. Brooks is no artist, needless to say; he wants to prove something, as if the proof weren't planted in the material. Truman Capote, who wrote the book, expressly intended to keep his distance like Flaubert, to reconstruct the abhorrent crime with a minimum of editorial intrusion. Brooks succumbed to the obvious temptation—obvious when homemade sociology is in popular demand. He kept his distance from the murdered family right enough—he simply lacks inventive powers—but he paid excessive attention to the case histories of the two criminals. With the victims we never became sufficiently familiar for our sympathy with them to become binding, fearful, absolute, and outraged. Brooks simply gave us four likable but quite blank people whose domestic life was characterized chiefly by bad homey music on the track whenever their frame house appeared in the shot. The killers, on the other hand, were created in the round and more so, from womb to doom. (Agreed that a fox is more attractive than a chicken; Brooks should have faced that probability.) Critics who scorned, with a condescending titter, what they called Freudianism in *Reflections in a Golden Eye* and *Bonnie and Clyde* accepted the far clumsier instances of it in Brooks's movie, where phantoms of adulterous mother and avenging father materialize conveniently to upset a psycho's sex life and underline a thesis which appears to read, "I hated my mother, so I became a homicidal maniac." A mixed-up, sensitive kid! Further, Brooks confessed (to a European TV interviewer) that with the close of the film he had entered a plea against capital punishment. You would have thought the story, as it came to his hand, was sufficiently loaded without introducing a major argument barely within the province of the tragedy. A familiar trap. Brooks as citizen interferes with Brooks as film-maker. (André Cayatte suffers from the same division, but he has a better excuse: he was a lawyer before he made movies. It might be brutal of me to suggest that he has a finer intelligence.) . . . There *were* good things in the Brooks film, we recall, after screening out the coordinate social psychology: the hypnotic drag of the American highway leading everywhere and nowhere, encouraging flight and deferring resolution; the loathsomely executed murders, fleetingly witnessed by flashlight in the darkness of that tasteless house; and the *complete* credibility of Robert Blake and Scott Wilson, playing the pathetic assassins.

Bonnie and Clyde is a test case for American film-making as it is for American criticism. Having seen it for a third time, I feel more favorably toward it than at first, when I suppose I was resisting the publicity. While I don't want further to abuse that all-purpose word *classic* (which should mean something long established rather than something newly definitive), I feel more than ever persuaded that Arthur Penn's film has no superior in the past twenty years of American commercial cinema. If this is not authentic Americana, I'm too far out to be entrusted with the subject. The time, the place, the people: nobody makes a false movement (and there's movement all the way—and that, my friends, is your America!); nobody takes a stance that doesn't embody his occupation; nobody speaks out of character and much of the lingo is choice: the incongruous formality when C. W. Moss, the little toad from the gas station, asks Buck's wife, "What was your family's religious affiliation?"—and the dogged irrelevance with which Old Man Moss demands of his son in an abrupt querulous whine, as they're gingerly carrying the wounded Bonnie and Clyde into the house, "What you go 'n git that damned tattooin' done on yousself fur?" The feeling of the thirties in sectional America is recaptured with just enough vernacular history to fill you in without reminding you of the wardrobe department or old newsreels: the Roosevelt posters, Eddie Cantor on the radio, "Giant Cheeseburgers" (probably 35 cents, you recollect with a groan), the Burma-Shave signs single-filing across grassless plains where once the buffalo ran, the shin-length dresses, the caps (all things return), dust-bowl evacuees, and names like Velma.

Warren Beatty (Clyde) is perfect: all little-boy strut, bashfulness hiding pathic conceit, impotent anger, and the vigilance of a wildcat. He's a card, too, this kid poised to shoot (elbows held down and back, torso quick to swivel); nobody can tell a cornier joke, unless it's big brother Buck. And he's an expert at sensing what other people (at his emotional level) really want; he knows everything within his field of operation, *everything*—except that he himself has a kink in his brain. "We're Bonnie and Clyde. We rob banks." So they play out their little day of glory—funny, outlandish, sickening—and fatality is the payoff as the rhythm of the ballad accelerates: that awful woman screaming and screaming when the police attack the house they're holed up in, the all-out carnage of the raid on the motel, the stopover in the cow pasture when the police move in again and Buck gets his, and that frightful woman yelling her head off, *"Don't die, Daddy, don't die!"*; Clyde's fierce clambering race for the river, then the long false calm of recuperation before

392 | *Vernon Young on Film*

the squeal and the shambles—and the slow-motion roll of Bonnie and her Clyde as they're whipped to death by a tempest of bullets.

Of course, you'll kill the film in America. You will talk it half to death. Then you'll imitate it. Fifteen times—and it will get worse every time. How you worship "originality"! And how you sack it!

Later. The sextons have already gathered. *Bonnie and Clyde* is socially damaging. Yes, indeed. Which came first, the social damage or the film? When you have a society in which violence is not regarded as admirable, you will have fewer films that "exploit" the supervising value. The other prong of the argument is that we have been cajoled into identifying ourselves with that reprehensible couple, Bonnie and Clyde. Who is tipping whose hand?

Identification is a whimsical category. Last year two engaging American films (engaging, not engagé) included Steve McQueen as the leading actor. In *Bullitt*—certainly lightweight but suavely directed by Peter Yates—McQueen was a personable (if virtually mute) detective given a very dangerous assignment, which he fulfilled with far greater relish than his girl friend (a terrible bore) appreciated. She was kin to the critics I roughly cited above; she believed you could make an omelet without breaking eggs. I'm sure that all of us were securely on the side of Bullitt, cheering his attempt to bring the bad citizen to justice and incidentally envying his seat behind the wheel of that leapfrog automobile. Then, McQueen was cast as the top-drawer felon (smart showmanship) in Jewison's elegant thriller *The Thomas Crown Affair*. Now, don't let anyone tell me he wasn't delighted to see Crown working out his ingeniously plotted caper (to the fascinating accompaniment of those monitor images and a catchy theme song that had nothing to do with anything), getting away with all that bullion, and frustrating not only the cuckoo-clock Swiss but the female bloodhound hired by the bank. (If a good actress had played the part, the film would have been more equal in its central contest, but Faye Dunaway, if born to play Bonnie, is otherwise a stinkingly bad actress.)

Here is where the bluenose makes his entrance, whispering lasciviously a text from, I think, C. J. Jung, to the effect that each of us harbors a criminal within; we are indulging by proxy the subconscious wish to rob a great big bank. (I'll not protest; I don't know how *sub*-conscious is my wish.) By the same kind of reasoning, however, and by reference to *Bullitt,* each of us is harboring a cop within! Can we have it two ways? Are we subconsciously law abiding or subconsciously illicit? While I pause for replies from rival schools of psychology, I'll suggest that this is more feasibly a simple equation in the art of theater: the spell of personality in the appropriate context. We want McQueen to win the day, as a dick *or* as a criminal, because we like McQueen. (My fancy argument hinges on a presumption, to be sure; anyone who doesn't want to play, just run along home.)

So far I have heard no outburst from the home guards on the possibly insidious effects of Noel Black's *Pretty Poison*. Excellent in its homespun way—homespun by a disciple of Charles Addams—the film predicates an unhinged young man (Anthony Perkins) (he had once burned down a house in which his aunt just happened to be) who gets out of prison, takes a job in a chemical plant, and involves an eighteen-year-old drum majorette in his wanton fantasy: that of being a CIA agent. The twist is that while his lies are relatively harmless, the girl, who looks like one of Henry James's candid provincial heroines, is the genuine lethal article. This revelation is developed with deceptive leisure and wit that suddenly piles up into cold-blooded murder. It's an infernal little tale with enough reality of characterization to persuade you that this sort of thing happens daily in Winslow, Massachusetts. While Anthony Perkins, after fifteen years in film, still looks like a mule deer about to be rushed by a cougar, he displays somewhat more confidence in this role than he has done in the company of Melina Mercouri and Orson Welles. The girl is very convincing, probably by accident (she is played by someone with a marvelous name, Tuesday Weld, right out of Hardy!) , and her mother is done to a turn, with expert dryness and a species of weathered-Yankee sex appeal, by Beverley Garland. The film is altogether a modest contribution toward the destruction of a myth—that of American innocence. Seemingly the guardians of our mental health didn't believe in this entertainment, whereas they had to believe in *Bonnie and Clyde;* perhaps, after all, they *are* esthetes, bless them: they find truth more unpalatable than fiction.

When tempted to regret that I do not work at the heart of a special context—London, Paris, New York—where I would know precisely the audience for which I was writing and to what its assumptions were immediately related, I have only to glance at current reviews —from New York, especially—to feel relieved that I am not at the distracting hub, that beyond the reach of death and Barbra Streisand I customarily write in ignorance of the *débat du jour* and the latest quotations from the market. Whenever I do manage to focus on American film criticism, I find that it tends to get surprisingly worked up, quite as much as French criticism does, about overheard opinions, from which a given individual wants fanatically to dissociate himself and pronounce a last word of his own. I can understand the nature of the pressure and I am not suggesting that criticism can or should remain consistently aloof from gossip, the loose ends of the universally shaping voice: it is the character of the *occasion* that so often puzzles me. For example, I find difficult to realize, barely two years after the event, that *The Graduate* could have ever been thought a controversial film. I went to see it as I do most films of the heavy-commercial category, mercifully unaware at the moment that American filmgoers, generally, received it as, in some meaningful way, a statement about the war of the generations. What I saw was an amusing enough farce, on the sour side, sweetening abjectly as it progressed, in a special setting of rather empty and secretly vicious people. Any sententious undertones were quickly dispelled by the strange determination of that weird boy (delightfully played by Dustin Hoffman) to marry his less than scintillating fiancée, despite his initial attitude of being a confused onlooker at any social convention whatever. This was a bit of a letdown for me; I was expecting a far more revolutionary decision. I mean, clearly, the girl's mother was by far the more interesting object for any male of sanguineous appetite. I never discovered why *The New Yorker* devoted an almost entire issue (so I was told) to a serious comparison of the movie with the book: one has to limit one's experiences somewhere.

Now I have been reading sundry notices of the latest westerns, and I see that the merits of, respectively, *The Wild Bunch* and *Butch Cassidy and the Sundance Kid* are being argued with a zeal usually conserved for disputing the superiority of Milton to Dante. From a high-altitude view I would suppose that neither film leaves you with anything to think about at breakfast the following morning. However, the object even of film criticism is to discriminate qualities, and I have observed in the past that this is the last enterprise you can expect of most critics when it comes to the western. They are always looking for the Big Idea. After all these years, that's a waste of time. Here and there in Peckinpah's film (*The Wild Bunch*) there are characterizations more meat than bone; thanks to the actors, mainly, the relationships among the men ring with a certain crude moral veracity. But this promising earnestness is effectually canceled by the usual big-production showing-off: the elaborated mayhem, slow-motion falls from horses and cliffs, and the *opéra bouffe* battle in Mexico at the end. The most effective sequence is a virtually silent takeover of a U.S. Cavalry train—the only sound the stertorous exhalation of the steam engine. At that moment Peckinpah was making *movie*. Because he was making music.

The *Butch Cassidy* film (directed by George Roy Hill) was obviously an attempt to make a kind of *Bonnie and Clyde* western, only funnier, with the principals ruefully aware that they're deadbeat outlaws and had best make their exit from a too dangerous game. Predictably, it doesn't wholly come off, chiefly because the director, or whoever, wanted to hold on to the heroic bite. Meanwhile there are some lamentably Camp excursions, and Bacharach was clearly being paid by the foot for his music. Like *The Wild Bunch* (I don't know which was manufactured first), this film ends with a holocaust in which our gallows-humored heroes hold off what looks like the entire Bolivian Army. Still, it was an entertainment, and I don't see why the many critics I have been reading should have been so condescending, in view of some westerns they have taken seriously. The actors were, on the whole, fun, Robert Redford covering for Newman in an agile and ingratiating performance of the Kid. Newman gets by; he's just Newman, which means that, as ever, he's being protected by closeups to divert us from noting how badly—and how un-western—he carries himself. He smiles his way through most of his parts and always seems to be the same cheap, affable gambler that he played in *The Hustlers*. But again, there's one fine stretch of film-making here which seems not to have impressed the quasi-sociologists I've been reading: the flight-and-pursuit rhythms when Cassidy and the Kid are being followed by brilliant trackers and are outwitted every foot of the way. The persistence of the pursuers and the increased panic of the pursued are enormously effective because, until the end of the game, Hill never cuts to those pursuers; they remain at distance, inexorable and anonymous. Very impressive is the moment in near-darkness when these mounted hunters become just a malevolent and rhythmic cluster of bobbing torches. Directors should be commended when they work out action poetry like that.

Years ago the inevitable *cul de sac* of the western was pleasantly prophesied by a scene in Danny Kaye's *The Secret Life of Walter Mitty*. The whole genre was reduced to its common denominators.

The town was nothing but a mock-up of facades: those of the saloon, the hotel, the stable, the blacksmith shop. Beyond, through the windowless frames in these building fronts, a line of hills and some cacti (I don't now recall the sparse details) and, in the foreground, nothing but The Stance: Kaye himself, loping down the board sidewalk, ankles relaxed, face petrified, hands idly hovering near the pearl-handle guns, worn low for the ready draw. This crystallizing of elements has now been seriously achieved—by seriously I mean calculatedly—above all by the Italian contrivers of the so-called *spaghetti western,* shot in Italy and sometimes in Mexico. Italians, naturally enough, have a lyrical or operatic sense of the West, which they exploit with tongue in cheek. Most of their stuff, answerable to big investments, is junk: a killing every four and a half minutes, interminable closeups in-between of men like Clint Eastwood whose faces are made of adobe, a sex brawl or two, quaint Mexican accents dubbed by stranded Americans in Rome, and usually a taste of revolution-honey for the Anabaptists necking with their girls. Perhaps once a year some Neapolitan dreams up a few good isolated effects and manages to sustain a musical curve in his narrative. For my taste, this is better than a sermon about the fatal consequences of individualism.

There were some good senseless eipsodes of this kind in Sergio Leone's *Once in the Glorious West,* a film that went on and on until my stomach thought my throat was cut and I simply had to escape for sustenance and in hope that I might still get Bach's *Magnificat* on the radio. About every twenty minutes I resolved to leave, but at that juncture Leone would arrange something that suggested he was going to repeat some of the better moments in the first quarter of the film: long leather dust coats flapping in the torrid breeze, a train arriving with the expected killer getting off on the other side of the tracks, the not-a-word massacre of a family as the man of the house prepares his second wedding feast outdoors. This was really done with a fine feeling for instinctive apprehensions, masterfully measured—the sound of wind along the desert floor, the call of a wild turkey, perhaps simulated by a foe, then the real feared thing: a sudden ripping of the air, a scramble and crumpling of the man and his sister, and a remaining small boy looking up the muzzle of a gun held by a man with no taste at all for mercy.

Men like Leone have visions of the West unsupported by any extended content; they see a configuration, a tableau, a confronting of one style with another, or of a movement with a countermovement in a different tempo. Then a hack writer connects these moments of lethal choreography. (My inference!) If they get the right actor for this formula—Henry Fonda, Charles Bronson, Lee Marvin, Richard Boone—and the right setting, something of the interest that inheres in ballet may ensue: visual drama in essence, though I am not for a moment equating Leone with Léonide Massine. (Henry James said of a puppet show: "What an economy of means! And what an economy of ends!") My point is that since we are obviously going to get a radically limited historical and psychological authenticity from western films, we had better judge them by their trapeze acts.

Critics are anyway in no position to judge the authenticity of a western, as far as I can make out. Reviews of these films, whether written in Paris, London, or New York, are at times equally comical, perhaps especially those authored by women. Shall we squarely face it? The western is a stag's vice, and even female reviewers who wear sensible shoes sound awkward when they are trying to say something admiring about Robert Ryan or a stampede of longhorns. When they're being intentionally funny, they're welcome. (One of the funniest disparagements I've read was that of Isobel Quigley, in *The Spectator,* on that unspeakable western made by Marlon Brando—on the wilds of the Carmel golf course, I would say!) Elsewhere, however, they follow the sociological guidance of their male colleagues. In New York you have perhaps a score, can I say, of "influential" movie critics, who are bounded geographically and in social attitude by Times Square, the Village, Madison Avenue, and the MMA. They wouldn't know an Apache from a Snake, or a Two Grey Hills from a hole in the ground (maybe—if they saw them both together). In lieu of lore they prefer theme; hence, they are impressed by trash like that Yul Brynner film (forgotten the title) in which he played a quadroon in Arizona and there was a lot of feathers about miscegenation (which is of course never consummated) and the usual drivel about the Spanish "culture" in the Southwest (there was little enough of that!) —while they pass up *Will Penny,* an unassuming film which had the real occupation flavor in its talk and in which the cowboys were dressed right for the year and the time of the year and there was, for once, a female you might want to be introduced to (Joan Hackett) and scenery which hadn't been used a hundred times by John Ford or the Oak Creek Canyon unit (it was high Sierra country, around Mono—my guess). No, it wasn't an "important" movie: didn't face the community with the individual or recommend itself to the Bureau of Ethnology, but it smelled of wet rawhide and smoked blankets and snow coming, and the men downed their whiskey with the right grimace, and the melodrama didn't get too much in the way of the common sense.

If most Hollywood scenarists were not such mediocrities, I would feel sorry for them when they face the problem of preparing a film about Indians. No matter what they do, they're going to be wrong with someone writing a review in Manhattan or San Francisco. If a movie depicts bad Indians, then the script-writer or director or both are allegedly exploiting a scapegoat; if it interprets the Indian as noble, it is repeating a cliché from Longfellow. In historical fact, of course, you can find evidence to suit any generalization you choose to illustrate. Geronimo and his skeleton crew, fewer than a score if I remember, and squaws among them, cunningly ran rings around the U.S. Cavalry in the West for months. But when this same brave Geronimo was first in solitary hiding, he killed defenseless men who had known and befriended him for years. In one and the same tribe—Omahas, for example—you could find an Indian who would make a present of his adulterous wife to the man she preferred, without rancor and with a dowry—another who would cut off the erring woman's nose or peg her out on the plain for thirty braves to enjoy. I know all about the "century of dishonor" and the definitive massacre of the Sioux at Wounded Knee. The Sioux have long been a metaphor of stoicism, endurance, mystic powers, and artistic skill (in the decoration of buffalo-hide shields and the like); yet Rufus Sage, one of the most knowledgeable of Western chroniclers, reminds us that their name came from a French-Canadian corruption of a word for *drunken* and that their own name for themselves was Lacota, or Cut-Throats! "The members of this nation," he wrote, in 1859, "so far as my observations extend, are a cowardly, treacherous, thieving set, taken as a body—and are well deserving the appellation of mean and contemptible. . . ."

On this subject, I think Elliot Silverstein should be congratulated for making a film (*A Man Called Horse*) in which he doesn't hesitate to portray as less than totally sympathetic a tribe of the Sioux. The opening of the adventure was so ludicrous I had no hopes (an experienced hunter, declaring he was bored, wearing a scarlet bathrobe in hostile-Indian territory and going for a swim without posting a guard!), but as the film goes on to treat his capture, his abasement, and his grueling initiation into the caste of Sioux warrior it develops an atmosphere of believable physical misery as well as a kind of savage splendor; becomes finally, after all hesitations have been allowed for, a testimony to the grandeur that unwittingly emerges from sheer survival in the harsh tooth of things: weather, war, and famine. The love interest worried me because the actress didn't have a mutton-and-smoke smell—I doubt that any Sioux seedbed would resemble her in any respect—but I was hugely gratified by the fact that the most convincing Indian of this tribe was Judith Anderson. Another aspect of the film's poetry, completely unique, was the abundance of wild life, thematically featured. You can see a hundred westerns in which there is pictured a West totally uninhabited by elk, coyotes, hawks, beavers, meadowlarks, or even jackrabbits!

American film-makers are always on the *verge* of an authentic subject. So far they have never wholly engaged one; the gist gets blurred or corrupted. Of the two most tragic events in American history, the settlement of the West and the Civil War, they have just brushed the first and have never sighted the second. There is always someone announcing that the American movie has come of age. The announcement is always premature. The reason, as I see it, is that the movie is a public art and Americans are not good at public speech. They are always conscious that someone in the audience needs an explanation. This is why the only pure art of importance in America today is poetry, where the artist can talk to himself and his friends; if you overhear him, very well, but you are not his primary object of address.   1967–1970

"A Sad Tale's Best for Winter": On Re-seeing *The Third Man*

"I came to Vienna to work for a friend of mine, but . . . he died."
"Oh, how awkward."
"Is that what you say when a man dies—how awkward?"

Walking home from *The Third Man* on a polar night in Stockholm, with not a *konditori* open that looks cozy enough to brood in, a hard white crust underfoot and everywhere faces as unyielding as the frozen pavements, to a flat in which I shall sit and work out the Christmas–New Year vacancy without, I know from experience, so much as a telephone call unless it's from a "foreigner," I am driven to examine some curious disparities in our conclusions—about a lot of things.

If the late films of Bergman, about which I am now, with as much sympathy as I can summon, writing, are accepted as serious art and Carol Reed's film as "merely" entertainment, there is something amiss with our categories. We can all recite the creed: art is created from the inside, melodrama from the outside; a good plot is a spurious asset (although Aristotle never thought so) ; the aim of the artist is to make the transcendent visible (Karl Jaspers said something like this but so did Redon, for example, which leaves much latitude for construing what is transcendent) ; Bergman has a world-view of his own, his films have a consistent intent; Carol Reed made three or four good films from someone else's stories—*Odd Man Out, The Fallen Idol, The Third Man, An Outcast of the Islands*—then he was finished, he had nothing to express.

Is that what you say when a man dies—how awkward?

The fact remains that, having seen *The Third Man* probably nine times over the years, I am as broken up by it as I was the first time. The deficiencies are simple to note: there's padding in this film and often glibness rather than facility, and there is rather more characterization than character. All the same, it casts a spell—the spell of heartbreak in an hour and a half that enshrines the end of Europe more indelibly than any film I know. It's all so sad and relentless and filled with wonderful oblique shots I always forget about until I see it again, and late-autumn light and glimpses of vernacular architecture I recognize, like the so-called fisherman's church; to the incessant and insolent march of the zither it all rushes by me again and I hope it will end differently but I know it won't. Things didn't.

"I want to get to the bottom of things here, Major."
"Death's at the bottom of things, Martins. Leave death to the experts."

Vienna, partitioned, is Europe. If you don't care about Europe you will hear no reverberations in this film. The people in this movie are caught in the deed; what they are is a consequence of the forces which have moved them—to sin, or to love, or to justice. They share the fate of Europe; they *are* Europe. They were Europe. Europe was yesterday—and I've never seen a Swedish face that looked as if it had shed a tear over the fact. Whenever someone tells me they found convincing the sham war of *The Shame* I remember Wurzburg, a baroque jewel of a town, the like of which never grew on Scandinavian soil, destroyed by Allied bombers (for no strategic reason whatever) in a matter of twenty-two minutes.

"Well, *they* started it, didn't they?"

Yes.

When I lived in Munich I used to eat frequently at the central-station restaurant, offensive to the gourmet within, perhaps, but there I knew I would meet Germans from every part of the country, as well as Austrians. It was an education. I remember a chap, about fifty then, who had been with the *Wehrmacht* on the southern front in Russia; they had been far into the interior. He was still dazed. "What a chance we missed," he told me. "The people *welcomed* us! They believed we were bringing God back to them!"

All the memorable films are ultimately about death. In the Chamber films of Bergman, death is in the head. There is no tragedy because there is no waste. Insofar as his characters are to be interpreted at a naturalistic level, they are given no value by history. Their shadows are short. They have consciousness in a void; since they love nothing, their agony is ersatz. They stand in no meaningful relationship to a cognizable society. Except perhaps for *Winter Light,* there is no single scene in a latter-day Bergman film as soaked in personal loss, against a juggernaut background, as the brief interchange between Holly Martins and Anna, the actress, in her one-room flat. Every time I see the film I mean to analyze the art of that scene but it always eludes me; I'm *in* it before I can think about it, then it's all over. There's little enough art in it, no doubt, it's a Graham Greene trick: everything is said you need to know with short-cut dialogue and in an incredibly few shots. You learn exactly what the worthless Harry Lime has meant to both of them, a big brother to Holly and everything there was to her. You see right off the hopelessness of Martins' infatuation with Anna; she talks to him because he was a friend of Lime and this is the suicide hour when Harry used to visit her. She wants to keep the wound open; to feel a wound is at least to be alive.

Holly Martins, the nice American, is a tourist, no more equipped to understand Anna than Europe, in ruins around him, or Lime, when he finds out how rotten a man can be. The sequel is inevitable: when he is finally convinced that his "third man" was a monster of unimaginable dimension, he agrees to the sticky bargain: trap Lime in order to save Anna from the Cossacks. Here is a stereotype of the postwar deal in Europe: the righteous Anglo-American tribunal imposing justice as if it could ever vindicate Europe or save it from its own infection. Anna couldn't be saved. Holly could help her survive unmolested, which he does, but she's beyond saving. Holly has the naive conviction that if she understood what a rotter Lime is she would unhesitatingly denounce him. A woman's logic is not a man's. And at the suicide hour there were so many rotters to denounce; sometimes they were all the family one had. So after a photogenic chase through the sewers, Holly kills Lime, after his nod of consent, and expects Anna to fall into his arms? She walks on by, as all those bloody leaves fall, and that, too, is an image that will remain. The nice American helps clean up the aftermath and Europe leaves him standing there with his packed suitcase and walks on past in its raincoat.

Call it *kitsch*, if you want to get out from under. It's *about something*. What are most Swedish films about? The unutterable boredom of being outside history. *Menschen ohne Profil*, my Austrian friend calls them. But the women photograph beautifully and Americans just adore them. I told an editor that Jorn Donner's films were not worth reviewing, and he wrote back with a gee-whiz: "He must have *something* if he's married to Harriet Andersson!"

He has something. He has Harriet Andersson.

The sentimental Martins is perhaps the least durable character as you revisit *The Third Man,* because Joseph Cotten was a lazy actor. When he liked a part he tried hard; when he didn't, he sulked his way. And I can certainly think of actresses who would have been more Viennese than Alida Valli—even non-Viennese actresses. It's no matter, finally; there is enough heart and visual force in the situation to deceive us about details; the Viennese and Hungarian actors were vile with immense charm, Trevor Howard in his duffel coat was a living cartouche of the British Zone, and Orson Welles as Harry Lime was so authoritative that many people I know are under the impression to this day that he made the film. (He *did* contribute the now well-worn line about the Swiss cuckoo clock.)

They made a wonderful movie, greater than they thought, Greene and Reed—and it was the fruit of both. "Carol Reed and I worked closely together," Greene has written, "covering so many feet of carpet a day, acting scenes at each other. No third ever joined our conferences: so much value lies in the clear cut-and-thrust of argument between two people." They were beneficiaries of an enthralled moment, one is led to believe. When Europe stood aghast at what it had done to itself, that was the hour to make a film on the subject. Later, it was too late without overreaching. I think the only other film that expresses a phase of the tragedy as deeply is *The True End of the Great War* (Kawalerowicz) but it's so unbearable one can't see it twice. Many I know couldn't sit it once. Yet neither Reed nor Greene believed he was making a tragedy. Greene, in fact, wanted to end the film with American Gets Girl; he felt his story was too light to carry an "unhappy ending." This was his only serious dispute with Reed, who, as he concedes, "has been proved triumphantly right." Reed thought that any other ending than the one we see would have been cynical, following Lime's death. And Greene concludes:

> I admit I was only half-convinced: I was afraid few people would wait in their seats during the girl's long walk from the graveside and that they would leave the cinema under the impression of an ending as conventional as mine and more drawn-out. I had not given enough consideration to the mastery of Reed's direction and, at that stage, of course, we neither of us could have anticipated Reed's brilliant discovery of Mr. Karas, the zither player. (*New York Times*, March 19, 1950.)

Out of this nettle, danger, they plucked "entertainment." They should see their own film, twenty years after, on a frigid night in Sweden.

Socialism is where Europe goes when it dies.   1969

The Brave American

Orson Welles is my favorite buccaneer. He has accepted the conditions of exile and the big squeeze. Not all the conditions: within these jaws he plays the game. Forever making errors of judgment, forever at the mercy of wolverines who make art untouchable by the stench they leave on it, he never wholly surrenders. He does not shrug, "All right, if that's the only way to survive, I'll be a complete louse." He is not a louse. He survives—somehow. He pays to make good movies (*he* thinks they're good) by acting in bad ones (not always as bad as he thinks they are, sometimes better than some of his own!).

Stanley Kauffmann has written of Welles, and I have quoted him before, that he has "no relation with his world of which his films are an expression. He is a scene and sequence maker, not a film-maker." As a Judgment Day verdict this is probably defensible, but I should personally recommend clemency. I believe that Welles's total contribution (to our enjoyment—hang the history of the medium!) is richer than the sum of its parts. His films are sometimes bad, but they are always interesting. Well, nearly always: I think of *Macbeth* and I groan. Welles told Francis Koval in an interview (*Sight and Sound,* December 1950) that nobody had judged the film on its own grounds; it was made in twenty-three days on a low budget. Mr. Koval didn't think quickly enough to reply (or perhaps he was too polite) : "Mr. Welles, if you're foolish enough to attempt a movie in twenty-three days of shooting you should be prepared to take the critical consequences." And what I like about Welles is that he would have answered Koval, if I'm not mistaken, by rumbling, "Yes, you're right. I should."

He's one of the few directors who doesn't pull punches when he's interviewed. He says what he believes, without pomposity, without hanging back; in fact he's positively, if genially, high-handed, and I find that a relief from the kind of snow job that most of these characters try to purvey. If Welles doesn't often enough succeed in doing the real thing, judged by our loftiest standards, he knows the real thing when he sees it. (Among film-makers, he's one of the few who realizes that De Sica has a kind of nobility.) One curious strategy he employs: he pretends to believe that critics are highbrows because they're impressed by visual brilliance to the exclusion of inner content. I'm sure he means what he's saying, but in reviewable fact his own films are distinguished by their great creative invention, infrequently wed to any fundamental definition of man. As for that "highbrow" talk, I'm sure he can't consider himself a lowbrow! I remember hearing him on a radio symposium about twenty years ago, with a panel of university professors. He was the only one present who said anything coherent. I think the world is in greater need of honest men than of perfect film-makers.

Pardonably, I hope, I feel as if I had a personal investment in this man. My memory goes back to his importunate and dazzling beginnings. I don't believe it now, but I saw him play Mercutio on the stage (to the Romeo and Juliet of Basil Rathbone and Katharine Cornell) when he was seventeen. He *couldn't* have been as good as I thought he was because I wasn't much older myself, and who at that age has judgment? Talent, perhaps; judgment, no.

Nor shall I ever forget his eruption into radio drama with his Mercury Theatre in the mid-thirties. "You want to know how to make radio theater exciting? I'll show you. Move over." Nobody before then, save perhaps a few rare individuals with the Columbia Workshop of the Air, had had such a dynamic conception of what you could do with the medium in terms of dialogue-and-sound montage. To this day it's a seldom occasion to hear anything as shaped to the ear (which in turn, of course, invokes the eye) as Welles's adaptations and his direction of them in those depression days. *The War of the Worlds* is a part of history; I'll tire nobody by repeating that story, but I remember (just!) other examples of his narrative virtuosity: *A Farewell to Arms, Heart of Darkness, The Count of Monte Cristo.* I don't know how he managed to tell the latter effectively in one hour, but he did so: that's why he's called Orson Welles. About seven minutes before the close-off, Edmond Dantès had yet to kill his third victim and explain himself to Mercedes-was-it? Welles got him killed and the *envoi* tucked in before having to give way to the signature, Tchaikowsky's *Piano Concerto No. 1.* I never hear the opening chords of that first movement without expecting them to fade as the fudgy voice rides over, like oil on water, with oh-such-diffident authority, "Good evening, ladies and gentlemen, this is Orson Welles"—as who should say, "superfluous as it is to remind you."

A great showman. Is he a great movie-maker? Yes, he's a great movie-maker. Perhaps he has never made a great movie, like Ophuls. And as with Ophuls, it doesn't matter. These men have style. They have a *way* of doing something filmic that makes it seem quite as enriching as anything else we might define as more "profound" or, in the contemporary sense, "relevant." Because thou art virtuous, shall there be no more cakes and ale? Ophuls, by the way, paid Welles the greatest of compliments by stealing his effects (he who had no need of borrowings from anyone!) for the film *Caught* (1949). The whole ambience of the Ohlrig mansion was that of Kane's Xanadu, even to the camera perspectives that exaggerated the longitude of a billiard table, the contours of a sculpture, or the cavity of a fireplace; *and* the overlapping, fervent conversations in which two people start to say something at the same time, then each stops, waits for the other, and once again re-launches his part of the dialogue simultaneously with the antagonist. Welles did that, with a *loud whisper* treatment, on the staircase in *The Magnificent Ambersons* (1942), and I don't think anyone had done it before.

The *Ambersons* film shows Welles at his most resourceful and is a fair indication of his most nagging problem: the style is precariously in excess of the subject and milieu. The doings in that family mansion are all terribly portentous and electrifying, filled with crystal-clear projections of figures in rear distance (process devised by Gregg Toland) and "from-under" shots to enhance interest; these imply an ominous aspect in figures who are seldom ominous. All very clever and articulate but not, squarely speaking, the world of Booth Tarkington. Yet seeing the film today, one's reservations from this standpoint are quickly overcome by admiration for Welles's unfailing purity of invention. Every shot and sequence is rewarding to those with a seasoned response to the audacity with which a film story can be told: the intersections of the off-screen narrative with the dialogue, the sharp economy with which the family crises are dramatized, with a critical eye to their gravity and to their unwitting absurdity, the loving accuracy with which a period custom, prejudice, or décor is without redundancy expressed. And among memorably weird performances, provoking laughter and pain in awkward partnership, that of Agnes Moorhead as the spinster buried alive by the Ambersonian ethos is surely in the foreground of our recall. If nothing else, *The Magnificent Ambersons* is a laudable contribution to Americana, affectionate and shrewd. Nevertheless, the principal tendency of the film, when elsewhere underlined, was to become the primary Welles hazard: in most of his efforts there is, if I may coin a word, a *baroquity* in the service of entertainment which can't rise to the pitch of the informing manner. Which may be why Welles periodically returns to Shakespeare: it's the adequate vehicle for his art of the grandiose.

To see *Citizen Kane* today—*the* film, I suppose, synonymous with Welles for most people—is to realize what a brilliant sorcerer he was, how much he lifted from precedent film-making and made his own (and how much others then lifted from him and simply made it Hollywood). No film with such a reputation could stand up to critical scrutiny without showing its seams. There *are* scenes-for-padding in this film; they are salient now as they were not when we were freshly mesmerized by the virtuoso sequences that preceded and followed: the singing lessons hammered into Kane's talent-less wife; her plaintive appeal, "What do you *do* when you go out there every night with the audience *hating* you?" and his growl—"You fight 'em"; and the domestic life of Mr. and Mrs. Kane fraying out inexorably, comprised in about three and a half minutes of film— the breakfast table over the years as communication dries up—each scene in the sequence cut in devaluating proportion, from eight frames to four and finally two. How many film-makers in 1941 could do that?

One of my favorite lines is from this film. When Kane picks up his future wife on the street corner (by offering to share his taxi), he says: "My name's Kane. I own a coupla newspapers. What do *you* do?"

The chilliest critical objections to *Citizen Kane* came from the social pragmatists. To them the film was irrelevant because it didn't document the consequences of Kane's career. Its indictment of one of the colossal Borgias of capitalist-monopoly enterprise was confined to the private life of the man himself and was conspicuously lacking in the evidential complexity of his empire, the prodigality of his corruption, his political and financial chicanery, the slaughtered reputations, and the rest. In short, no teeming social texture. The film for them took place in a baroque vacuum, sealed off from the multitudinous damage wrought by the ego which was being, not without a wry touch of sympathy, explored.

There is no argument because the questions were raised in another room. If theirs is the *only* way of making a film on such a subject, it is pointless to tell them this was the film Welles made, this was the angle that interested him, these were the limits he proposed, this is what he could handle. If they wanted the other treatment they could have read Theodore Dreiser—or Ferdinand Lundberg. If Welles had tried to do what some thought he should have done, after he had done what he did do in order to provide them with an objection—well, we wouldn't have had *Citizen Kane*. I don't know what we would have had. We might not have had Citizen Welles, making movies away from home.

The best comment on the film's leading gimmick came from an Irish friend of mine. "What would have become of the movie if that sled had been called *Fearless Flyer?*"

As late as the mid-fifties, Welles claimed that he had never made another film with complete independence before *Othello*. That independence was hard won. His backer pulled out and he paid for the film, which he made in Morocco, with his savings from sundry parts he had played in blockbusters. I am heartened to learn this because I have always thought that *Othello* was his most fully personal achievement after *The Magnificent Ambersons;* if more Welles than Shakespeare, that's more all right with me than it was with Eric Bentley when he first reviewed the film, and many other critics more conservative than Bentley. I think perhaps we are all readier today to allow (up to a point) a liberal measure of freedom to Shakespeare-in-the-movies. You simply can't have the text intact and have creative cinema. You can have a good photographed play, like the excellent *Othello* of Olivier recently post-prepared for the television. But something has to go when you're movie-making; that something is most of the lines. Strangely enough, the poetry is not thereby lost. (Never have I seen a spoken *Romeo and Juliet* as fabulous as the danced version of Russian ballet.) The poetry, if we mean the words, is still there; there in the back of our heads.

The paragraphs immediately following are from my notes, taken in 1954, I believe:

> In Welles's *Othello* you can't hear half the lines which *are* retained; the company is unsuccessfully trying to ape the throwaway skill of their director. It doesn't much matter. Every few minutes, as if sighting treasures rising to the surface from a sunken galleon, you hear something musically familiar go by. "Happiness to their sheets!" . . . "Lying with her—*on* her?" "What you will." . . . "Are you hurt?" "Aye, past all surgery." . . . "Othello's occupation's gone!" (This followed by the shot of a sail being lowered.) The great sense of *space* Welles has! No director is memorable without this sense. As they debate the actions of Cassio, Othello and Iago pace in a forever tracking-shot on the vast topside of that Moroccan castle. When at last, clutching suspicion as he might an unsheathed knife, Othello cries out, "But, oh, the pity, the pity of it, Iago!" his face is suddenly removed from moment and place, tossed against an emptiness of sky. As he walks swiftly away from Iago, then collapses, towers careen and a woman's laugh punctuates the screaming of the gulls. His encroaching suspicions are otherwise pictured in shadowed corridors, in trenches between adobe walls, or in the oubliette of a staircase well; he spies on Desdemona from behind grillwork or across a dry moat: gusts of jealousy are paralleled by billowing cloaks, veering birds, and flapping sails.
>
> I don't remember who, before Lytton Strachey, pointed out that Iago is a villain without an adequately expressed motive. But homosexual spite takes care of that motive completely, especially it explains his ruthless treatment of Emilia. In any case, the condition is explicit here and it works. One of the first shots in the film enforces it (we view the end of the tragedy at the beginning) —Iago, suspended in a basket, staring with mingled love and terror at the body of Othello as it is carried along the battlements. The actor, McLiammoir, is too mannered for my taste, but I think Welles's interpretation of Iago is a sound one.

Sergei Yutkevich tried to do an *Othello* as vivid as Welles's, but despite the added feature of color, his film is dead. Every effect is patently calculated: the shot is set up, the actor is moved into it, and every symbol clangs like a bell. In the Welles film we are always in the moving thick, conveyed either by the traveling shot or the quick, quick cut: we see objects and events when the actor glimpses them, not before (like very early Hitchcock) and some actions we see only as a brilliant blur—like the attack on Cassio. The murder of Desdemona is great. Othello's black head floats as if bodiless in a greater darkness; he moves into the sparse light cast by the candle, asks in an abrupt, casual, toneless voice, "Have you prayed tonight, Desdemona?" Then he grinds out the candlelight with the flat of his hand and strangles her with a gauzy coverlet, through which you see the contours of her face as you would on a death mask.

Welles didn't think too highly of his own performance, and while I won't rush to confirm his modesty I'll say that, if deficient in patience and depth, I never saw it conclusively excelled until a few years ago, by Laurence Olivier's incredible impersonation of the Moor with a West Indian accent. But the assignments were far different, were they not? Welles was not attempting to particularize the Shakespearean role in all its nuances; he was trying to generalize it for purposes of film. He caught its essence, and substantially he caught the essence of the play: the fruits of vanity, passion, and mindless jealousy; the inadmissible suspicion working like malaria in the bloodstream; the irreversible surrender—then calamity alone, and Iago nursing his wound (both his wounds) like a caged vulture. And all this Welles took into the open air, into a world of surf and seabirds and scalding sunlight. If not the most profound filming of Shakespeare to date—I'd reserve that concession for Kozintsev's *Hamlet*—it is, I think, the most inventive English-language Shakespeare of the cinema. *Chimes at Midnight* is more moving in some ways (Falstaff played by Welles as if his heart had already been broken), but its inspirations were less breathtaking and there are too many camp actors cluttering the battlegrounds.

For my sorrow, Welles's most brilliant failure was *The Stranger* (1946). In it he played a ghoul who had been an executioner at a Nazi concentration camp. Escaping from Germany, he had incredibly turned up as a teacher, in, of all places, a New England preparatory school for boys. His identity is not suspected and he's living the safe life, managing to choke down the quotes from Nietzsche that rise to his lips whenever the defeated Reich is impugned. His pedagogic idyll is shattered when a demented associate from his oven days arrives on the scene; this loony has seen the light of day, acquired a species of religion, and has looked up his old friend so that together they can repent and pay the penalty for their crimes. There is of course no solution to this contretemps except to murder the wide-eyed nuisance. Which Welles does; he strangles him in the woods and buries him under a carpet of autumn leaves. In one of the most striking film moments Welles ever devised, there is a beautiful sequence of inter-cutting here: between a troop of boys on a paper chase through the woods—refracted sunlight making church aisles of the maples, down which the boys leap, all eagerness and bright health—and the murderer skulking in the hollow, spreading leaves over the last smell of his past. Why—how—Welles managed to end such an adroit story, with its invocative geography (autumn in New England has never on the screen been so crisp to the touch), by means of a gimmick in the worst Hitchcock taste will be the first question I shall want answered if we ever meet.

Great aspirations constantly imperiled or vitiated by the melodramatic ruse—the wrong torso in the right museum. This is the perennial Welles predicament. Are these solecisms forced on him? I don't know; I'd like to give him the benefit of the doubt. In *Lady from Shanghai,* where he assembled a plausible colony of evil lotus-eaters off the coast of Acapulco, did he have to wind things up in a hall of distorting mirrors in a San Francisco amusement park? Did he *have* to cast Anthony Perkins as Joseph K. in *The Trial?* I mean . . . after all! And having succumbed to the vogue of the sex movie (*An Immortal Story*)—in his own handsome and meditative way, to be sure—was it necessary to employ a male who was so obviously immune to seduction by any Moreaus whatever?

Even so, he's Orson Welles. A brave American. He lives uprooted; he works in no social context of his own. And in what social context would he work if he were making films in the United States? The chances are that he never gets financed for his most fruitful ideas. Freer than he would be in Hollywood, he's nonetheless dependent on the whims of the wealthier—the stealthier. The miracle is that he gets any films made at all. He stands for something—hard to define, perhaps, but when you say "Orson Welles" people know what you mean. I've noticed they always smile. His films surprise by a fine excess (to put it mildly); there's usually a current of energy running through them, and a feeling of discovery, sometimes hazily resolved. Don't we still always expect something from a new Welles movie? And don't we usually get something? Not a solemn perfection; sometimes an outrageous evasion; often an honorable failure. And he does have a preferred subject which provides at least half his films with a perceptible unity: the unheroic titan, sometimes evil, sometimes comic, sometimes just big, who is never as formidable as he sees himself—the pathos of deflation.

Famous without being popular, Welles doesn't attract crowds, bless him. There is no Welles cult. That's something he has to be grateful for; not even Americans confuse him, as they do Bergman, with the Saviour. He is safe from endorsement by the Now Chows, the Festival Cats, the New Leftovers, and the unchuckling postgraduates who soberly sniff in the tracks of Susan Sontag.

"The waste remains, the waste remains and kills." If he knows the Empson refrain he must appreciate it, but I don't see him crying over it. He shares the fool belief of all those who won't say yes: tomorrow is Redemption Day. In that wise story of Anatole France, *Le Jongleur de Notre Dame,* the juggler who had no suitably reverent offering performed a few expert acts before the high altar. Our Lady found them acceptable. Why should we be less generous?

1969

Index

Abramson, Hans, 204, 295
Academy of Motion Picture Arts and
    Sciences, 349
ACCATONE, 235
Accent, vii
ACCIDENT, 14, 312ff., , 317
Ackland, Rodney, xi, 29
ADALEN, 351–352
Ådams, Henry, 385
Addams, Charles, 213, 393
Aeschylus, 205, 207
Aguayo, Jose F., 163
Agee, James, 14
AGOSTINO, 232
Aimée, Anouk, 306
Akutagawa, R., 53, 102n.
ALEXANDER NEVSKY, 86, 153
ALFIE, 300
Allegret, Yves, 80
Allen, J. H., 84
ALPHAVILLE, 282, 324ff.
ALTE UND DER JUNGE KÖNIG, DER, 143, 179
Alvarez, A., 381–382 quoted
AMALIE, 255
American Federation of Arts, 68n.
AM GÄLGEN HANGT DER LIEBE, 142
AMICHE, LE, 278
Amiel, Frederic, 241
AMORE, 145
AMOURIST, THE, 311
Andersen, Hans C., 251
Anderson, David, 118
Anderson, Judith, 399
Anderson, Lindsay, 350–351
Andersson, Bibi, 198, 203
Andersson, Harriet, 83, 200, 201, 403
Andrade, J. P. de, 363
ANGELS OVER BROADWAY, 13
Anger, Kenneth, 323
ANGES DU PÉCHÉ, LES, 106

ANGRY SILENCE, THE, 140
AN IMMORTAL STORY, 412
ANITA G. (*Yesterday Girl*), 307
Anna Karenina, 330
Antioch Review, 53n.
Antonioni, Michelangelo, 4, 14, 126n.,
    137ff., 184, 188, 193ff., 198, 199, 210,
    230–232, 238, 274, 276, 278, 282, 283,
    288, 300, 313, 323, 327, 329, 362, 385,
    389
Architecture of Humanism, The, 75
Arnaud, Georges, 78n.
ARNE'S TREASURE, SIR, 154
Arnold, Matthew, 294, 296
AROUND THE WORLD IN NINETY NIGHTS,
    230
Art Film Publications, vii
Arts, magazine, vii, 72; Year Book,
    viii, 122n.
ASCENSEUR À L' ÉCHAFAUD. *See* Frantic.
Astruc, Alexandre, 10
ATLANTIS, 21
Auden, W. H., 104 quoted, 139, 385
AU HASARD, BALTHAZAR, 335
AVEC DES SI, 258, 307

Baalsrud, Jan, 104ff.
Bach, J. S., 240ff., 380, 396
Bacon, Francis, 326
BAD DAY AT BLACK ROCK, 9, 92
Baker, Carroll, 169
Baker, Stanley, 313
Ballets Suédois, Les, 186
BANDA CASAROLI, LA, 234
BANDE À PART, 281
BANDIT, THE (*O Cangaceiro*), 12, 83ff.,
    362
BANDITS OF ORGOSOLO, THE, 4, 209, 239,
    274
Baratier, Jacques, 221

BARBARIAN IN ASIA, A, 56
Bardem, Juan Antonio, 225
Bardot, Brigitte, 10
Barreto, Lima, 85
Barry, Iris, 48
Bate, Anthony, 355
Bates, Alan, 168, 319
Battcock, Gregory, 322ff.
Battestin, M. C., 329
BATTLE OF CULLODEN, THE, 340, 345
BATTLE OF SAN PIETRO, THE, 13
Baumbach, Jonathan, 329
Baumeister, Willi, 72
Bazin, Herve, 81
BBC, 300, 341, 354
BEAST WITH FIVE FINGERS, THE, 380
Beatty, Warren, 391
BEAUTY AND THE BEAST, 20, 99, 191, 254
Becker, Jacques, 145ff., 255, 360
Beckett, Samuel, 186, 211
Belasco, David, 18, 91
Bel Geddes, Barbara, 26
BELL' ANTONIO, IL, 131ff., 135, 173, 232, 233
BELLE DE JOUR, 310ff.
Bellero, Carlo, 237
BELLE VIE, LA, 221
Belmondo, Jean-Paul, 135
Benedetti, Nelly, 262
BENJAMIN, 335ff.
Benôit-Lévy, 180
Bentley, Eric, 410
Berggren, Thommy, 308, 336
Bergman, Ingmar, ix, 7, 82, 119, 123, 126n., 142, 160, 168, 196ff., 210, 214ff., 274, 276, 282, 284ff., 295, 296ff., 305, 327, 333, 335, 344, 362, 379, 384ff., 400ff., 402
Bergman, Lillevi, 200
Berkovic, Zvanimir, 339
Berlanga, Luis, 226
BERLIN, 143
Berliner Ensemble, 110
Berlin International Film Festival, 282, 331n., 361
Bernanos, Georges, 334
Berto, Giuseppe, 61
BEZHIN MEADOW, 152ff.
BICYCLE THIEF, THE, 4, 210
BIDONE, IL (*The Swindler*), 60, 99
Bierce, Ambrose, 221, 363
Bierstadt, Albert, 90
BILLY LIAR, 9, 224
Bingham, George Caleb, 90
BIRTH OF A NATION, THE, 15, 19
Bischof, Werner, 49
BITTER RICE, 4, 61

Bitzer, William, 147
Björck, Staffan, 154
Bjornstrand, Gunnar, 216
Black, Noel, 393
BLACKBOARD JUNGLE, THE, 332
BLACK GOD, WHITE DEVIL, 12, 361
BLACKMAIL, 179
Blackmur, R. P., 347 quoted
Blake, Robert, 390
BLISS ON EARTH, 102
Blom, August, 21
Blom, Frederik, 216
BLONDE VENUS, 179
BLOOD OF A POET, 145
BLOW-UP, 300
BLUE ANGEL, THE, 9, 177ff.
BLUE DAHLIA, THE, 13
Bogarde, Dirk, 312, 313
Bogart, Humphrey, 280, 328
Bois, Kurt, 26
Bolen, Francis, 70
Bolero, 53
Boleslawski, Richard, 91
Bolitho, William, 259
Bolognini, Mauro, 131ff., 172, 232
Bolt, Robert, 317
Bonnefoy, Yves, 72, 73, 74
Boone, Richard, 397
BONNIE AND CLYDE, 13, 389, 391–392, 393
Bonne, Richard, 397
Bosch, Hieronymus, 74
Bosio, Gianfranco de, 220n.
Bouchard, Thomas, 70
Bourguignon, Serge, 300
Bouts, Dirk, 74
BOY IN THE TREE, THE, 252
Boys, Arthur, 29
Bracelli, 186n.
Bradbury, Ray, 293
Brando, Marlon, 397
Braque, Georges, 20
Brass, Tinto, 221
Brasseur, Pierre, 133
Brault, Michel, 264
Braunberger, Pierre, 77, 79ff., 80n., 281
BRAVE SLEEP WELL, THE, 286
BREAKUP (*Uppbrott*), 246
BREATHLESS, 144, 145, 255, 280
Brecht, Bertolt, 110
Brel, Jacques, 333
Bresson, Robert, 10, 106ff., 211ff., 255, 334ff., 363, 378
Breton, André, 194
BRIDE WORE BLACK, THE, 338
BRIDGE, THE, 119, 142
Bridges, Alan, 355
BRIG, THE, 323

Briot, René, 106
Broca, Philippe de, 254
Bronson, Charles, 397
Bronte, Emily, 8
Brooks, Richard, 389–390
Brown, Pamela, 74
BROWNING VERSION, THE, 9
Brueghel, Pieter, 47, 71
Brunius, Jacques, 192, 193n.
Brynner, Yul, 397
Buck, David, 355
BULLFIGHT, 77, 79ff.
BULLITT, 392
Bunin, Ivan, 158
Bunraku theatre, 57
Buñuel, Luis, 11, 80n., 161ff., 209, 256n., 275, 276, 281, 288–289, 295, 310ff., 377–386
BUTCH CASSIDY AND THE SUNDANCE KID, 394ff.

CABIRIA, 17
Cacoyannis, Michael, 124–125, 205–207, 274, 275, 276
Cahiers du Cinéma, 189, 362, 378
Cannes International Film Festival, 162, 236, 260, 282, 300, 308, 327n., 349, 351
Cantor, Eddie, 391
CAPO IL MONDO, 221
Capote, Truman, 54, 389–390
CARABINIERS, LES, 281
Card, James G., 20–21
Cardinale, Claudia, 135, 173
Carné, Marcel, 22–23, 170
CARNIVAL IN FLANDERS, 20
Carrez, Florence, 212
Carrière, Mattieu, 301
Carroll, Lewis, 251, 329, 377 quoted
Carruthers, Ben, 282
Cartier, Jacques, 264
Cartier-Bresson, H., 49, 334–335
CASE, THE, 311
CASQUE D'OR, 83, 145
Cassavetes, John, 145
Catseli, Aleka, 213
CAUGHT, 26, 407
Cavalcanti, Guido, 20, 80n.
Cayatte, André, 80, 112, 257, 333ff., 379, 390
Cézanne, 142
CELA S'APPELLE L'AURORE, 384, 385
Chabrol, Claude, 253 quoted, 255, 274, 275, 281, 330
Chaconne, 380
CHANS (*Chance*), 199
Chaplin, Charles, 66n., 386

Chappell, Fred, 329–330
CHARLEY, 348–349
Chartres, 386
CHARULATA, 11
Cheka, 152
Chekhov, 6, 9, 123, 356
Chiaki, Minoru, 120
Chiarini, Luigi, 218
CHIEN ANDALOU, UN, 381
CHIENNE, LA, 80n.
CHILDREN ARE WATCHING, THE, 4
CHILDREN OF PARADISE (*Les Enfants du Paradis*), 22–23
CHIMES AT MIDNIGHT, 411
Chirico, Giorgio de, 184ff.
Chopin, Frédéric, 256
Christie, Julie, 294, 319
CHRISTMAS MORN, 248–249
Churchill, Sir Winston, 315
CHUSHINGURA, 102
Cinema, The, 34
Cinema Eye, Cinema Ear, 378
Cinema 16, 322
Cintron, Conchita, 79
CIOCIARIA, LA (*Two Women*), 127ff., 134
CITIZEN KANE, 408–409
CITY LIGHTS, 289
Clair, René, 20, 80, 179
Clark, Sir Kenneth, 144
Clarke, Shirley, 221
Clemenceau, Georges, 336
Clément, René, 30–31, 133, 180
Clementi, Muzio, x
Clementi, Pierre, 336
CLEO, 221, 260
Cocteau, Jean, 20, 61n., 99, 190, 191, 254, 281, 295, 323
COEUR GROS COMME ÇA, UN, 210, 221, 274
College Art Association, 68n.
Collinson, Peter, 345ff.
Columbia Workshop of the Air, 407
Comfort, Lance, xi, 9
CONCRETE JUNGLE, THE, 139
CONDAMNÉ À MORT S'EST ÉCHAPPÉ, UN. *See* A Man Escaped.
Connaissance des Arts, 186n.
Conrad, Joseph, 116, 215, 379
Constantine, Eddie, 282
COOL WORLD, THE, 221
Cornell, Katharine, 406
Cotten, Joseph, 27, 403
Count of Monte Cristo, The, 407
Couperin, François, 336
COUSINS, LES, 254
Cousteau, Jacques-Yves, 10, 222, 323
CRAINQUEBILLE, 145

Crawford, Broderick, 99
CRIME WITHOUT PASSION, 13
CRIMINAL, THE, 312
CRISS CROSS, 92
CUBA 58, 269
CUL DE SAC, 307n.
Cuny, Alain, 233
Curie, Eve, 10
Curtiz, Michael, 24

Dagens Nyheter, 156n., 197
Dali, Salvador, 186, 190
DAMES DU BOIS DE BOULOGNE, LES, 106
Damiani, Damiano, 137, 232
D'Annunzio, Gabriele, 17
DARLING, 300, 319
Dassin, Jules, 80, 170, 275
David, Jacques Louis, 152
DAVID AND BATHSHEBA, 20
David Copperfield, 294
Davidson, James F., 53
Death in Venice, 64
Dedalus, Stephen, 330, 346
Defoe, Daniel, 383
Degas, Edgar, 241, 290
Degermark, Pia, 308
Dekeukeleire, Charles, 74
Delannoy, Jean, 180, 257
Delluc, Louis, prize, 260
Delon, Alain, 131
Delvaux, Paul, 186, 188
DeMille, Cecil B., 20
DEMONIO, IL, 225
Demy, Jacques, 10, 254, 260
Deneuve, Catherine, 310, 336
Desailly, Jean, 261
Descartes, René, 10
De Seta, Vittorio, 209, 231, 239, 265, 270, 300
De Sica, Vittorio, 59, 96, 118, 127ff., 131, 172, 231, 336, 406
DESTROYING ANGEL, THE, 295, 382
DEVIL IN THE FLESH, THE, 102
Deville, Michel, 336
DEVIL'S GENERAL, THE, 81
DEVILS OF LOUDUN, THE, 213
DIABOLIQUES, 80
Diaghilev, 186
Dialogue, vii
DIAMONDS OF THE NIGHT, 279
DIARY OF A CHAMBERMAID, 256n.
Dickens, Charles, 372
Dickinson, Thorold, 9, 28–30, 150ff.
Dietrich, Marlene, 179, 183
DILEMMA, 221
Dillard, R. H. W., 329
DISHONORED, 179

DIVIDED WORLD, A, 240ff.
DIVORCE—ITALIAN STYLE, 172ff., 235, 282, 328
Dmytryk, Edward, 92
DR. KILDARE, 330
DR. STRANGELOVE, 295
DOLCE VITA, LA, 4, 5, 127, 132 159, 277, 288
DOLPHINS (I Delfini), 127, 135ff.
Don Giovanni, 100
Doniol-Valcroze, Jacques, 80n., 134, 145, 171, 255
Donner, Jorn, 162, 204, 220n., 283n., 295, 403
Dorleac, Françoise, 262
Dostoievsky, Fyodor, 216, 235, 285, 354ff.
Dover Beach, 294
Dovzhenko, Alexander, 90, 155, 190
Downer, Alan, 329
Drach, Michel, 255
DRAGÉES AU POIVRE, 221
Drda, Jan, 226
Dreiser, Theodore, 409
Dreyer, Carl-Theodore, 44–50, 363
DRUNKEN ANGEL, 58
DUEL IN THE SUN, 20
Dunaway, Faye, 392
DUPED TILL DOOMSDAY, 107ff.
Dupont, E. A., 178
Duvivier, Julien, 180

EARRINGS OF MADAME DE . . ., THE, 80
EASY LIFE, THE (Il Sorpasso), 228
EASY RIDER, 353–354
ECLIPSE, THE (L'Eclisse), 194, 210, 278, 328
Edelfeldt, Albert, 154
Edwall, Alan, 216
EIGHTH DAY OF THE WEEK, 171
Eisenstein, Sergei, 18, 28, 34, 45, 96, 147ff., 380
Ekberg, Anita, 129, 282
Ekborg, Lars, 201
Ekman, Hasse, 141, 204
EL, 382
ELEKTRA, 205ff.
Eliade, Mircea, 298
Eliot, T. S., 160 quoted, 385
ELVIRA MADIGAN, 308ff.
Empson, William, 413
EMPTY CANVAS, THE (La Noia), 232
Encounter, 192, 353n.
END OF ST. PETERSBURG, THE, 211
Engström, Clas, 331
Enrico, Robert, 221
Epstein, Jean, 45, 190, 191

Erasmus Foundation Prize, 291
ESTATE VIOLENTA, 134
Euripides, 207
EVA, 312
Evans, Dame Edith, 29, 321
Evein, Bernard, 260
Evergreen Review, 189
EXTASE, 200
EYE FOR AN EYE, AN, 112ff.

FACE OF ANOTHER, THE, 311
FAHRENHEIT 451, 293ff., 325
Falck, Ake, 204
Falconetti, Maria, 46ff., 48, 50, 125
FALLEN IDOL, THE, 401
FALL OF THE HOUSE OF USHER, THE, 191, 254
Fant, Kenne, 197
Farewell to Arms, A, 407
FAR FROM THE MADDING CROWD, 318ff.
FARRÉBIQUE, 264
Farrow, Mia, 307n.
FATHER SERGIUS, 155
Faulkner, William, 280
Faure, Elie, 54–55 quoted, 95 quoted
FAUST: Gründgens, 318; Murnau, 99
FEARLESS VAMPIRE KILLERS, THE. *See* Your Teeth in My Neck.
Feeling and Form, 119
Fellini, Federico, 5, 59ff., 97, 99, 131, 231, 232, 236, 275, 282, 284ff., 299
FELLINI 8½, 5, 231, 236, 274, 277, 282, 295
Fellini, Ricardo, 220n.
Fertes, Yannis, 207
FEU FOLLET, LE. *See* My Life Is Mine.
Fiedler, Leslie, 329
FIÉVRE MONTE EL PÃO, LA, 384
"Film and the Radical Aspiration," 324
Film Culture, 52, 183, 210
Film Makers on Film Making, 322
Film Quarterly, viii, 131, 270
Film, the Creative Process, 327ff.
Finch, Peter, 319
FIN DE FIESTA, 369ff.
Fini, Leonor, 186
Fitzgerald, F. Scott, 158
Fjelstad, Jack, 105
Flaherty, Robert, 23–25, 34, 243
Flaiano, Ennio, 61, 99, 226
FLAMING CREATURES, 324
FLUTE AND THE ARROW, THE, 250
Fonda, Henry, 397; Peter, 353
Forbes, Bryan, 320
FORBIDDEN CITIES, 230
FORBIDDEN GAMES, 30–31, 133, 180
FORBIDDEN SEX, 230

Ford, Ford M., 313
Ford, John, 88–94, 118, 397
FORTY-SEVEN RONIN, 268
Fossey, Brigette, 31
FOUR DAYS IN NAPLES, 237
FOUR HUNDRED BLOWS, THE (*Les Quatre Cents Coups*), 119, 144, 175, 180–182, 254, 266, 295, 299, 328
Fowle, Chick, 83
Franc, Helen, 71
France, Anatole, 363, 413
Francen, Victor, 380
Franju, Georges, 172, 256n.
FRANTIC, 338
Freud, Sigmund, 33, 38, 194, 206, 248, 284, 310, 327, 390
Friedländer, Max, 273 quoted
Friedrich, Caspar David, 185
From Caligari to Hitler, 178
FUGITIVE, THE, 92
Fuhmann, Franz, 107
Fujiwara, Kamatari, 120
Fulchignoni, Enrico, 71, 72

Gahlin, Salon, 176
Gance, Abel, 41
Gandhi, Mahatma, 48
Garbo, Greta, 98, 147, 156, 273
GARÇON SAUVAGE, LE, 180, 254
Gardiner, Reginald, 260
Garfein, Jack, 169–170
Garland, Beverley, 393
Gassman, Vittorio, 133–134, 229
GATE OF HELL, THE, 52–55, 99, 100
Geduld, Harry, M., 322n., 323
GENERAL LINE, THE, 152
Gentleman from San Francisco, The, 158
George, Heinrich, 179
GEORGY GIRL, 9, 300
Gerardi, Roberto, 134
Germi, Pietro, 127, 136, 172, 282, 371
Geronimo, 398
Gilliatt, Penelope, 203
Girardot, Annie, 131
GIRL AND THE GUNS, THE, 307
GIRL WITH THE HYACINTHS, THE, 141
GLADIATORS, THE, 341ff.
GLINKA, 155
Godard, Jean-Luc, 80n., 212, 227, 234, 255, 259, 275, 280ff., 306, 322n., 324ff., 327n.
Goethe, J. W. von, 318
Gogh, Vincent van, 185, 290
GOLDEN AGE OF PRIMITIVE FLEMISH PAINTERS, THE, 74
Golden Bear, prize, 282, 331n.

GOLDEN DEMON, 102
GOLDEN FERN, THE, 226–227
GOLD OF NAPLES (*Oro di Napoli*) , 97–99
Goldwyn, Samuel, 88
Gonzales, Manolo, 79
Good Soldier, The, 313
GOOD TIMES, WONDERFUL TIMES, 343ff.
GOYA, 71
Goya, Francisco, 97
GRADUATE, THE, 394
GRANDE GUERRA, LA, 133ff., 235
GRAPES OF WRATH, THE, 90, 91, 92
GREAT ADVENTURE, THE, 52, 248ff.
Great Gatsby, The, 157–158
Great River, 166
Greene, Graham, 28, 92, 335, 402ff.
Greenfeld, Howard, 286n., 290
Gregoretti, Ugo, 234–235
Grierson, John, 139
Griffith, D. W., 15–21, 34, 91, 147, 381
Grohmann, Will, 72
Gruault, Jean, 175
Gründgens, Gustav, 318
Grünewald, Mattias, 73
GRYNING (*Dawn*) , 248
Guinness, Alec, 70, 351

Haas, Ernst, 49, 50
Hackett, Joan, 397
Haesaerts, Paul, 73, 74, 75, 76
HAMLET, 9, 58n., 171, 411
Hamsun, Knut, 202ff.
Handel, 163
HAND IN THE TRAP, 372
HANDS ON THE CITY, 220, 234, 236
HAPPINESS (*Le Bonheur*) , 309
Hardison, O. B., 330
Hardy, Thomas, 8, 16, 90, 381ff.
HARP OF BURMA, 103
Harrison, Edward, 52
HARSH AWAKENINGS, 369–372
Harte, Bret, 388
Hartmann, Karl R. E. von, 248n.
Hasegawa, Kazuo, 55
Hatch, Robert, 77ff.
Hawks, Howard, 93
HÄXAN (*The Witch*) , 213
HEAD AGAINST THE WALL, 81
Heart of Darkness, 407
Hecht, Ben, 13
Heller, Erich, 174
Heller, Otto, 29
HELL IS A CITY, 139
Hellström, Gunnar, 199–200
Hemming, David, 345
Hendin, Herbert, 7, 287n., 291
Hendricks, G., 53

Henning-Jensen, B., 202
Henreid, Paul, 350
HENRY V, 58n.
HENRY VIII, 101
Henze, Hans Werner, 302
HERE IS YOUR LIFE, 8, 298ff., 331n.
HIDDEN FORTRESS, THE, 115–121
HIGH AND LOW, 223, 285
HIGH FIDELITY, 235
HIGH NOON, 101
HIRED KILLER, THE (*Il Sicario*), 136f., 232
Hiroshige, 6, 52
HIROSHIMA, 52
HIROSHIMA, MON AMOUR, 52, 144, 189ff., 279
Histoire de la Peinture Surréaliste, 184n.
Hitchcock, Alfred, 8, 90, 137, 139, 179, 261, 293, 330, 337, 338
Hitler, 34ff.
Hodier, André, 189ff.
Hoffman, Dustin, 394
HOLE, THE, *See* Night Watch.
Holst, Gustav, 38
Horgan, Paul, 166
HOUR OF THE WOLF, THE, 8
HOUSE OF THE ANGEL, THE, 371
Housman, A. E., 8
Howard, Trevor, 27, 403
Howarth, David, 105
HOW GREEN WAS MY VALLEY, 91
HUD, 220
Hudson Review, The, vii, x
Hughes, Thomas, 351
Hulsker, Jan, 72
HUMANISM, VICTORY OF THE SPIRIT, 75, 76
HUMAN VOICE, THE, 61n.
HUNCHBACK, THE, 234
HUSTLERS, THE, 395
Huston, John, 13, 24, 328
Huston, Penelope, 113, 335
Huxley, Aldous, 213, 268, 342

I AM CURIOUS, 309ff.
Ichikawa, Kon, 6, 282
Idestam-Almquist, B., 148
IDIOT, THE, 354ff.
IF, 350–351
Ignez, Helena, 364
ILUSION VIAJA EN TRANVIA, LA, 384
Image, 21
Imamura, Shohei, 311
Importance of Being Earnest, The, 260
IMPOSTER, THE, 52, 55, 57
IN COLD BLOOD, 389–390

INDIAN VILLAGE, 251
Industria Annual, viii, 156
INFORMER, THE, 88, 91, 289
IN JENEN TAGEN (*In Those Days*) , 143
INNOCENT SORCERERS, THE, 170
I NOMMI DEL LEGGE (*In the Name of the Law*) , 172
IN THE HEART OF THE NIGHT, 388–389
INTOLERANCE, 15–21
IRON HORSE, THE, 88, 92
Isaaksson, Ulla, 201
Island Sinks, The, 331
I SPY, 330
IVANHOE, 20
IVAN THE TERRIBLE, 153ff.

Jacopetti, G., 378
James, Henry, 11, 107, 393, 397 quoted
Jancso, Miklos, 357ff.
Jannings, Emil, 91, 179
Japanese Quarterly, 302
Jaspers, Karl, 278, 401
Jealousy, 192
Jean, Marcel, 184n.
Jeffers, Robinson, 64, 142, 205–206 quoted, 208 quoted
Jerome, Saint, 298 quoted
Jessua, Alain, 336
Jesus, 48
JEU DE MASSACRE, 336ff.
Jewison, Norman, 388–389, 392
Johnson, Eyvind, 299
JOLI MAI, LE, 220n., 221
Jongleur de Notre Dame, Le, 413
Jonson, Ben, 170
José, Paulo, 364
JOURNAL OF A COUNTRY PRIEST, 106
Joyce, James, 330
JULES ET JIM, 174ff., 221, 274, 295, 298, 339
JULIET OF THE SPIRITS, 286n., 289ff., 295
Jung, C. J., 392
Jung-Alsen, Kurt, 107, 110
Jurgens, Curt, 81, 112

Kabuki theatre, 51, 57
Kafka, Franz, 6
Kalatozov, M., 224
Kamaraden, 107
Karas, Anton, 404
Kast, Pierre, 254
Kastner, Peter, 266
Katcha, Vahe, 113
Kauffmann, Stanley, 405
Kautner, Helmut, 143
Kawalerowicz, Jerzy, 110ff., 213, 321, 404

Kaye, Danny, 395
Kazan, Elia, 101, 118
Keaton, Buster, 217, 224
Keats, John, 8
Keene, Donald, 102n.
Kellner, W., 29
KERMESSE, 142
Kezich, Tullio, 286, 290
KILLERS, THE, 92
Kimura, Keigo, 99
KIND OF LOVING, A, 167ff., 225
KING AND COUNTRY, 312
Kino, 224n.
Kinoshita, Keisuke, 373ff.
Kjellin, Alf, 198
Klee, Paul, 192
Kluge, A., 307, 343
KNACK, THE, 281–282
KNIFE IN THE WATER, 274, 339, 366ff.
Kobayashi, Masaki, 266–268
Koestler, Arthur, 6, 7, 380
Koval, Francis, 406
Kozintsev, 411
Kracauer, Siegfried, 178
Kramer, Hilton, vii
Kramer, Stanley, 118
Krauss, Werner, 179
Kubrick, Stanley, 110
Kulle, Jarl, 202
Kurosawa, Akira, 5, 6, 58, 85, 115–121, 223, 284ff., 299, 302ff., 361
Kyo, Machiko, 55, 99

L 136 (*A Diary with Ingmar Bergman*) , 287n., 290
LABBRA ROSSE (*Red Lips*) , 274
LADY FROM SHANGHAI, 412
LADY MACBETH OF MTENSK, 212
LADY WITH A DOG, 123, 274
L'ÂGE D'OR, 80n., 166, 380, 381
Lagerkvist, Hans, 204
Lagerlöf, Selma, 154, 197
Lamb, Charles, 318
Lambetti, Ellie, 124–125
L'AMÉRIQUE INSOLITE, 169
LAND WITHOUT BREAD, 162, 209, 382
Lang, Fritz, 143, 155
Langer, Susanne, 119 quoted, 205 quoted
LARK, THE, 274
LAST DAY OF SUMMER, 171
LAST LAUGH, THE (*Der Letzte Mann*) , 178
LAST TEN DAYS, THE, 81
LAST YEAR IN MARIENBAD, 4, 187ff., 254, 278, 279, 327
Lattuada, Alberto, 59, 133, 231

Laurel and Hardy, 378
Laurents, Arthur, 26
Lauritzen, Bertil, 252n.
Lavi, Daliah, 225
L'AVVENTURA, 4, 158, 159, 160, 189, 193, 210, 274, 288, 290, 328
Lawrence, D. H., 8, 126 quoted, 127, 135, 138 quoted, 141, 353
Lawson, John Howard, 327ff.
Lazarevic, Mile, 213
LEAGUE OF GENTLEMEN, THE, 139
Lebrun, Rico, 87
Lehman, Leo, 355f.
Lelouch, Claude, 258, 306
Leni, Paul, 155
Lenin, 150
Leonardo, 71, 72, 360
Leone, Sergio, 396
LEOPARD, THE, 236
Leskov, Nikolai, 212
Lester, Richard, 281ff., 308, 343, 344, 345
Leterrier, François, 107, 255ff., 256n.
Levi, Carlo, 61, 100
Leyda, Jay, 148, 151, 152, 224n., 327
LIAISONS DANGEREUSES, LES, 257n.
Life, 221
LIFE BEGINS TOMORROW, 79
LIFE OF OHARU, THE, 58
Life of the Bee, The, 35, 39
LIFE UPSIDE DOWN (*La Vie à l'Envers*), 336
LIMELIGHT, 31–33
Linder, Carl, 323
Linder, Max, 217, 224
LIPSTICK, THE, 137
LITTLE ROAD, THE. See Pather Panchali.
Livet, Roger, 72, 73
LIVING (*Ikiru*), 58, 117–118, 285
Lizzani, Carlo, 234
LOLA, 10, 254
Lolita, 158
Lollobrigida, Gina, 129
LONG DAY'S DYING, A, 345–346
Longfellow, H. W., 398
LONG VOYAGE HOME, THE, 90ff.
LOOK BACK IN ANGER, 118, 139
Loren, Sophia, 129, 134
Lorre, Peter, 57
Losey, Joseph, 14, 223, 378
LOUISIANA STORY, 23–25, 243
LOVE '65, 282
LOVELY IS THE SUMMER NIGHT, 141
LOVERS, THE, 222
LOVES OF ISADORA, THE, 349
LOVING COUPLES, 295
Lulli, Folco, 112

Lundberg, Ferdinand, 409
L'UOMO DI PAGLIA, 136
Luther, Martin, 290, 317

Macaulay, Thomas, 296
MACBETH, 212, 318
McCann-Erickson, 67
McCarten, John, 56
McCullers, Carson, 13
Macdonald, Dwight, 323
McLaglen, Victor, 91
Maclaren, Norman, 266
McLiammoir, M., 410
McLuhan, M., 328
McQueen, Steve, 392
Madame Bovary, 330
Madame Butterfly, 100
MADE IN U.S.A., 306
Magarshack, David, 354n.
MAGICIAN, THE (*The Face*), 274, 277, 289, 298
MAGNIFICENT AMBERSONS, THE, 407ff.
MAGNIFICENT SEVEN, THE (*Seven Samurai*), 85, 101n., 303
Magnum, 306
Magritte, R., 186
MALEDETTO IMBROGLIO, UN, 135, 172
Mallarmé, Stéphane, 241
Malle, Louis, 222, 223, 255, 257, 301, 338
Malraux, André, 10, 40, 275, 284 quoted
MAMMA ROMA, 235
MAN, THE, 224
MAN AND A WOMAN, A, 306
MAN CALLED HORSE, A, 398ff.
MAN ESCAPED, A, 106–107
MAN FOR ALL SEASONS, A, 317
Manfredi, Nino, 226
Mangano, Silvana, 98f., 129, 133f.
MAN OF ARAN, 243
Man of the Renaissance, The, 73
Man on His Nature, 247
MANO SUL FACILE, LA (*Hand on the Gun*), 237ff.
Man Who Died, The, 64
Marc, Franz, 77 quoted
MARCELINO, PAN Y VINO, 97
Marchand, Corinne, 225
Marcuse, Herbert, 355
Marker, Chris, 220n., 221, 234, 308, 335
Marlowe, Christopher, 317
Marxism, 327
Maselli, Francesco, 135ff.
Masina, Giulietta, 60, 66n., 99
Mason, James, 26
Massine, Léonide, 397
Mastroianni, Marcello, 133, 173, 174, 277

Maté, Rudolf, 46
MATERNELLE, LA, 180
Matisse, Henri, 260
MATKA JOANNA, 213–214
MATTER OF DIGNITY, A, 124, 134, 274
Mattsson, Arne, 7, 196, 295
Mauriac, François, 256
MAUVAIS COUPS, LES, 255ff., 274
Meeker, Ralph, 169
MEETING ON THE ELBE, 155
Mekas, Jonas, 323
MELODY OF THE WORLD (*Melodie der Welt*) , 143, 179
Memling, Hans, 74
Mercouri, Melina, 393
Mercury Theatre of the Air, 406
MER PROMISE, LA, 257n.
Messel, Oliver, 29
Metsys, Quentin, 74
MEXICAN BUS RIDE, 382
Mexican Journal, 87
Michalek, Boleslav, 214
Michaux, Henri, 56 quoted, 59 quoted
Michelangelo, 76
Michelson, Annette, 324ff.
Mifune, Toshiro, 58, 86, 119, 120
Milestone, Lewis, 24, 92
Milian, Tomas, 136
Milosz, Czeslaw, 379
Miracle, The (Reinhardt) , 36
MIRACLE, THE (Rossellini) , 61
MIRACLE IN MILAN, 59, 235
Mirbeau, Octave, 256n.
Miró, Joan, 70
MISCHIEF MAKERS, THE (*Les Mistons*) , 180
MISS JULIE, 7, 190, 254
Miyagawa, K., 52
Mizoguchi, 96
MOBY DICK, 14
Modern Japanese Literature, 102n.
MONDO CANE, 230
Monicelli, Mario, 133ff., 231, 235
Monroe, Marilyn, 129, 330
Montaigne, 10
Montand, Yves, 349–350
Montherlant, Henri de, 19
Monument Valley, 94
Moore, Henry, 192
Moorhead, Agnes, 408
Morassi, Mauro, 230
Moravia, Alberto, 127, 135, 167
More, Sir Thomas, 10, 317
Moreau, Jeanne, 161, 174, 257, 338
Morelli, Rina, 133
MORGAN, 9, 300
Morgan, Frederick G., vii

Morgan, Michele, 80
MOROCCO, 179
Morris, Glen, 41
MOUCHETTE, 334
MOURNING BECOMES ELECTRA, 57
Mozart, W. A., 110, 163, 309
Murder for Profit, 259
MURDER MY SWEET (*Farewell, My Lovely*) , 13
MURDERER, THE, 295
MURIEL, 220n.
Murnau, F. W., 45, 99, 178
MUSASHI, 58, 101
MUSIC ROOM, THE, 11
Musil, Robert, 301
Myberg, Per, 198
MY DARLING CLEMENTINE, 89, 90
MY FIRST LOVE, 373ff.
MY HOME IS COPACABANA, 271, 282
MY LIFE IS MINE (*Le Feu Follet*) , 222, 222n., 224
MY SISTER, MY LOVE, 295
MYSTERIES OF ROME, 221
MYTH, THE, 295

Nakadai, Tatsuya, 267
NAKED ISLAND, THE, 208
NAKED NIGHT, THE (*Sawdust and Tinsel*) , 82
NANOOK OF THE NORTH, 243
Nanuzzi, Armando, 133
Napoleon, 48
Naruse, 277n.
Nascibene, Mario, 135
Nation, The, 77
NAZARIN, 384
Nemec, Jan, 279
NEON NIGHT LIFE, 230
NETTEZZA URBANA, 279
"New American Cinema", 322
Newhaven-Dieppe. See Temptation Harbor.
Newman, Paul, 395
Newton, Robert, xi
New Yorker, The, 336, 354, 394
New York Times, The, 88, 296, 404
Nichols, Dudley, 92
Nicholson, Jack, 353
Nigger of the Narcissus, The, 379
NIGHT GAMES, 295ff.
NIGHT JOURNEY IN RUSSIA, 1943, 143
NIGHTMARE, 295
NIGHT WATCH, THE (*Le Trou, The Hole*) , 144, 255, 274
Nilsen, Vladimir, 150
NINE LIVES, 105ff.
NOBLESSE DU BOIS, 73

NOBODY WAVED GOODBYE, 265
Noh drama, 55, 56, 57
NOIA, LA. *See* The Empty Canvas.
NO LOVE FOR JOHNNY, 138
NOTTE, LA, 157–161, 192, 194, 210, 288
NOT TO SPEAK OF ALL THOSE WOMEN, 276, 291.
NOZO NO YUREISEN, 101
Nude, The, 144
NUNCA PASA NADA, 225

Observer, The, 301
OCTOBER, 150
ODD MAN OUT, 93, 401
O DREAMLAND, 350
Of Fear and Freedom, 100
O'Flaherty, Liam, 93
OKASAN, 102
OLE DOLE DOFF, 8, 331ff.
OLIVER TWIST, 9
Olivier, Sir Laurence, 9, 57, 70, 171, 334, 355n., 410, 411
OLVIDADOS, LOS, 162, 182, 328, 378, 380, 385
OLYMPIAD, 34–43
OMICRON, 235
ONCE IN THE GLORIOUS WEST, 396
ONE-EYED, 97
O'Neill, Eugene, 18, 92
ONLY ANGELS HAVE WINGS, 93
Ophuls, Marcel, 254
Ophuls, Max, 10, 26–27, 80, 254, 261, 407
ORGANIZER, THE (*I Compagni*), 235, 238n.
Ortega y Gasset, 289
Oscarsson, Per, 332
OTHELLO: Welles, 318, 409ff.; Olivier, 410; Yutkevich, 411
OUTCAST OF THE ISLANDS, AN, 401
Owen, Don, 265
Oxford Theatre Society, 317
Ozu, 5, 6, 102n., 277n., 376

Pabst, G. W., 81
Pagnol, Marcel, 98
PAISAN, 25
PAN (*Short Is the Summer*), 201ff.
Panofsky, Erwin, 102
Papas, Irene, 207, 350
Paradise, 76
PARIS 1900, 79
Paris-Match, 165, 221
PASSION OF JOAN OF ARC, THE, 44–50, 107
PATHER PANCHALI (*The Little Road*), 11, 95f.

PATHS OF GLORY, 110
Paxinou, Katina, 57, 131
PEAU DOUCE, LA (*Soft Skin*), 260ff.
Peck, Richard, 330
Peckinpah, Sam, 394
PENTHOUSE, THE, 346
Perelman, S. J., 215
Perkins, Anthony, 393, 412
Perrault, Pierre, 264, 270
Perrin, Jacques, 350
PERSONA, 296ff., 304
PETULIA, 343
PHAEDRA, 170
PHANTOM CARRIAGE, THE, 197
Philipe, Gérard, 80
Philosophy of the Beautiful, 248n.
Philosophy of the Unconscious, 248n.
Piccoli, Michel, 336
PIERROT LE FOU, 326
Pinelli, Tullio, 99
Pinga, Ben, 52
Pinter, Harold, 312, 317
Pirandello, Luigi, 127, 297, 381
Piscator, Erwin, 236
PLACE IN THE SUN, A, 118
Planets Suite, The, 38
PLAY ON THE RAINBOW, 198
Poggi, Gianfranco, 130
POIL DE CAROTTE, 180, 254
Point Counter Point, 342
Poitier, Sidney, 388–389
Polanski, Roman, 307, 307n. 318, 327n., 366ff.
Polish Perspectives, 213
Portman, Eric, 321
POSTO, IL (*The Job*), 274
POTEMKIN, 45, 149–150
Pound, Ezra, 18
Poussin, 73
POWER AND THE GLORY, THE. *See* The Fugitive.
Pratolini, Vasco, 61
Pravda, 152
PRETTY POISON, 393
PRISONER OF SHARK ISLAND, THE, 93
PRIVILEGE, 312, 316, 341
Prix International des Critiques Cinéma et Télévision, 362n.
Prokofiev, Sergei, 153
PROUD AND THE BEAUTIFUL, THE, 80
Pudovkin, V. I., 18, 90, 155
PURPLE NOON (*Plein Soleil*), 255
Pushkin, A., 30

QUEEN OF SPADES, THE, 9, 28–30, 58n.
QUIET ONE, THE, 13
Quigley, Isobel, 372 quoted, 397

QUO VADIS, 17

Rabal, Francisco, 311
RAGAZZA CON LA VALIGIA, LA, 134ff.
RAICES, 97
RASHOMON, 52, 58, 64, 86, 117, 119, 285, 287, 289, 346
Rathbone, Basil, 406
Ray, Nicholas, 92
Ray, Satyajit, 11, 96, 323
Real Thing, The, 107
RED AND THE WHITE, THE, 358ff.
RED BALLOON, THE, 290
RED BEARD, 286
RED DESERT (*Deserto Rosso*) , 278, 288
Redford, Robert, 395
Redgrave, Michael, 9, 355n.; Vanessa, 349
RED RIVER, 93
RED SHOES, 57
Reed, Carol, 9, 19, 27–28, 400ff.
REFLECTIONS IN A GOLDEN EYE, 13, 390
Reggiani, Serge, 146
Reichenbach, François, 10, 80n., 169, 210, 255, 258, 300
Reinhardt, Max, 254
Reisz, Karel, 349
Religion of the Future, The, 248n.
Renoir, Auguste, 290, 352
Renoir, Jean, 96, 254, 257
Reporter, The, 101
REPULSION, 307n.
Resnais, Alain, 6, 144, 184ff., 220n., 227, 279, 307, 311
REVOLT OF THE FISHERMEN, 236
Ribeiro, Milton, 84
Richardson, Tony, 203
Richie, Donald, 7, 118, 119, 267, 270, 285, 288, 291
Richter, Hans, 211
RIDEAU CRAMOISI, LE (*The Crimson Curtain*) , 10
Riefenstahl, Leni, 34ff., 143
RIEN QUE LES HEURES, 80n.
Riesman, D., 67
RIFIFI, 80
RÍO Y LA MUERTE, EL, 384, 385
Risi, Dino, 228ff.
RISQUES DU MÉTIER, LES, 333ff.
Ritt, Martin, 220
Riva, Emmanuele, 334
RIVER, THE (Lorentz) , 24
RIVER, THE (Renoir) , 96
Riwkin-Brick, Anna, 49
ROAD TO HEAVEN, 248
Robbe-Grillet, A., 187ff., 223, 326
Robertis, Francesco de, 25
ROBINSON CRUSOE, 382

Roca, Daniele, 173–174
Rocha, Glauber, 362
Roché, Henri-Pierre, 175
Rockefeller Foundation, x
Roeder, Ralph, 73
Roeg, Nicholas, 319
Rogosin, Lionel, 343ff.
ROI SANS DIVERTISSEMENT, UN, 257n.
Romeo and Juliet, 100
ROMEO AND JULIET (Soviet film) , 9, 410
Rondi, Brunello, 225
RONDO, 339
ROOM AT THE TOP, 9
Roosling, Gösta, 248
ROSEMARY'S BABY, 307n.
Rosenberg, H., 354
Rosi, Francesco, 220, 233, 236, 282
Rosif, Frederic, 270
Rossellini, Roberto, 59
Rossen, Robert, 24
Rotha, Paul, 273
Rotunno, Giuseppe, 134
Rouch, Jean, 227, 265, 343
ROUND-UP, THE, 357–358
Rouquier, Georges, 264
Rousseau, Jean Jacques, 380
ROYAUMES DE CE MONDE, 72
Rubens, 74
RULES OF THE GAME, 254
Rustichelli, Carlo, 238
Ruttman, Walter, 45, 143, 179
Ryan, Robert, 26, 397

St. Joan (Shaw) , 48
SALKA VALKA, 7
SALT FOR SVANETI, 224
SALVATORE GIULIANO, 234
Salvatori, Renato, 131
SAMURAI (*Musashi*) , 101
SANJURO, 268
Santos, Roberto, 362
SATURDAY NIGHT, SUNDAY MORNING, 8–9
SAVAGE EYE, THE, 170
SCARLET EMPRESS, THE, 179
Schapiro, Meyer, 70
Schlemiel, Peter, 315
Schlemmer, Oskar, 191
Schlesinger, John, 168, 225, 318ff.
Schlöndorff, Volker, 301
Schnabel, Arthur, 290
Schollin, Christina, 201
Schopenhauer, Arthur, 248
Schorer, Mark, 101
Scott, Geoffrey, 75
Scott, Nathan A., Jr., 329
SCOTT OF THE ANTARCTIC, 105
SEA GULL, THE, 355n.

SEARCHERS, THE, 89
SECRET LIFE OF WALTER MITTY, 395
SECRET SHARER, THE, 215
SEDUCED AND ABANDONED, 371
Sellers, Peter, 139
SENHIME *(Princess Sen)* , 99, 102
SENILITA, 232
Sennett, Mack, 176, 281
SEPPAKU *(Hara-kiri)* , 267ff.
SERPENT, THE, 295
Serre, Henri, 174
SERVANT, THE, 223, 312
Seton, Marie, 148
SEVEN SAMURAI. See The Magnificent Seven.
Seyrig, Delphine, 191
SHADOWS, 170, 282
SHADOWS OVER SNOW, 245
SHAME, THE, 8, 344, 401
SHANGHAI EXPRESS, 179
Shaw, G. B., 48
Sherrington, Sir Charles, 104 quoted
SHE WORE A YELLOW RIBBON, 88
Shindo, Kaneto, 208, 224, 247
Shinoda, 311
SHOOT THE PIANO PLAYER, 255
Short Cut, The, 61
Sibelius, Jean, 319
SICARIO, IL. See The Hired Killer.
SIEGFRIED, 155
Sight and Sound, 113, 406
SIGNAL, 149
SIGN OF TE GLADIATOR, 279
Signoret, Simone, 146, 257ff., 334
SILENCE, THE, 8, 277, 287, 290, 295
SILENT WORLD, THE, 222
Silverstein, Elliot, 398ff.
Simenon, Georges, xi
Sinclair, Upton, 151
Singer, Burns, 192
Siodmak, Robert, 92
Sioux, 398
SISKA, 201
Sjöberg, Alf, 7, 82, 190, 248, 254, 298
Sjöman, Vilgot, 198, 201, 287, 290, 295, 309
Sjöström (Seastrom) , Victor, 147, 374
SKOPJE 63, 269–270
Sleepwalkers, The , 157
Sluys, Felix, 186n.
SMILES OF A SUMMER NIGHT, 204
Smith, Jack, 323
Smutna, Dana, 227
SOLITI IGNOTI, I, 134
SOMETHING WILD, 169ff.
SONG OF CEYLON, 96
SONS AND LOVERS, 139

Sontag, Susan, 324, 326, 330, 413
Sordi, Alberto, 60, 133
SORPASSO, IL *(The Easy Life)* , 228
S.O.S. SUBMARINE *(Uomini del Fondo)* , 25
SOUND OF MUSIC, THE, 330
SOUS LES TOITS DE PARIS, 179
Southwest Review, viii
Spectator, The, 372, 397
STAGECOACH, 88, 91
Stalin, 154, 326
Steffens, Lincoln, 162
Steichen, Edward, 48
Steig, William, 352
Steiger, Rod, 388f.
Steinhoff, Hans, 143
Stendhal, 211, 256, 385
Sternberg, Josef von, 91, 177ff., 182
Stiller, Mauritz, 147, 154, 156
STORIES OF THE REVOLUTION, 269
STORY OF A LOVE, 278
STOTEN, 141
Strachey, Lytton, 410
STRADA, LA, 52–67, 82
STRANGER, THE, 411
Strauss, Harold, 54
Strauss, Richard, 38
STRAY DOG, 299
STREET OF SHAME, 102
Streisand, B., 394
STRIKE' 149–150
Stroheim, Erich von, 385
Sturges, John, 9, 92
Suarès, André, 66n.
SUCCESSO,IL, 230
Sucksdorff, Arne, 7, 52, 210, 240–252, 271ff., 282, 298, 299
Sugiyama, K., 52
Suicide in Scandinavia, 287n.
SUMMER WITH MONIKA, A, 7
SUNDAY IN SEPTEMBER, A, 220n.
SUNDAYS AND CYBÈLE *(Les Dimanches de Ville d'Avray)* , 254, 274
SUSANA, 384
Sydow, Max von, 198, 216

Tadic, Ljuba, 213
Tanguy, Yves, 188
Tarkington, Booth, 408
TASTE OF HONEY, A, 9, 203
Taylor, Elizabeth, 318
Tchaikowsky, Peter, 407
TEMPEST, THE, 279
TEMPTATION HARBOR, xi, 9
TERM OF TRIAL, 9, 334
TERRACE, THE, 335
TERRA TREMA, LA, 264

TERRORISTA, IL, 220n.
Teshigahara, 6, 311
THÉRÈSE DESQUEYROUX, 256
THEY LIVE BY NIGHT, 13
THIEF OF BAGHDAD, THE, 100
THIRD MAN, THE, 9, 20, 27–28, 112, 400–404
THIS SPORTING LIFE, 350
THOMAS CROWN AFFAIR, THE, 392
Thomas, Dylan, 30 quoted, 280
Thomson, David, 328
Thompson, Virgil, 24
Thoreau, Henry David, 18
Three Musketeers, The, 100
THRONE OF BLOOD, THE, 100n, 118, 268
THROUGH A GLASS DARKLY, 142, 160, 168, 215, 290
Through the Looking-Glass, 377 quoted
Thulin, Ingrid, 215
THUNDER OVER MEXICO, 151
TIGHT LITTLE ISLAND (*Whisky Galore*), 9
Time, 78
TIME AND HOUR OF AUGUSTO MATRAGA, THE, 362
TIME OUT OF WAR, 13
Times, The (London), 306
Times Literary Supplement, The, 381
Times, The New York, 404
TIME STOOD STILL, 4
Tintoretto, 40, 73, 76
Tisse, Edward, 147–155, 156n.
TITAN, THE, 76
Titian, 73
TO DIE IN MADRID, 270
TO HAVE AND HAVE NOT, 93
TOKYO MONOGATARI, 5, 376
Toland, Gregg, 408
Tolnay, Charles de, 74
Tolstoi, Leo, 285, 361
Tom Brown's Schooldays, 351
TOM JONES, 9, 329
TORMENT (*Hets, Fury*), 8, 82, 102
Torre-Nilsson, Leopoldo, 11, 274, 275, 327, 369ff.
Tours, Festival of, 73
Tower Beyond Tragedy, 205 quoted
TOWER OF LILIES, 102
TRAGIC PURSUIT OF PERFECTION, THE, 71, 72
TREASURE OF THE SIERRA MADRE, 116
TRIAL, THE, 326, 412
TRIAL AT VERONA, 234
TRIAL OF JOAN OF ARC, THE (Bresson), 211ff.
TRICHEURS, LES (*The Cheats*), 170
Trieste, Leopoldo, 60, 174
Trintignant, Jean-Louis, 134, 229–230, 306, 349–350
Tristan and Yseult, 100
TRIUMPH OF THE WILL, 35
Troell, Jan, 8, 298ff., 331n.
Troilus and Cressida, 340 quoted
Trotsky, Leon, 326
TRUE END OF THE GREAT WAR, THE, 110, 171, 214, 274, 321, 404
Truffaut, François, 10, 119, 174ff., 255, 260ff., 272, 275, 280, 281, 293ff., 298, 299, 327n., 330, 337ff.
TRUTH, THE. See La Vérité.
TUNES OF GLORY, 139
Turgenev, 285
Turolla, Luigi, 237
TWENTY-FOUR EYES, 102
Twain, Mark, 388
Twilight in Italy, 135–136
TWO WOMEN (*La Ciociaria*), 127ff.
Tynan, K., 300
Typhoon, 116

Udet, Ernst, 81n.
Uehara, Misa, 119
UFA, xii, 352
UGETSU, 52, 55, 56, 96, 100
Ullman, Liv, 203
UMBERTO D, 4, 67, 118, 127
UMBRELLAS OF CHERBOURG, 259ff., 260
Uncle Vanya, 9
UNDERCURRENT, 102
UNIVERSE, 266

Vadim, Roger, 212, 257n., 282
VAGHE STELLE DELL'ORSA, 329
Vailland, Roger, 257n.
Valéry, Paul, 342
Vallentin, Antonina, 71
VALLEY OF DREAMS, 247
Valli, Alida, 403
Van Doren, Mark, 244
Varda, Agnes, 260, 307, 309
VARIETY, 28, 178
Vèdres, Nicole, 80n.
Veidt, Conrad, 155
Venice International Film Festival, 3, 60, 82, 100n., 217ff., 236, 302, 308, 310
VERDUGO, EL, 226
Verga, Giovanni, 126 quoted, 127
VÉRITÉ, LA, 134, 255
Vermeer, 260
Vertov, Dziga, 323
Verve, 61n.
VIACCIA, LA, 135, 232
VIDAS SECAS, 12
Vidor, King, 163
Vierzehnheiligen, 336

Vigo, Jean, 180, 190
Villon, Francois, 386
VIRGIN SPRING, THE, 7n., 8, 119, 123, 274, 277
VIRIDIANA, 161–166, 274, 277, 289, 360, 383, 385
Visconti, Luchino, 129ff., 231, 236, 264, 329
VITELLONI, I, 4, 5, 60, 61ff., 124, 299
Vitti, Monica, 161
Vogel, Amos, 70
Vogue, 319
VOICE OF ANXIETY, 361
Voit, Mieczyslaw, 214
VOYAGE AU BALLON, 197

WAGES OF FEAR, THE, 78n.
Wagner, Richard, 40, 80
Wajda, Andrzej, 170, 212
Walbrook, Anton, 29, 57, 58n.
Waley, Arthur, 54
WALK IN THE SUN, A, 92
WAR GAME, THE, 315ff., 340ff.
War of the Worlds, The, 407
Watch, The, 61
WATER IN THE MOUTH, 255
Watkins, Peter, 312, 315ff., 340ff., 351
Watteau, 336
Waugh, Evelyn, 351
WAX DOLL, 196
WAX-FIGURE CABINET, THE, 155
WAY DOWN EAST, 19
Wayne, John, 89, 93
WAYS OF LOVE, 61n.
WE ARE ALL ASSASSINS, 80, 113, 379
We Die Alone (NINE LIVES), 104ff., 105–106
WEEKEND, 343
Weiss, Jerry, 182
Weiss, Jiri, 226
Weld, Tuesday, 393
Welles, Orson, 27, 307, 323, 326, 393, 403, 405–413
Werner, Oskar, 81, 174, 293
Weyden, Rogier van der, 74
WHEAT WHISTLE, 102
WHISPERERS, THE, 9, 320
WHITE SHEIK, THE, 59ff., 235

Wicki, Bernhard, 119
Widerberg, Bo, 271, 282ff., 308ff., 351, 352
WILD BUNCH, THE, 394ff.
WILD STRAWBERRIES, 374
Williams, T., 170
WILL PENNY, 397
Wilson, Harold, 342
Wilson, Scott, 390
WIND AND THE RIVER, 252
WIND FROM THE WEST, 244, 247
Windt, Herbert, 38
Winnicka, Lucyna, 214
Winsten, Archer, 53
WINTER LIGHT (*The Communicants*), 204, 214ff., 274, 287, 287n., 291
WOMAN OF THE DUNES, 6, 311, 364
WOMAN'S LIFE, A, 58
WONDERFUL ADVENTURES OF NILS, THE, 196
Wordsworth, W., 8, 315
WORLD WITHOUT SUN, 323
Worringer, F., 160
Wright, Basil, 96
Wright. Frank Lloyd, 51

YANG KWEI-FEI, 99
Yates, Peter, 392
Yeats, W. B., 64, 211 quoted, 214 quoted
Yepes, Narciso, 31
YOJIMBO, 268
Young, Victor, 24
YOUNG ONE, THE, 384
YOUNG TÖRLESS, 300ff.
YOUR TEETH IN MY NECK, 307n.
Yutkevich, Sergei, 318, 411

Z., 349–350
Zampa, Luigi, 231
Zavattini, 61, 127, 137, 147, 221
ZAZIE IN THE METRO, 255
ZÉRO DE CONDUITE, 145
Zetterling, Mai, 198, 271, 295ff.
Zinnemann, Fred, 10, 317
ZORBA THE GREEK, 275
Zuckmayer, Carl, 81
Zurlini, Valerio, 134ff.